AF235279

The Tree Of Knowledge

A Novel

by

Mrs. Baillie Reynolds

The Tree Of Knowledge
A Novel
by Mrs. Baillie Reynolds

Copyright © 2024

All Rights reserved.

No part of this publication may be reproduced, stored in a retrieval system, or transmitted in any form or by any means, electronic, mechanical, photocopying or Otherwise, without the written permission of the publisher.
The author/editor asserts the moral right to be identified as the author/editor of this work.

ISBN: 978-93-69077-80-9

Published by

DOUBLE 9 BOOKS
2/13-B, Ansari Road
Daryaganj, New Delhi – 110002
info@double9books.com
www.double9books.com
Tel. 011-40042856

This book is under public domain

ABOUT THE AUTHOR

Gertrude Minnie Robins, born in Teddington, United Kingdom, was an accomplished English author renowned for her vast literary contributions. Writing under the pen name Mrs. Baillie Reynolds after her marriage, she authored over fifty novels spanning various genres. Her works were often centered around human emotions, relationships, and personal growth. Gertrude's literary career was marked by a keen understanding of her characters' internal struggles and the challenges they faced in their pursuit of happiness and fulfillment. Her novels often explored deep themes of love, loss, and the complexities of human nature. She had a child, P. K. Baillie Reynolds, and her works remain a testament to her enduring legacy in the world of literature. Some of her notable books include The Tree of Knowledge: A Novel (1889), The Man Who Won (2024), and The Judgment of Charis (1921), among others. Gertrude's writings continue to be appreciated by readers for their emotional depth and engaging storytelling. While she may not have achieved the widespread fame of some of her contemporaries, her works have left a lasting impact on the literary world.

CONTENTS

CHAPTER I

Where I will heal me of my grievous wound.

Mort d'Arthur.

Anyone who has read the *Mort d'Arthur* can hardly fail, if he traverse the Combe of Edge in early summer, to be struck by its resemblance to the fairy Valley of Avilion.

A spot still by good fortune remote from rail, and therefore lying fresh and unsullied between its protecting hills, waiting, like the pearl of great price, to reward the eye of the diligent seeker after beauty. It seems hard, at first glance, to believe that the rigors of an English winter can ever sweep across its sunny uplands.

"Where falls not rain, nor hail, nor any snow,
Nor ever wind blows loudly; but it lies
Deep-meadowed, happy, fair with orchard lawns
And bowery willows, crowned with summer sea."

As regards the falling of rain and hail, and the buffeting of winds, it is to be supposed the place does not, literally speaking, resemble the mystic Isle; but it was a fact, as Allonby had just elicited from the oldest inhabitant, that snow had only three times lain on the hills within his memory.

To the young man himself, as he sat in a patch of shade just outside the rural inn, with a tankard of cider in his hand, and his long legs extended in an attitude of blissful rest, it seemed as if the remainder of the description must be also true.

Up over his head, the sky was blue—how blue! An unseen lark trembled somewhere in its depths, and its song dropped earthwards in trills of melody.

It was that loveliest season of the English summer which comes before the cutting of the grass. All up the sides of the valley the meadows were ripe for the scythe; the dark-red spires of the sorrel and the white stars of the ox-eye daisy bent softly in the warm south breeze. Down below the level of the eye, in the very heart of the Combe, a fringe of reeds and little willows marked the lowly course of the brook. No one who noted its insignificant proportions would have guessed—unless he were a true disciple of Isaak Walton—what plump trout glided over its clear gravel bed.

In the fine pasturage of the glebe meadows, the red-brown cows were gathered under a tree, out of the hot sparkle of the sun. The orchards had lost their bewildering glory of bloom, except just here and there, where a late apple-tree shoot was still decorated with coral-tinted wreath.

And beyond the orchards was the crown of summer sea—

"The liquid azure bloom of a crescent of sea,
The silent sapphire-spangled marriage-ring of the land,"

thought Allonby, who was altogether in a Tennysonian frame of mind that morning. He could not help it. The fresh loveliness of his surroundings impressed him with a dreamy delight, and he loved nothing so well as the luxury of yielding to his impressions. He was filled with a blending of indescribable emotions, longings, desires; wondering how anyone managed to live in London and yet retain any powers of mind and thought.

"I have been here two days," he sighed, "and my range of ideas is stretching, stretching, like the handkerchief in the fairy-tale which stretched into a gown. My horizon is widening, my standard of perfection is rising; I shall either die, if it goes on much longer, or become a totally different person. Farewell, my old self, with your trivial daubs, your dingy studio, your faded London models. Let us go in for the shearing of sheep under burning skies, for moon-rise on the waters of an endless sea, for the white, dusty perspective of the village street, or for Mary, the maid of the inn!"

Mr. Allonby, as will have been gathered from this fragment, was not a strikingly coherent thinker; but to-day he was certainly more wool-gathering than usual, and he had not even strength to be angry with himself for the same.

"Temperament," he went on, lazily "national temperament, is entirely the result of climatic influence. I fancy I've heard that sentiment before—I have a dim idea that I have heard it frequently; but I have never till this moment realised it thoroughly. I now give it the sanction of my unqualified assent. They say of us, that no Englishman understands how to *flâner*. How the devil could anyone *flâner* in the shades of a London fog? Is east wind conducive to lounging in the centres of squares? or a ceaseless downpour the best accompaniment to a meal taken out of doors? No, indeed! Give me only a landscape like the present, and six weeks of days such as this, and I will undertake to rival the veriest *flâneur* that ever strolled in a Neapolitan market. How sweet-tempered I should grow, too! Even now I recall, dimly as in a dream, the herds of cross and disagreeable people who struggle into omnibuses at Piccadilly Circus. Why, oh, why do they do it? Do they really imagine it worth the trouble? Why don't they tear off their mittens and mackintoshes, fling away their tall hats, their parcels, their gamps, and make one simultaneous rush for the Island Valley of Avilion?"

And, as he thus mused, arose straightway before his imagination — which was keen — a vision of such a crowd as emanates, on a wet night, from a Metropolitan railway-station — of such a crowd pouring from an imaginary terminus, and flocking down that poetic village street, inundating the grass-grown curve of beach in the bay, swarming in a black herd up the warm red sides of the peaceful cliff.

"Jove!" he ejaculated, under his breath, "how they would spoil the place!"

And he checked his philanthropic desire that all his fellow Londoners should come to learn lounging in this ideal village. His beatific musings were broken into by the appearance of the inn-keeper's young daughter, "Mary, the maid of the inn," as he had named her, though her parents had christened her Sarah.

She came walking awkwardly through the cool dark passage, and poked her pretty, tow-colored head round the doorway, to obtain a side scrutiny of her father's guest, who was an object of great interest to her.

"Me mother said I was t'ask yer if yer was goin' to get your dinner aout, same as yesterday, or if yer'd get yer dinner here to-day?"

This question brought Allonby's thoughts home to a sense of forgotten duty. The spot he had yesterday selected, whence to paint his projected picture, was a mile along the valley, and the day was passing; so far he had been conspicuously successful in his efforts to become a lounger.

"I wonder if your mother would tie me up some dinner in a handkerchief?" said he. "I had none yesterday, because it was too far to come back."

Then, as the girl disappeared, he rose, stretched, and told himself that he was a fool to have put off his tramp till the hottest hour of the day, when it would be quite impossible to get an inch of shade, either side of the way.

However, he had come to Edge Combe brimful of good resolutions, and he meant at least to try to keep them, in spite of the strange fermentation which seemed to be taking place in his brain. As he shouldered his camp-stool and other paraphernalia, it occurred to him to bestow a smiling pity on a poor fool who could allow all his ideas of life to be revolutionized by a sudden plunge from London dirt and heat into the glamor of a Devonshire summer.

"However," he reflected, "it won't last. I've been overturned in this way before. Look what an ass I made of myself in Maremma! It doesn't increase one's self-respect to recall these things. But after all, either I am a singularly unappreciative person, or my insular prejudices are very strong, or—I like best to imagine this third—there is a something in the fickle beauty of an English summer which surpasses even Italy. I don't think anything there ever moved me quite as the Valley of Avilion does. There is something so pure, so wholesome, in this sea-scented, warm air. There is no treachery, no malaria lurking under the loveliest bits of foliage—no mosquitoes either," he suddenly concluded, somewhat prosaically, as he lifted his soft cloth helmet, and wiped his big forehead. "Only one drawback to an English summer," he continued, as he started on his way, with his dinner tied up in a blue handkerchief and began to tramp, with long strides, along the curve road, with its low stone wall, which skirted the deep blue bay. "Only one drawback, and that one which enhances its beauty, and makes it all the more precious: one is never sure of keeping it for two days together. Its uncertainty is its charm."

He paused and keenly surveyed the purple and hazy horizon. No signs, as yet, of the weather breaking; all was fair, and all was very, very hot. He rested his dinner on a stone, and again passed his handkerchief over his brow. The swish, swish of the scythes in the long grass made him glance up. The mowers were mowing the steep hill to his right, and the long sweep of their muscular arms was fine to see, as they advanced, step by step, in regular order, the fragrant crop falling prostrate in their path.

"It's a grand day!" cried Allonby, in the joy of his heart.

"Ay, sir, and it'll be a grand week. We'll dû all we've got to dû before the rain comes."

This was said with a cheery authority which gladdened Allonby afresh, and seemed to put a final touch to his riotous delight. Scarcely a moment before he had affirmed that the uncertainty of the weather was what pleased him; but the dictum of this rural prophet was none the less encouraging and reassuring.

Just beyond the mowers, under a clump of very fine ash-trees, stood the forge, and in its shadow the furnace roared, and the sparks leaped out. The young man must needs pause here again to enjoy the contrast of the fierce dark fire on the one side, and on the other the musical trickle of a limpid rill of water, which fell from a spout, and dropped into a roughly hewn stone basin, shooting and sparkling in the light.

As he stood, absorbed in gazing, the shrill call of some bird came clearly to his ear, and made him glance up. He was standing at the foot of a very steep hill thickly grown with trees, and high up, between the leaves, he could descry peeps of a long white house, and a sunny terrace, blazing with geraniums. His keen eyes noticed at once a big brass cage wherein doubtless a cockatoo was enjoying the sunshine, and then he saw a little lady in white come slowly along, with a wide black straw hat to shield her from the sun. He was far-sighted enough to know that the little lady was middle-aged and wore spectacles, but she had a sweet and pleasant countenance, and at once Allonby longed to know what favored mortal this was who made her home in Avilion.

How lovely was that sunny terrace! How soothing the cry of that unseen bird! What a lovely wicker-chair that was which stood so invitingly just in the shadow of the porch! A great longing to enter these precincts, to penetrate into the mysteries of that dusky, cool interior, took possession of him, and he had gazed for many minutes before it occurred to him that he must present something the appearance of a little street urchin, flattening his nose against a confectioner's window.

Turning sharply, he saw that the grimy smith, with his blue eyes looking oddly from his blackened face, was standing at the door of the smithy, regarding him with much curiosity.

"Good morning," said Allonby. "That's a pretty house up the hill there. Who lives in it?"

"The Miss Willoughbys," was the answer. "It's the only big house in the village, sir."

Allonby breathed freely. He had dreaded lest he should receive for answer that Mr. Stokes the tanner, or Noakes the varnish-maker, dwelt in that poetic house; but no! All was in keeping with the valley of Avilion. The Misses Willoughby! He said to himself that the name might have been made on purpose.

With a strong effort he tore himself away, and continued his tramp in the broiling sun, and still, as he went up the valley, between the steep banks of harts-tongue, over the musical brooks, he could hear the hot and sleepy cries of the bird on the terrace growing ever fainter and fainter.

CHAPTER II

Let no maiden think, however fair,
She is not fairer in new clothes than old.

Tennyson.

Miss Fanny Willoughby, when the unseen Allonby saw her pass on the terrace, had just come from feeding her fowls. The poultry-yard was quite a feature at Edge, as the house was always called for brevity's sake, though its full name was Edge Willoughby. This year had been a very fortunate one for Miss Fanny's pigeons, and her mind was full of happy and contented thoughts as she carried back her empty tin dishes and deposited them carefully, along with her gardening gloves, in the little room known as the gardening-room.

Beside her walked the very bird whose call had attracted the artist's attention. Jacky was a Cornish chough, coal-black in plumage, with brilliant orange-tinted beak. He strutted along sideways and with great dignity, casting looks of exultant triumph at the imprisoned cockatoo, who was his sworn foe. Puck, the stout and overfed terrier, solemnly accompanied them, as was his invariable habit, walking very close to the neat box-border, and now and then sniffing at the glowing geraniums.

"Dear me!" said Miss Fanny, "how warm it is—quite oppressive."

She would not for worlds have said that it was hot, but her dear little face was pink with her exertions, and her small plump hands so moist that to pull off the gloves was quite a business.

The sound of a piano was loudly audible—a jingly piano, very much out of tune, up and down which scales were being rattled lightly and evenly.

"I really think I shall tell the child not to practise any more," said Miss Fanny. "Charlotte is certainly a trifle exacting this warm weather."

So saying, she opened a door to her right, and entered a room which was evidently sacred to the purposes of education—the education of a former day. A reclining-board and two large globes were its principal features. The book-shelves were stocked with such works as "Mangnall's Questions," "Child's Guide," "Mrs. Markham's England," and the like. On the square table in the window was a slate full of sums, and what used to be known as a "copy slip"—bearing a statement of doubtful veracity:

"Truth is better than flattery."

This sentence comprised exactly the system on which Elaine Brabourne's aunts had brought her up.

They loved her very dearly, but they would have thought it a criminal weakness to tell her so. They acted always on that strange system which was in vogue when they were young—namely, that you always would be naughty if you could, and that the only thing to keep you under was a constant atmosphere of repression. If you learned your lesson, you were given to understand that the fact was due to the excellence of the manner in which you were taught—not to any effort of your own. If you did not learn it, you were conscious that this deficiency on your part was only to be expected from one who habitually made so small a use of such exceptional advantages. You were never encouraged to form an opinion of your own. It was an understood thing that you accepted that of your elders. For example: "A plate basket," said Miss Charlotte, "should always be kept in the parlor closet;" and her niece Elaine would have regarded the woman who ventured to keep hers elsewhere as out of the pale of civilization.

This plan of education had answered very well for the Misses Willoughby, whose lives had been peaceful and secluded as modern lives rarely are, and who passed their days always in the same place, and in nobody's society but their own. Their delightful unanimity of opinion was the great bond of peace between them; but they had never reflected that Elaine Brabourne could not pass her life in Avilion as they had done, nor paused to consider what would be the result when this girl, who had never been allowed to think for herself, even in such a matter as the color of her gowns, should be suddenly precipitated into London life as the eldest daughter of a rich man.

Elaine did not cease her scales, nor look round as her aunt entered. The metronome's loud ticks were in her ear, and she dared not halt; but sweet-tempered little Miss Fanny crossed the room with light step, and stopped the instrument of torture with a smile.

"Oh, Aunt Fanny! Aunt Char said I was to play scales for an hour!"

"My dear, it is so excessively warm," said Miss Fanny, apologetically, "I feel sure you should lie down till the luncheon-bell rings. It is really quite exceptional weather; I am so glad for the hay-makers."

Elaine, like a machine, had busied herself in closing the piano and putting away her music. Now she rose, and followed her aunt to the table by the window.

She was such a very odd mixture of what was pleasing and what was not, that it was hard to say what was the impression she first conveyed.

She was a head taller than her aunt, and looked like an overgrown child. She wore a hideous green and white cotton frock, and a black holland apron. The frock had shrunk above her ankles, and was an agonising misfit. Of the said ankles it was impossible to judge, for their proportions were shrouded in white cotton stockings and cashmere boots without heels.

She was quite a blonde, and her hair was abundant. It was combed back very tightly from a rather high forehead, plaited and coiled in a lump behind, which lump, in profile, stuck straight out from the head.

The eye seemed to take in and absorb these details before one realised the brilliancy of the complexion, the delicate outline of the short nose, the fine grey eyes, perhaps a shade too light in color, but relieved by heavy dark lashes, and the almost faultless curve of the upper lip.

Such was Miss Brabourne at nineteen. A child, with a mind utterly unformed, and a person to match. The dull expression of the pretty face when at rest was quite noticeable. It looked as if the girl had no thoughts; and this was sometimes varied by a look of discontent, which was anything but an improvement. She felt, vaguely, that she was dull; and that her life bored her; but her mind had not been trained enough to enable her to realise anything.

She had read astonishingly little. There was a deeply-rooted conviction in the minds of her aunts Fanny, Charlotte and Emily that reading was a waste of time,—except it were history, read aloud.

It was hard to see wherein the great charm of this reading aloud lay; it had sometimes occurred to Elaine to wonder why she was made to read "Markham's France" aloud to her aunts by the hour together, yet, if found perusing the same book to herself in the corner, it was taken away, and she was told to "get her mending."

She did not care conspicuously for reading. She did not care for anything much, so far as she knew. The only thing which evoked any warm interest was music, and the one piece of restraint which she deeply resented was the being forbidden to play on the beautiful grand piano in the drawing-room. It never occurred to her aunts for a moment that their pupil could play far better than her teachers; it never dawned upon them that she was fifty times more able to do justice to the grand piano than they were. Elaine was the child—under their authority. It stood to reason that she must not play on the best piano, any more than she might loll in arm-chairs, stand on the hearthrug, or go up and down the front staircase. And so, at an age when most girls are going out to balls, admiring and being admired, Elaine was playing her scales, getting up at half-past six, going to bed at half-past nine, not happy, but quite ignorant of what she needed to make her so.

There was one aunt who did not quite agree with the plans adopted for their niece's education, but she was far too gentle to tell her sisters so. This was Aunt Ellen, the eldest, and Elaine's god-mother.

She was far the most intellectual of the four sisters, but had resigned any active part in her god-daughter's education because of her ill-health. She reserved to herself the task of amusing the child, and this she wished to do by teaching her fancy-work, and occupations for the fingers. But if there was one thing Elaine disliked, it was fancy-work, or occupation of any sort for the fingers. In fact, it puzzled them to know what she did like, though it never occurred to them to think how narrow was their range of interests—so narrow as to make it quite likely that the girl might have a thousand, and they not discover them. Miss Ellen was a great reader, and would have dearly liked Elaine to read the books she read; but out of deference to her sisters' theories she lent her only such books as they approved—memoirs, essays and biographies; and Elaine hated memoirs, essays and biographies.

She did not decline to read them, any more than she declined to do fancy-work—she was too well-trained for that. Her individuality was not powerful enough to resist that of her aunts, three of whom were women of strong character, accustomed to be obeyed. And so the days went on, and she passed from child to woman, no one but Aunt Ellen being aware of the fact; and Ellen Willoughby dreaded unspeakably the day, which she felt certain must come soon, when the girl would awake to all the possibilities of life, and find her present existence intolerable.

It might have been a presentiment which made her mind so full of this thought on this hot, beautiful summer's day, when she lay on her low couch beside the great window, gazing out at the glowing valley, and watching the shadows change as the sun slowly advanced.

Presently there was a tap at the door, and Elaine came in. She brought fresh roses for the invalid's glasses, and, as she crossed the room, her godmother watched her keenly. The girl shut the door quietly and crossed the carpet, neither stamping nor scuffling. Her manners had been well attended to, but as she advanced it struck Miss Willoughby that her step lacked the elasticity which one associates with youth; she thought at that moment she would have preferred to see Elaine hurl herself into the room, and skip and dance for joy of the beautiful weather.

The niece kissed her aunt in her usual methodical fashion, and then, fetching the vases, began the duty of putting fresh flowers and water, much as she would have begun to fold a hem or stitch a seam. This done, she sat still for some few minutes, thinking apparently of nothing, and with her dull, handsome eyes fixed on the distance.

At last she said:

"Martha's field is being cut to-day, and they say, if we get some rain by-and-by, there ought to be a fine aftermath."

"Dear me! Martha's field being cut already! How the years fly!" said Miss Ellen, with a sigh.

"Oh, do you think so? I think they drag," said Elaine, rather suddenly; and then repeated, as if to herself, "They drag for me."

Miss Willoughby felt for the girl, but her sense of what was fitting compelled her to utter a platitude.

"Time always passes more slowly for the young," she said. "When you are my age—"

"That will be in twenty-two years," said Elaine.

She said no more, but somehow her tone implied that she did not wish to live twenty-two years, and to the elder woman it sounded very sad.

She looked wistfully at her niece, wondering if it would be possible to get her sisters to see that some amusement beyond the annual school-feast and tea at one or two farmhouses was necessary for the young.

She longed to say that youth seemed so long because of the varied emotions and experiences crowded into it—emotions which were lifelong, minutes of revelation which seemed like years, hours in which one lived an age. But she knew Charlotte would feel it most unfitting to talk of emotions to a child, and dimly she began to feel sure that Charlotte must be wrong, or that somebody was wrong, that Elaine's was not a happy nor a normal state of girlhood.

Just then Miss Emily Willoughby entered the room. She was the youngest of the four, and rather handsome, though her style of hair was unbecoming, and her dress an atrocity.

"Is Elaine here? Oh, yes, I see she is. Elaine, Jane is ready for your walk, and I should like you to go along the valley to Poole, and tell Mrs. Battishill to send up twenty pounds of strawberries for preserving, as soon as they are ripe."

Elaine rose, with a face expressing neither displeasure nor distaste. She merely said, "Yes, Aunt Emily;" and, taking up her tray of dead flowers, left the room and closed the door behind her.

Miss Ellen's eyes followed her anxiously, and, as the footsteps died away along the passage, she lay back among her cushions and a slight flush rose in her white face.

"Emily," she said, "I should like to have a little talk with you."

"That is just what I have come up for," said her sister, seating herself in Elaine's vacated chair, and taking out her knitting. "About this work from Helbronner's, isn't it? Well, my dear, we have just been discussing it among ourselves, and have come to the conclusion to send back the design. It will not do, my dear Ellen, as I know you will agree. It would be considered quite Popish by the villagers, and, as Mr. Hill would not like to object to it if it were our work, it would be placing him in a *most* awkward position."

Miss Ellen fixed her soft, questioning eyes on her sister's face, but soon removed them, with a sigh of resignation. Emily's mind was full of the design for the new altar-cloth, and it would be useless at such a moment to appeal to her on the subject of her niece's future. She could but lie still and hear the pros and cons respecting a design of cross intertwined with lilies, which design Miss Emily, for some inscrutable reason, seemed to consider appropriate only to the Church of Rome. Presently, through the open window could be heard Elaine and the maid setting out for their walk, and again Miss Willoughby caught herself wishing that the girl's footfall had had more of girlish buoyancy about it.

CHAPTER III

The champaign, with its endless fleece
Of feathery grasses everywhere!
Silence and passion, joy and peace,
An everlasting wash of air.
Browning.

Elaine Brabourne's feelings, as she went up the Combe, along the path which Allonby had trod before her, were about as different from his as anything that could possibly be imagined. She was not thinking much of anything in particular, but her predominant sensation was annoyance and resentment that her aunt should send her all the way to Poole on such a hot afternoon.

It was about a quarter-past four, and the sunbeams were beginning to take that rich golden tinge which tells that the middle day—the "white light" so worshipped by Constable—is past. Tea at six and light supper at nine was the rule at Edge Willoughby, and so Elaine always went for a walk at four o'clock in the summer-time—at which hour her aunts affirmed "the great heat of the day to be past."

The girl had never in her life been for a walk by herself. Jane had been her companion for the last fifteen years, and Jane's legs preferred an equable and leisurely method of progression along a good road, with, if possible, some such goal as Mrs. Battishill's farm, and a prospect of new milk, or perhaps junket. Consequently, country-bred though she was, Elaine was almost a stranger to rambles and scrambles up the cliff, to running races, scaling precipices, bird's-nesting, or any of those pursuits which usually come as naturally to the girl as to the boy who is reared "far from the maddening crowd."

Had she had a companion to suggest such sports, they would have been delightful to her; but hers was eminently an imitative and not an original mind, so she walked along passively at Jane's side, letting the parasol, which had been given her to protect her complexion, drag behind her, its point making a continuous trail in the white dust.

She was walking through a scene of beauty such as might have moved a far less emotional temperament than Allonby's. Behind her back were the waters of the bay, one sheet of flame in the vivid light, while here and there gleamed the sails of some proud ship steaming slowly down the Channel. The road she was treading ran along the western side of the valley; to her right all was deep, mysterious shadow, and beyond it the lofty swell of the more easterly of the two hills which bounded Edge Combe. High on the side of the Copping, as this eastern hill was called, was the long white front of Edge Willoughby, and a full view of the terrace glowing with its crimson and scarlet glory of climbing geraniums.

Every gateway that they passed disclosed a wealth of luxuriant grass, almost as tall as Elaine herself, ready and waiting for the mower's hand. The white butterflies flew here and there, dancing with glee. The sunshine, striking through the larch plantation on the left, flung bars of light and shadow across the road; and under the trees the fern-fronds were rearing their lovely heads, uncurling in crown-like grace and beauty.

All so still; nothing but the sleepy, hushed murmur which comes from nowhere and yet fills the air of a summer's day. In the silence the call of the chough on the terrace could be distinctly heard right across the combe.

"Hark at Jacky!" said Elaine, with a little laugh. She rested her arms on the stile, and gazed away over the laughing meadow at the terrace. "I can see Aunt Ellen's head at the window," said she, "and here comes Aunt Char with a watering-pot. I hope she won't forget to water my nasturtiums just around the corner. Do you know I've got one of those new coral-colored ones, Jane?"

"If we don't push on, miss, we'll not get to Poole and back before tea," was Jane's remark.

"I do think it's a shame to send me all the way to Poole such a day as this," sighed the girl, as she reluctantly rose and continued her way.

She did not care in the least for the beautiful landscape. Its monotony was thoroughly distasteful to her. What mattered it whether beautiful or not, so long as it never changed? Variety was the need of her young life: something fresh—something different. Had she come upon a cargo of bricks and mortar, and workmen hacking down the finest trees in order to erect a villa, the sight would have afforded her the liveliest relief.

Presently they left the high-road, and crossed a bit of furzy common—just a small piece of waste ground, with the water lying in picturesque pools and clumps of starry yellow blossoms brightening the sandy soil.

As they passed along this marshy tract, Elaine raised her eyes to the road they had just quitted, which now ran along to their left, rather above the level on which they were walking; and she saw something which made her stop stone still and gaze round-eyed up at the road in a fashion which Jane could not understand till her own eyes followed the direction of her young mistress'. Then she beheld what was sufficiently unusual amply to justify the girl's surprise.

A broad back, covered with a light tweed coat, a soft, shapeless felt hat, two unmistakably masculine legs appearing on the further side of a camp stool:—a folding easel, bearing a canvas of fair dimensions, and a palette splotched thickly with color. The painter's back was towards them. His point of view lay inland, up the valley, and took in a corner of Poole farmhouse, and the grove of ash-trees behind it.

It may at first sound somewhat contradictory that an artist should be such a *rara avis* in so beautiful a spot as Edge Combe. But it is, nevertheless, true, and this for two good reasons. Firstly, the place is quite out of the beat of the usual Devonshire tourist. It is nowhere near Lynton, nor Clovelly, nor the Dart, nor Kingsbridge. No railway comes within five miles of it, and very few people have ever heard its name. Secondly, many landscape artists are dispirited by the cruel difficulty of getting a foreground. It is embarrassing to paint with the ground descending sheer away from your very feet, so as merely to present to you the summits of several trees, and the tip of a church spire in violent perspective. Equally inconvenient is it to take your seat at the foot of a steep hill, with intention to paint the side thereof. And so, as level ground there is none, the artists at Edge Combe are limited to those who, like Allonby, fall so headlong in love with the place that they make up their minds to paint somewhere, regardless of difficulties. Again it may be added that there is no bold coast-line at Edge Combe, no precipitous granite rocks, with white breakers foaming at their base, no mysterious chasms or sea-caves,—all is gentle and smiling. The cliffs are white chalk, riddled with gulls' nests, or warm red-brown crumbling sand-stone. The blackberries ripen at their sunny summits, the park-like trees curve over almost to the water's brim; and the only danger attaching to these cliffs is their habit of now and again quietly subsiding, breaking away and falling into the sea without the slightest warning.

Allonby had chosen his painting-ground with rare felicity, and had, as was his wont, gently congratulated himself on the pleasing fact. Elaine longed, with a longing which was quite a novel emotion, to be near enough to see what he was doing.

He was not painting, at this moment, but sitting idly, leaning his head on his hand.

Oh, if he would but turn round and look at her! The usually dull grey eyes gathered a strange intensity; even Jane, as she looked at the girl, noticed her odd expression, and was rendered vaguely uneasy by it.

"Come on, miss," said she.

"Oh, but, Jane—he is painting—see! He looks like a gentleman. I wonder who he is!"

"I heard Hutchins say there was a gentleman staying at the Fountain Head. That might be him," said Jane.

"I daresay. Most likely. I wonder what his name is?"

"I don't see it matters to you, miss. You don't know him, nor your aunts don't know him, and if we loiter like this we'll not get home afore the dumpsie" (twilight).

Elaine reluctantly tore away her feet, which seemed rooted to that charmed spot. Her thoughts were not coherent—they were hardly thoughts at all, but there was a sudden passionate wish that she were a man, and free. It was no good to grow up if you were only a girl. She was nineteen, and had no more liberty than when she was nine. Oh, to be able to travel about alone, to stay at an inn, to go from one part of England to another, with no one to ask the why and wherefore of your actions! She looked almost with hatred at Jane's homely, well-known features. Why must she always have a Jane at her elbow?

The evil hour to which Miss Ellen looked forward with mournful prophecy was hard at hand.

"Well, now, I dû say that it's nice to see you, Miss Ullin," said Mrs. Battishill, with delight. "And Jane tû! Come along in out of the heat—come into the rhûme. Is all the ladies well? How dû they like this weatherr, and how dû like it yourself, Miss Ullin, my dearr?"

The Devonshire dialect was one of Allonby's keenest sources of delight, particularly the soft liquid French sound of the *u*, contrasting with the rough burr of the *r*. On Elaine it produced absolutely no effect whatever; she had heard it all her life. Her idea of bliss would be to hear something completely different. She went mechanically into Mrs. Battishill's best parlor, neat and clean as a new pin, but with the strange stuffiness which comes of never opening the windows.

She ate the cakes provided, and drank the milk with healthy girlish appetite; but her thoughts were centred on the artist in the lane, and she did not hear a word that Jane and the farmer's wife were saying.

Jane was admiring a large fine silver cup gained by Mr. Battishill at the last agricultural show for the best cultivated farm of more than a hundred acres. This prize was offered every year to his tenantry by Sir Matthew Scone, who owned nearly all the surrounding country.

"Yes, it's a fine coop," said Mrs. Battishill, with pride. "I shown it yesterrday to a young fellow who's making a picturre out there in the lane, and coom oop to the farrm for a drink o' milk."

These words suddenly fixed Elaine's attention.

"He's painting out there now," said Jane, with interest; "we see him as we came threw the waste."

"I dessay you will have," returned Mrs. Battishill, benevolently. "I showed him all over the hoose, and he was that taken oop with it. He said he never see such a queer place in his life. He didn't seem half a bad chap, to me," she was kind enough to add.

Poole Farm had never before presented itself to Elaine in such a pleasant light. It was most certainly a very queer house, for it was built right against the side of a hill, so that you could walk in at the front door, ascend two or three flights of stairs, and then walk out of a door at the back, and find yourself unexpectedly on *terra firma*. It had never occurred, to the girl till to-day that this eccentricity was attractive; but now the house, the farmer's wife, the whole surrounding landscape seemed to borrow new dignity from the potent fact of this unknown artist having admired them.

She did not join in the conversation, but listened with feverish interest as Jane asked if Mrs. Battishill knew his name.

No, she had not asked it. He had said he was staying at the "Fountain Head," and, when she asked him how long he meant to stay in these parts, he laughed and answered "as long as the fine weather lasts."

"Eh, well, we'll hope the rain'll hold off till he's done his picture," said Jane, as she rose to take her leave.

The farmer's wife protested against such a short visit, but Jane reminded her that tea at Edge was at six o'clock, and that they were bound to be home in good time; and so they started out again into the golden evening, where a circle of rose-color was just beginning to rim the intense blue of the pure sky.

When they had shut the wicket-gate, and crossed the brook by the miniature bridge of three crazy planks, Elaine took her courage in both hands and ventured a petition.

"Jane," said she, "don't go across the waste. Let us go home by the road; it will be—a change."

As she spoke, she turned crimson, and almost despaired, for it was a longer way to go home by the road.

Jane guessed with perfect accuracy the thoughts which were busy in her young mistress' mind; but she herself was a true daughter of Eve, and she wished to go home by the road as much as ever Elaine could do. She just sent one keen look at the girl's flushed face, and then said:

"It was more than a bit boggy across the waste; you'll get home dry-shod if we go the other way."

So these two dissemblers, neither of whom would own her secret motive, turned into the road, and walked along until a sudden bend in it brought them in sight of the artist's easel, and then Elaine's heart seemed to spring up to her throat and choke her, and she cried out, regardless of whom might hear,

"Oh, Jane! He's gone!"

CHAPTER IV

Give her time—on grass and sky
Let her gaze, if she be fain:
As they looked, ere *he* drew nigh
They will never look again!

Jean Ingelow.

"Gone!" was Jane's quick response; "but he'd never go and leave his picture sticking out there by itself for the first shower to spoil—he can't be far off."

For a moment Elaine recoiled, every nerve thrilled with the thought that the stranger, concealed in some bush in the immediate vicinity, had heard her reckless and incautious exclamation. There was no movement and no sound, and, after a pause fraught with more suspense than she could remember to have ever felt before, she stepped about two paces forward, and took another timid look. Something was lying on the ground near the easel—a confused heap of gray, which outlined itself clearly in the long rank wayside grass; and for a moment Elaine turned white and looked as if she were going to faint; then, no longer hesitating, but urged on by a wild impetuosity, she ran to the spot, and stood gazing down at Allonby's pallid and stiffened features.

All her life long she would remember that moment—every detail, every sensation, stamped on her brain with indelible distinctness. The soft whisper of a newly-awakened diminutive breeze in the ash-trees, the grass all yellow as corn in the golden evening light, the hot sweet perfume that arose from the fragrant hedgerow, and the still hard face, bloodless under its newly-acquired bronze. It was death—she was certain of it. Death, that mystery in whose existence she had never really believed, though she knew, as matter of history, that both her parents were dead.

Into the heart of this strange, awful secret she seemed suddenly hurled with a force which bewildered her. For a few moments she stood quite speechless, swaying to and fro, and seeing through a mist, while Jane, with her back towards her, was staring down the lane in hopes of seeing the artist reappear.

Allonby had evidently come to the ground with force. His fall had crushed the camp stool under him. He had fallen forward, but slightly sideways; one arm was flung out under his head, and, owing to this, his face was turned upward, leaving clearly visible a livid purple mark on the left side of the forehead. The other hand was clenched, and the lower limbs slightly contracted, as if from a sudden shock; the eyes were closed and the brows drawn together with an expression of pain.

To this girl, who had scarcely in her life come into contact with a young man socially her equal, this strange experience was overwhelming. A moment she remained, as has been said, trembling and erect; then she dropped on her knees in the long grass, and cried out, piercingly,

"Jane! Jane! come here! What are you doing? He is dead! He is dead!"

Jane turned as if she had been shot.

"Lawk-a-mercy, Miss Elaine," she cried, hurrying to the spot; and then, as is the manner of her class, she began to scream, and her shrill cries rent the air three or four times in rapid succession. "Oh, good Lord! Oh, mercy on me! What can have happened? He's been murdered, sure enough! Oh, Miss Elaine, come away! Come away from the corpse, my dear! You know your aunts would never hold with your touching a corpse. Oh, dearie, dearie, all the years I've lived I never come across such a thing! Never!"

"*Murdered!*"

The word dropped from Elaine's trembling lips with a wailing sound. Such a thing had never suggested itself to her mind. Probably had she had the usual training in the way of sensational novels, had she been accustomed to read of crimes and follow up the details of their detection with the zest of the true lover of late nineteenth-century romance, the idea of murder would have at once occurred to her, and she might have proceeded forthwith to search the long grass around for footprints, fragments of clothing, or a blood-spattered weapon. But she never once thought of the criminal, only of the victim. Neither did it dawn upon her that the mysterious danger which had lurked for the artist in that smiling landscape might lurk there also for her. She thought of nothing but him: that idea swallowed up and eclipsed all others.

Poor Allonby! Barely four hours ago he had rejoiced over the straightforward sincerity of the English summer. He had quoted with smiling satisfaction the words in which a French writer describes the Maremma:

"Cette Maremme fertile et meurtrière qui en deux années vous enrichit et vous tue."

Nothing less murderous could well be imagined than this peaceful Devonshire lane. Here were no ghastly exhalations, no venomous reptiles to glide through the long flowery grass: an Eden without the snake it seemed at first gaze, and yet some unseen malign power had exerted itself, and felled the lusty manhood of this young Englishman with a blow.

To Elaine, the sight was horror and agony untold; it acted physically on her nerves, and produced a dizzy faintness from which it took her several moments to recover. Feverishly she laid her hand on that of the young man, then on his brow, which was cold and rigid; she recoiled, filled with panic, from the touch, and leaped impulsively to her feet.

"Oh, help! Help! Will nobody help? Will nobody hear us if we call?"

"Oh, dear heart, he's bleeding under his coat here somewhere," cried Jane, holding out her hand, on which was something wet and glistening.

This sight robbed the girl of whatever nerve she might have possessed, and she recoiled with a gasp of terror.

"Stay with him," she cried, frantically, "I will run for help;" and, without waiting for reply, she started off to run at her topmost speed, feeling only that the one need of her soul at the moment was violent action, that something must be done at once.

The emergency, the first emergency of her life, had utterly scared away her wits.

She ran blindly, not in the least knowing where she was running—almost with an instinct of flight—escape from that terrible cold, still, bleeding form among the grass.

She could see his face in fancy as she ran, could remember how a tall daisy bent over and touched his brown moustache, and a huge curled dock-leaf flung its shadow over his forehead. All so still, so stiff—ah! how dreadful it was, dreadful beyond the bounds of belief.

In her dire perplexity, she never once thought of what was the only obvious thing to do,—namely, to run to Poole, and tell the Battishills to send down some men with a hurdle. She simply tore along the lane like a mad thing, never stopping to ask herself what she intended, uttering from time to time short sobs of terror and pity.

A little way beyond Poole, the lane joined the high coach-road which runs from Stanton to Philmouth; into this road she dashed, and along it her flying feet bounded, whither she neither knew nor cared. For the first time in her life she was alone—alone and free. She was beyond reach of her aunts and Jane, out by herself, alone in the wide road; and without her being conscious of the fact, this unwonted loneliness added to the terribleness of the situation. She soon lost her ugly hat, with its prim bows of drab ribbon edged with black lace; but she never even noticed its loss. On, on she flew, till at last the sound of wheels met her ear, and her tearful eyes caught sight of a carriage approaching.

It was an open carriage, just large enough for two, very compactly built. The man on the box looked like a private servant; within were a lady and a gentleman.

It did not matter to Elaine who they were—they might have been the Queen and the Prince of Wales for all she cared. Her one idea was that she must stop them. She ran pantingly on till the carriage was within a few yards of her, and then flung up both her arms, crying,

"Oh, stop, stop! I want to speak to you! Stop!"

The sudden apparition in the lonely road of a tall girl without a hat, running as if hunted, was so astonishing, that the coachman reined in his horses before he was quite clear of what he was doing, and the lady in the carriage leaned forward with an eager expression, hearing the cry, but not having clearly descried the speaker.

"What now, Goodman?" she said.

"A young lady, my lady," said Goodman. "Wants to speak to you, my lady, I fancy."

"Here, Claud," said the lady, with a laugh, "is your adventure at last! Make the most of it."

"This is the third time you have promised me an adventure. If this proves to be as futile as the other two, I shall turn it up, and go home. I have had too many disappointments—they begin to tell on my nerves. Only a girl begging, is it?"

"Hush!" cried Lady Mabel, laughingly holding up a finger to her brother; and by this time Elaine, crimson, trembling, on the verge of tears, was at the carriage door.

The Honorable Claud Cranmer's eyes fell on the girlish figure, and took in everything in an instant. He thought her the most beautiful girl he had ever beheld; and beautiful she was in her passion and her excitement.

Her hair-pins had all been scattered freely along the road as she ran— the huge plait of her deep gold hair hung down her back half uncoiled. It had been all loosened by her vehement motion, so that it framed her lovely face in picturesque disorder. The most exquisite carnation glowed in her transparent skin, crystal tears swam in her large eyes, her whole face was alight and quivering with feeling, her ivory throat heaved as if it would burst.

Never in his life had he seen anything so totally unconventional, never heard anything to equal the music of the broken voice as she gasped out the only words that occurred to her—

"Oh, I beg your pardon—do come—I must have help at once!"

"What is it?—something wrong?—an accident?" said Lady Mabel, rapidly, in her deep, sympathetic, penetrating voice. In a flash she saw that the girl was a lady, and that her tribulation was no acting, but terribly sincere. "Try to tell me," she said, laying her hand over the trembling one with which Elaine grasped the edge of the carriage.

"A gentleman has been murdered," cried the girl—"he has been murdered, there!" waving dramatically with one arm. "He is lying in the grass, dying, or dead. Perhaps it is only a faint—Jane is with him—won't you come?"

Lady Mabel cast a sweeping glance at her travelling companion, as if to ask if here was not his adventure with a vengeance.

"But oh, my dear child, I think and hope you are mistaken," said she. "People are not murdered out in the road in broad daylight here in England."

"Oh, won't you come?—won't you come? I tell you he is bleeding—I saw the blood on Jane's hand!" cried Elaine, with a shudder of irrepressible repugnance.

"Let us drive on at once and see to this," said Claud, with sudden energy, rising and letting himself out into the road. "I will go on the box with Goodman, if this young lady will take my seat—she looks fearfully exhausted."

"I have run so fast," said Elaine, with a smile of apology, as, nothing loth, she sank into the vacant seat. "Tell him to drive quickly, won't you? He must take the first turning to the right."

Mr. Cranmer mounted to the box, and the horses started briskly, Goodman being by no means less excited than his master and mistress at this novel experience.

The girl leaned back in the carriage and hid her face. The whole of her frame was shaking with feeling she could not repress.

Her companion looked at her with eager sympathy, and presently it seemed as if the magnetism of her wonderful eyes drew Elaine to look up at her, which she did in a timid, appealing way, as if imploring some solution of the mysteries of life which were bursting upon her so suddenly.

It was a very remarkable face which bent down to hers—a face not so much beautiful as expressive. The features were so strong that they would have been masculine but for the eyes—such eyes! Of the darkest iron-grey, darkened still more by the blackness of brows and lashes—eyes which could flash, and melt, shine with laughter, brim with tears—eyes which were never the same two moments together. Their effect was heightened by the fact that, though Lady Mabel Wynch-Frère was certainly not yet forty, her hair was ashen grey, as could be seen under her travelling-hat.

She was very small, slender, thin, and active—a person impossible to describe—genial, impetuous, yet one with whom no one dared take a liberty; a creature of moods and fancies, delighting in the unusual and the Quixotic.

To-day's adventure suited her exactly; her eyes were full of such unutterable sympathy as she bent them on the frightened girl beside her, that whatever secret Elaine might have possessed must infallibly have been told to her; but Elaine's life, as we know, possessed no secrets.

"Don't you trouble," said that wonderful vibrating voice, "we shall find it not so bad as you think. You have been sadly frightened, but it will all come right. Do you live near here?"

"About three miles."

"Will you tell me your name?"

"Elaine Brabourne."

"Mine is Mabel Wynch-Frère, and that is my brother, Claud Cranmer."

"Taking my name in vain, Mab?" asked the Honorable Claud, half turning round.

"Claud, this young lady's name is Brabourne," said Lady Mabel, in her gracious way.

Claud lifted his hat and bowed, as if it were a formal introduction.

"Any relation of poor Val's, I wonder?" he said.

"Who was Val?"

"Colonel of the 102nd before Edward got it."

"Oh, I remember. Are you by chance related to the late Colonel Brabourne?"

"He was my father," said Elaine, timidly.

"Oh, ho!—then this is one of the wards in chancery," said Claud, with amusement in his eyes. "I beg your pardon, Miss Brabourne, but is it not your unenviable lot to be a ward in Chancery?"

But Elaine heeded him not. The carriage had turned swiftly down the lane, and she had caught sight of Jane's sunbonnet crouching over that motionless figure in the grass. The sound of wheels made Jane look up; and it would be beyond the power of any pen to describe the dismay depicted in her countenance as the carriage stopped, and she caught sight of her young mistress—flushed, dishevelled, her hat gone, and the light of a tremendous excitement burning in her eyes.

Mr. Cranmer had opened the door in a moment, and Lady Mabel, in her neat little travelling-dress, sprang to the ground as lightly as a girl of eighteen, Elaine scrambling awkwardly after her.

"My word!" said Lady Mabel, impetuously, "what can be the meaning of this?"

"I don't know who you are, mum," said Jane, bluntly, "but I can tell you I'm right glad to see a fellow-creature's face. It's give me such a turn as I never had in all my born days, sitting here alone, not knowing any minute whether the hand that struck this poor young man mightn't strike me next. There's been foul play here, sir, as sure as my name's Jane Gollop; and not an hour back he was sitting here a-painting quite quiet and happy, for Miss Elaine and me seen him as we went by to the farm."

CHAPTER V

The past was a sleep, and her life began.

Browning.

"Oh, indeed I think you must be mistaken," said Mr. Cranmer. "It can't be murder—it must be a sunstroke, or a fit."

"Queer sunstroke, to wait till five o'clock in the evening to strike, and queer fit to break a man's arm," said Jane, with some warmth. "I've seen apoplexy, sir, and I've seen epilepsy, and I've seen many and many a sunstroke; I know 'em when I see 'em. This here isn't nothing of that sort."

Claud approached, hastily cramming an eyeglass in one eye, and, stooping over the wounded man, without further ado pulled open his flannel shirt and laid a hand over his heart. His face grew grave.

"We must have help for him quickly," he said, in an alert, decided tone, which did not seem to match his dilletante exterior. "Where is the nearest place to run to?"

"Poole is quite close—the farmhouse yonder—I thought Miss Elaine had gone there," said Jane.

He just touched the arm which lay powerless, the coat-sleeve soaked in blood, and shook his head.

"You're right enough—it's no fit; it's a brutal assault," he said. "A robbery, I suppose. I'll run to the farm—who'll show me the way?"

"I—I can run fast!" cried Elaine, who seemed to have pinned her faith on Mr. Cranmer.

They scrambled down through the gap in the hedge, and ran breathlessly across the Waste. It was hard to believe that the animated, emotional creature whose feet seemed to fly over the uneven ground was the same as the dull, spiritless girl who had trailed the tip of her parasol along unwillingly in the dust such a short time back.

"Do you know the people—at—the—farm?" panted Claud, who was not in training.

"Oh, yes. Mind the bog—don't get over the stile, it's broken—come through the gap. There's Clara come back from the milking. Clara! Clara! call your father, call the men, quick! Something most dreadful has happened!"

These ominous words, pronounced at the top of the shrill young voice, filled the farmyard as if by magic. The men and girls, the boys, the farmer and his wife, all rushed out of doors, and great indeed was their astonishment to see Miss Brabourne arrive on the scene with a perfectly strange gentleman as her escort. It was well that some one was at hand who could tell the story more coherently than poor Elaine, who by this time was quite at the end of her powers.

No sooner did Mr. Battishill comprehend what was wanted than his fastest horse was saddled and his son was galloping for a doctor, while the farm-laborers pulled down a hurdle, and, spreading a blanket over it, proceeded briskly to the scene of the disaster, accompanied by the farmer himself.

Mrs. Battishill urged Elaine to stay with her, but, though white and almost speechless, the girl vehemently refused—she must go back and see what had happened.

Claud Cranmer took her hand as if she had been a little girl, and she clasped his vehemently with both hers.

"Oh, do you think he will die?" she whispered hoarsely.

"I hope not; he looks a big strong fellow. It will depend, I should think, on whether or not his skull is broken. He is not a friend of yours, is he?"

"Oh, no, I never saw him in my life before. They say he is staying in the village."

"You will be dreadfully tired after this," he said, sympathetically.

"Oh, it, does not matter in the least. I am never tired; I never have anything to tire me. You don't really think his skull is broken, do you?"

"If the man that struck him could break the bone of his arm in two, I'm afraid it looks bad for the poor chap. It's a most ghastly thing, 'pon my word. I never heard of such an outrage! Broad daylight in a little country place like this! It's horrible to think of."

But he was not thinking wholly of Allonby and his mysterious fate; he was marvelling at the utter unconsciousness of the girl who walked beside him, her hand confidingly clasped in his. He had never met a girl so vilely dressed—never seen even a housemaid who wore such astounding boots; but this Miss Brabourne was evidently not in the least aware of how far her toilette came short of the requirements of an exacting society. In spite of the urgency of the moment, by the time they arrived back at the scene of action, he was lost in a speculation as to how long it would take this anomaly in the way of girlhood, if suddenly transported into the midst of fashionable London, to discover her own latent capabilities.

Lady Mabel had not been idle in their absence. She had slit Allonby's coat-sleeve, pulled his jointed mahl-stick to pieces, and contrived an impromptu splint for the broken arm therewith. She was supporting his head in her lap, and bathing it with the contents of her vinaigrette.

The wounded man's eyes were open, and he was moving his head uneasily and slowly, groaning deeply every now and then. It was plain that he was quite unconscious of his surroundings, and that he suffered much.

Elaine crept up with a fixed stare of wonder, and crouched down on the grass near. His eyes fell on her a moment,—they were big, honest, hazel eyes,—and the girl shivered and shrank, turning crimson as she met his gaze, though it was vacant and wild, and wandered off elsewhere in another second.

"Oh, if he would not groan so! Oh, how he suffers; he is going to die," she cried, mournfully.

Jane came up and drew her away, as the men assembled round the prostrate figure, and lifted it on to the hurdle, Mr. Cranmer carefully supporting the head, which was laid on a soft shawl of Lady Mabel's.

All the sky was scarlet and rose, and all the fields tinged with the same hue, as the small procession started to carry the sufferer with as little jolting as possible. The sun caught the windows of Poole and made them flare like torches.

Among the crushed grass where Allonby had lain was a dark wet stain. How sad the easel looked, with its picture just begun! The palette had fallen face downwards, the brushes were scattered hither and thither.

Lady Mabel began to collect them, and to pack them into the open color-box.

"Come, Miss Elaine, dear, we must run home. Your aunts will be sending out to see after us," said Jane, nervously re-tying her bonnet strings.

"I cannot walk a step," said the girl, who was seated on the grass, as white as marble. "You must go and tell them so—go and leave me."

"Miss Elaine, my dear!" cried Jane, totally at a loss. Elaine was usually perfectly obedient.

"I will drive Miss Brabourne home," said Lady Mabel, coming forward. "She is quite over-wrought. I should like to see her aunts, for I am nearly sure my husband knew Colonel Brabourne. Claud, what are you going to do?"

Her brother jerked his glass suddenly out of his eye and turned towards them; he had been apparently contemplating the distance with an abstracted air.

"Is there an inn in your village?" he asked of Jane.

"Yes, sir."

"Could we stay the night there?"

"Dear heart, sir, no, this lady couldn't. It's very rough, clean, and they're decent folks, but just a village public, sir. This poor young man was staying there, they say. I make no doubt but Mrs. Clapp'll be wondering after him."

"What do you want to do, Claud?" said his sister.

"I want to investigate this highway robbery a little," he answered. "It is interesting to me—very. I should have liked to have Goodman with me; so I thought, if there was any accommodation at the village, you might drive on, put up, and send Goodman back to rejoin me here."

"And let him find you also lying by the wayside with a broken head?" said Lady Mabel.

He smiled.

"Not likely to attempt two such outrages in the same spot, on the same evening," he said. "No. I'll tell you what I will do: I must go up to the farm and see to this poor fellow. He may have friends who should be telegraphed to. I'll get a bed here for the night, if you will give me my bag out of the carriage; you must drive through the village, stop at the inn to let the good folks know what has become of their lodger, and then on to the Stanton hotel as we planned. The farmer shall lend me a trap to-morrow, and I'll join you."

"You think of everything," said his sister, admiringly, "but, Claud, I wonder if these people know anything of nursing—I am so uneasy till the doctor has delivered his verdict—is there a nurse in the village that I could send up, I wonder?"

"There's a very good nurse in the village," said Jane Gollop, "the Misses Willoughby let her have a cottage rent free, and all her milk, and eggs, and butter from their own farm. We pass her cottage, if you please, 'm."

"Very good. Tell Mrs. Battishill I shall send her up," said Lady Mabel, getting into the carriage. "It is so light now, we shall get to Stanton before dark, don't you think so, Goodman?"

"Yes, my lady. It's not dark at nine o'clock now."

"No, no. Take care of yourself, Claud."

Her brother nodded, then turned to lift Elaine from the grass, where she sat motionless, staring at the road where the lifeless form of Allonby had been carried.

"Come," said Mr. Cranmer, gently.

"It's all over now," sighed Elaine.

"What is over?" he asked.

"What happened. Nothing ever happens in Edge Combe. This is the first thing that ever happened to me in my life, now it is over."

"Miss Elaine, my dear, don't stay talking," cried Jane, in a fright. She thought her charge was light-headed with the excitement she had gone through. The girl said no more, but submitted to be put into the carriage with Lady Mabel, and sank down with a sigh into the corner, turning her face away from that fateful patch of roadside grass. Goodman helped Jane gallantly to a seat beside him. Claud lingered, with his hands resting on the top of the carriage door, his eyes on Elaine's face.

"You do look pale," he said, "a lily maid indeed."

The rich color flew to her face as he had hoped it would, but he could see by the look in her eyes that she had not understood his allusion in the least.

"Breathes there a girl within the four seas who has not read the Idylls of the King?" he pondered, wondering. Then, just as the carriage was starting, he cried out,

"Hi! Goodman! One thing more—as you go through the village, send me up the constable."

CHAPTER VI

Too often, clad in radiant vest,
Deceitfully goes forth the morn;
Too often evening in the west
Sinks, smilingly forsworn.

Wordsworth.

Claud Cranmer stood still in the road, watching the carriage till it disappeared round a bend in the winding way.

Then he turned, and gravely surveyed the scene of action. The hedge on one side of the lane—the side on which they had found Allonby—was broken and full of gaps. The lane on this side was skirted, first by a hay-field, and further on by the piece of ground known as the "Waste," through which, as has been before stated, an oblique footpath led to the wicket-gate in Mrs. Battishill's flower-garden.

Persons crossing this Waste were in full view of the windows of Poole. The field which adjoined the Waste was to be cut to-morrow. It was full of tall rich grass, through which no mortal could have passed without leaving most evident traces of his passage behind him.

On the further side of the lane was a very tall, quick-set hedge, thick and compact, without a hole or a rent anywhere. Below it was a deep ditch, along the brink of which Mr. Cranmer walked, eyeing the long grasses and weeds keenly for the smallest trace of trampling or disorder.

There was none.

Crossing the road again, he sat down on the stile leading to the Waste, and reflected.

Jane and Miss Brabourne had come up the lane from the direction of Edge Combe. They had crossed this piece of ground, noticed the artist at work, and proceeded to the farm beyond. In about half-an-hour they had returned by the road, to find the outrage committed and no traces of the robber to be seen.

It appeared unlikely, then, to say the least of it, that this robber should have come from the direction of Poole Farm.

Any loitering man would have been noticed by them as they passed; there was not a single clump of bush on the Waste large enough to conceal a man from the view of anyone crossing by the footpath. It seemed also to Mr. Cranmer to be exceedingly improbable that the villain should have approached along the road by which the carriage had come—that is to say, that he had been walking *towards* Edge Combe, because the artist had been sitting directly facing anyone who came from that direction, and must have seen and noticed a passer-by on that lonely road.

Probability then suggested it as most likely that the tramp, or whoever it was, who had struck to such purpose, had approached his victim from the direction of the village of Edge Combe—had simply walked along the lane, come up behind the unsuspecting artist, and without warning administered the blow on the head, which was quite enough to leave the strongest man helpless in his hands. Of course, it was all mere speculation, still, it might afford a clue; for, if a stranger, a tramp, or a suspicious-looking person had passed through the village that afternoon, he was certain to have been noticed, and probably there were several who could identify such a one.

Then, if he had approached along the lane, how had he escaped?

Most probably by simply walking on along the solitary lane till he came to the high-road. Here was another negative piece of evidence. If this had been his course, he must, when he reached the high-road, have turned to the right, towards Stanton, because Lady Mabel and her brother, driving from Philmouth, must have met him if he had turned to the left; and Mr. Cranmer clearly recollected that they had met no such person.

All this, of course, was very elementary reasoning; because there were a thousand places in which a tramp might have concealed himself, out of the main road. Yet it appeared to the young man likely that one who presumed sufficiently on the isolation of the neighborhood to commit such an assault in broad daylight, almost within view of the windows of a large farmhouse, would be hardy enough to adopt the course of simply walking off down the road after securing his booty,—a far safer plan and less likely to attract suspicion than skulking in fields or outhouses.

But, altogether, the more he thought of it, the more incredible, the more outrageous the whole thing appeared to be.

Surely the artist would not be likely to have enough of value on him during a sketching-tour, to make the robbing of him worth such an enormous hazard! His costume, as Claud remembered, had been simplicity itself—white flannel shirt and trousers, with rough, short grey coat and cloth helmet.

He would carry a watch and chain—most likely; a signet ring—very probably. About a pound's worth of loose silver; aggregate value of entire spoils, perhaps ten pounds, for the watch would be very likely silver, or the chain worthless. Could there be more—far more in the affair than met the eye? Could this artist be a man who had enemies? Was there some wildly sensational tale of hatred and vengeance underlying the mysterious circumstances?

Claud pondered, as he raised his neat brown felt hat and wiped his forehead. He was overcome with a desire to see and question the victim. From him something might be ascertained, at least, of the plan of attack.

He set out to walk to Poole Farm, remarking casually to himself, in a depressed way, that nature never intended him for a detective.

"But I wonder what a detective would have done under the circumstances?" he mused. "I could not observe mysterious footprints in the grass near, for Miss Brabourne's well-meaning but clumsy handmaiden had trodden it all flat by the time I arrived on the scene. I have examined the road and banks for shreds of evidence. I have picked up a hairpin, which I have reason to believe is Miss Brabourne's. Ought I to put it in my pocketbook to show to the real *bona-fide* detective when he arrives on the scene? It would hardly be of service, I suppose, to preserve any of the blood? Ought I to have left the paints and messes in the exact order in which they fell, I wonder? It's too late to reflect on that now, however," he added, with a glance at the paint-box, which he carried strapped up in one hand, the easel being over his shoulder. The beautiful calmness of the evening seemed to him horribly at variance with the tragedy just enacted. "It's like that funny hymn which little Peggy sings,

'Every prospect pleases, and only man is vile.'

Certainly man in his worst aspect is a contemptible reptile," he sighed, as he walked up the little pebble walk, where the wall-flowers drowned the air with sweetness.

Inside, in the kitchen, a lively scene presented itself. Mrs. Battishill, having deposited the sick man in bed, had just come down for towels and hot water, and was flying from linen-press to boiler-tap with a volley of words and some agitation. Her daughter Clara, a slight, delicate girl who would have been pretty had she not attempted to be fashionable, wearing steels in her dress, and a large imitation gold watch chain, was trying somewhat feebly to help her mother, and holding the kettle so unsteadily that the water splashed on the clean flags. A group of men and boys stood round awestruck, anxious to glean every bit of information that could be given.

There was a murmur as Claud appeared, and everyone made room for him to enter.

"Missis—here be the London gentleman," said a great benevolent-looking laborer who stood near the door.

"Eh? Oh, come in, sir. Declare I near forgot you in the hurry of it. Saul, my boy, take the things from the gentleman, there's a dearr lamb."

A tall boy about sixteen came forward, and held out his hands for the easel with a lovely smile.

Mr. Cranmer resigned his burden with a momentary admiration of the beauty of the West of England peasantry, and came forward to where Mrs. Battishill was standing.

"As I was saying, sir, I grudges nothing; the time, nor the food, nor the bed, nor anything; but if he could have managed to fall ill at any other time than right on top o' my hay harvest! Lord knows how I'm going to dû! There'll be thirty men to feed to-morrow, sir, count heads all round, and it's one woman's work to get ready the victuals, I can tell you, and Clara and the gal doing everything wrong if I so much as turns my head away! And if I'm to be up all night——"

He was able to calm her considerably with the hope of the village nurse's speedy arrival, and was on the point of asking to go up and see the patient, when a clatter of hoofs was heard, and the doctor appeared on the scene.

He was a rough, surly, middle-aged man, totally without any modern ideas of comfort or consideration, but with broken limbs and broken heads he was in his element, for he had a sharp practice amongst the quarrymen.

Mrs. Battishill went upstairs with him, and Claud sat on the kitchen-table, swinging his legs.

"Clara," said he, "I am most fearfully hungry."

A giggle went round the assembly, as Clara, blushing rosy red, ran to get him some bread and cream, and a draught of cider.

"This is food for the gods," said the hungry Claud, as he covered his bread thickly with scalded cream. "This is indeed a land flowing with milk and honey."

"I can get yer some hooney tû, if yer wants it," murmured Clara, very low, with drooping eyes.

"No, no, I was only speaking metaphorically," said he, laughing. "How old are you, Clara?"

"A'm seventeen, sirr."

"Ah! That's a fine age. And how old's your brother?"

"A've tû broothers, sirr."

"Oh, two—which be they?" said Claud, wiping his lips, and surveying his admiring audience.

The two Battishills stepped forward, grinning.

"Oh! isn't that tall fellow with the light hair your brother?" he said, indicating the boy whom Mrs. Battishill had called Saul.

She shook her head, and there was a general titter, while the words "sorft," "innocent," could be heard, by which means he gradually gathered that Saul was the village idiot, at home everywhere and beloved everywhere. Finding himself the object of general attention, the boy crept behind Clara, who was a head shorter than he, and hid his face in her neck till only his beautiful golden curls were visible.

She leaned back, her arms on his hips, blushing and laughing.

"He's turrible shy with strangers," she said, "he can't bear 'em. Stan' up straight, thee girt fule, Saul!"

Claud thought it as picturesque an interior as Teniers ever painted. The great hearth, with its seats each side of the chimney, the glowing fire, the white washed walls, the shining tins on the dresser, the amused, absorbed faces of the peasantry, and through the open door a waft of pure air with a glimpse of trees and evening sky.

He turned next to Joe Battishill, a comely young man of one and twenty.

"What do you think of this affair?" he asked. "You know these parts—I don't. Has such a thing ever happened before?"

There was a chorus of "No!" and at least half a dozen started forward to vindicate their country side of such a charge. All were convinced that it was the work of some tramp, and then Claud proceeded to give them his ideas on the subject. It was agreed that the stranger spoke sound sense, and several volunteered to organize search parties. This was just what he wanted them to do, and he despatched some towards Edge Combe, some along the highroad to Stanton, and with these last he sent a scribbled note, enclosing his card, to the Stanton constabulary.

He begged them to watch every tramp, every suspicious character that passed through the town. Just as he was in the act of writing, and waxing quite excited in his converse with the men, the doctor was heard lumbering downstairs.

A dozen eager faces darted forward to hear the news, but the doctor marched in solemn silence through the group, and took up his position in front of the great fire, facing the assembly.

"A won't speak a worrd till he's had his ciderr," whispered Mrs. Battishill to Claud, and Clara went flying past him into the cellar.

Meanwhile Dr. Forbes' sharp eyes had travelled round the room till they rested on Claud, and the two stood staring at one another in a manner irresistibly comic to the latter.

Certainly Mr. Cranmer introduced a foreign element into the society, an element the doctor would scarcely be prepared to find in Mrs. Battishill's kitchen. He was not above middle height, and slightly built. In complexion he was somewhat fair, with closely cropped, smooth dust-colored hair and moustache, and a pale face. His eyes were grey and usually half shut, and he might have been any age you please, from five and twenty to forty. He had no pretence to good looks of any kind, but he possessed an elegance not very easy to describe—a grace of bearing, a gentleness of manner, a readiness of speech, which no doubt he owed to his Irish origin. He was a conspicuously neat person, never rumpled, never disarrayed, and now, after his very unusual exertions, his collar and tie were in perfect order, his fresh, quiet, light suit was spotless, and his neat brown felt "bowler" lay on the table at his side without even a flack of dust.

His glass was in his eye, and he held a piece of bread and cream in his hand. Feeling the doctor's eyes upon him, he deliberately ate a mouthful; then, rising his mug of cider:

"I drink your good health, sir," he said. "How do you find your patient?"

"My patient, sir," said Dr. Forbes, in a loud, resonant voice, "has had as foul usage as ever I saw in my life. He'll pull through, he has a splendid constitution. I never saw a finer physique; but he'll have a fight for it."

At this point Clara brought up the cider, which the doctor drained at one long steady pull, after which he wiped his large expressive mouth.

"If the blow on his head had been as hard as those that followed it, he'd have been a dead man by now," he said presently. "But luckily it was not. It was only strong enough to stun him. But there's a broken arm and a couple of broken ribs, and wounds and contusions all over him. Sir, if the weapon employed had equalled the goodwill of him who employed it, there would have been a fine funeral here at Edge Combe to-morrow."

"Then," said Claud, eagerly, "what do you think the blows were inflicted with?"

"A stick—a cudgel of some sort," said the doctor, "but I'll swear they were given by a novice—by a man that didn't know where to hit, but just slashed at the prostrate carcase promiscuously. Why, if that first blow on the head had been followed by another to match—there would have been the business done at once! But I can't conceive the motive—that's what baffles me, sir."

"But—don't you think the motive was robbery?" cried Claud, excitedly.

"What did he rob him of?" said the doctor; and opening his enormous hand, he showed a handsome gold watch and chain, a ring with a sunk diamond in it, a sovereign or two, and some loose silver.

CHAPTER VII

Where the quiet-colored end of evening smiles,
Miles on miles
On the solitary pastures, where our sheep,
Half asleep,
Tinkle homeward in the twilight—stay or stop
As they crop.

Browning.

There was a general hush, during which the doctor surveyed Mr. Cranmer keenly.

"What *can* be the meaning of it?" cried Claud, thoroughly disconcerted and at fault.

"That's past my telling, or the telling of anybody else, I think," said Dr. Forbes, slowly. "It's the most mysterious thing in the whole course of my professional experience." He eyed Claud again. "Will you be a friend of his?" he asked.

"No, no—I know nothing of him at all," said the young man, proceeding briefly to relate how strangely he had been summoned to the scene of the tragedy. The Scotchman listened attentively, and then asked abruptly:

"Since ye take so kindly an interest in the poor lad, will ye come up and see him?"

"I should like to," said Claud at once.

"Should we go after all, sir?" asked Joe Battishill, diffidently.

"What—on the search expeditions? Yes, it would be as well to rouse the neighborhood," said Cranmer, after a moment's consideration; "but tell the Stanton constables this extraordinary fact about the property not being taken. If only I could get a word with the poor fellow himself,—if only he were conscious!"

"He'll not be conscious yet awhile," said the doctor.

They ascended the old stairs with their weighty bannisters, the loud tread with which the doctor crossed the kitchen having vanished entirely. His step was noiseless as he opened the bed-room door. It was a big room, airy and clean, and the bed was a large and cumbersome four-poster, with pink hangings. Among a forest of pillows lay Allonby, his fine proportions shrouded in one of Farmer Battishill's night-shirts. His eyes were wide open, and with the arm which was not strapped up he was beating wearily on the counterpane.

The farmer's wife, having no ice, was laying bandages of vinegar and water on his head to cool him. The doctor had set the casement window wide open, and the low clucking of the fowls in the farmyard was softly audible. Mr. Cranmer approached the bedside and looked down at the sufferer.

Allonby was a fine-looking young man—perhaps thirty years old, with strongly defined features and a pale complexion. He had a rather long, hooked nose, his eyes were set in deep under hollow brows, and his chin was prominent, giving a marked individuality to the face, which was, however, too thin for beauty. It was the face of a man who was always rather anxious, to whom the realities of life were irksome, but who had nevertheless always to consider the question of £ s. d.—a worn face, which just now, in its suffering and pallid aspect, looked very sad. The soft dark brown hair lay in a loose wave over a fine and thoughtful forehead. It was with an instinct of warm friendliness that the gazer turned from the bedside.

"Oh, what a shame it is!" he said, indignantly. "I think I never heard of such a butchery. But now, the thing is to find his friends. Had he a pocket-book with him? If not, I must walk down to the inn and inquire—he must have left letters or papers somewhere."

"Here's a pocket-book," said the doctor, holding out a leathern pouch of untidy and well-worn appearance.

Claud carried it to the window, and opened it. It contained several receipted bills, six postage-stamps, two five-pound notes, a couple of photographs of a racing crew in striped jerseys, with the name "Byrne, Richmond," on the back of them, an exhibitor's admission to the Royal Academy exhibition, and several cards of invitation and private view tickets. These served to elucidate the fact that the artist's name was Osmond Allonby, but no more.

He lifted the grey coat which hung over a chair, and felt in all its pockets. At last, from the outer one, he unearthed a pocket handkerchief and a letter addressed to

O. Allonby, Esq.,
At "The Fountain Head,"

Edge Combe,
South Devon.

"I hope he'll forgive my opening it, poor chap," said Claud, and he pulled the paper from its envelope.

The address, as is customary in letters between people who know each other intimately, was insufficient. It was merely "7, Mansfield Road." He glanced over the beginning—it was quaint enough.

"How are you getting on, old man? We are being fried alive here, and the weather has put old C— — into such an unbearable rage that Jac says he has brought out the old threat once more, all the girls are to be turned out of the R. A. schools!"

The reader was sorely tempted to continue this effusion, but nobly skipped all the rest of the closely-written sheet, and merely looked at the signature.

"Always your loving sister,
"Wyn."

"How much trouble young ladies would save, if only they would sign their names properly!" said Claud, somewhat exasperated. "However, if she is his sister I suppose it is fair to conclude her name to be Allonby. Wyn Allonby!"

He turned to the envelope, and in a moment of inspiration bethought him of the postmark. It bore the legend, London, S. W.

"That's enough!" he said, "now I can telegraph. That's all I wanted to know. Mrs. Battishill, will you kindly take all these things and lock them up in a drawer, please, for Mr. Allonby's people to have when they come."

He proceeded to wrap the watch, chain, pocket-book, etc., all together in a paper, and deposited them in a drawer which Mrs. Battishill locked and took the key.

Claud could hardly restrain a smile as he busied himself thus. The idea would occur to him of how ridiculous it was that he, Claud Cranmer, should be so occupied!—of what Mab would say if she could only see this preternatural, this business-like seriousness!—of what all the men at the "Eaton" would say!—of how they would shout with laughter at the idea of his posing as the hero of such a predicament!—of what a tale it would be for everyone down in the shires that autumn!

A voice from Allonby suddenly recalled him to the present. He approached the bed-side full of pity, trying to catch the fragments of speech which the sick man uttered with difficulty from time to time.

"And now farewell!—I am going a long way," said Allonby, and after a pause again repeated, "I am going a long way ... if indeed I go,—for all my mind is clouded with a doubt,—to the island valley of——"

A pause, then again.

"To the island valley of—what is it? where is it? I forget—I cannot say it,—to the island valley of——"

"Avilion?" suggested Claud.

There was a sigh of relief.

"Yes—that's it! that's it! The Island Valley of Avilion, where I will heal me of my—grievous wound."

"Now I wonder what has put that into his head?" said Claud.

"Following up some previous train of thought most probably," said the doctor. "The subject for a picture I should say very likely. Let him be, poor lad."

Clara here tapped softly at the door, to say that the nurse had arrived; and Claud was despatched downstairs to send her up, the doctor remaining to give her directions.

Joe Battishill and another young laborer were waiting at the door for "the gentleman's orders," and when he had sent up the nurse—a nice motherly, clean-looking woman,—he sat down to write out his telegram.

"Beg pardon, sir," said a big man, pushing past the others to the table, "but I should like half-a-dozen words wi' ye. I'm Willum Clapp as keeps the 'Fountain Head,' and my missus be in a fine takin' about this poor young chap, an' I wants to hear all that's took place."

"Oh, you're the landlord of the 'Fountain Head,' are you?" said Claud, "you're just the man I wanted to see. Can you account in any way for this that has happened? What sort of man was your lodger, quiet?—peaceable?"

William Clapp broke out into a warm eulogium on the virtues of "Muster Allonba!"

He was quiet, gentle, good-humored, and had his word and his joke for everyone. He had only received two letters since he came to Edge, one of which he put in the fire after reading it. This Mr. Clapp specially remembered, because his lodger had to come into the kitchen to accomplish the said feat, there being, naturally, no fire in the sitting-room. He had started from the inn that morning a little before mid-day, with his dinner done up in a blue handkerchief—

"And that minds me, sirr, to ask if Missus Battishill could let my missus have back the handkercher and the pudding-dish, as there'll be sooch a-many dinners to send out to the hayfields to-morrow."

"Oh—certainly, I suppose Mrs. Clapp can have her things; just ask after them, some of you fellows. And now tell me," said Claud, "did Mr. Allonby know anybody down in these parts?"

"No, sirr, I don't think he did."

"Are you sure?"

"Sure as can be, sirr. At least, if a did, a said nowt abaout it to me or the missus."

"Nobody ever came to see him?"

"No, sirr, that I'm certain on!"

"Did he seem as if he had anything on his mind?"

"No, that a didn't, for my missus said as haow she neverr see such a light-hearted chap in herr life!"

Claud pondered deeply, nursing one knee and staring at the kitchen floor.

"You see, this is what bothers me, Mr. Clapp," he said. "It was an assault apparently without any motive whatever, for Mr. Allonby was not robbed."

"Eh, it's as queer a thing as ever I heard on, and as awful," said William Clapp. "In the meedst of life we are in death, as I've often heared in church, sirr! Why, the mowers in Miss Willoughby's grass, and Loud at the smithy, they see him go by a-laughing and a-giving everyone good-morning as perlite and well-mannered as could be; and the next one hears of him— —!"

The farmer made an eloquent gesture with his hand.

"Well, I'm just writing a message to his people, Mr. Clapp," said Claud. "I found a letter from his sister in London, and I thought the best thing to do was to telegraph for her to come straight."

"If *you* please, sirr," said the landlord, "anything me or my missus can do— —"

"I am sure of it, and thank you kindly. I may want a bed at your house to-morrow night, but I'll let you know."

He rapidly pencilled a message to—

Miss Wyn Allonby,
7 Mansfield Road,
London, S. W.

Then paused a minute.

"I don't even know whether she's married or not," he reflected. "However, I should think this would find her any way; people usually open telegrams."

He wrote:

> "Accident to Mr. Allonby. Serious. Has been taken to Poole
> Farm. 11.30 train Waterloo to Stanton shall be met to-morrow."

He glanced up at the landlord.

"I will add your name," he said, "and address,—it will be better."

So he added, "Clapp, Fountain Head Inn," and passed the paper over to Joe Battishill, who gravely began to count the syllables.

"One and twopence, please, sir," said Joe.

Claud tossed him half-a-crown.

"You'll want something when you get to Stanton," he said; "you can keep the change."

Clara came creeping down the stair, looking white and nervous.

"Please, sir, mother say she never saw no blue handkercher nor pudding-basin neither."

"Eh?" said Claud. "Well, now I come to think of it, no more did I; I suppose it was left by the wayside."

"I'll be bold to say it wasn't," said William Clapp, "for I walked oop right past the place, and I should a known my missus's dish-clout, bless yer."

"I suppose it's hidden among the grass," said Mr. Cranmer, after a moment's thought. "Let us go and look. Is your mother sure it was not brought here, Clara?"

"Certain sure, sir. Nobody carried away anything but mother, who took the peecture, an' you as carried the box and easel."

"Could Miss Brabourne's servant have taken it?" suggested Claud.

"Nay, sir, a think not," said Clapp, "for a stopped to speak to my missus, and she would ha' gi'en her the things if she had 'em."

"Let's go and look!" cried Claud, seizing his hat again.

The sun had set at last—what a long lime it seemed to have taken to-night! The rosy afterglow dyed all the heavens, and the trees were outlined black against it. As they hurried through the Waste, it seemed to the young man as if he had known the neighborhood for years; ages appeared to have elapsed since the afternoon, when he had been soberly driving with Mab along the coach-road, accomplishing the last stage in their pleasant, uneventful ten days' driving-tour. How little he had thought, when he planned that driving-tour for Mab, who had been thoroughly wearied out with an epidemic of whooping-cough in her nursery, that it would lead to consequences such as these. He was profoundly interested in the mysterious circumstances of this affair in which, somehow, he had been made to play such a prominent part. Come what might, he must stay and see it out. Mab might go home if she liked—in fact, he thought she had better telegraph to Edward to come and fetch her. The children were all at Eastbourne with the nurses, and she would have a chance of quiet if she went for a few days to the "mater's" inconvenient dark little house in Provost Street, Park Lane; and——

"Here you are, sirr," said William Clapp, in his broad Devon. "Where's the missus's dishclout?"

In fact, it was not to be seen. They searched for it high and low, in vain. Mr. Cranmer felt as if he were in the toils of that mixture of the ghastly and the absurd which we call nightmare. This last detail was too ridiculous! That a gentleman should be waylaid and murdered on the king's highway, and all for the sake of a blue handkerchief and a pudding-basin! In his mingled feelings of amusement and annoyance, he did not know whether to laugh or be angry—the whole thing was too incredible, too monstrous.

CHAPTER VIII

"Thy steps are dancing towards the bound
Between the child and woman,
And thoughts and feelings more profound
And other years are coming;
And thou shalt be more deeply fair,
More precious to the heart,
But never canst thou be again
The lovely thing thou art."
Sidney Walker.

"My dear, I cannot understand it!" said Miss Charlotte Willoughby.

"It is most strange—you don't think Mrs. Battishill can have kept them to tea?" hazarded Miss Fanny, in her gentle way.

Miss Charlotte crushed her, as usual.

"Jane stay out to tea without leave? She has never done such thing a before."

"It's very warm. They may be lingering on account of the heat," put in Miss Ellen's quiet voice.

"The heat is not too great for any healthy girl," said Miss Emily, with decision. "I have noticed lately in Elaine a very languid and dawdling way of doing things. I shall speak to her on the subject. I don't know what she has to occupy her thoughts, but she evidently is never thinking of what she is doing."

"She is a dear good child, on the whole," said Miss Fanny, comfortably.

"I cannot help thinking that she sometimes finds her life dull," said Ellen.

"Dull!" cried the three ladies in chorus; and Charlotte added, in high and amazed tones:

"Why, she is occupied from morning till night!"

"It was only to-day I let her off a quarter-of-an-hour practising on account of the heat," continued Fanny.

"If you think she might devote more time to her calisthenics——" began Emily.

"It was not that I meant at all," said Ellen, when she could get a hearing. "I do not complain of want of occupation for hers, but want of amusement."

"I was always taught to consider," said Charlotte, in a tone of some displeasure, "that those who were fully employed need never complain of *ennui*. Occupation is amusement."

"Then, to follow on your argument," said Ellen, half playfully, "the convicts who are sentenced to hard labor must have a most amusing time of it."

This remark, savoring dangerously of irony, was received by the three sisters with utter silence, and Charlotte thought, as she often did, what a pity it was that Ellen read so many books; really it quite warped her judgment.

"Of course everything should be in moderation," she said frigidly, after a pause; "too severe labor would be as bad for the body as too little is for the mind."

This speech sounded rather well, and Charlotte's temper was somewhat soothed by the feeling that she had made a hit.

Miss Ellen sighed. She felt that nothing could be done on Elaine's behalf, if she began by setting up the backs of the entire council of education. Yet so narrow had the minds of these excellent women grown, by living so perpetually in one groove, that it seemed impossible even to hint that they were mistaken without putting them out of temper.

"Of course I know that occupation is most necessary," said she, "and I agree with you that every woman should be well employed; but I only wanted to suggest that perhaps a little more variety than we find necessary might be good for the young. We are glad to live our quiet, untroubled days through; but for Elaine,—don't you think that some diversion now and then would be beneficial? Remember, as girls, we went to London for a month each spring, our dear father always gave us that treat; and I know that I, at least, used to get through my work here with all the greater zest because of looking forward to that month's enjoyment."

"And what is the result?" burst out Miss Charlotte, with quite unusual energy. "What is the result of all this going to London, pray? I am sure I heartily wish, and Fanny for one agrees with me, that we had never gone near the place! If we had not gadded about to London our poor pretty Alice would never have met that vile Valentine Brabourne with his deceitful face, and the family tragedy would never have taken place— —"

"And we should never have had Elaine to brighten our home and give us something to care for," said Ellen, speaking bravely, though the remembrance of her favorite sister brought the color to her wan face, and dimmed her eyes.

"You know the reason we never took Elaine to London was to keep her as much as possible dissociated from her step-mother and step-brother," went on Miss Charlotte, combatively.

"Yes, I know," answered her sister, quietly, "and that is where I think we have been so wrong. Because, much as we may have disliked Mrs. Brabourne, she was Valentine Brabourne's wife, and we had no right to allow Elaine to grow up quite estranged from her brother."

This took Charlotte's breath quite away. It was rare to hear Ellen assert herself at all, but to hear her deliberately say that Charlotte was wrong——!

"I am much more to blame than any of you," went on Ellen, "because I will admit that, at the time Elaine came to us, I was very, very sore at the conduct of Mrs. Brabourne and her relations, and I was only eager to get possession of the child and keep her from them all; but I was quite wrong, Charlotte. Think what an interest her little brother would have been to her."

"Well, I do think, Ellen, you cannot quite reflect on what you are saying," said Charlotte, her tongue loosed at last in a perfect torrent of words. "I have always said you read too many books, and I suppose you have some romantic notion of reconciliation in your head now. I have every respect for you, Ellen, as the head of this family, but you must allow me to say that, invalid as you are, and always confined to the house, you are apt to be taken hold of by crotchets and fancies. Let us look for a moment at the facts of the case: do you consider that Mrs. Brabourne was a fit person to have the bringing-up of Elaine?"

"No, I frankly say I do not. I am not suggesting that Mrs. Brabourne should have brought her up."

"Do you consider that the Ortons would be a nice house for Elaine to be constantly visiting at?"

"No, Charlotte, I cannot say I do."

"Do you imagine it at all likely that we could have been on terms of any intimacy with Mrs. Brabourne and her brother *without* allowing Elaine to visit there?"

"It might have been difficult," Miss Ellen, with rising color was constrained to admit; "but I was not advocating intimacy exactly; only that Elaine should be on friendly terms with little Godfrey."

"Is she *not* on friendly terms? I am sure then it is not my fault. She sends him a card every Christmas and a present every birthday, and always writes to her step-mother once a year. I really do not see how one could go much further without the intimacy which you admit is undesirable," cried Charlotte, in triumph.

"I do not admit that it is undesirable for Elaine to be intimate with her brother," said Ellen, with firmness.

"And pray how is the brother to be separated from the Orton crew, with their Sunday tennis-parties, their actors and actresses, their racing and their betting?"

"By asking him down here to stay with his sister," said Ellen, quietly.

A pause followed, an awful pause, which to good little Miss Fanny boded so darkly, that she hurled herself into the breach with energetic good-will.

"Dear me!" she cried, "what a good idea! What a treat for dear Elaine! I wonder nobody ever thought of it before!"

"Do you? *I* do not," said Charlotte, with withering contempt. "I wish, Fanny, I really wish you would reflect a little before you speak—you are as unpractical as Ellen is!"

Miss Fanny rejoiced in having at least partially diverted the storm to her own head—she was well used to it, and would emerge from Charlotte's ponderous admonitions as fresh and smiling as a daisy from under a roller.

"Do you know the atmosphere in which that boy has been brought up?" went on the irate speaker. "Do you know the society to which he is accustomed—the language he usually hears—and, very probably, speaks? He smokes and drinks, I should say—plays billiards and bets, very probably—a charming companion for our Elaine."

"My dear Charlotte, he is not fourteen yet, and he is being educated at the most costly private school—he can scarcely drink and gamble yet, I really think," remonstrated Ellen.

"Oh, of course, if you choose to invite him, there is no need to say more—no need to consult me—the house is not mine, as no doubt you wish to remind me," said Charlotte, with virulent injustice.

"Char!" cried Ellen, in much tribulation, "you know, my dear, so well that I would not for worlds annoy you—I would do nothing contrary to your judgment. You know how I lean upon you in everything. But think, dear, if this poor little boy is brought up, as you say, in a house-hold of Sabbath breaking, careless people, is it not only right, only charitable on our part to ask him here and see if we cannot show him the force of a good example? Are we so uncertain of the results of our teaching on Elaine that we feel sure he will corrupt her? May we not hope that the contrary will be the case—that the care we have lavished on our girl may help her to serve her brother?"

"My dear Ellen, I never yet put a rotten apple into a basket of good ones with the idea that the sound apples would cure the rotten one," said Miss Charlotte, grimly.

"Oh, surely the case is not the same," cried Miss Ellen, too flurried to search for the fallacy in her sister's analogy.

"Put it in this way: In two years—only two years, mind—Elaine will be her own mistress, whether or not she inherits the fortune which we think is hers by right, she will at least have a handsome allowance. With what confidence will you be able to launch her out into the world if you fear now that, in her own home, and surrounded by her home influences, she will not be able to withstand the corrupting power of a little boy of fourteen?"

"There again, that is all rhodomontade," cried Charlotte, "talking on, without reflection, which is very surprising in a woman of your sound sense. 'Launch her out into the world,' indeed! As if we were going to turn Elaine out of the house on her twenty first birthday, and wash our hands of her. What is to prevent her staying here always, if she pleases?"

"What is to keep her here a moment, if she chooses to go?" asked Ellen.

Charlotte hesitated a little.

"She is not likely to choose to go," she said.

"I am not so sure. There is a great deal—oh, a great deal in Elaine which none of us have ever seen," replied her sister. "It sometimes frightens me to think how little I know about her."

"I cannot imagine what you mean," said Charlotte, in the blank, dry tone she always used when she could not understand what was said.

"You will see some day," said Ellen, which Micaiah-like prophecy exasperated her sister the more.

"I think Ellen is right," said Emily, suddenly.

She had taken very little part in the discussion, but it was always assumed in the family that Emily would agree with Charlotte. The open desertion of this unfailing ally bereft the already much irritated lady of the power of speech.

"I mean about having the boy Brabourne to stay here," said Emily, "I have thought of the same thing myself more than once—that Elaine ought to get acquainted with him, and that the only way to do it would be to have him here, as we dislike the Ortons so much. I don't want people to think that we grudge him his share of the inheritance, and I think it looks like that, if we ignore him so persistently."

This was putting the matter on a ground less high than Ellen's, and one, therefore, more easily grasped by the others.

"I quite agree with you," murmured Fanny, and Charlotte raised an aroused face from her work.

"I daresay," said Emily, "that the Ortons all laugh at us for nasty covetous old maids, and that they think we dislike the boy simply because we are jealous, I don't exactly like to have people imagine that."

"Naturally not," Charlotte was beginning, in muffled tones, when Fanny exclaimed, in consternation,

"Bless us all! Look at the clock! Where can that child be?"

All looked up. The urn had long ceased to sing, the hot cake was cold, the fried ham had turned to white lumps of fat, and the finger of the clock pointed to seven.

They had been so absorbed in discussing Elaine's future that her present whereabouts had entirely been forgotten. Now at last they were thoroughly anxious.

Fanny rang the bell to have the tea re-made and the food heated, Emily hurried out to see if there were any signs of the wanderers on the road across the valley. Charlotte went to Acland, the coachman, to tell him to go and look for them.

"You had better harness Charlie, and take the carriage," she said, "I am afraid something is wrong—Miss Elaine has sprained her ankle, or something; anyway, it is getting so late, they had better drive home. It is very strange; I can't understand it at all."

"No, miss, not more can't I, for Jane's mostly a woonderful poonctual body for her tea," said Acland, chuckling.

"Never known her late before; something *must* have happened."

She walked nervously across the stable-yard, and looked down the drive.

Lo! and behold a trim little carriage was just entering, and perched on the box beside a strange coachman was Jane herself.

"Jane!" screamed Charlotte, "where's Miss Elaine?"

The carriage came to a standstill, and Elaine, white, and, somehow, altered-looking, stood up in it.

"Here I am, Aunt Char," she said; "I am quite safe."

"But what—what—what has happened?" gasped Miss Charlotte, staring at Elaine's travelling-companion. "Jane, what has happened?"

For all answer, Jane went off into a perfect volley of hysterics. It was scarcely to be wondered at, for her day's experience had far exceeded anything which had previously happened to her in all her fifty years of life.

Miss Charlotte was greatly alarmed, however, as Jane's usual demeanor was staid and unemotional to a degree. She ran for sal volatile, salts, for she hardly knew what, and soon her agitated and broken utterances drew Fanny and Emily out into the stable-yard.

Elaine did not go into hysterics. She stood up, very white, with shining eyes, which seemed bluer and larger than usual, as Lady Mabel introduced herself to the ladies, and began a clear and graphic description of what had taken place. It seemed too incredible, too horrifying to be true, that their little Edge Combe had been the scene of such violence and bloodshed.

So overcome were they that they quite forgot even to thank Lady Mabel for her kindness in bringing Elaine home, until she said, with a charmingly graceful bow, "And now I will not keep you, as I know you are longing to be rid of me;" and extended a hand in leave taking.

Then Miss Charlotte suddenly rallied, and said,

"Oh, but we could not on any account allow you to go on without taking some refreshment."

CHAPTER IX

So it would once have been—'tis so no more,
I have submitted to a new control;
A power is gone which nothing can restore,
A deep distress hath humanized my soul.
Wordsworth.

Lady Mabel did not require much pressing to induce her to accept the eagerly-offered tea and rest. She was tired and wet, hungry and thirsty, and in her graceful, Irish way, she made her acceptance seem like the conferring of a favor.

It was with some amused and speculative interest that she entered the house which had produced such an anachronism of Miss Elaine Brabourne.

The sisters greeted her with some nervousness, but as much cordiality as they knew how to show. Hospitality was a virtue they all possessed, though their opportunities of displaying it were few and far between. A grateful coolness was the first sensation which her ladyship experienced on entering the low-ceiled dining-room. A real Devonshire "high tea" was spread on the table in tempting profusion. There were chudleighs and cream, cakes and honey, eggs from the poultry-yard, and such ham as could only be cured in perfection at Edge Willoughby.

Miss Ellen lay on her couch near the window, and, as she stretched her thin hand in kindly greeting, her guest was much impressed by the refined and intellectual type of her features, and their lovable expression. In the blue, shadowy eyes, with their long lashes, underlined as they were with the purple marks of suffering, and wrinkling in the corners with advancing years, could be clearly traced the wreck of the same beauty which was budding in Elaine. Miss Emily too was handsome, though a hard expression robbed her face of the charm of her sister's. Little Miss Fanny, in her plump and plaintive amiability, was also prepossessing in her way, Charlotte only, with massive jaw, large features, high forehead, and stony gaze, conveyed a feeling of awe.

This forehead was not only high but *polished*. It shone and twinkled in the light, as though the skin were too tightly stretched on the bony knobs of the skull beneath. The sparse hair was tightly strained away from it above—

the frowning sandy eyebrows failed to soften it below. Lady Mabel guessed at once who was the ruling spirit of this unconventual sisterhood.

The furniture of the room was the furniture of a by-gone day, when art had not been promulgated, and nobody thought of considering beauty as in any sense an important factor of one's happiness. In that sad period the fated Misses Willoughbys' youth had been cast. Alas! for the waste of good material which must then have been the rule! Girls intended by nature to be beautiful and charming, yet who, by dint of never comprehending their mission, managed only to be ugly and clumsy. The parents of these girls had forgotten the sweet and harmonious names of their Anglo-Saxon ancestry. There were no more Ediths, or Ethels, or Cicelys, or Dorothys. Even the age of Lady Betty had passed and gone. Amelia, Caroline and Charlotte, Maria and Augusta were the order of the day.

It agonizes one only to think of the way those unlucky girls violated the laws of taste. Their fathers surrounded them with bulky mahogany furniture, and green and blue woollen damask. No wonder they dressed themselves in harrowing mixture of magenta and pink and mauve. Why should they trouble to arrange their hair with any view to preserving the *contour* of their head, when every tea-cup they used was a monstrosity, every jug or bowl the violation of a law?

The delicate fancy of Wedgewood and his school was banished and ignored with the Chippendale furniture and all the other graces of their grandfathers. Everything must be as large as possible, and as unwieldy. The questions of beauty and of usefulness were as nothing if only the table or chair were sufficiently cumbersome.

Mercifully for us that terrible time of degradation was short. A violent reaction soon set in. But the period left its marks behind it—left a generation which it had infected and lowered, out of whom it had knocked all the romance, from whom it had extracted, in some fatal way, the faculty to appreciate the beautiful, and the Misses Willoughby, house and all, were a living monument of its hideous influence.

The furniture remained as it had been in the life-time of their father. The sisters never wore anything out, so what would have been the object of renewing it? Everything looked as it used to look, and was arranged as it had been arranged in the days of their wasted girlhood, what could Elaine desire further? She would fare as they had done. It seldom occurred to them that their mode of life left anything to be desired.

Let it not for a moment be thought that the study of art is here advocated as a remedy for all the ills that flesh is heir to, or that the laws of beauty are in any way suggested as a substitute for those higher laws without which life must be incomplete. It is of course more than possible for a woman with no eye at all for color, and an absolute disregard for symmetry, to lead the life of a heroine or a saint. And yet an innate instinct seems to suggest a close connection between the beauty of holiness and all the other million forms in which beauty is hourly submitted to our eye; and it seems just within the limits of possibility that a link should exist between the decadence of taste and the undoubted and unparalleled stagnation of religious life which certainly was to be found side by side with it.

If we believe, as it is to be supposed Christians must, that a purpose exists in all the loveliness which is scattered about so lavishly through the natural world, then surely it follows that we can hardly afford to do quite without the help so afforded us, lest, in forgetting the loveliness of nature, we lose our aspiration towards the perfection of nature's God.

Certainly, in the Willoughby family, the sister who evidently had the strongest feeling for beauty was the sister who most strongly suggested the Christian ideal of the spiritual life.

The world in which Lady Mabel Wynch-Frère now found herself was a world so altogether new to her as to be exceedingly interesting to her restless mind.

She did not find the particular grade of society in which her own lot was cast conspicuously fascinating. She had ability enough to despise the superficial life of a large portion of the fashionable world; and her delight was to seek out "fresh fields and pastures new."

Elaine had inspired her with a peculiar interest. She was confident that the girl was a unique specimen in our essentially modern world. To watch the gradual unfolding of a mind behind the magnificent blankness of those enormous eyes, would be a study in emotions entirely after her ladyship's own heart. She knew that she already exerted a certain influence over this uncouth result of the Misses Willoughbys' attempts at education.

As the girl sat at table, not eating a mouthful, her gaze was steadily rivetted on the new comer. To every word she uttered, a breathless attention was accorded. In vain the aunts remonstrated, and urged their usually meek charge to eat. She seemed dazed—in a dream—and sat on as if she did not hear them.

"My youngest brother and I are the best of friends," said Lady Mabel to Miss Ellen. "We are the most alike of any of the family, and it is always a pleasure to us to be together. My little ones have had the whooping-cough—I adore my children, and I quite wore out myself with nursing them. When they were quite recovered, Claud thought I should take a little rest. My husband is just now in command of his regiment, and could not come with us, so we planned this little tour. To-day's tragic incident has been most unexpected. Stanton is our goal—we propose returning to London from thence, as we hear there is not much to see beyond. We have come along from Land's End—all the way! It seems perhaps a little heartless to say so, but in one way this tragedy will be of great interest to my brother. He has so desired to get a glimpse of the inner lives of these people. We have felt such complete outsiders, he and I—we have seen the country, but we cannot know the natives. At each inn, everybody puts on their company manners at once. We feel that they are endeavoring to suit their conversation to our rank. They will not appear before us naturally and simply; but you see, in a calamity like this, they have no time to pick their words. Like the doctor, one sees right into their hearts in such a moment; my brother will be deeply interested, I feel sure."

"I am sure I hope the Battishills will remember to treat Mr. Cranmer with all due respect," said Miss Charlotte, with her manner of blank incomprehension of a word that had been said.

It was such a conspicuously inapposite remark, that even Lady Mabel had no answer ready, and felt her flow of conversation unaccountably impeded.

"They are very respectable people, as a rule," went on Miss Charlotte, "but Mrs. Battishill is apt to be short in her temper if flurried. I hope she was not rude to you, Lady Mabel?"

"I scarcely saw her," answered her ladyship, perusing the speaker earnestly from her intense eyes.

"I can understand that desire to win the hearts of the people," said Miss Ellen, quietly; "and I think perhaps our Cornish and Devonshire folk are particularly hard for strangers to read; they are very reserved, and their feelings are deep, and not easily stirred."

"I am sure they are very ordinary kind of people, *I* never find any difficulty in getting on with them; I don't approve of all this rubbish about feeling," said Miss Charlotte, shortly.

Before the visitor had been half-an-hour at table, she knew that "I am sure" of Miss Charlotte's by heart, and a deep feeling of pity for those who had always to listen to it sprang up within her. There seemed to be no point on which the excellent lady was not sure, yet the mere statement of an opinion by anyone else appeared to rouse in her breast a feeling of covert ire.

"Elaine, my child, come here," said Miss Ellen, softly.

Elaine started, rose, and came round the table. Her aunt took her hands.

"You are eating nothing," she said, "and your hands are very hot. Don't you feel well? Are you tired?"

"I am sure," remarked Miss Charlotte, "she has had nothing to tire her—she drove all the way home from Poole."

"Yes, but she has been agitated—she has had a shock," said Miss Ellen, anxiously; with a strange feeling, as she looked into the girl's dilated eyes, that Elaine was gone, and that she was perusing the face of a stranger. "Do you feel shaken, dear child?"

"Yes," said Elaine at last, in her unready way.

"She had better have a little wine and water, and lie down," said her aunt, sympathetically. "Go and lie on the sofa, Elaine dear, and rest. I am so vexed—so grieved for her to see such a terrible thing," she said to Lady Mabel. "One would always keep young girls in ignorance even to existence of crime."

"Oh, would you?" said her ladyship, in accents of such real surprise that each sister looked up electrified at the bare idea of questioning such orthodox teaching. "I mean," she explained, with a smile, "that I think women ought to be very useful members of society, and I should not at all like to feel that the sight of a wounded wayfarer by the roadside only inspired one with the desire to faint. I shall wish all my girls to attend ambulance classes, so that a broken limb may always find them a help, not a hindrance. One cannot shut up girls in bandboxes nowadays, and I would not, if I could. Let them be of some use in their generation—able to stop a bleeding artery till the doctor comes, as well as able to bake a cake or make their clothes. Do you agree with me, Miss Willoughby?"

Ellen hardly knew. The doctrine was to her so utterly novel. Charlotte's breath was so taken away that she had not a word to offer.

"Every woman is sure to have emergencies in her life, is she not?" asked her ladyship, in her earnest winning way. "If not of one kind, then of another. If she marries, her children are certain to call forth her resources, if she does not marry, her nephews and nieces very probably will do so instead. How can a girl take a serious view of life if she does not know its realities? Of course there are limits—there are things which had better not be discussed before girls, because it would do them no good to know them, and there is no need to intrude the ghastly and the wicked unnecessarily into their lives; but I certainly would train a girl's nerves so that a shock should not utterly prostrate her. I would teach her courage and presence of mind."

There was no answer whatever to this speech. Miss Charlotte, having never reflected on the subject in her life, had no opinion to offer. She had always taken it for granted that a lady should do nothing beyond needlework, and perhaps a little gardening. "Accomplishments" were the order of her day, in which list were bracketed together, with grim unconscious irony, watercolor painting and the manufacture of wax flowers!

Her ladyship rose, and crossed the room with her light energetic step to where Elaine had seated herself on the sofa. The girl had not lain down, but remained with her eyes fixed on the visitor, drinking in every word she uttered. A cool hand was laid on her forehead, and a pair of wonderful eyes gazed down into hers!

"Oh, yes—her forehead is very hot. I would not give her wine; give her some iced milk and soda water and let her go to bed, she is quite exhausted," she said. "And now I must bid you good-night, if I do not wish to be benighted," she added, rising.

"Oh, but indeed we cannot let you go on to-night," said Miss Ellen eagerly. "You must be good enough to stay with us here. We have many more rooms than we can occupy, and we shall be glad to be of use——"

There was some polite demur, but it was overruled; all the sisters seconded Ellen's invitation, and finally Lady Mabel gratefully accepted it, and sent her coachman up to Poole, to apprise her brother of her whereabouts, and to bring back the latest news of the invalid.

Meanwhile the night had come. With all its stars it hung quietly over the fairy valley in solemn and moonless splendor. Elaine, sent to bed, had crept out from between the sheets, and knelt, crouched down by her window, awaiting the return of the messenger from Poole.

So irregular a proceeding was a complete novelty in her career; but oh! the strange, new, trembling charm of having such a day's experiences to look back upon!

It had all happened so rapidly, in such a few hours. That afternoon had begun, dull and eventless; now, how different was everything. In an undefined, vague way she felt that things could never more be quite as they had been. A boundary line had been passed. The world was different, and for the first time in her nineteen years she was engaged in the perilous delight of contemplating her own identity.

Up to the dark purple vault of heaven were sighed that night vague aspirations from a heart which had never aspired before; a prayer went with them, which, brief and shapeless as it was, was nevertheless the first real prayer of Elaine Brabourne's heart:

"Oh, if only he may not die!"

After all, the Misses Willoughby were but human, and had all the feelings of the English provincial middle-classes.

Their reverence for the aristocracy had something well-nigh touching in its simple faith. Determined as they were against anything unconventional, they yet almost dared to think that Lady Mabel Wynch-Frère had a right to hold opinions—a right conferred on her by that mystic handle to her name, which sanctioned an eccentricity that would have been unpardonable in any woman less strongly backed up—any woman supported by a social position less unquestionable.

Moreover, they could not but be sensible that the sojourn of this star of fashion at Edge Willoughby would set all the neighborhood talking, and that to them would be assigned, for a time at least, all the local importance they could possibly desire. Her ladyship's heresies were more than condoned, in consideration of her ladyship's consequence.

CHAPTER X

... For me,
Perhaps I am not worthy, as you say,
Of work like this; perhaps a woman's soul
Aspires, and not creates; yet we aspire...
... I,
Who love my art, would never wish it lower
To suit my stature. I may love my art,
You'll grant that even a woman may love art,
Seeing that to waste true love on anything
Is womanly, past question.

E. B. Browning.

The heat of the blazing day was just beginning to be tempered with light puffs of sea-scented air as the sun declined, when the Honorable Claud Cranmer stepped upon the platform at Stanton, and asked the station-master if the London train were due.

"Yes, it was—just signalled from Coryton;" and Claud, after the manner of his race, put his hands behind him, wrinkled up his eyelids on account of the sun, and gazed away along the flat marshy valley of the Ashe river, to catch the first glimpse of the approaching train.

On the other side of the sandy river mouth lay the little old village of Ashemouth, picturesquely nestling at the foot of the tall cliff. It was a pretty view, but not to be compared at all with the beauty of Edge Combe.

"I do hope the young lady will arrive," soliloquised the young man. "The poor fellow ought to have some one with him who knows him. I only wish I could hit upon some clue to the mystery; it's the most baffling thing!"

He sighed, and then he yawned vigorously, for he had been up the greater part of the night, and he was a person whom it did not suit to have his rest disturbed. The village nurse had been quite inadequate to the task of holding poor Allonby in his bed, and so had aroused "the gentleman" at about two, since when he had only had an hour's nap. The day had been most distressing. Lady Mabel had sent Joseph, the coachman, into Stanton for ice, which he had obtained with difficulty, but it seemed as if nothing would abate the fierce heat in that sick-chamber, they longed for cool wind and cloudy skies to obscure the brilliant weather in which the haymakers were so rejoicing. As the fever grew higher, Dr. Forbes' face grew graver, and it was with a sickening dislike to being the bearer of such tidings that Claud set out for the station to meet the patient's sister, and drive her up to the farm.

The train appeared at last, curving its dark bulk along the gleaming metals with the intense deliberation which marks the pace of all trains on branch lines of the South-Western.

"No need to hurry oneself this hot weather," the engine appeared to be saying, comfortably, while Claud was feverishly thinking how much hung on every moment. He had formed no pre-conceived idea as to what Miss Allonby's exterior would be like. His eyes dwelt anxiously on the somewhat numerous female figures which emerged from the carriage doors. Most of them were mammas and nurses, with two or three small children in striped cotton petticoats, whose cheeks looked sadly in want of the fresh salt air of Stanton.

At last he became aware of a girl, who he guessed might be the one he sought for, merely because he could not see anyone else who could possibly answer to that description.

This girl must have alighted from the train with great celerity, for her portmanteau had already been produced from the van and laid beside her. She was rather tall and particularly slight—somewhat thin, in fact. She wore a dust-colored tweed suit very plainly made, and a helmet-shaped cap of the same cloth. Her face was pale, with an emphasis in the outline of the chin which faintly recalled her handsomer brother. Her eyes were keen, and her expression what Americans call intense.

She was walking towards Mr. Cranmer, but her gaze was fixed on a porter who stood just behind him.

"Is there a cart or anything in waiting to take me to Poole Farm?" she asked, with the thin clearness of voice and purity of accent belonging to London girls. Claud stepped forward, raising his cap.

"I'm afraid I can't lay claim to being a *cart*," he said, modestly, "but perhaps you would kindly include me in your definition of a *thing*. I am in waiting to take you to Poole Farm."

An amused look broke over the girl's face, a look not of surprise but of arrested interest; in a moment it changed, a shadow fell on the eyes as if a cloud swept by, she made a step forward and spoke breathlessly.

"You come from Poole Farm? What news do you bring me of my brother?"

Claud felt a sudden movement of most unnecessary emotion; there was such a feverish, pathetic force in the question, and in the expression of the mouth which asked it, that he was conscious of an audible falter in his voice, as he replied, as hopefully as he could:

"Mr. Allonby has had a very bad accident, it is folly not to tell you that at once. He is very ill, but the doctor says he has a fine constitution, and hopes that everything—that all—in short, that he'll pull through all right. You will want to reach him as quickly as possible. Will you come this way, please?"

He hurriedly took her travelling-bag from her, not looking at her face, lest he should see tears; and hastened out of the station to where Joseph stood with the trap.

By the servant's side stood an unclassified looking man of quiet appearance, and plain, unostentatious dress. As Mr. Cranmer approached he stepped forward and touched his hat.

"Mr. Dickens, sir, from Scotland Yard," he said, in a low voice.

"Oh, ah! Yes, of course. You came down by this train. Just get on the box, will you, and we will take you straight to the scene of the tragedy, as I suppose all the newspapers will have it to-morrow," and Claud motioned Joseph to his seat with a hurried injunction "to look sharp." When he turned again to Miss Allonby, she was quite quiet and composed. Nobody could have guessed that she had received any news that might shock her. "Wasting my pity, after all, it seems," thought Claud, as he helped her into the carriage. "I hope you will excuse my driving up with you," he said, as he took his place beside her. "It's a good long walk, and I'm anxious to be back as fast as possible."

"I can only thank you most sincerely for taking so much trouble on our account," she answered, at once, "and I should be so grateful if you would tell me something of what has happened. I am quite in the dark, and—the suspense is oppressive."

"I shall be only too glad to help you in any way," he said, with one of his deft little bows, which always conveyed an impression of finished courtesy. "You are Miss Allonby, I presume?"

"Yes—and you?"

"My name's Cranmer, and I am a total stranger to your brother, whom I have never seen but in a state of perfect unconsciousness."

He proceeded to relate to her all the incidents of the eventful yesterday.

She listened with an interest which was visible but controlled, and with perfect self-possession. Her eyes rested on his face all the while he was speaking—not with any disagreeable persistency, but with a simple frank desire to comprehend everything—not the mere words alone, but any such shade of meaning as looks and expression can give.

With his habit of close observation, Claud studied her as he spoke, and by the end of his narration had catalogued her features and attributes with the accuracy which was an essential part of him. There are men to whom girls are in some sense a mystery, who take in dreamy and comprehensive ideas of them, surrounded by a little idealization or fancy of their own, these could never tell you what a woman wore, how her dress was cut, not even the arrangement of her front hair—that all important detail!—nor the color of her eyes or size of her hands. It is to be conjectured that a certain loss of illusion might result to these men when, on being married, they find themselves unavoidably in close proximity to one of these heretofore mistily contemplated divinities, and by slow degrees make the inevitable discovery that their "phantom of delight" eats, drinks, sleeps, brushes her hair, and dresses and undresses in as mundane a fashion as their own.

Claud Cranmer, though doubtless he lost much delight by never surrounding womanhood with a halo of unreality, yet would certainly be spared any such lowering of a preconceived ideal, since he took stock in a detailed and matter-of-fact way of every woman he met, and by the time Miss Allonby and he reached Poole Farm could have handed in a report as cool and unpoetically worded as Olivia's description of herself—"*Item* two lips, indifferent red—*item* two grey eyes with lids to them."

But his companion's eyes were not grey, they were hazel and were the only feature of her face meriting to be called handsome. As before stated, she was pale, and had the air of being overworked—though this might be partially the result of a long and hurried journey. Her skin was fair and pure, with an appearance of delicacy, by which term is here meant refinement, not ill health. Her impassive critic observed that her ears were small and well-set, that the shape of her head was good, her teeth white and even, and her eyelashes long, she had no claims at all to be considered beautiful, or even what is called a pretty girl—which being stated, the reader will doubtless rush at once to the conclusion that she was plain, which was far from the case. It was just such a face as scarcely two people would be agreed upon. One might find it interesting, another complain that it was hatchetty, the former would admire the clean-cut way of the features, the latter gloomily prophecy nut-crackers for old age, and lament over angular shoulders and sharp elbows.

It was not a face which attracted Claud. He was an admirer of beauty, and preferred it with a certain admixture of consciousness, he liked a woman's eyes to meet his with a full knowledge of the fact that they were of opposite sexes. He had a weakness for pretty figures, cased in dresses which were a miracle of cut; though of course the wearer must be more than an ornamental clothes-peg: he was too intelligent to admire a nonentity.

Miss Allonby's dress was not badly cut, neither was it put on without some idea of the way clothes should be worn; but it was shabby, and had evidently never been costly. Her gloves, too, fitted her, and were the right sort of glove, but they were old and much soiled. Her shoes gave evidence that her foot was not too large for her height, and her hands, as Claud mentally noted, *were size six and a quarter*. Her face wore an expression which can only be described as preoccupied. Of course it was natural that on this particular day she should be thinking only of her brother; but her new acquaintance had penetration enough to know that there was more than a temporary anxiety in her eyes. Had he met her on any other day, under any other circumstances, it would have been the same; he was merely a passing event—something which was in no sense part of the life she was leading. She seemed to convey in some indescribable fashion the fact that he was not of the slightest importance to her, and the idea inspired a wholly unreasonable sensation of irritation.

An unmarried doctor once somewhat coarsely engaged to point out all the portraits of unmarried women in a photographic album, on the theory that the countenance of all those who are single wears an expression of unsatisfied longing. Wyn Allonby's face would hardly have come under this heading. Hers was not a happy nor a perfectly contented look, but neither could it be said in any sense to express longing. It was the look of one who has much serious work to do, the doing of which involves anxiety, but also brings interest and pleasure—a brave, thoughtful, preoccupied look, more suggestive of a middle-aged man of science than a young girl.

Claud found something indirectly unflattering in such an expression; he liked to have the female mind entirely at his disposal, *pro tem*. Her age, too, puzzled him; it was necessarily provoking to such an adept to find himself unable to decide this point within five years. She might be twenty-one, and looking older, or she might be twenty-five, and looking younger, or she might claim any one of the three intermediate dates.

When he had told her all that there was to tell, he relapsed into silent speculation on these important points, now inclining to think that a life of hardship had made her prematurely self-possessed, now that her peculiarly unconscious temperament gave an air of fictitious youth. He would have liked to ask her some questions, or, rather, deftly to extract from her a few details as to who she was and what were her circumstances. But Miss Allonby gave him no opening. She was silent without being shy, which is certainly undue presumption in a woman.

Her first words seemed to be extorted from her almost by force.

They had left Stanton far behind. The distance from thence to Edge Combe was said to be about five miles; but these miles were not horizontal, but perpendicular, which somehow tended to increase their length considerably. They had climbed gradually but continuously for some time between tall hedges, up a lane remarkable only for its monotony; thence they had emerged, not without gratitude, into the Philmouth Road. This was a wide highway, somewhat indefinite as to its edges, which were fringed irregularly with hart's-tongue and other ferns, or clumped with low brambles bearing abundant promise of a future blackberry harvest. On either side a row of ragged and onesided pine-trees, stooping as if perpetually cringing before the stinging blows of the wild sou'-westers, which had so tortured them from their youth up that they habitually leaned one way, like children whose minds are warped from their natural bent by undue influence in one direction.

Behind these trees the sky was beginning to flame with sunset, making their uncouth forms stand out weirdly dark in the still air.

For a short way they drove quietly along this road, then turned down a precipitous lane to the left, and wound along till a white gate was reached. Mr. Dickens from Scotland Yard jumped down and opened the gate; and as the carriage went slowly through, and turned a corner, the effect was like a transformation scene, and a cry of wondering admiration broke from the silent girl.

They stood on the very edge and summit of a descent so steep as to be almost a precipice. Below them lay the fairy valley, half-hidden in a pearly mist, with a vivid stretch of deep-blue sea as its horizon. Well in evidence lay Poole Farm, directly beneath them, a sluggish wreath of smoke curling lazily up from its great chimney. The road curved to and fro down the abrupt hillside like a white folded ribbon, here visible, there lost behind a belt of ash trees.

"How beautiful," said Wynifred,—"how beautiful it is!"

The rest of evening was over it all—over the tiny, ancient grey church far, far away towards the valley's mouth; over the peaceable red cows which lay meditatively here and there among the grass; over the sun-burnt group of laborers, who, their day's mowing done, were slowly making their way down to their hidden cottages, with fearless eyes of Devon blue turned on the strangers and their carriage.

"What splendid terra-cotta-colored people!" said Miss Allonby, following them with her appreciative gaze. Mr. Cranmer was unable to help laughing. "They are a delicate shade of the red-brown of the cliffs," said the girl, dreamily. "How full of color everything is!"

Her companion mentally echoed the remark: it was the concise expression of a thought which in him had been only vague. She was right, — it was the color, the strange glow of grass, and cliffs, and sea, which so impressed eyes accustomed only to the "pale, unripened beauties of the north."

"That is Poole Farm, right beneath us," he said. "It is not so near as it looks."

"Oh, if I were only there!" she burst out; and then was suddenly still, as if ashamed of her involuntary cry.

"Get on as fast you can, Joseph," said Mr. Cranmer, and felt himself unaccountably obliged to sit so as not to see the pale face beside him, nor to pity the evident force which she found it necessary to employ to avoid a complete break-down.

When at last they stopped at the farm-yard gate, and he had helped her out, and seen her tall, slight figure disappear swiftly within the house, he experienced a relaxation of mental tension which was, he told himself, greatly out of proportion to the occasion; and, strolling into the big kitchen, was sensible of a quite absurd throb of relief when he heard that Dr. Forbes hoped his patient was just a little better.

"It is strange how people vary," he reflected. "I have met two girls, one to-day, one yesterday, neither of whom is in the smallest degree like any girl I ever saw before."

By which it will be inferred that his acquaintance with modern developments of girlhood had been limited pretty much to one particular class of society. The girl art-student he had never met in any of her varieties; and this opportunity of contemplating a new class, of perusing a fresh chapter in his favorite branch of study, was by no means without its charm.

CHAPTER XI

The clouds that gather round the setting sun
Do take a sober coloring from an eye
That hath kept watch o'er man's mortality;
Another race hath been, and other palms are won.
Thanks to the human heart by which we live,
Thanks to its tenderness, its joys and fears,
To me the meanest flower that blows can give
Thoughts that do often lie too deep for tears.
Wordsworth.

The mellow coloring of the third evening which Claud Cranmer had spent at Poole Farm was inundating the valley with its warm floods of light.

He was leaning meditatively against the stile which led from the farm garden to the Waste, and his eyes were fixed on the stretch of summer sea which, like a crystal gate, barred the entrance to the Combe. His thoughts were busy with a two-fold anxiety—partly for the man who lay fighting for life in the farmhouse behind him, partly concerning the mystery which attended his fate.

Mr. Dickens of Scotland Yard had so far succeeded in discovering merely what everybody knew before, and was in a state of complete bewilderment which, he begged them to believe, was a most unusual circumstance in his professional career. The mystery of the pudding-basin and the blue dishcloth was as amazing and as incomprehensible to him as it was to William Clapp himself and his scared "missus."

The good people of the district were sensible of a speedy dwindling of courage and hope, when it became evident that the London detective could see no farther through a brick wall than they could.

They did long to have the stigma lifted from their district by the discovery that the murderer had been a stranger, an outlander, anybody but a native of Edge Combe; but, if Mr. Dickens had an opinion at all in the matter, it was that he was inclined to believe the crime perpetrated by some one who knew where to find his victim, and had probably walked out of the village purposely to give him his quietus. But why? What possible animus could any dweller in the valley have against the inoffensive young artist?

The detective was privately certain that the entire motive for this affair must be looked for under the surface.

"It's probable," said he to Mr. Cranmer, "that the victim himself is the only person likely to tell us anything about it. If he has enemies, it is to be supposed that he knew it. Mrs. Clapp has told us that he burnt a letter he received. That letter may have contained a warning which he thought fit to disregard. I have tried to make Mrs. Clapp recall any particulars she may have noticed as to its appearance, handwriting, or post-mark. But she seems to have noticed nothing; these rustics are very unobservant. I should like to ask Miss Allonby a few questions. She might be able to give us a clue."

But Miss Allonby, being summoned, could not help them in the least.

She came down from her brother's sick-room, with a tranquil composed manner, which encouraged Mr. Dickens to hope great things of her. She seated herself in one of the big kitchen chairs, and looked straight at him.

"You want to ask me something?" said she.

Claud spoke to her.

"Yes," he said, "we want to ask you certain personal questions which would be very rude if we had not a strong warrant for them. I am sure you are as anxious as we are that the mystery of your brother's accident should be cleared up?"

"Oh, yes," said Wyn.

"Well, Mr. Dickens thinks that the motive we have to search for was a good deal deeper than mere robbery; he wants to know if Mr. Allonby had enemies. Do you know of anyone who wished him ill?"

"No, certainly I don't," she replied at once. "Osmond is a most good-natured fellow, he never quarrels with a creature—he is too lazy to quarrel, I think. I don't know of a single enemy we have."

"Will you tell me your brother's motive in coming down here to Edge Combe?"

"Certainly. He came here to sketch. He had sold his landscapes at the Institute very well, and a friend of the gentleman who bought them wanted two in the same style. Osmond thought a change to the country would do him good. An artist friend of ours recommended Edge Combe, and so he came here."

"Do you know the friend who recommended Edge Combe?"

A slight hint of extra color rose in the girl's cheeks.

"Yes, I know him; he is a Mr. Haldane, a student in the Academy Schools."

"On good terms with your brother?"

"Yes, of course; but he knows my sister Jacqueline better than he knows Osmond."

"Would he be likely to write to Mr. Allonby?"

"No, I hardly think so. He never has, that I know of. He sent the address of the inn on a postcard. Mrs. Clapp would know him—he stayed here several weeks last year."

The detective pondered.

"You are sure there was no quarrel—no jealousy—nothing that could——"

"What, between my brother and Mr. Haldane? The idea is quite absurd. They are only very slightly acquainted, and Osmond is at least six years older than he is!"

"Will you tell me, on your honor, whether you yourself can account in any way at all for what has occurred? Had you any reason whatever to think it likely such a thing might happen? Or were you absolutely and utterly horrified and surprised by such news?"

"I was horrified and surprised beyond measure; so were my sisters. We are as much in the dark about the matter as you can possibly be. I can offer no guess or conjecture on the subject; it is quite inexplicable to me."

"And you would think it quite folly to connect it in any way with Mr. Haldane?"

She laughed rather contemptuously.

"I'm afraid, even if he did cherish a secret grudge, Mr. Haldane is not rich enough to employ paid agents to do his murders for him; and, as he was at work in the R.A. schools when the crime was committed, it does seem to me unlikely, to say the least of it, that he had anything to do with the matter. What can make you think he had?"

"Merely," answered the detective, somewhat confused, "that in these cases sometimes everything hangs on what seems such a trifling bit of evidence; and as you said this gentleman recommended your brother to come to this particular place——"

"You thought he had an *arrière pensée*. I am afraid you are quite wrong. I cannot see how Mr. Haldane could possibly serve any ends of his own by compassing my brother's destruction," she said, evidently with ironical gravity. "Besides, I hardly think that either he or his agent would have troubled to carry away an empty basin as a momento of the deed."

"The people all declare that no stranger passed through the village on that day," put in Claud.

"No; and none of the inhabitants walked out towards the farm in the afternoon except Miss Brabourne and her maid. I have ascertained that past a doubt. I don't see any daylight nowhere," said poor Mr. Dickens, becoming ungrammatical in his despair.

Claud could not but echo the remark. He walked over to Edge Willoughby in the afternoon with the same dreary bulletin. His sister was still there; she was anxious not to leave till the crisis was over, and her hostesses were proud to keep her. Elaine he scarcely saw; she was practising. He declined to stay to tea, as the good ladies urgently invited him. With a mind less absorbed he might have found them and their niece most excellent entertainment for a few idle hours; but, as it was, he was only anxious to get back to the farm, while every hour might bring the final change and crisis in the young artist's condition.

Was everything to remain so shrouded in mystery? he wondered. Was there to be no further light shed on the details of so mysterious a case? Would Allonby die and go down in silence to the grave, unable to name his murderer, or to give any hint as to the motive of so vile an assault? Over all these things did he ponder as he leaned against the stile, and saw with unseeing eyes the loveliness of the dying day change and deepen over the misty hollow of the valley.

He looked at his watch. It was past eight o'clock, and the quiet of dusk was settling over everything. He wondered what was passing in the sick-room—he longed to be there, but did not like to go, lest he might disturb the privacy of a brother and sister's last moments. But he did wish he could persuade the pale Wynifred to take some rest—she had never closed her eyes during the twenty-four hours she had been at Poole.

As these thoughts travelled through his mind, he heard a slight sound, and, raising his eyes, saw the subject of his meditations emerge from the open farmhouse door. She did not see him, and moved slowly forward, with her eyes fixed on the western sky. Down the little path she passed, and then stepped upon the grass of the little lawn, and, with a long sigh almost like a sob, sat down upon the turf, and buried her face in her hands.

"Was it all over?" Claud wondered, as he stood hesitatingly by the stile. "Should he go to her, or should he leave her to the privacy of her grief?"

Unable to decide, he waited a few moments, and presently saw her raise her head again, and look around her like one who took in for the first time the fact of her surroundings.

Stretching her hand, she gathered some white pinks from the garden border and inhaled their spicy fragrance; and Claud, slowly approaching, diffidently crossed the grass to where she sat.

"Good evening," he said, raising his hat politely.

"Good evening," she said, "and good news at last. I know you will be glad to hear. He is sleeping beautifully. Nurse and Dr. Forbes sent me away to get some rest, and I came out here into this air—this reviving air."

"You don't know how glad I am," said Claud, from the bottom of his heart. "I was so anxious; it seemed as if that terrible fever must wear him out. But he'll do well now. Let me wish you joy."

"Thank you," she said, with a smile, and her eyes fixed far away on the distance. "I feel like thanking everyone to-night—my whole heart is made up of thanksgiving. You don't know what Osmond is to us girls. We are orphans."

"Ah! indeed!" said Claud, giving a sympathetic intonation to the commonplace words.

"Yes; the loss of him would have been——"

She stopped short, and, after a pause, began to talk fast, as though the relaxed strain of her feelings made it imperative that she should pour out her heart to somebody.

"I had been sitting all the afternoon with my heart full of such ingratitude," she said. "I felt as if all the beauty was gone out of the world, and all the heart out of life. You know

> 'The clouds that gather round the setting sun
> Do take a sober coloring from an eye
> That hath kept watch o'er man's mortality.'

I could not help thinking of that, and of how true it was, as I watched the little red bits of cloud swimming in the blue, and it kept ringing in my head till I thought I must say it out loud—

> 'Another race has been, and other palms are won.'

I do not want him, my brother, to win his palm yet; I wanted to look at sunsets with him again, and hear him enjoy this beauty as he can enjoy it—so thoroughly. Oh, we are very selfish in wanting to keep people we love on earth, when they might win their palms! But it is only human nature after all, you know; and I do think Osmond's life is a happy one, though it is so full of care."

"I am sure it must be," said Claud, quietly, as he sat down on the grass beside her. "Life is a pleasant thing to every man who is young and has good health, more especially if he has love to brighten his lot. I think your brother a fort right, because you would have thought my denial an empty protestation, designed to make you say it again, with more decision; so I thought it better to let it drop."

"Do you think we are the best judges of our own courage, or, in short, of our own capabilities any way?" asked Mr. Cranmer, following her example by gathering a few pinks and putting them in his button-hole.

"I don't know; I think we ought to be—what do you think about it?" asked she, evidently with a genuine interest in the subject itself, and none to spare for Claud Cranmer.

It was strange how this manner of hers non-plussed him. He was accustomed enough to hear girls discuss abstract topics, inward feelings, and the reciprocity of emotion—who in these days is not? But in his experience the process was always intended to serve as a delicate vehicle for flirtation, and however much the two people so occupied might generalise verbally, they always mentally referred to the secret feelings of their own two selves, and nobody else.

He felt that Miss Allonby expected him to give a well thought out and adequate answer to her question, while he had been merely trifling with the subject, and had absolutely no intention of entering upon a serious discussion.

He hesitated, therefore, in his reply, and at last calmly remarked that he believed he knew his faults, intimately—he saw so much of them; but that his acquaintance with his virtues was so slight that he scarcely knew them by sight much less by heart.

She laughed, a clear fresh laugh of appreciation; but objected that this was not a fair answer.

"But, perhaps," said she, "you are one of those who don't think it right to analyse their own emotions?"

He shrugged his shoulders.

"I don't know about thinking it right," he said. "Of course I have to do it, or pretend to do it, if I don't wish to be voted a fool by everyone I meet. And that reminds me, I have discovered, here in these wilds, a young lady who never even heard of the current topics of the day—who, far from dissecting the sentiments of her inmost being, does not even know herself the possessor of such a morbid luxury as an inmost being. You ought to see her; she is the most curious sample of modern young lady-hood it was ever my lot to meet. She has the mind and manners of an intelligent girl of ten; my sister tells me she is nineteen, but I really can scarcely believe it. She lives with some maiden aunts who have brought her to this pass between them. My sister is enthusiastic about her, and most anxious to have the pleasing task of teaching this backward young idea how to shoot. If she is as free from the follies as she is from the graces of girlhood, she is certainly unique."

"You make me very anxious to see her. She must be like one of Walter Besant's heroines—Phyllis, in the "Golden Butterfly," or one of those. I have often wondered if such a girl existed. Is she charming?"

"N—no. I don't think I could truthfully say I thought so; and yet she has all the makings of a beauty in her; but you can't attempt conversation—she wouldn't understand a word you said. She has seen nothing, heard nothing, read nothing. That last remark is absolutely, not relatively true; she really has read nothing. It gives, one an oppressive sense of responsibility; one has to pick one's words, for fear of being the first to suggest evil to such a primeval mind."

Wyn laughed softly, and took a deliberate look at him as he lay on the turf. He had put up his arms over his head, and looked very contented and a good deal amused. He enjoyed chattering to a girl who had some sense, and was for the moment almost prepared to pardon the paleness and thinness, and even the unconsciousness of his companion, which latter characteristic affected him far the most seriously of the three.

"Most undeveloped heroines turn out very charming when some one takes them in hand, and sophisticates them," said the girl. "I wonder if your discovery would do the same?"

"I can't say. She has a very fine complexion," said Claud, inconsequently. "Her skin is rather the color of that pinky reach of sky yonder. What a night it is! It feels like Gray's elegy to me. I wonder if you know what I mean?"

"Yes, I know. What an amount of quotations come swarming to one's mind on such a night! It is a consolation, I think, in the midst of one's own utter inadequacy to express one's feelings, to feel that some one else has done it for you so beautifully as Gray."

A step behind them on the gravel, and, turning quickly, Wyn beheld Dr. Forbes.

"Get up, young woman, get up this minute. I sent you to rest, not to come and amuse this young sprig of nobility with your conversation. Very nice for him, I've no manner of doubt; but, nice or not, you've got to bid him good-night and go to bed."

Wyn rose at once, but attempted to plead.

"I have been resting, doctor, indeed—drinking in this lovely air. I had to go out of doors—one must always go out of doors when one is feeling strongly, I think—roofs are so in the way. I wanted to look right up as far as that one star, and to send my heart up as far as my eyes could reach!"

The doctor looked down at the face raised to him—pale with watching, but alive with happiness.

"I'm of the opinion, Miss Allonby," said he, with a mouth sterner than his eyes, "that if the Honorable Claud Cranmer finds you so interesting when you're worn out with waking and fasting, you'll be simply irresistible after a good night's rest."

The girl had vanished almost before this dreadful remark was concluded. The doctor chuckled as he watched her flight.

"There's girls and girls," he remarked, sententiously; "some take to their heels when you joke them about the men. Some don't. I thought she'd go."

"I had rather," said Claud, nettled, "that you indulged your humor at anyone's expense but mine."

"Oh, that'll never hurt you," said the doctor, placidly, rubbing his eyeglasses with his red silk handkerchief, "nor her either. Young people get so fine-drawn and finikin now-a-days."

Claud smiled.

"I perceive, doctor, that you do not hold with the modern ideas concerning introspection. You are a refreshing exception. I regret that I was born a generation too late to adopt your habits of thought."

"Habits of thought! Why, t'would trouble you mighty little to adopt all I've got," was the genial reply. "I've avoided all habits of thought all my life, and that's what makes me so useful a man. I just think what I think without referring to any book to tell me which way to begin. Hoot! I'd never think on tram-lines, as you do: I go clean across country, that's my way, and I'm bound to get to the end long before you, in your coach-and-four."

"Yes," conceded Claud, "I expect you would; that is, if you didn't come a cropper on the way."

CHAPTER XII

A low cottage in a sunny bay
Where the salt sea innocuously breaks,
And the sea-breeze as innocently breathes
On Devon's leafy shores.
Wordsworth.

"May I come in, Miss Willoughby? My brother is here, and has brought good news from Poole."

"Come in, pray, Lady Mabel; and Mr. Cranmer too," said Ellen, raising herself eagerly on her couch. "Tell me all about this good news. Mr. Allonby will live?"

"He will live, and is doing finely," said Claud, shaking hands with the invalid. "He has recognised his sister this morning, and spoken several coherent sentences. Dr. Forbes is much elated, and I must say I am greatly relieved; it would have been very tragic had he not recovered."

"I am deeply thankful," said Miss Ellen, with a sympathetic moisture in her eyes. "How delighted his sister must be!"

"She is. I fancy, from what I can gather, that she and her sisters are quite dependent on their brother; she told me they were orphans."

"Poor children!" said Lady Mabel, in her impulsive way. "It would have been terrible had it ended fatally. I feel quite a weight lifted from my mind. Miss Willoughby, I must express to you my hearty thanks for having been so long troubled with me. I have sent Joseph into Stanton with a telegram telling Edward to come and fetch me, as Claud does not seem inclined to come back to London just yet awhile."

"I want to try to get a clue to this affair before I go," said Claud, "for it has piqued my curiosity most amazingly. The fellow from Scotland Yard has quite made up his mind that we shall get the whole truth from Mr. Allonby's own lips; I'm inclined to think he must be right; but, of course, one can't torment the poor fellow about it while he is so weak."

"How very reserved Englishmen are!" burst out Lady Mabel. "All of them are alike! Claud tells me that this Miss Allonby knows absolutely nothing of her brother's affairs, though, from what she said, they seem to be on the most confidential terms. She had never heard that he had an enemy. Claud, my dear boy, draw a moral from this sad story. Write the names and addresses of your secret foes upon a slip of paper, seal it in an envelope, and give it to me, not to be opened till you are discovered mysteriously murdered in an unfrequented spot."

"A good idea, that, Mab," responded Claud, cheerfully, "and one that I shall certainly act upon. How would it be if I were to add a few memoranda to every name, hinting at the means of murder most likely to be employed by each? So that if I were knocked down with a cudgel, you might lay it to Smith; if prussic acid were employed, it would most likely be Jones; while a pistol-shot could be confidently ascribed as Robinson. Save the detectives a lot of trouble that way."

"Oh, how can you jest on such a subject!" said Miss Ellen, reproachfully.

The brother and sister were abashed, and Claud at once apoligised in his neat way.

"We're Irish, you know, we must laugh or die," he said. "Only an Irish mind could have evolved the idea of a wake; they feast at their funerals because the sources of their laughter and their tears lie so close together, if they didn't do the one they must do the other. I am so relieved this morning—such a load's off my mind. Faith! if I didn't talk nonsense, I'd explode, as sure as a gun."

"Bottle up your nonsense a bit, my boy, for the ears of one who's more used to it than Miss Willoughby," said Lady Mabel, patting him on the head admonishingly. "It's been something quite out of his line," she went on, explanatorily, "these last few days of anxiety and gravity. It has told upon him, poor fellow, and he must let off some steam. I am going to walk up to Poole with him, if you'll allow it, to call upon Miss Allonby. May we take Elsa with us?"

Lady Mabel had shortened Elaine's name into Elsa, because she declared her to be like the Elsa of the old German myth.

"She has just the expression," she said, "which I should imagine to have been worn by Elsa of Brabant, before the appearance of the champion on the scene. She has an unprotected appealing look, as if she were imploring some one to take her part. If I could get her to London she would not long appeal in vain."

Elsa worshipped Lady Mabel, as it was natural she should; and the idea of a visit to London being held out to her had caused such excitement as prevented her sleeping and almost bereft her of appetite. Every turn of their visitor's head, every sweep of her tasteful draperies, every puff of the faint delicate perfume she used, every tone of her deep vibrating voice was as the wave of an enchanter's wand to the bewildered girl. She looked now with aching misery on her own ill-cut, misfitting garments; she pondered with sharp misgivings over her face in the glass, as she remembered the thick artistic sweep of Lady Mabel's loose grey hair, as it made dark soft shadows over those mysterious, never-silent eyes. A passion of discontent, of longing, of unnamed desire was sweeping like a summer storm over the girl's waking heart and mind. The feminine impulses in her were all arousing. Slowly and imperfectly she was learning that she was a woman.

With the strange reticence which she had imbibed from her bringing up, she mentioned none of this. Lady Mabel had very little idea of the seething waves of feeling which every look and smile of hers was agitating afresh. She talked to the girl on various subjects, to be surprised anew at every venture by the intense and childish ignorance displayed; but on the subjects which were just then paramount in Elaine—dress, personal appearance, love—of these she never touched, and so never succeeded in striking a spark from the smouldering intelligence. It was Miss Charlotte who most noted a difference in her pupil.

In the old days, when the girl first came Edge, she had been the possessor of a temper which was furious in its paroxysms. This temper the combined aunts had set themselves soberly to subdue and to eradicate. They had succeeded admirably as far as the subduing went; no ebullition was ever seen; rebellion was as much a thing of the past as the Star Chamber or the Inquisition; but as regards eradication they had not succeeded at all.

In some dumb indescribable way, Miss Charlotte was now made by her pupil to feel this daily. In her looks and words, but chiefly in her manner, was an unspoken defiance. She still came when she was called, but she came slowly; she still answered when spoken to, but her manner was impertinent, if not her words. She was altered, and the fact of not being able to define the change made Miss Charlotte irritable.

Poor lady! she sat stewing in the hot school-room, hearing Elaine read French with praiseworthy patience and fortitude, little thinking how entirely a work of supererogation such patience was, nor how much more salutary it would have been for both if, instead of goading her own and her niece's endurance to its last ebb over the priggish observations of a lady named Madame Melville—who gave her impossible daughter bad advice in worse French with a persistency which would certainly have moved said daughter to suicide had she not been, as has been said, impossible—if instead of this Miss Charlotte had taken Elsa to see the world around her, the pleasant, wholesome world of rural England, with its innocuous society, its innocent delights, its tennis-parties and archery meetings, its picnics and pretty cool dresses, and light-hearted expeditions. Above all, its youthfulness.

To be young with the young—that was what this poor Elsa needed. That was what her aunts could not understand, and they could not see, moreover, what consequences might spring from this well-intentioned ignorance of theirs.

Says Mrs. Ewing, who perhaps best of all Englishwomen understood English girlhood:

"Girls' heads are not like jam-pots, which, if you do not fill them, will remain empty."

Every girl's head will be full of something. It is for her parents and guardians—spite of Mr. Herbert Spencer—to decide what the filling shall be.

Nothing of this recked Elaine's instructress, as she sat with frowning brow and compressed mouth, listening while the intolerable Madame Melville accosted her daughter thus:

"You are happy in your comparisons this morning, and express them pretty well."

In dreary monotone and excruciatingly English accent the girl read on, as the obsequious dancing master wished to know.

"Vous ne voulez point que je la fasse valser?"

"Non," replied his prophetic patroness, "je suis persuadee que cette mode n'est pas faite pour durer!"

And this volume bore date 1851.

To waltz! The very word had a secret charm for Elaine. What was this waltzing? she ignorantly wondered. Something pleasant it must have been, as Madame Melville declined to allow poor Lucy to learn it, and her meditations grew so interesting that she lost her place on the dreary page, and was only recalled to the present by Miss Charlotte's irritable tones:

"I am sure I cannot think what has come over you, Elaine! You seem quite unable to fix your attention on anything."

Meanwhile, upstairs in Miss Ellen's room, Elaine was the subject of conversation.

"May we take your Elsa with us on our walk to Poole? She will like to see Miss Allonby?" Lady Mabel suggested, instigated thereto by a hint from

Claud that he should like to renew the acquaintance of the Sleeping Beauty in the Wood.

"If you could wait half an hour—Charlotte does not like her hours interfered with," said Miss Ellen, deprecatingly. "She will be free at four o'clock."

"Does Miss Brabourne never take a holiday?" asked Claud, tracing patterns with his stick on the carpet.

"Well—not exactly. She is not hard worked, I think," said Miss Ellen, feeling bound to support the family theory of education, in spite of her own decided mistrust of it. "It is very bad for a young girl to have nothing to occupy her time with—my sister considers some regularity so essential."

"I should have thought," Lady Mabel was unable to resist saying, "that a young woman of nineteen could have arranged her time for herself, if she had been properly taught the responsibilities of life."

The wavering pink flush stole over the invalid's kind face.

"I am afraid we middle-aged women forget the flight of years," she said, with gentle apology. "To us, Elaine is still the child she was when she came to us twelve years ago."

"It's most natural," said Claud. "Will Miss Brabourne always live with you? I remember, when Colonel Brabourne died, hearing that the terms of the will were confused, or that there was some mess about it. Was not the estate thrown into Chancery? I hope it is not rude of me to ask?"

"Not at all," answered Ellen, "I should be really glad to talk over the child's future with some one not so totally ignorant of the world as I am. The whole story is a painful one to me, I own, but it has to be faced," she added, with an effort, after a short pause; "it has to be faced."

"Don't you say a word if you would rather not," said Lady Mabel, earnestly. "But if you would really like my brother's opinion, he will be most interested to hear what you have to say. He is a barrister, and might be of some use to you."

The Honorable Claud grew rather red, and laughed at his sister.

"Don't let Mab mislead you, Miss Willoughby," he said. "I was called to the Bar in the remote past, but I have never practised. Still, I learnt some law once, and any scraps of legal knowledge I may have retained are most entirely at your service."

"You are very kind, and I will most willingly tell you as well as I can how matters stand," said Miss Ellen. "We had formerly another sister—Alice—she was the youngest except Emily, and she was very pretty."

"I can well believe it," said Lady Mabel, purely for the pleasure of seeing Miss Willoughby's modest blush.

"In those days," she went on, "we went every year to London for the months of May and June; my father was alive, you understand, and he always took us. There we met Colonel Brabourne, and he fell in love with our pretty Alice. My father saw no reason against the match, except that he was twenty years older than she; but she did not seem to mind that, and was desperately in love with him. When they had been engaged only a few weeks, my father died very suddenly, and, as soon as the mourning would allow, Colonel Brabourne insisted on being married. It was a very quiet wedding, of course, and there were no settlements of any kind—nothing that there should have been. Everything was very hurried; his regiment was just ordered to India, he wished her to accompany him; we knew nothing of business, and we had no relations at hand to do things for us. They were just married as soon as the banns could be called, and away they went to Bengal. My father left his fortune to be divided equally among his daughters, and secured it to their descendants, so that Elaine will have, in any case, more than £200 a year of her own; but now comes the puzzling part of the story. The climate of India proved fatal to my sister. She was never well after her marriage; and, when Elaine was born, her husband got leave to bring his wife and child to England, to see if it were possible to save her. It was not. She flagged, and drooped, and pined, and gradually we got to know that she was in a deep decline. It was just at this time, when her husband and all of us were almost crazy with anxiety, that Alice's godmother, a rich widow lady named Cheston, living in London, died. In consequence of Alice being named after her, she left her all her fortune—about fifty thousand pounds. This was left quite unconditionally.

"We were all so anxious about our sister, I think we scarcely noticed the bequest. She died about a fortnight afterwards, leaving a little will, dated before she knew of this legacy, bestowing everything she could upon her husband, with whom, poor darling, she was madly in love, then and always. She was, of course, sure of his doing all he could for little Elaine. My experience of the world is very limited," said Miss Willoughby, wiping her eyes, "but I must say I think men are the most incomprehensible beings in creation. You would have thought that Valentine Brabourne was absolutely inconsolable for the loss of his wife. He threw up his commission, and went to live in seclusion, taking his baby daughter with him. We saw nothing of him."

"Did he live on his wife's money?" asked Claud.

"He lived on the income of it chiefly. He had very little of his own, besides his pay. I did not see how we could interfere. His wife's will left the money to him, by implication, and of course I thought it would be Elaine's. But when she was three years old he married again—a person who—who——" Miss Willoughby faltered for an expression. "Well, a person of whom my sisters and I could not approve. She was a Miss Orton, and lived with her brother, who was what they call a book-maker, I believe. It did seem so strange that, after mourning such a wife as Alice, he should suddenly write from the midst of his retirement to announce himself married to such a person. We did not wish to be selfish or unpleasant—we invited him and his wife down here, but we really could not repeat the experiment."

Tears of pleading were in the poor lady's eyes.

"I hope you will not think me narrow," she said, "I know we lead too isolated a life; but I could not like Mrs. Brabourne. She smoked cigarettes, and drank brandy and soda water. She was always reading a pink newspaper called the *Sporting Times*, and I think she betted on every horse-race that is run," said poor Miss Willoughby, vaguely. "She talked about Sandown and Chantilly, and other places I had never heard of. She never went to church, and appeared, from her conversation, to do more visiting and gambling on the Sunday than on any other day. She was a handsome young woman, with her gowns cut like a gentleman's coat. She drove very well, and used to wear a hard felt hat and dogskin gloves. I cannot say I liked her. My sisters could none of them approve. She was unwomanly, I cannot but think it, and I am sure she influenced her husband for evil. Soon after her stay here, she had a baby, but it died within twenty-four hours of its birth; so the next year, and the next. I am sure she took no proper care of herself, but when she had been four years married, she had a son, who did live, and was called Godfrey. Six months after his birth, his father was thrown in the hunting-field and killed. He left a will bequeathing the whole of his property—this fifty thousand which had been poor Alice's,—to his son Godfrey. Mrs. Brabourne was to have three hundred a year till her death, and a certain sum was set aside for the maintenance and education of both children till they were of age. And all this of Alice's money—our Alice! Do you call that a just will, Mr. Cranmer?"

"I call it simple theft," said Claud, shortly; "but, if the will your sister left be legally valid, I don't see what you are to do in the matter."

"So our solicitor said," sighed Miss Willoughby. "He thought we had no grounds at all for litigation; but I think that everyone must confess that it is a hard case. I wish it had been possible to throw it into Chancery, but it was not."

"I can just remember there being some talk about it," said Lady Mabel. "I call it a very hard case."

"If it had been half!" said Miss Willoughby. "I would not have grudged the boy half my sister's fortune; but that he should leave it all to him!"

The clock struck four as she spoke, and the sound of a closing door was heard.

"Here comes Elaine," she said. "Please mention nothing of all this to her. She does not know."

"Does she not? Why not tell her?" asked Lady Mabel.

"I thought it might set her against her brother," answered Miss Ellen, "or make her disrespect the memory of her father. But I cannot feel as I should towards the Ortons I must confess. There was something very underhand; something must have been done, some undue influence exerted to induce him to leave such a will, for I know he loved Alice as he never loved his second wife."

"Is she alive still, the second Mrs. Brabourne?" asked Claud.

"No; she died two years ago. The boy is more than twelve years old. The money will be worth having by the time he attains his majority; when Elaine is twenty-one, I shall make another effort on her behalf."

"I am sure I wish you success, but I am afraid you have no case," said Claud, regretfully.

As he spoke the door was opened, and Elaine walked in.

CHAPTER XIII

Ankle-deep in English grass I leaped,
And clapped my hands, and called all very fair.
In the beginning, when God called all good,
Even then was evil near us, it is writ;
But we indeed, who call things good and fair,
The evil is upon us while we speak;
Deliver us from evil, let us pray.
Aurora Leigh.

As the young girl entered the room Claud Cranmer rose, with a quick gesture of courtesy.

Elaine, not prepared to see strangers, paused, and the ingenuous morning flush of youth passed over her face in a wave of exquisite carmine. Claud thought he had never beheld anything more lovely than that spontaneous recognition of his presence. She had not blushed when he met her first—her anxiety for Allonby had been paramount. And the pale girl up at Poole, with the sculptured chin, never blushed at all, but looked at him with frank and limpid eyes as if he were entirely a matter of course.

But for Elsa, dawn had begun; the sun was rising, and naturally the light was red. Oddly enough, an old country rhyme floated in Claud's mind—

"A red morning's a shepherd's warning."

He did not know quite why he should think of such a thing, but a good many varying emotions were stirred in him as he scrutinised this girl who had so nearly escaped the inheritance of a considerable fortune.

What a complexion she had! Her inexorable critic mentally compared her with the slim Wynifred. A throat like a slender pillar of creamy marble, lips to which still clung that delicate moist rose-red which usually evaporates with childhood, a cheek touched with a peach-like down, eyelashes long enough to shadow and intensify the light eyes in a manner most individual, but hard to describe. What a pity, what a thousand pities, that all this effect should be marred and lost by the cruel straining back of the abundant locks, and the shrouding of the finely-developed form in a garment which absolutely made Mr. Cranmer's eyes ache.

The girl smiled at him—a slow smile which dawned by degrees over her lovely, inanimate face. The look in her eyes was enough to shake a man's calmness; and when she asked, "How is Mr. Allonby?" he felt that she had some interest to spare for Mr. Allonby's messenger.

Here was a type of girlhood he could understand, for whose looks and smiles he could supply a motive.

He watched her every moment keenly, and soon found out that her awkwardness was the result of diffidence and restraint, not of native ungainliness. He determined that Mabel must have her to stay with her, and civilize her. She would more than repay the trouble, he was confident.

He saw the sudden ardent glow of pleasure succeed the restless chafing of suspense when at last permission was accorded for her to walk to Poole with Lady Mabel.

"Run and put on your hat," said Miss Ellen, indulgently, and away darted the girl with radiant face.

"Jane," she cried, bursting into the *ci-devant* nursery where Miss Gollop reigned supreme, "where's my best hat—quick! I am going out with Lady Mabel and Mr. Cranmer!"

"Your best hat's in its box, where it'll stop till Sunday," answered Jane, placidly. "You ain't going trapesing along the lanes in it, I can tell you, Lady Mabel or no Lady Mabel."

"Oh, Jane, you are unkind! Do let me wear it."

"You shan't wear it, Miss Elaine, and that's flat. Once take it out in this sun, you'll have the straw burnt as yaller as them sunflowers."

"Where's my second best?" grumbled the girl, turning to the press.

"On the Philmouth Road, for all I knows; at least, that's where you last left it, ain't it?"

"And am I to go out in my garden-hat—with Lady Mabel Wynch-Frère?" cried Elaine, aghast.

"I don't see no other way for it," said Jane, calmly, drawing her thimble down a seam to flatten it, with a rasping noise which set her charge's teeth on edge.

"Well, Jane, I never heard of such a thing!" she burst forth after a pause of speechless indignation.

"I can't help it, miss; I must teach you to take care of your clothes. You're not going flaunting over to Mrs. Battishill's in that ostrich feather o' yours. Maybe, next time you drop your hat in the road, you'll remember to pick it up again."

Surely Elaine's fairy godmother spoke through the untutored lips of Jane Gollop!

Instead of presenting herself to Claud in a headgear covered with yellow satin ribbon and a bright blue feather, Elsa appeared downstairs in her wide-brimmed garden-hat, simply trimmed with muslin; and narrowly escaped looking picturesque.

How different was the road to Poole, now that she trod it with such companions! Her heart was light as air, her young spirits were all stretched eagerly, almost yearningly forward into the unknown country whose border she had crossed so lately.

Her fancy played sweetly around the image of the artist-hero, her pulses beat a glad chime because he was living, and not dead. She waxed less shy, and chatted to her companions,—even daring to ask questions, a thing her aunts never permitted. She gave them reminiscences of her childish days, when she lived in London, and of a dream she had constantly of streets full of houses, one after another, in endless succession, with very few trees among them.

"That is all I know of London," she said, "and I hardly remember anything that happened, except hearing the baby cry in the night. It was Godfrey. I used to wake up in my little bed, and see nurse sitting with the baby near the lamp, rocking him in her arms. I remember being taken in to kiss papa when he was dead; but that was not in London—it was somewhere in the country—at Fallowmead, where Godfrey's uncle has his racing-stud. I remember mamma; she was not my real mamma. I could not bear her. She used to whip me, and once I bit her in the arm."

"My dear Elsa!" said Lady Mabel.

"I did. I was a very naughty little girl—at least, Jane always says so. I remember being shut up alone for a punishment."

As she spoke, they turned a bend in the road, and came in sight of the spot where the crime had been perpetrated.

Two men stood there talking together. One was Mr. Dickens of Scotland Yard, the other Elsa greeted with a glad wave of the hand in greeting.

"Oh," cried she, springing forward, "it's Mr. Fowler, it's my godfather! I did not know he had come back!"

At the sound of her voice, Mr. Fowler turned round, and his face lighted up as she came towards him.

"Why, Elsie!" he said, "there you are, my child! And I'm hearing such doings of yours, it makes me quite proud of you. And you, sir," he went on, addressing Claud, "are Mr. Cranmer, I suppose, and entitled to my very hearty goodwill for your behavior in this matter."

Claud had heard of Mr. Fowler before, as a local justice of the place, and he gladly shook hands with him, scrutinizing, of course, as he did so, the general mien and bearing of his new acquaintance.

Mr. Fowler was short, square, sturdy, and plain. His hair and thick short beard had once been jet black, but were now iron grey. His skin was exceedingly dark, almost swarthy, and his eyes, big, soft, and luminous, were his one redeeming feature. His manner was a curious mixture of gentleness and strength; he never raised his voice, but his first order was always instantly obeyed. Something there was about him which invited confidence; he was not exactly polished, yet his manner to women was perfect. Gentle as was his eye, it yet had a curiously penetrating expression, and Lady Mabel, used as she was to what should be the best school of breeding in England, was yet struck with the simplicity and repose of his address.

"I only came back to Edge Combe yesterday," he said, and, though he had lived all his life in South Devon, Claud noticed at once that the rough burr of the "r" was absent from his quiet voice. "I am often absent for some months, on and off, managing some tin mines in Cornwall; and it was through the medium of the newspapers I learned what had been going forward in our little valley. And now, Mr. Cranmer, what do you think about it?"

"I'm afraid I must postpone my opinion till Mr. Allonby himself has been questioned," said Claud.

"Exactly what I've been telling Mr. Fowler," observed Mr. Dickens, who wore a baffled and humbled look. "Nothing can be done till Mr. Allonby speaks. It's a case of *vendetta*, I'll go bail; and it's done by one that's accustomed to the work, too; accustomed to cut the stick and leave no traces."

"Cut the stick—the stick they knocked him down with?" asked Elsa in low, horrified tones.

Claud smiled.

"Your theory hardly holds with Dr. Forbes, Mr. Dickens," he said rather shortly. "He declares the blows were given by a novice—by a hand that didn't know where to plant his blows."

"Well, I don't know what to say," snapped the detective. "Here's a man beat almost to death on the high-road in broad daylight; some one must have done it. Where is he? There ain't a trace of him. Nobody has met a single soul that could be taken up on suspicion—nobody has seen anybody as so much as looked suspicious. Miss Brabourne and her servant met nobody as they came along not half-an-hour afterwards. It ought to be some one uncommon deep, and not a tramp nor a fishy-looking party of any kind."

All this was true. Claud was inclined to think that the detective had done his best, and his ill-success was owing to the very strange nature of the case, and not to his inability.

They left him sadly ruminating by the wayside, and crossed the Waste to the farm, Elaine with her hand clasped tightly in the square, short, hard palm of her godfather.

"This has been an adventure for you, little woman," he said. "What do the aunts say?"

"They are surprised," answered she, with her usual paucity of vocabulary.

"I should think they were! And horrified too—eh?"

"Yes, very. Aunt Fan nearly had hysterics."

"Poor Aunt Fan! I don't wonder. I have a great respect for the Misses Willoughby," he said, turning to Lady Mabel. "I have known them all my life."

His voice seemed to soften involuntarily as he said it, and, as his eyes rested lingeringly on Elaine's face, Lady Mabel could not help framing a romance of twenty years ago, in which he and pretty Alice Willoughby were the leading characters; and a swift bitter thought of the complications of life crossed her mind. Had Alice mated with the deep patient love that waited for her, and chosen a home by "Devon's leafy shores" instead of the hot swamps of the Ganges, she had probably been a happy blooming wife and mother now, with the enjoyment of her godmother's fortune duly secured to her children.

And now here stood Elsa, comparatively poor, fatherless, motherless; while Henry Fowler, like Philip Ray, had gone ever since "bearing a life-long hunger in his heart." All this, of course, was pure surmise, yet it seemed to invest the homely features and square figure of the Devonian with a halo of tender feeling in her eyes; for Lady Mabel had a romance of her own.

"Did you have hysterics, Elsie?" asked Mr. Fowler.

"No; I lost my hat," answered she, in a matter-of-fact way which made them all three laugh.

"It was a wiser thing to do," he answered, in his quiet voice. "But the whole affair must have been a great shock to you, lassie."

"Yes," said the girl—an inadequate, halting answer.

Dimly she was feeling that that day had been not all darkness—that it was the beginning of life. She did not know the inviolable law of humanity, that no new life is born without a pang; but imperfectly she felt that her pain had been followed by a feeling of gladness for which she could not account, and that the days now were not as the days that had been.

"What a solitude," says somebody in some book, "is every human soul." At that moment the solitude of Elaine Brabourne's soul was very great. She was standing where the brook and river met; vaguely she heard the sound of coming waters foaming down into the quiet valley. It awed her, but did not terrify. There was excitement, but no fear. And of all this those who walked beside her knew nothing.

Henry Fowler was one of those who surround womanhood with a halo, and his feminine divinity had taken form and shape. It had borne a name, the name of Alice Willoughby—for Lady Mabel's surmise had been correct.

Had he known how near the torrent stood near the untried feet of Alice's daughter, he would have flung out his strong right arm, caught her in a firm hold, and cried, "Beware!"

But he did not know. He saw only with his waking eyes, and those told him that Elaine had grown prettier—nothing more. She was safe and sound—she was walking at his side. The vital warmth of her young hand lay in his. No care for her future troubled him just then.

He chatted to Claud about the details of the mysterious assault. There seemed but one subject on which it was natural to converse, in the Combe, in those days.

When they came to the bridge, he made the girl pass over its crazy planks before him, and jumped her from the top of the stile.

As they neared the farm-house, a sound of loud crying, or rather roaring, greeted them; and when Mr. Fowler, with the privilege of old custom, walked into the house, and through to the kitchen, there lay Saul the idiot, his whole length stretched on the floor, his face purple with weeping, and kicking strenuously.

Clara Battishill stood against the table, the color in her pretty little cheeks, her chest heaving as with recent encounter, her mien triumphant.

"Saul Parker, hold your noise at once—get up off the flags—stand up, I say! What's all this about, eh?" said Mr. Fowler, in his even, unruffled tones.

Saul left off howling directly, and, after taking a furtive look at the company, hid his tear-strained visage with a wriggle of anguish.

Clara burst out in her shrill treble.

"I've give him a taste of the stick, I have," said she, brandishing a stout ash twig, "for killing o' my turkey. He's a cruel boy, he is, and I'm very angry wi' him. He took an' threw great rocks over into the poultry-yard, and Miss Allonby, she was there wi' me, and he might ha' killed both of us; but 'stead o' that, he goes an' kills my best turkey I set such store by. I'll l'arn him to throw stones, I will! I's take an' tell me mother I won't have un abaout the place if he's going to take to throwing stones."

"It won't do," said Mr. Fowler, lightly touching the recumbent Saul with his foot. "I always said it wouldn't do when the poor lad grew up. He's getting mischievous. Up, Saul!—up, my lad, now at once. You've had a beating, which you richly deserved. What made you so naughty, eh?"

For answer the big lad raised himself on his hands and knees, crawled towards Clara, and flung his arms humbly about her knees, saying, in his imperfect way,

"Poor! poor!"

His castigator was melted at once. She took his beautiful head of golden curls between her hands, and patted it energetically.

"There, you see, he don't mean anything; he's as good as gold all the time," she said. "But mind, you leave my birds a-be, Saul. If I ketch you in my poultry-yard, I'll give you such a licking! I will! So mind!"

He began to whimper penitently. Lady Mabel looked sorrowfully at him.

"Poor boy!" said she, "what an affliction! He ought to be put into an asylum."

"Please, your ladyship, his mother won't part with him," said Clara; "and he never does no harm, not if you're kind to him. There, there, boy, don't cry. I've got some butter-milk for you in t' dairy."

He began to smile through his tears, which he wiped away on her apron. Claud thought it the oddest group he had ever seen. The sight of the great fellow prone on the ground, meekly taking a beating from a girl half his size, was a mixture of the pathetic and the absurd. It half touched, half disgusted him. Suddenly a light step on the wooden stair made him turn.

Wynifred stood in the doorway.

"Oh,—Mr. Cranmer," she said, faltering somewhat at the presence of three strangers. "I beg your pardon, I thought you were alone. My brother would like to see you."

"I'll come at once, but first of all you must let me introduce you to my sister."

CHAPTER XIV

"Till the lost sense of life returned again,
Not as delight, but as relief from pain."
The Falcon of Sir Federigo.

Allonby's return to full consciousness had been a very gradual affair. Each lucid interval had been eagerly watched by Dr. Forbes, who feared the loss of memory, partial or entire, which often results from such brain attacks. Were the young man to forget—as it was entirely probable that he would—the circumstances immediately preceding his illness, the difficulty of Mr. Dickens' mission would be increased tenfold.

When it became evident that the sick man recognised his sister, the excitement began to culminate. But hours went by, he slept, ate, awoke, and dozed again, quite tranquil, and apparently not at all solicitous as to how Wynifred came to be at his side, or where he was, or what was the reason of his illness.

But at last, one afternoon, the "light of common day" broke in upon the calmness of his musings, and sent his mind tossing restlessly to and fro in all the tumult of newly aroused consciousness.

He awoke from a delicious sleep with a sense of returning vigor in all his big limbs, and, essaying to throw out his left arm, behold! It was immovable.

He held his breath, while he surveyed the bandaged limb, and all the glittering visions which had been the companion of his delirium came showering to earth in a torrent of shining fragments.

Throughout his illness, the idea of the Island Valley of Avilion had never left him. No doubt the fact that his dominant idea had been a beautiful and a peaceful one had greatly served to help him through. His talk, when he rambled, had been all of "bowery willows crowned with summer sea," and of the rest of the exquisite imagery with which he had mentally surrounded Edge Combe in his holiday dreams. Now, the mirage of imaginary loveliness had fled. Like a flash it was gone, and only the commonplace daylight of every day remained.

This sudden departure of the baseless fabric of his vision was by no means a novelty to Osmond. Often and often before he had had violently to recall his winged thoughts to earth: to set aside the sparkling beauties of the life he lived in fancy, in order to cope with the butcher's bills, the rates and taxes of the life he lived in reality.

But this last dream had been passing sweet, and he thought it had lasted longer than was common with the airy things. It had rivetted itself in his mind, till he felt that he could close his eyes and commit it to canvas from memory alone. He could see the soft dim outline of the mythic barge, he could "hear the water lapping on the crags, and the long ripple washing in the reeds," and he could see, feature for feature, the face of the sorrowing queen. A young, lovely face, with the light of morning on it, but with anguish in the eyes, and sympathy of tears upon the cheeks.

For a moment he closed his eyes to recall it all. Then he boldly opened them, to confront a world with which he felt too weak to cope.

Not much of the said world was visible just then, and what there was seemed calculated to soothe and cheer. It was bounded by the four walls of a not very large room, the whitewash of whose ceiling was spotlessly white, the roses of whose wall paper were aggressively round and pink. To his right, a casement window hung wide open; and through it came the sighing of a summer wind rustling through elm-trees.

Near this window stood the well-known figure of his sister Wynifred, stepping leisurely to and fro before the board on her sketching easel, to which she was transferring, in charcoal, some impression which was visible to her through the window.

Her straight brows were pulled together so as to make a perpendicular furrow in the forehead between them; the soft scratching of her charcoal brought back to Osmond common-place memories of the Woodstead Art School, wherein he passed three days of every week as a master, when it was not vacation time.

Wynifred and Wynifred's occupation were familiar enough. They let him know the folly of his dreaming; but there yet remained one puzzling thing. How came he to be lying there in bed, with a bandaged arm, in a room that was utterly strange to him?

It was rather a remarkable room, too, when one came to study it attentively. It possessed a heavy door carved in black oak, which door was not set flat in the wall, but placed cross-ways across the corner—evidently a relic of great antiquity.

The invalid pondered over that door with a curiosity which was somewhat strange, considering that the answer to his puzzle, in the shape of his sister, stood so close to him, and that he had only to ask to be enlightened.

But it is to be supposed that there is something fascinating in suspense, or why do we so often turn over and over in our hands a letter the handwriting of which is unknown to us—exhausting ourselves in surmise as to who is our correspondent, when we have but to break the seal for the signature to stare us in the face? There is no saying how long Allonby might have amused himself with conjecture, for it was, truth to tell, a state of mind peculiarly congenial to him. He liked to feel that he did not know what was to happen next—to wait for an unexpected *dénouement* of the situation. He had often, when exploring an unknown country, been guilty of the puerile device of sitting down by the roadside, just before a sharp bend in the road, or just below the summit of a high hill, while he pleased himself with guessing what would be likely to meet his eye when the corner was turned, or the hill-crest reached. So now he lay, speculating idly to himself, and by no means anxious to break the spell of silence by pronouncing his sister's name; when suddenly she looked up from her work, half absently, and, finding his eyes gravely fixed on her, flung down her charcoal, and came hastily to the bedside, wiping her fingers on her apron.

"How are you, old man?" she said, meeting his inquiring look with one of frank kindliness. There was no trace of the burst of feeling with which she had told Dr. Forbes that her heart was soaring up to the evening star in the quiet heavens in gratitude and love. Evidently Miss Allonby kept her sentiment for rare occasions.

"I believe I feel pretty well," said he, using his own voice in an experimented and tentative way. "But I feel rather muddled. I don't quite recall things. I think, if you were to tell me where I am, it would give me a leg up."

"Take a spoonful of 'Brand' first," said Wyn; and, taking up a spoon, she proceeded to feed him. He ate readily enough; and philosophically said no more till she had turned his pillows and arranged his head in comfort; all of which she did both quietly and efficaciously, though in a manner all her own, and which would have revealed to the eye of an expert that she had been through no course of nursing lectures, nor known the interior of any hospital.

"There!" she said at last, seating herself lightly on the edge of the bed. "Now I will tell you—you are in a place called Poole Farm. Does that help you?"

"Poole Farm? Yes," he said, reflectively. "I was sketching near there. Did I have a fall? I have managed to smash myself somehow. How did I do it?"

"Don't you remember?" asked Wyn, earnestly.

He lifted his uninjured hand and passed it over his forehead. It came in contact with more bandages. He felt them speculatively.

"Broken head, broken arm, broken rib," he remarked, drily. "Broken mainspring would almost have been more simple. How did it happen, now? How did it happen? I can't understand."

"You were painting, in the lane by the wayside," said the girl, suggestively. "A picture with a warm key of color, and a little bit of the corner of the farm-house coming into it—evening sky—horizon line broken on the left by clump of ash-trees."

"Yes, I know. I recollect that," he said. "I walked over from Edge Combe in rather a hot sun. I felt a little queer. But a sunstroke couldn't break one's bones, Wyn. I must have had a fall, eh?"

"You fell from your camp-stool to the grass," she returned, "but that could hardly have hurt you to such an extent."

He lay musing. At last,

"I don't remember anything," he said, with a sigh. "I think the sun must have muddled my head. Tell me what happened."

"My dear boy," cried she, "that is exactly what we want *you* to tell *us*!"

"What! Don't you know?" he asked, with a sudden access of astonishment.

"Nothing! Nobody knows anything except that you were found by the roadside, all in fragments. Ah! I can laugh now. But oh, Osmond! when they telegraphed to me first!"

She leaned over him, and kissed his forehead.

"My dear boy," she said, "I could eat you."

He caught his breath with a weary sigh.

"What's become of Hilda and Jac?" he asked.

"Oh! they are all right—gone to the Hamertons at Ryde, and having a delightful holiday. Don't fret," she said, answering fast, and with an evident anxiety at the turn his inquiries were taking. But he would go on.

"And how long have I been lying here?" he asked, grimly. "I suppose there are some good long bills running up, eh? Doctors not the least among them." A pair of very distinct furrows were visible on his forehead.

"And that commission of Orton's," he sighed out.

Wyn had slipped down to her knees by his bed, and now she took his hand and laid her cheek upon it.

"Listen to me, old man," she said; "there is no need to fret, I've managed things for you. I wrote first thing to Mr. Orton, and he answered most kindly—his friend will be satisfied if the pictures are ready any time within six months, so do unpucker your forehead, please. As to expense, it won't be much. Mrs. Battishill is the most delightful person, but becomes impracticable directly the money question is broached. She says she never let her rooms to anybody in her life, and she isn't going to begin now. The room would be standing empty if you didn't have it, and you are just keeping it aired. As to linen, it all goes into her laundry: "She don't have to pay nothing for the washing of it, so why should we!" Ditto, ditto, with dairy produce. "It all cooms out of her dairy. It don't cost her nothing, and she can't put no price on it!" I have been allowed to pay for nothing but the fish and meat I have bought; and I don't apprehend that Dr. Forbes' bill will ruin us. There! That's a long explanation, but I must get the £ s. d. out of your head, or we shall have no peace. I've kept my eyes open and managed everything. You are *not* to worry—mind!"

He heaved a long breath of relief.

"Bless you, Wyn!" he said. "But we must not be too indebted to these good folks, you know."

"I know! I'll manage it! We must give them a present. They are really well-to-do, and don't want our money. Besides, they are, owing to us, the centre of attraction to the neighborhood. All Edge Combe is for ever making pilgrimages up here to know how you are faring. You are the hero of the hour."

"And you can't tell me what it all means?" he asked, with corrugated brow.

"I can tell you no more at present," she answered, rising as she spoke. "I must feed you again, and you shall rest an hour or two before you do any more talking, and, if you are disobedient, I shall send for Dr. Forbes."

Whether Osmond found this threat very appalling, or whether what he had already heard supplied him with sufficient food for meditation, was a matter of doubt; but some cause or other kept him absolutely silent for some time; and Wyn, who had retired to her easel, the better to notify that conversation was suspended for the present, by-and-by saw his eyes close, and hoped that he was dozing again. So the afternoon wore on, till voices struck on her ear—voices of persons in eager conversation. They were floated to her through the open window, but came apparently from round the corner of the house, for she could not see the speakers when she looked out.

As the sounds broke the stillness, Osmond's eyes opened wide.

"Who is there?" he asked, hurriedly.

"I don't know," said his sister, peering forth, "I hear Mr. Cranmer, but there is some one else."

Then suddenly a little gush of laughter, high and clear, sailed in on the hot summer air, followed by the distinct notes of a girl's voice.

"Saul! Saul! Get up, you stupid boy!"

Osmond stirred again. He rolled right over in bed, and turned his eager face full to the window.

"Wyn—who is it?" he asked, uneasily.

"I'll go and see if you want to know."

"Stay one minute—I want to hear—who found me by the wayside, as you say, in fragments?"

"A young lady and her maid," was the reply, "She is a Miss Brabourne, I believe, and lives near here. She ran in search of help, and accidentally met a carriage containing two tourists——"

"Brabourne? Isn't that the name of that horrible imp of a child who lives with the Ortons?"

"Yes—I believe it is," said Wyn pausing. "*My nephew, the heir to a very large property*," she presently added, mimicking a masculine drawl, apparently with much success, for her brother laughed.

"That's it," he said. "Well—but who is Mr. Cranmer?"

Wynifred now became eloquent.

She told him all that Claud had done—his kindness, his interest, his unwearying attention, his laying aside all plans for the better examination of the mystery.

Of course she greatly exaggerated both Mr. Cranmer's sacrifice and his philanthropy. He had been interested, that was all. It had amused him to find himself suddenly living and moving in the heart of a murderous drama, such as is dished up for us by energetic contributors to the sensational fiction of the day. Vol. I. had promised exceedingly well: Vol. II. seemed likely to be disappointing. In all the "shilling horrors," though of course the detective does not stumble on the right clue till page two hundred and fifty is reached, still he contrives to be erratic and interesting through all the intermediate chapters, by dint of fragments of a letter, the dark hints of an aged domestic, the unwarranted appearance of a mysterious stranger, or the revelations of a delirious criminal.

Since Allonby had burned the sole letter which could have been of any importance, and in his delirium talked only of a place and persons alike mythical and useless, it really seemed as if the story must stop short for want of incident. Mr. Dickens had all but succeeded in persuading Claud that they had to deal with a modern English *vendetta*—a thing of all others to be revelled in and enjoyed in these days when the incongruous is the interesting.

Our jaded palates turn from the mysteries of Udolpho, where all was in keeping, where murders were perpetrated in donjon keeps, ghosts were fitly provided with arras as a place to retire to between the acts, and mediæval knights and ladies were to the full as improbable as the deeds and motives assigned to them. Now something more piquant must be provided, above all something *realistic*. Mr. Radcliffe and Horace Walpole are relegated to the land of dreams and shadows; give us *vraisemblance* to whet our blunted susceptibilities. Let us have mystic ladies, glittering gems, yawning caverns, magic spells; but place the nineteenth century Briton, chimney-pot hat and all, in the centre of these weird surroundings. Make him your hero; jumble up what is with what could never have been, and the first critics in English literature shall rise up and call you blessed! They thought themselves dead for ever to the voice of the charmer: you have given them the luxury of a new sensation; what do you not deserve of your generation? Join the hands of the modern English nobleman and the mythical African princess—link together the latest development of Yankeeism and dollars with the grim tragedy of the Corsican bandit—your fortune is made; you are absolutely incongruous; you have out-Radcliffed Radcliffe. She gave us the improbable; to you we turn for the absurd.

That Allonby was going to miss such an opportunity as this was, to the mind of Mr. Dickens, a *bêtise* too gross to be contemplated. He had already caused the local newspapers to bristle with dark hints. He awaited, in a state of feverish suspense, the waking of the lion.

Could he have seen that lion's unfurrowed brow and unenlightened expression, his heart would have sunk within him.

As to Claud, the upshot of it all would not materially affect him, whichever way it turned. After all his personal taste for melodrama was only skin-deep. He preferred what was interesting to what was thrilling. He had taken a liking to the unconscious victim; he was struck with the loveliness of the Devonshire valley; the weather was fine; he had nothing else to do; and that was the sum of all. Considerably would he have marvelled, could he have heard Wynifred's description of his conduct as it appeared to her. Nobody that he knew of had ever thought him a hero; neither did any of his relations hold self-sacrifice to be in general the guiding motive of his conduct.

When Miss Allonby, after instilling her own view of his actions into her brother's willing ear, slipped off her apron, hung it over the back of a chair, and went to summon this good genius to receive the thanks she considered so justly his due, he was totally unprepared for what was to come.

To have his hand seized in the languid, bony grip of the sick man, to see his fine dark grey eyes humid with feeling, to hear faltering thanks for "such amazing kindness from an utter stranger," these things greatly embarrassed the ordinarily assured Claud.

He jerked his eye-glass from his eye in a good deal of confusion, he pulled the left hand corner of his neat little moustache, he absolutely felt himself blushing, as he blurted out a somewhat vindictive declaration that,

"Miss Allonby must have given a very highly-colored version of the part he had taken in the affair."

"Oh, of course you would disclaim," said Allonby, with an approving smile. "That's only natural. But I hope some day the time may come when I shall have a chance to do you a kindness; it doesn't sound likely, but one never knows."

"But this is intolerable," cried Claud, fuming, "I haven't been kind—I tell you I haven't! I have been merely lazy and more than a trifle inquisitive! I won't be misrepresented, it isn't fair!"

"Could some fay the giftie gie us," said Wyn, smiling softly at him across the bed.

"Oh, well," said the young man, with a sudden softening of voice and manner, "it's not often that others see me in the light that you two appear to have agreed upon. I don't see why I am to disclaim it. It's erroneous, of course; but rather unpleasant on the whole; and, after all, we never do judge one another justly. If you didn't think me better than I am, you might think me worse; so I'll say no more."

"Better not, it would be labor lost," said Wyn, seriously. "When we Allonbys say a thing, we stick to it."

"Do you?" said he, with an intonation of eager interest, as if he had never before heard such a characteristic in any family.

The girl nodded, but turned away, and beckoned to him not to talk any more.

"We must leave him a little," she said, gently. "Dr. Forbes will soon be here, and I don't want him to think him unduly excited."

"Wyn," said Osmond, as his sister and the Honorable Claud reached the door, "is Miss Brabourne downstairs?"

"Yes."

"It was she who found me by the roadside?"

"Yes."

"Ah!" He said no more, but turned his face to the window and lay still, with his poetic and prominent chin raised a little. It was impossible to guess at his musings.

CHAPTER XV

Since you have praised my hair,
'Tis proper to be choice in what I wear.
In a Gondola.

When Miss Allonby and Mr. Cranmer emerged into the garden, they found a pleasing group awaiting their arrival.

Lady Mabel was sitting in a wicker chair, her gloves were removed, and lay rolled up in her lap, her firm white hands were employed with tea-cups and cream jug.

On the grass near sat Elsa, her hat off, her eyes dilated with wonder and enjoyment. Mr. Fowler stood near her ladyship, cutting bread-and-butter.

"Come along, Claud," she cried, as they appeared. "That good Mrs. Battishill provides an *al fresco* tea for us! Sit down and take the gifts the gods provide you. Did you ever see such a view?"

"Never," said Claud, with conviction. "Of all the lovely bits of rural England, I do think this is the loveliest. What makes its charm so peculiar is that it's unique. Half a mile along the high-road either towards Philmouth or Stanton, you would never guess at the existence of such an out-of-the-way spot of beauty. It really does remind one of what your brother called it," he went on, turning to Wynifred, "The 'Island Valley of Avilion.'"

"That's in Tennyson, I think," said Mr. Fowler. "I am ashamed to say how little poetry I read; we are behind the times here in the Combe, I'm afraid—eh, Elsie?"

"I don't know," said the monosyllabic beauty, confused.

Her large eyes were resting on Miss Allonby, drinking her in as she had drunk in Lady Mabel. They were not alike, most assuredly, yet from Elaine's standpoint there was a similarity. Both of them were evidently at ease. Each knew how to sit in her chair, what to do with her hands, and, above all, what to say.

When her aunts received company they were excited, disordered. They ran here and there, for this and that—they fidgetted, they were flurried.

Wynifred Allonby looked as if she did not know what to be flurried meant.

She wore the simplest of grey linen gowns, with an antique silver buckle at her waist. Into her belt she had fastened three or four of the big dark red carnations which grew in profusion in the farm-house garden, and were just beginning to blossom. She was in the presence of an earl's sister, whom she had never seen before, yet her calm was unruffled, and her manner perfectly quiet. In Elsa's untutored eyes, this was inimitable.

Though she herself had now met Mr. Cranmer several times, yet she found herself blushing more and more every time she met his eye. Consciousness was awake—her quick feminine eye told her that her clothes did not resemble those of either of the women beside her.

Both were most simply attired, for it was the whim of Lady Mabel, when in the country, to wear short woollen skirts, leaving visible her shapely ankles, and otherwise to cast away the conventions of Bond Street by the use of wash-leather gloves and a stout walking stick. To-day, under a short covert coat of dark blue cloth, she wore a loose scarlet shirt, the effect of which was coquettish and telling. Her well-looped skirts were also of dark blue, and there was a rough and ready suitableness to the occasion about her which was most effective. The poor little watching, unfledged Elsa felt a soreness, an intolerable jealousy. Why was she so unlike others? Why could she not have different gowns? She almost thought she could sit and talk as easily as Miss Allonby, if only her dress fitted, and she could wear buckles on her shoes.

There was Mr. Fowler, who had always been her own especial property, her godfather, the one human being who had ever dared to say, "Let the child have a holiday." "Let the child stay up another hour this evening." There he was, talking to Miss Allonby in his gentle way, looking at her with his honest eyes, laying himself out to entertain her, and not so much as throwing a glance at his forlorn Elsa.

Nobody knew what purely feminine sorrows were vexing the young heart.

Lady Mabel was in a frame of mind inclined to be very regretful. She, like her brother, had taken a vehement fancy to Edge Combe, and she knew she must leave it, and return to London. She wanted to make the most of these sunshiny, peaceful hours, these interesting people, this lovely landscape.

Her fine eyes gazed down the valley, at the mysterious deeps below them, thick with foliage, and the deep glowing sea which formed the horizon.

"What a color that ocean is!" she said. "Do look, Claud, it's quite tropical!"

Mrs. Battishill was placing a big dish of clotted cream on the table.

"Eh, for all the world like a great basin of hot starch, isn't it? I've often thought so," said she, good-humoredly.

Her prompt exit into the farm-house allowed the smiles to broaden at will on the countenances of four of her five auditors.

"Oh, Mab," said Claud, with tears in his eyes, "what a slap in the face for your sentiment!"

"I'm not sure that it's not a very apt illustration," cried Wyn, when she could speak. "It is really just the same color, and the dip of the valley holds it like a basin! Imaginative Mrs. Battishill!"

"You draw, I think, Miss Allonby?" said Mr. Fowler.

"Yes, I am very fond of it," she answered.

"You will be able to do some sketching, now that your mind is at ease about your brother."

"Yes; but I am a poor hand at landscape. That is Osmond's province. I prefer heads. I should like," she paused, and fixed her eyes on Elsa, "I should like to paint Miss Brabourne."

Elsa started as if she had been shot. Up rushed the ungoverned color to face, throat, and neck. She could not believe the hearing of her ears.

"To paint me?" she cried. The water swam in her glorious eyes. "Are you making game of me?" she passionately asked.

"Making game of you? No!" said Wyn, in some surprise. "I am very sorry—I beg your pardon—I am afraid I have distressed you."

Lady Mabel reached out her hand towards the girl as she sat on the grass; and, placing it under her chin, turned up the flashing, quivering, carmine face and smiled into the eyes.

"Should you dislike to sit for your portrait, Elsa?"

"I don't know—I never tried—I know nothing about it!" cried she, enduring the touch, as it seemed, with difficulty, and ready to shrink back into herself.

"You would try to sit still, if it would be a help to Miss Allonby, I am sure?"

"I don't think she means it," cried the tortured Elsa, with a sob.

"I meant it, of course," said Wynifred, very sorry to have been so unintentionally distressing. "But I am ashamed of having asked so much. Sitting is very tedious, and takes up a great deal of time."

"I should be very anxious to see what you would make of her," said Mr. Fowler, with interest. "Elsa, little woman, you must see if you can't keep still, if Miss Allonby is so kind as to take so much trouble about you."

"Trouble! It would be both pleasure and education," said Wyn, with a smile; "she will make a delicious study, if— —"

"If?" said Lady Mabel, turning swiftly as she hesitated.

"If I might do her hair," said Wyn, laughing, and throwing a look of such arch and friendly confidence towards Elaine that the shy girl smiled back at her with a sudden glow.

"Oh, you may do as you like with my hair, if the aunts will only let me sit to you!" she said, with eager change of feeling.

"Leave the aunts to me, Elsie—I'll manage them," said Mr. Fowler, reassuringly.

"To think that I must go home and lose all this interest and enjoyment," cried Lady Mabel, in some feigned, and a good deal of real regret.

"Why need you go, Mab?" asked Claud.

"Oh, my dear boy, I must! Edward is coming down to fetch me, and there are my darlings to see after. My holiday is over. But I shall comfort myself with hoping to have Elsa to stay with me when I am settled. Edward writes me word that we shall be obliged to have a house in town this winter—my husband has been so ill-advised as to get into Parliament," explained she to Mr. Fowler.

"Oh, yes; I remember hearing very gladly of his success," was the cordial response. "Also that his electioneering was most ably assisted by Lady Mabel Wynch-Frère, who was received with an ovation whenever she appeared in public."

He was bending over her as he spoke, handing her the strawberries, and she smiled up at him with sudden passion of Irish eyes.

"Any effort in the good cause," she said, with fervency.

The Tree Of Knowledge A Novel | 109

"Exactly, in the good cause," he responded. "You may speak out—we are all friends here."

"How do you know?" asked Claud. "You don't suppose I sympathize with Mab's political delusions, do you? A younger son must be a Radical, as far as I can see. The idea of plunder is the only idea likely to appeal to his feelings with any force."

Mr. Fowler laughed pleasantly.

"You put me in a difficulty," said he. "I was going to try to persuade you to come and take up your quarters in my bachelor diggings in the Lower House for awhile and try my shooting; but if you are going to vote against the government——"

"You'll have to drive me out of the Lower House—stop my mouth with a peerage, eh?" cried Claud.

"Miss Allonby doesn't see the joke," said Mr. Fowler; "my dwelling is called the Lower House," he proceeded to explain, "receiving that title merely because it happens to be further down the valley than Edge Willoughby."

"I see," said the girl, laughing. "Well! as a representative of law and order, I'm shocked to hear you advocating shooting, Mr. Fowler!"

"To an Irishman, eh? Yes, it's risky, I own. But what say you, Mr. Cranmer, seriously? Come and try my covers?"

It was exactly the invitation Claud wanted. He had no compunction in becoming the guest of a well-to-do bachelor, whose birds were probably pining to be killed; and it would keep him in this lovely part of the country, and within reach of Allonby and his mystery, not to mention Elsa Brabourne.

His face lighted up with pleasure.

"But——" he began.

"But it's not the 12th, yet—no, you're right. I can offer you a trout-stream to begin with, and a horse if you care about riding. If you are bored, you can run up to town, and come down again for the shooting."

"I shan't be bored," said Claud.

In point of fact, the whole thing promised most favorably.

A visit to a house with no mistress—where doubtless you might smoke in your bed-room, and need never exert yourself to get off the sofa, or put on a decent coat, or make yourself entertaining, or go to church twice on Sundays.

His bachelor soul rejoiced.

All this, with the ladies within reach if by chance he wanted them or their society, why, it was the acme of luxury!

"I was wondering how you were going to begin shooting so soon," said Lady Mabel; "but I assure you, Claud will be perfectly happy if only you let him loaf about and dream by himself. He likes a contemplative existence."

"Yes," said Claud, modestly and even cheerfully accepting this description of himself. "I like leisure to congratulate myself that I have none of the vices, and few of the failings, of my fellow-creatures in this imperfect world."

"*Few* of the failings—have you *any*?" asked Miss Allonby, with innocent surprise, holding a strawberry ready poised for devouring. "Do you really admit so much? I am curious to know to what human weakness you are free to confess?"

"Would you really like to know? Well—it is a very interesting subject to me, so doubtless it must be interesting to other people," said Claud, in his debonair way. "Know, then, that I have a fault. Yes, I know it, self-deception was never a vice of mine; I see clearly that I am not without a defect; and I deeply fear that time will not eradicate it, though haply indigestion may do so. This weakness is—strawberries." He heaved a deep sigh, and helped himself to his fourth plateful with melancholy brow.

"Only one consolation have I," he went on, placing a thick lump of cream on the fruit. "It is that the period of degradation is transient. A few short weeks in each year, and I recover my self-respect until next June. Peaches smile on me in vain, dusky grapes besiege my constancy. My friends tempt me with pine-apples, and wave netted melons before my dazzled vision; but I remain temperate. Strawberries are my one vulnerable point; which, being the case, I know you'll excuse my further conversation."

"Say no more," said Wyn, in solemn accents. "A confidence so touching will be respected by all."

"Ah! sympathy is very sweet," sighed he. "Have you a failing, by chance, Miss Allonby?"

"I am sure I do not know," she answered, with great appearance of reflective candor. "My self-knowledge is evidently not so complete as yours. If I were conscious of one, I fear I should not have your courage to avow it; perhaps because my defect would most likely be chronic, and not a mere passing weakness like yours."

During this passage, Lady Mabel had been abundantly occupied in studying Elsa's face. Its expression of incredulity and dismay was strange to behold. That, two grown-up persons should deliberately set to work to talk the greatest nonsense that occurred to them at the moment had never struck her as in any way a possibility. What made them do it? Were they in earnest? Their faces were as grave as judges, but Mr. Fowler was laughing. She hoped that nobody would ever speak to her like that, and expect her to reply in the same vein. It overwhelmed, it oppressed her. Involuntarily she drew near Lady Mabel, and shrank almost behind her, as if for protection from the two who were, like Cicero, speaking Greek.

Lady Mabel amused herself in thinking what Miss Charlotte Willoughby's verdict would have been, had she been present.

"I am sure you both have a pretty good opinion of yourselves," she might have remarked, or more probably still, "Strawberries are wholesome enough when eaten in moderation, but I am sure such excessive indulgence must be bad for anybody."

"I don't wonder," said Mr. Fowler, with sly playfulness, "that Miss Allonby is unwilling to follow Mr. Cranmer's fearless example, and proclaim herself uninteresting for eleven months out of twelve."

"Uninteresting!" cried Claud.

"What so uninteresting as perfection? I am glad I first made your acquaintance when you were under the influence of your one defect. I doubt I shouldn't have invited you to Lower House if I had met you a month later."

"Ah! you have invited me now, and you must hold to it," cried Claud, in triumph; "but, as I must admit I have deceived you, and owe you reparation, why—to oblige you—I will try to hatch up a special defect for August."

"I don't think you'll find it very difficult, dear boy," said Lady Mabel, sweetly.

"Difficult to make myself interesting? No, Mab, that has always come easily to me; you and I were never considered much alike," was the impudent answer.

"His desire to have the last word is really quite—lady-like, isn't it?" said his sister to Mr. Fowler; and all four burst out laughing. "Claud, I am ashamed of you—get up and put down those strawberries. Here is Elsa looking at you in horror and amazement! Do mind your manners."

"As I have devoured my last mouthful, I obey at once. I am like the ancient mariner after telling his story. The feverish desire for strawberries has passed from me for a while. I become rational once more."

"Such moments are rare; let us make the most of them," retorted she, "and tell me seriously what your plans are."

"If you'll allow me, I'll walk back with you and Miss Brabourne, and expound them on the way. Oh, look, Mr. Fowler, there's that ass Dickens; I must go and speak to him a minute, and tell him we're more in the dark than ever."

He rose hurriedly, his nonsense disappearing at once, and went down to the gate, followed by Henry Fowler.

"We can never be grateful enough to your brother, Lady Mabel," said Wyn, gently, when they were out of hearing.

"I am sure he is only too pleased to have had a chance of being of use. He is as kind a fellow as ever breathed, and hardly ever does himself justice," said Claud's sister, warmly. "He is a real comfort to me, and always has been; so thoughtful and considerate, and never fusses about anything."

"No, he does everything so simply, and as if it were all in the day's work," said Wynifred, as if absently. "It is the kind of nature which would composedly perform an act of wild heroism, and then wonder what all the applause was for."

Lady Mabel looked swiftly at the speaker. It seemed to her that it was the most un-girlish comment on a young man that she had ever heard. Perhaps the strangeness of it lay more in manner than in words. Wynifred leaned one elbow on the table, her chin rested in her hand; her pale face and tranquil eyes studied Mr. Cranmer, as he stood pulling the gate to and fro, and eagerly talking to the detective. Her expression was that of cool, critical attention. Something in Lady Mabel's surprised silence seemed to strike on her sensitive nerves. She looked hurriedly up, and colored warmly.

"I beg your pardon," she said, confusedly, "I am afraid I am blundering" ... and then broke short off, and pushed back her chair from the table. "We have a bad habit at home," she said, "of studying real people as if they were characters in fiction; but we don't, as a rule, forget ourselves so far as to discuss them with their own relations."

Lady Mabel smiled; it was a pretty and an adequate apology. She thought Miss Allonby an interesting girl, and was inspired with a desire to see more of her.

"You must come and see me when I am settled in London, Miss Allonby," she said, kindly, "I should like to know your sisters."

"I should like you to know them," was the eager response. "Osmond and I are very proud of them."

"They are both younger than you?"

"Yes; Hilda is three years younger, and Jacqueline four. There is only just a year between them."

"And you are orphans?"

"Yes."

At this moment Claud approached.

"Miss Allonby," he said, "I wonder if you would get your brother's permission for Mr. Dickens to rifle the things he left behind him at the 'Fountain Head' with Mrs. Clapp?"

"Oh, certainly, I am sure he would have no objection. Perhaps I had better come myself," said Wynifred. "I have been wanting to fetch up some paints."

"It would be far the best plan," said Claud, with alacrity. "I am going to walk down with my sister and Miss Brabourne. Will you come to? I will see you safely home again."

"You are very kind," she answered, simply. "I will go and tell Osmond, and see whether nurse has given him his tea."

"We shall have to set out soon," said Lady Mabel, "or we shall be late for tea at Edge Willoughby."

"The amount of meals one can get through in this climate!" observed Claud, pensively. "Why, you have this moment finished one tea, Mab,—I'm ashamed of you! Mr. Fowler, how many meals a day am I to have at the Lower House?"

"Oh, I think I can promise you as many as you can eat, without taxing my cook or my larder too far. We are used to appetites here."

"A fellow-feeling makes us wondrous kind," mused Mr. Cranmer. "The fact that King Henry died of a surfeit used to impress me, I remember, with an unfavorable view of that monarch's character. But"—he heaved a sigh, and, with a side-glance of fun at Elsa, took another strawberry—"*nous avons changé tout cela! Vive* Devonshire and the Devon air!"

CHAPTER XVI

We read, or talked, or quarrelled, as it chanced.
We were not lovers, nor even friends well-matched:
Say rather, scholars upon different tracks,
Or thinkers disagreed.
Aurora Leigh.

With his usual forethought, Mr. Cranmer had made out in his own mind a plan of the coming walk. He meant to walk from Poole to Edge with Elsa Brabourne, the anachronism, and return from Edge to Poole with Wynifred Allonby, one of the latest developments of her century.

He felt that there must needs be a piquancy about the contrast which the dialogue in these two walks would necessarily present. No doubt one great cause of his happy, contented nature was this faculty for amusing himself, and at once becoming interested in whatever turned up.

It is scarcely a common quality among the English upper classes, who mostly seem to expect that the mountain will come to Mahomet as a matter of course, and so remain "orbed in their isolation," and, as a natural consequence, not very well entertained by life in general. It was this trait in Claud which drew him and his eccentric sister together. She was every bit as ready as he to explore all the obscure social developments of her day. Anything approaching eccentricity was a passport to her favor, as to his; and these valley people had taken strong hold on the fancy of both.

He was standing just outside the door, when Wynifred came down ready for her walk, and he noted approvingly that the London girl was equipped for country walking in the matter of thick shoes, stout stick, and shady hat. On the shoes he bestowed a special mental note of approval. Lady Mabel had once said that she believed the first thing Claud noticed in a woman was her feet. Miss Allonby was intensely unconscious that her own were at this moment passing the ordeal of judgment from such a critic, and passing it favorably.

"Osmond is very quiet and comfortable, and nurse thinks I can well be spared," she announced.

"I must reluctantly bid you all good-bye for the present," said Mr. Fowler, regretfully. "I am obliged to go on to visit a farm up this way. I wish you a pleasant walk."

He raised his hat with a smile, and stood watching as they started. Lady Mabel, urged on by her active disposition, went first, and Wynifred went with her. Claud dropped behind with Elaine, and this was the order of the march all the way to the village. Mr. Cranmer was resolved to make Elsa talk, and he began accordingly with the firm determination that nothing should baulk him, and that he would not be discouraged by monosyllables. It was well that this resolution was strong, for it was severely tried.

The first subject he essayed was the beauty of the scenery, and the joy of living in the midst of such a fine landscape. He could have waxed eloquent on this theme, and shown his listener how much happier are the dwellers in rural seclusion than they who exist in towns, and how it really is a fact that the dispositions of those born among mountains are freer and nobler than those of denizens of flat ground—with much more of the same kind. But he soon became aware that he spoke to deaf ears. The girl beside him was not interested: he could not even keep her attention. Her feet lagged, her head seemed constantly turning, without her volition, back towards the direction of Poole Farm.

"But perhaps you don't share my enthusiasm for the country?" he broke off suddenly, with great politeness.

Elsa grew red, stretched out her hand for a tendril from the hedge, and answered, confusedly:

"I hate living in the country!"

There was a note in her young voice of a defiance compelled hitherto to be mute, and consequently of surprising force. The very fact of having broken silence at last seemed to give her courage; after a minute's excited pause, she went on:

"I want people—I want companions. I want to be in a great city, all full of life! I want to hear people talk, and know what they think, and find out all about them. Do you know that I have never met a girl in my life till I saw Miss Allonby! And—and—" with voice choked with shame—"I am afraid to speak to her. I don't know what to say. I should show her my ignorance directly. Oh, you can't think how ignorant I am! I know nothing—absolutely nothing. And I do so long to."

"Knowledge comes fast enough," said Claud, impetuously. "You will know—soon enough. Don't fret about that. In these days you cannot think what a rest it is to find anyone so fresh, so unspoiled—so—so ingenuous as yourself, Miss Brabourne! You must forgive my venturing to say so much. But, if you only knew what a power is yours by the very force of the seclusion you have lived in, you would be overwhelmed with gratitude to these wonderful ladies who have made you what you are!"

"Then," said Elaine, shyly, stealing a wary glance at him, "you *do* see that I am very unlike any girl you ever met?"

Claud laughed a little, and hesitated.

"Yes, you are—in your bringing up, I tell you frankly," he said. "As regards your disposition, I don't know enough to venture on an opinion."

They walked on a few minutes in silence, and then she said:

"Tell me about London, please."

He complied at once, but soon found out that it was not theatrical London, nor artistic London, nor the London of balls and receptions which claimed her attention, but the world of music, which to her was like the closed gates of Paradise to the Peri.

When he described the Albert Hall, and the Popular Concerts, she drank in every word. It was enchanting to have so good a listener, and he talked on upon the same theme until the village was reached, when his sister faced round, and said that Miss Allonby wished to stop at the "Fountain Head," but she and Elsa must hasten on, so as not to be late for the Misses Willoughby's tea-time.

It was accordingly settled that Claud should walk up with them as far as the gate of Edge and return to fetch Wynifred in half-an-hour. On his way back he called at the postman's cottage to see if there were any letters for Poole Farm. They put two or three into his hands, and also a packet which surprised him. It was addressed to Miss Allonby, and obviously contained printer's proofs.

He stared at it. A big fat bundle, with "Randall and Sons, Printers, Reading, Llandaff, and London," stamped on a dark blue ground at the top left-hand corner.

"So she writes, among other things, does she?" said he, speculatively, as he turned the packet over and over. "What does the modern young lady not do, I wonder? what sort of literature? Fiction, I'll bet a sovereign, unless it is an essay on extending the sphere of feminine usefulness, or on the doctrine of the enclitic De, or on First Aid to the Sick and Wounded. Strange! How the male mind does thirst after novelty! I declare nowadays it is exquisitely refreshing to find a girl like Miss Brabourne, who has never been to an ambulance lecture, nor written a novel, nor even exhibited a china plaque at Howell and James'!"

For Claud had that instinctive admiration for "intelligent ignorance" in a woman which seems to be one of the most rooted inclinations of the male mind. Theoretically, he hated ignorant woman; practically, there were times when he loved to talk to them.

Wynifred was seated in the porch of the inn, talking to Mrs. Clapp, when he came up. The subject of conversation was, needless to relate, the missing pudding-basin.

"When we find that, miss, the murder'll be aout," was the good lady's opinion.

Claud thought so too.

"First catch your hare," he murmured, as he paused at the door. "Have I kept you waiting, Miss Allonby?"

"Scarcely a minute," she answered, rising, and nodding a "good evening" to Mrs. Clapp.

"I called in at the postman's," he said, as they turned homewards, "and have brought you this, as the result of my enterprise."

He produced the packet of proofs, with his eyes fixed on her. Her face did not change in the least.

"Thanks," she said, "but what a heavy packet for you to carry—let me relieve you of it."

"Certainly not; it goes easily in my pocket;" and he replaced it with a curious sense of being baffled. Should he leave the subject, or should he take the bull by the horns and tax her with it? It might be merely a sense of shyness which made her unwilling to talk of her writings.

"I did not know you were an authoress, Miss Allonby," he said.

"No? I have not written very much," she answered, frankly.

"May I venture to ask what you write? Is it novels?" he asked, tentatively.

"It is singular, not plural, at present," she answered, laughing. "I have published a novel, and hope soon to bring out another."

"You seem to be a universal genius," he observed.

"That is the kind of speech I never know how to reply to," said Wynifred. "I can't demonstrate that you are wrong—I can only protest: and I do hate protesting."

"I am very sorry—I didn't know what to say," apologised he, lamely.

"Then why did you introduce the subject?" she answered, lightly. "You can't accuse me of doing so. Let us now talk of something on which you are more fluent."

He laughed.

"Do you know you are most awfully severe?"

"Am I? I thought you were severe on me. But, if you really wish to know, I will tell you that I don't care to talk of my writings, because I always prefer a subject I can treat impartially. I can't be impartial about my own work—I am either unjust to myself or wearisome to my audience. I don't want to be either, so I avoid the topic as much as possible. This letter is from my sisters at Ryde—will you excuse me if I just peep to see if they are quite well?"

"Most certainly," replied Claud, strolling meditatively on, with a glance now and then towards his companion, who was absorbed in her letter. He thought he had never beheld such an ungirlish girl in his life. That total absence of consciousness annoyed him more than ever. Elsa Brabourne was one mass of consciousness, all agitated with the desire to please, all eager to know his opinion of her. It really did not seem to matter in the least to Wynifred whether he had an opinion concerning her at all. Evidently he did not enter into her calculations in any other relation than as her brother's benefactor. Her burst of gratitude had been very pleasant to the young man's vanity; he had hoped at least to arrest her attention for a few days, to make her sensible of his presence, intolerant of his absence; but no. He had to confess that she was new to him—new and incomprehensible. He could not know that her state of impartiality and unconsciousness was an acquired thing, not a natural characteristic, the result of a careful restraint of impulse, a laborious tutoring of the will. It sprang from a conviction that, to do good work as a novelist, one must be careful to preserve the moral equilibrium, that no personal agitations should interfere with quiet sleep at night, and the free working of ideas. She met everybody with the preconceived resolution that they were not to make too deep an impression. They were to be carefully considered and studied, if their characters seemed to merit such attention; but this study was to be of their relation to others, not herself. She, Wynifred, was to be a spectator, to remain in the audience; on no account was she to take an active part in the scenes of passion and feeling enacting on the stage.

No doubt this was not a normal standpoint for any young woman to occupy; but she was scarcely to be judged by the same standards as the average girl. If blame there were, it should attach to the circumstances which compelled her, like an athlete, to keep herself continually in training for the race which must be run.

"Hilda and Jacqueline are quite well," she said, folding her paper with a smile. "They are having great fun. There is a mysterious yacht at Ryde which is causing great excitement; have you heard about it, by chance?"

"I wonder if it is the same that I heard about from a man I know at Cowes? Is it called the *Swan*?"

"Yes, that is the name. It belongs to a Mr. Percivale, of whom nobody seems to know anything, except that he is very rich and very retiring— nobody can get up anything like an intimacy with him. He speaks English perfectly; but they do not seem to think that he is English in spite of his name. It is interesting, isn't it?"

"Yes, I think it is; but I expect, after all, it is nonsense. Why should a man make a mystery about his identity, if you come to think of it, unless he's ashamed of it? But, as a novelist, I suppose you have an appetite for mystery?"

"Yes, I do think I must own to a weakness that way; you see mystery is rare in these days," said Wynifred, meditatively.

"Well, I don't know; we have a good rousing mystery up here in the Combe just now—a mystery that I don't think we shall solve in a hurry," said Claud, with a baffled sigh, as they drew near the fatal spot in the lane.

The girl's face grew grave.

"Yes, indeed," she said, abstractedly.

As if by mutual consent they came to a stand-still, and stood gazing, not at the grassy road-side where the crime had been perpetrated, but down the fair valley, where the long crescent of the waxing moon hung in the dark-blue air over the darkening sea.

"The worst of an untraceable crime like this seems to me," she said, "to consist in the ghastly feeling that what has been once so successfully attempted, with perfect impunity, might be repeated at any moment—on any victim; one has no safeguard."

"Oh, don't say that," he said, hurriedly, "it sounds like a prophecy."

She started, and looked for a moment into his dilated eyes, her own full of expression. For the first time in their mutual acquaintance he thought her pretty. In the isolation of the twilight lane, rendered deeper by the shadow of the tall ash-trees, with the memory of a horrible crime fresh in her mind, a momentary panic had seized her. She came nearer to him; instinctively he offered his arm, and she took it. He could feel her fingers close nervously on it.

"It is so dreadful," she said, in a whisper, "to think of wickedness like— like *that*, in such a beautiful world as this."

"It is," he answered, in sober, reassuring tones, "therefore I forbid you to think about it. I ought not to have brought you home this way; I am an idiot."

"It is I who am an idiot," said the girl, smiling at her own weakness. "Ever since I have known you—I mean, you have grown to know me at an unfortunate time. I suppose I am a little overdone; you mayn't believe it, but I—I hardly ever lose my head like this."

"I can believe it very well," was the prompt reply. "You will be all right again in half a minute." He had turned so that their backs were towards the fatal spot; and, as if absently, he strolled back a little way down the road, her hand still on his arm. He began to speak at once, in his easy tones. "Look!" he said, "what a superb night it is! I thought I saw a sail, just going behind that tree. Ah! there it is! How bright! The moon just catches it."

"Perhaps it is the *Swan*," she answered, struggling valiantly for a natural voice. "The girls said I was to look out for it—it is going to cruise westward."

"Perhaps it is," he answered. "How phosphorescent the water is in its trail—do you see? How the little waves are full of fire!"

"'The startled little waves, that leap
In fiery ringlets from their sleep,'"

she managed to quote, with a feeling of amazement that she should have re-conquered her self-possession enough to be able to speak and think at all.

Her whole heart was going out to Claud in gratitude for his most delicate consideration. The whole affair had lasted but a few moments, but she had been very near a breakdown that evening—nearer than she herself knew. She had needed to say nothing—one look into her eyes had told him just what she was feeling, and instantly all his care had been to help her. She had no time to apply any of her habitual restraints to the spontaneous rush of kindness with which she was regarding him. All of a sudden she had discovered in him a delicacy of sympathy which she had never met with in his sex before. He appeared to know exactly what she stood in need of.

It seemed to give her whole nature a species of electric shock; the carefully-preserved moral equilibrium was being severely strained.

"Will you come now?" he said, presently, in her ear. "I think it would be better for you afterwards if you can walk quietly past; but don't if you had rather not; we will go the other way round."

"I will walk past, please."

He turned, and walked at her side.

"I heard an anecdote of the mysterious owner of the *Swan* the other day," said he. "I fancy it was worth repeating;" and proceeded to relate said anecdote in even tones, making it last until they stood at the gate of the farm. There he broke off abruptly.

"I have brought you home just in time to say good-night to your brother," said he, brightly.

She turned, and gave him her hand.

"Thank you with all my heart," said she. "You don't know how grateful I am. Good-night."

She was gone—her tall slim form darting into the shadow of the doorway.

Claud propped himself against the gate, slowly drew out his cigar-case and matches, and lighted up. Then he turned, and leaning both arms on the topmost rail, smoked placidly, with his eyes fixed on the vanishing white sail, and its track on the phosphorescent water. Presently he withdrew his weed from his mouth a moment, and turned to where the lights of Edge gleamed in the valley.

"Elsa Brabourne," he mused. "A pretty name: and a lovely girl she will be in a year or two. Even if her brother allows her nothing, she will have more than two hundred pounds a year of her own, and the Misses Willoughby are sure to leave her every penny they possess. A younger son might do worse."

CHAPTER XVII

And he came back the pertest little ape
That ever affronted human shape:
And chief in the chase his neck he periled
On a lathy horse, all legs and length,
With blood for bone, all speed, no strength.
The Flight of the Duchess.

"Colonel Wynch-Frère? Glad to see you, sir! Fine day for the wind-up, isn't it? Never seen Ascot so full on a Friday in my life! Everybody's here. Seen my wife, by chance?"

"Yes, a minute ago: in Mrs. Learmorth's box. I've got a little bet on with her about this event," answered the gentleman addressed, tapping his little book with a gold pencil-case, and smiling.

It was the lawn at Ascot: and it was brilliantly thronged, for the rain, which had emptied itself in bucketfuls on Cup day, had at last relented, and allowed the sun to burst forth with warmth and brightness for the running of the Hardwicke Stakes.

"Ah! I don't know when I have been so excited over a race in my life," said the first speaker. "I'm of the opinion that Invincible is going to the wall at last. Carter's on Castilian, you know, and he's going to ride to win."

"Can't do it," said the colonel, shortly.

"*Can't he?*"

"No. He'll try all he knows, but Invincible is—Invincible, you know."

"I know he has been hitherto; but he's never met Castilian in a short distance; I say all that bone will tell. I'll give you two to one on it."

The bet was accepted, and Frederick Orton nodded to himself in a confident way, which also made his companion anxious, for he knew his was an opinion not to be despised.

"Haven't seen my young nephew, have you?" asked Orton, as he made a memorandum in his book.

"Not that I know of. What nephew?"

"My young limb of Satan—confound him!" said Orton, with a laugh. "He's made his book as carefully as if he had been fifty years old. I've fetched him twice out of the ring by the scruff of his neck to-day; but Letherby, my old groom, is with him, so I suppose he's all right."

"He's beginning early," observed Colonel the Honorable Edward Wynch-Frère, in his slow way.

"He is. What do you think? He wants to ride Welsh Rabbit for the Canfield Cup. What do you think, eh? Should you let him do it?"

The colonel meditated for some moments.

"Is he strong enough in the wrists? That's where I should doubt him," he said, reflectively. "He rode splendidly at those private races of yours at Fallowmead; but then he knew his ground as well as his horse; he'd have to carry weight at Canfield."

"Of course. But Letherby says he could do it. The only thing is the risk of a bad throw. These things are done in a minute, you know; and he's heir to a big property. It's been well nursed, and, if anything happened to the poor little beggar, plenty of people would be kind enough to say— —"

"I rode in a steeple-chase when I was sixteen," observed Colonel Wynch-Frère.

In fact, he looked more like a stud-groom than anything else you could fancy. No wonder; he had but two ideas in the world: one was horse-racing, the other was his wife. It seemed, on the whole, rather a pity that Lady Mabel's very wide range of sympathies should include neither horse-racing nor her husband. It was purgatory for her to go and stay at the house of Lord Folinsby, his father, the great Yorkshire earl, where the riding-school was the centre of attraction to all her brothers and sisters-in-law, and where the young men seemed always in training for some race or another, cut their whiskers like grooms, walked bandy-legged, and talked of the stables. Thus, the colonel indulged in his horse-racing and his wife separately; and endeavored, with all the force of his kind heart and limited intellect, not to talk of the first when in the presence of the second.

But to-day every faculty he had was centred on the question as to whether or not the duke's marvellous chestnut, Invincible, would have to lay down his laurels; and he moved along by Mr. Orton's side talking quite volubly, for him, on the all-engrossing theme, and the reports as to who was likely to drop money over the race.

Be it stated that he was eminently a racing, not a betting man; he was no gambler, though always ready to back his own opinion.

The grand stand was packed, and the ladies' dresses as brilliant as the June sky.

The two men, moving slowly on, at last caught the eyes of two ladies who were beckoning them, and accordingly went up and joined them.

"You are only just in time—they have cleared the course," said Mrs. Learmorth, a lady sparkling in diamonds but deficient in grammar.

"My dear Fred, where's Godfrey?" asked Mrs. Orton, a handsome, very dark young woman, with a high color and flashing eyes.

"Oh, he's somewhere about: Letherby's looking after him," was the nonchalant reply, as he lifted a pair of field glasses to his eye, and presently announced, in a tone of keen excitement; "They'll be out directly. Wait till they canter past the stand. Mrs. Learmorth, you've never seen Invincible, have you?"

"Never!" cried the lady, eagerly. "Mind you point him out to me."

"Here they come," said the colonel. "Look—that's Lord Chislehurst's Falcon—I've backed him for a place—lathy beast: but a good deal of pace. This one and this are both outsiders. There's the duke's daffodil livery, but that is only a second horse put on to make the running. Here comes the Castilian, Orton."

Mr. Orton was watching with an absorbed fascination.

"Ay, there's Carter," said he, studying the well-known jockey's face. "He means business, I tell you."

The Castilian was a large dark-brown horse, and the crimson and pale-blue colors of his rider set him off to advantage; but, like many good race-horses, he was not singularly beautiful to the eye of the unlearned. He cantered by with some dignity, amid a good deal of cheering, when suddenly there was a rush, something like a flash of light, a bright chestnut horse, with a jockey in daffodil satin, darted like a fairy thing past the stand, followed by a spontaneous shout from the crowded onlookers. The magic hoofs seemed scarcely to touch the turf over which they swept; and Mrs. Orton, watching with a somewhat sardonic smile, observed,

"You'll lose your money, Fred."

"You wait and see," said her husband, oracularly.

"I'm sure I hope he has been careful," she went on, with a laugh, to Mrs. Learmorth, "for he has promised to take me to Homburg if he wins."

"Don't talk, Ottilie," cried Frederick Orton, irritably; "don't you see they are just going to start!"

The race began—the memorable race which crowned Invincible with the chief of his triumphs. Not even with "Carter up" was the Castilian able to make so much as a hard fight for it. The lovely chestnut was like a creature of elfin birth—it seemed as if he went without effort; the field toiling after him looked like animals of a lower breed.

The wild yells of applause rang and echoed in the blue firmament— the mad excitement of racing for the moment mastered everyone, from the youth whose last sovereign hung on the event to the pretty, ignorant girl upon the drag, who had laid her pair of gloves with blind devotion on the daffodil satin as it flashed past.

One small boy, held up on the shoulders of an elderly groom, added his shrill screams with delight to the tumult around.

"Well done, Invincible! Well rode, Bartlett! Bravo! bravo! Didn't I tell my uncle he'd do it! Pulled it off easy! Knew he would! Look at poor old Carter! What a fool he looks! Ain't used to coming in a bad second! Let me down, Letherby, I want to find my uncle! I say, though, this is proper! I've made five pounds over this."

"You just wait one minute, Master Godfrey, till the crowd is cleared off a trifle—you'll be jammed to death in this 'ere mob if you don't look out, and the master said I was to see to you. You stop where you are."

"You old broken-winded idiot," shouted the child, a boy of fourteen, very small for his age, but handsome in a dark, picturesque style. "Do move on a bit, you are no good in a crowd. I can't stay here all day—elbow on!"

Letherby accordingly "elbowed on" through the yelling, shouting mass of betting-men, followed by the excited, dancing boy, who kept on talking at the top of his voice.

"Isn't it a sell for aunt, by Jove! She said she wouldn't give me five shillings to spend at Homburg next month, and now I've got five pounds! Why, Letherby, I knew a fellow who went to the table with five pounds, and came back with five hundred. I warrant you I have rare sport at Homburg!"

"That I can answer for it, you won't," said his uncle's voice suddenly in his ear, and the urchin felt himself abruptly seized by his coat-collar with no gentle hand. "Thanks to the upshot of this confounded race," said Mr. Orton, angrily, "you won't go to Homburg at all, for I can't afford to take you; and what the deuce do you mean by hiding away here when you're wanted? Your aunt's going home, and you'll go with her. I'll have you out of harm's way."

Godfrey Brabourne made no reply. He skulked at his uncle's heels with a look of sulky fury on his face which was not good to see. The spoilt boy knew that, on the occasions when his uncle was out of temper like this, silence was his sole refuge; but, if he did not speak, he thought, and his thoughts were not lovely, to judge from the expression of his eyes.

Letherby hurried away to put-to the horses, knowing that in this mood his master would not brook waiting; and, in half-an-hour from Invincible's winning of the Hardwicke Stakes, Mr. Orton and his party were spinning along towards the Oaklands Park hotel, where they were spending Ascot week.

A very subdued party they were. Spite of his winnings, Godfrey was silent and sullen. Mrs. Orton's temper was not proof against the shattering of all her plans for next month; she knew that, if she spoke at all, it would be to upbraid her husband, so she held her tongue; and he was in a state of mute fury, less at the loss of his money than at his own error of judgment in such a matter.

The very impression of his silent wife's face irritated him. "I told you so," seemed written on every feature.

When they arrived at the hotel, he petulantly flung his reins to the groom, and went indoors by himself, "as sulky as a bear with a sore head," mentally observed the wife of his bosom.

At dinner there was Colonel Wynch-Frère, who had come in a couple of hours later, having been invited by some other friends.

He was sitting at a table some distance from the Ortons, but afterwards joined them in the drawing-room. The dinner had been good, and Frederick's temper was improving; he was not an ill-tempered man, as a rule, and he was now half-ashamed of his late annoyance. Mrs. Orton was less placable; she sat aloof, and secretly longed to be able to say her say.

The colonel strolled up.

"Where's the boy?" he asked.

"In the stables, I suppose—where he always is," said the boy's aunt, snappishly.

How she had wanted to go to Homburg! The Davidsons were going, and the Lequesnes, and Charley Canova; what parties they would have got up! And now — —

"Godfrey's not always in the stables, Ottilie," said Fred, seating himself on a sofa at her side. "He has only gone now with a message from me. He'll be back directly."

The Tree Of Knowledge A Novel | 127

Frederick Orton was a rather picturesque young man of about five-and-thirty. He was dark, with brown eyes, and a short, pointed, Vandyck beard and moustache. The moustache hid his weak mouth. He was slight and pale, and looked delicate, which was probably the result of late hours and pick-me-ups.

His wife was handsome, and rather large, a year or two younger than he, and showing an inclination to stoutness. Her eyes and complexion were striking, her voice deep and rather loud—a fine contralto—and her disposition energetic.

She was very handsomely dressed for the evening in a dark-green dress covered with green beetle's wings, which flashed as she turned. The colonel rather liked her, though he never dared say so to Lady Mabel.

"How is your Lady Mabel?" she asked of him, just as this thought was crossing his mind.

"Lady Mabel is, as usual, having a good many adventures," he said, taking a chair near. "She has been on a driving-tour with her brother—"

"Mr. Cranmer? I know him slightly," said Frederick.

"Yes; they are in Devonshire, at a little place called Edge Combe, near Stanton."

"Dear me! Isn't that where all those old maids live—the Miss Willoughbys?" said Ottilie, turning to her husband.

He made one of the many English inarticulate sounds representing "Yes."

"I wonder if Lady Mabel has come across Godfrey's step-sister, Elaine Brabourne?" she went on, in her deep contralto accents.

"Oh, yes, certainly; she mentions a Miss—is your nephew's name Brabourne? I never knew it. Then his father used to be colonel of my regiment."

"That's it," said Frederick, calmly. "Yes, he has a step-sister, I'm sorry to say, who has been brought up by a set of puritanical old maids—old hags, my poor sister used to call them."

"Lady Mabel is staying with the Miss Willoughbys," said the colonel, rather red in the face.

There was an uncomfortable pause; then Mr. Orton laughed lazily.

"Put my foot into it," he said. "I usually do. Very sorry, I'm sure. I don't know the good ladies myself, and I expect my poor sister made them all sit up; she was as wild a girl as ever I saw, and they used to take her and set her down for hours in a rotting old church which smelt of vaults, and where the damp used to roll down the walls in great drops. She said it gave her the horrors. But that's a good many years back now, and I daresay they have changed all that."

"My wife says they are—well—very primitive," said the colonel. "But she speaks of Miss Brabourne as a most lovely girl, who only needs a little bringing out."

"Ottilie, you must have that girl up to town," remarked Frederick.

"Why?" said his wife, stifling a yawn.

"Because I think Godfrey ought to know her."

"Godfrey hates girls."

"Yes, because he is always alone, and gets spoilt—he ought to know his sister."

"She is coming to stay in town with Lady Mabel in the autumn, when we are settled," said the colonel; and at that moment some one came up and claimed his attention, so he bowed to Mrs. Orton and withdrew.

Later that night, Frederick, coming up to bed, tapped at his wife's door, and, on receiving a muffled "Come in," entered with a face full of news.

"I say, what do you think Wynch-Frère has been telling me? Poor old Allonby has got smashed up in this very place—I mean Edge Combe—and Elaine Brabourne found him lying by the roadside! So now we shall be able to hear whether she really is as good-looking as Lady Mabel wants to make out."

A ray of interest warmed Ottilie's face, and encouraged him to proceed. He acquainted her with all the details of the accident which he had been able to glean from the colonel; while she sat brushing out her long thick dark hair, and listening. When he had apparently chatted her into a better humor, he sat down on the dressing-table, and, leaning forward, looked at her wistfully.

"I say, old girl, were you fearfully set on Homburg?"

Her face hardened.

"You know I was," she said, shortly.

"Well, look here—can you think of anything we could do with that blessed child? I can't bear to disappoint you. I think it would run to it if we could get rid of him. He means an extra room and some one to look after him, and even then he's eternally in the way. Could we get rid of him for a little while? If so, I'll take you."

"You're very good, Fred," she said, with alacrity. "I—I'm sorry I was so cross. I'll think that over about Godfrey. It would be a hundred times nicer without him."

"My word, though, won't there be a shindy?" said Frederick, laughing. "I wonder what the young cub will say! He isn't used to being left behind; you've spoilt him, Ottilie."

"I indeed? I like that! Why, from the moment he was born you allowed him to do just whatever he chose, and taught him such language——"

"All right—of course it was all my fault, as usual; but now, am I a good boy?"

"Yes, you are."

"Well, then, kiss me."

So a peace was sealed for the time.

On their return to London, on the Monday following, two letters awaited them. One was from Wynifred Allonby, explaining that her brother was ill, and that she had gone to nurse him, and asking that he might have time allowed him to finish his commission pictures; the other was from Miss Ellen Willoughby, begging that Godfrey might spend his holidays at Edge.

"Just the very thing! I'll pack him off there the first minute I can!" cried Mrs. Orton, joyful and exultant.

Frederick smiled prophetically.

"He will probably try his sister's temper," he remarked, placidly, "and that in no common degree; but then, on the other hand, he will doubtless enlarge her vocabulary considerably, so he cannot be looked upon in the light of an unmixed evil."

CHAPTER XVIII

"'Go to the hills,' said one remit a while
This baneful diligence—at early morn
Court the fresh air, explore the heaths and woods;"
... 'I infer that he was healed
By perseverance in the course prescribed'
"You do not err; the powers that had been lost,
By slow degrees were gradually regained
The fluttering nerves composed; the beating heart
In rest established; and the jarring thoughts
To Harmony restored."

The Excursion

The fresh air had never seemed so gloriously sweet to Osmond Allonby before.

He sat in a roomy, comfortable arm chair, a shawl round his big limbs, and the light warm breeze that puffed up the valley bringing a faint color to his white face.

He had two companions, Wynifred and Mr. Fowler. The girl sat on the grass, busy over some little piece of needle-work; Henry Fowler lay beside her, throwing tiny pebbles idly at the terrier's nose. A great peace brooded over Poole Farm—a peace which seemed to communicate itself to the three as they sat enjoying their desultory conversation.

"And so," said Mr. Fowler, "Mr. Dickens returned to his own place yesterday, rendered absolutely despairing by his interview with your brother."

"I know; it was laughable," said Allonby, laughing gently. "He almost gave me the lie, so determined was he that I had a secret enemy somewhere; I was quite sorry I couldn't oblige him with one, his disappointment was so painful to witness."

"The worst of these detective police," returned his friend, "is that they will always pin their faith on some one particular feature of the case; they become imbued with a theory of their own, and in consequence blind and deaf to all that does not bear upon it. Mr. Dickens had settled that this was a vendetta, and he would entertain no other hypothesis."

"The notion is absurd in the highest degree," said Osmond, with animation. "No! It was some tramp, you may be sure, and he was frightened, and made off before securing his booty. I must have looked a very easy prey, for I was sitting, as I have told you before, with my head on my hands, feeling rather done up. I have a dim recollection of a violent blow; I suppose it stunned me at once. Not a soul had passed me, I am sure; whoever it was came up behind, along the Combe road."

"It would not be at all difficult for anyone who knew the country to conceal himself," said Mr. Fowler, meditatively, "but yet—the police watched well. Every neighboring village was searched, and all along the coast ... but these local police are easily deceived, you know. I wish I had been at home at the time."

"I wish you had," said Wynifred, impulsively; and then half repented her impulse, for she received such a very plain look of thanks and pleasure from Mr. Fowler's kind eyes.

From the first moment, he had been deeply struck with Miss Allonby; her character was as new to him as it was to Claud Cranmer, but he found her perfectly charming. Presents of fresh trout, of large strawberries, plump chickens, and invalid jellies daily arrived from the Lower House; and most afternoons the master would follow his gifts, and walk in, arrayed in his rough country clothes, very likely with a reminiscence of bricks or mortar somewhere on his coat sleeve, for he was building a house in the valley for some relations of his, and, as he was his own architect, the work necessitated a good deal of personal attention.

Wynifred had been down to see the house in question, and then to tea at Edge Willoughby, and had been escorted back to Poole by Mr. Fowler in the starlight; and a most interesting walk it had been, for he knew every constellation in the heavens, and exactly where to look for each at any season of the year.

A thorough liking for him had sprung up in her heart. The simplicity of his courteous manner was a rare charm; he was singularly unlike the London men of her acquaintance, with a modesty which was perhaps the most remarkable of his attributes.

The little silence which followed her remark was broken by Osmond.

"When is Cranmer coming down again?" he said.

"Next week, I hope; sooner if he can. I had a letter from him this morning; he asked to be most particularly remembered to you and Miss Allonby, and inquired much after your health," said Mr. Fowler.

"I am glad he was not down last week; the weather was so bad, he would not have known what to do," said Wyn.

In fact, Claud had been reluctantly torn from Edge Combe by his despotic sister, who, when she got to London, found that to choose a house without his assistance was quite an impossibility. In such a matter, the colonel's opinion was never even asked; neither did he resent the omission in the least. If Mabel liked the house, he liked it too, and Claud would see after the stabling.

So Claud went, and tramped Belgravia and even Kensington with submission; and, when at last a selection was made, found himself doomed to go down to Hunstanton with his tyrant and fetch up the children, the nurses, and the little governess for a week's shopping, previous to their being all swept off to Yorkshire, to be out of the way during the autumn at the castle of the earl, their grandpapa, whilst their mother went to make herself agreeable to her husband's constituents; in which last respect she certainly did her duty.

In Mr. Cranmer's absence, the wounded man had grown stronger daily; had sat at his bedroom window, had made the circuit of his chamber, and now was promoted to sit in the garden; and Dr. Forbes exulted in the rapidity of his convalescence.

"You see, there's everything in his favor," he said, complacently. "A fine constitution, a fine time of year—youth, and the best climate in England."

It was highly satisfactory that he should make such excellent use of his advantages.

"I feel to-day as if I could walk a mile," he said, with pride, stretching his long legs and arms and tossing his head.

"I am glad you are feeling so well. You are going to have a visitor this afternoon—Miss Brabourne, who found you lying by the roadside; she is so eager to see you."

Osmond blushed—actually blushed with pleasure. He was not very strong yet, and his heart beat stormily at thought of the coming meeting.

All through his delirium a certain face had haunted him—a girl's face, which he always seemed to see when he closed his eyes. With returning consciousness the vision fled—he could not recall the features, but he had a feeling that they were the features of Elsa Brabourne, and that, if he saw her again, he should know her.

"I'll go down as far as the stile, and see if I can see her," said Wyn; and, tossing her work to the ground, she rose and went wandering off among the flower-beds, singing to herself, and picking a rosebud here and there.

"I envy you your sister, Mr. Allonby," said Henry Fowler.

"Who? Wyn?" asked Osmond. "Yes she is a very good sort; but you should see Hilda and Jacqueline; they are both uncommonly pretty girls, though I say it."

"I think Miss Allonby pretty."

"Wyn? Oh, no, she isn't," was the fraternal criticism. "I've seen her look well, but you can't call her pretty; but I suppose she is attractive—some men seem to find her so."

"Ah!" said Mr. Fowler.

"But she is not at all impressionable," said Wyn's brother.

Meanwhile Wyn was walking down the Waste in happy unconsciousness of being the subject of discussion, and presently was seen to wave her hand and begin to run forward. She and Elsa met in the middle of the Waste, and exchanged greetings. Jane Gollop was far behind—she was growing used to this now, and took it as a matter of course that the young feet which for years had dragged listlessly at her side should now, for very gaiety and youth, outstrip her.

Now that Elsa's face wore that sparkling look of animation, now that her luxuriant tresses were piled classically on the crown of her beautiful head, the barbarity of her costume really sank into insignificance, triumphed over by sheer force of her fresh loveliness. Her glow of color made the pale Wynifred look paler, the girls were a great contrast.

"How is Mr. Allonby? Is he going on well?" panted Elsa, before she had recovered her breath.

"Capitally, thank you. Dr. Forbes says he never knew such a quick convalescence."

"Oh, how glad I am! Is he ... do you think ... it is so very fine to-day ... is Mr. Allonby in the garden?"

The shyness and confusion were very pretty, thought Wyn.

"Yes," she said, delighted to be able to call the warm clear color into the speaking face. "He is sitting in the garden, and is so impatient to see you. Come this way."

No need to speak twice. Elsa's feet seemed scarcely to touch the ground in their transit across the space which intervened between her and the hero of her dreams.

Osmond would insist on rising from his chair to greet her; and his tall form looked taller than ever now that he was so thin.

Elsa drew near, hardly knowing where she was or what she was doing — little recking that he was to the full as excited as she.

They met; their hands touched; the girl could hardly see clearly through the mist of tears in her large speaking eyes. He looked straight at her, saw the crystal mist, saw one irrepressible drop over-brim the lid, and rest on the delicate cheek. A storm of feeling overcame him; he grew quite white.

It was the face of the mystic queen in his visions of Avilion — it was beauty of the type he most passionately admired; and beauty which was stirred to its depths by pity and sympathy for him.

He could say nothing articulate, neither could she. Their greeting was chiefly that of eyes, and of warmly grasping hands, for she had stretched both to him, and he had seized them.

How long did it last? They did not know. To Osmond it seemed, like the dreams of his fever, to last for hours, and yet be gone like a flash. He only knew that presently he found himself seated again in his chair, his fingers released from the warm touch of hers; that she was sitting by him on Wynifred's vacated seat; that the skies had not fallen, nor the shadows on the grass lengthened perceptibly; and that neither Wyn nor Mr. Fowler expressed any surprise in their countenances, as if anything unusual had transpired.

Apparently he had not openly made a fool of himself. He heaved a sigh of relief, and lay back among his cushions. There sat the lady of his dreams, no longer a phantom, a real girl of flesh and blood, with large eyes of morning grey fixed on him.

He fancied how those calm eyes, like the misty dawn of a glorious day, would gradually warm and deepen into the torrid splendor of noon; when what was now only sympathetic interest should have strengthened into passionate love, when his voice, his touch should alone have power to— —

Alas! as usual, he was building an airy cloud-palace for his thoughts to live in; and here was the real earth, and here was himself, a poor, struggling young artist, a competitor in one of London's fiercest and most crowded fields of competition, and with three unmarried sisters to think of.

And there was she—could he dream of it for her? The future of a poor man's wife. *Wife!* The exquisite delight of that word, by force of contrast, calmed this enthusiast utterly. No. To him nothing nearer than a star, an ideal. His Beatrice, only to be longed for, never attained.

And all this he had time to think of, while Wyn was cheerfully telling Elsa that he had that day eaten a piece of lamb, and "quite a great deal" of milky pudding for his dinner, which hopeful bulletin of his appetite was received with marked interest both by Mr. Fowler and his god-daughter.

And then Elaine turned her bashful eyes on him, and he heard her voice saying,

"I am so glad you are getting well so fast. I was very unhappy when they thought you would not live."

"Were you?" he said, hoping his voice did not sound as queer to the others as it did to himself. "It was very philanthropical of you. That gift of pity is one of woman's most gracious attributes."

Elsa was developing very fast, but she was not yet equal to replying to this speech.

"I think I have been altogether far more fortunate than I deserve," went on Osmond. "Everyone in this fairy valley had vied in their efforts to be kind to me. Your good aunts, Mr. Fowler here, Mr. Cranmer and Lady Mabel, not to mention Dr. Forbes, Mrs. Battishill, and Mrs. Clapp."

Elsa was still tongue-tied; and, oh! it was hard, when she had so much to say to him. How kindly he spoke! How handsome he looked when he smiled! If only she knew what to say!

At this embarrassing juncture, Jane scrambled over the stile, grasping a covered basket. Like lightning the girl leaped up, ran to her nurse, and, taking her burden, carried it back to the young man's side.

"I brought these for you," she faltered. "The strawberries are over, but here are white currants and raspberries ... raspberries are very good with cream. Do you like them?"

"Like them? I should think so! My appetite is quite tremendous, as Wyn told you. Will you carry back my sincere thanks to Miss Willoughby for her kind thought?"

She blushed, and then smiled, rising her face to his.

"It was my thought," she said, timidly; "the aunts said they were not good enough to bring, and I went to Lower House for the currants," she concluded, nodding mischeviously to her godfather.

"Like your impudence!" he answered, pretending to shake a fist at her. "Now, Miss Allonby, I must be going; won't you show me the picture you are doing of Saul Parker?"

"Oh, yes, I should like to. I hope you will think it a good likeness," answered Wyn, eagerly.

She rose, and walked slowly into the house with Mr. Fowler, leaving the two seated together on the lawn, conscious of nothing in all the world but each other's presence.

There was a little pause; then Elaine gathered courage. It was easier for them to talk with no listeners.

"I saw you before you were hurt," she announced, blushing.

"You saw me?" cried Osmond, devoured with interest. "Where? I never saw you."

"No; I was behind your back. I was coming up to the farm; you were sitting at your easel. Your head was resting on your hands. I wanted to go and ask you if you were ill; but Jane hurried me on."

"And I never knew," said Osmond, in a slow, absorbed way.

"And so I asked Jane to go back round by the road because—because I wanted to see your face; and when we got there you were lying on the grass."

Here the lip quivered. Allonby threw himself forward in his chair, his chin on his elbow.

"I saw your face," he said, earnestly. "Tell me, did you not—were you not kneeling by me, and—and *weeping*?"

The girl nodded, hardly able to speak.

"You opened your eyes," she said, very low, after a pause, "and looked at me for a moment; but not as if you knew me."

"But I saw you. Do you know"—sinking his voice—"that your face was with me all through my illness—your face, as I saw it to-day, with tears on your eyelashes?... I knew even your voice, when I have heard it in the garden, and I have been lying in bed. I knew when you laughed and when you spoke ... and I counted the hours till I should be well enough to see you and thank you. You'll let me thank you, won't you?"

He took her hand again. The child—for she was no more—could not speak. It seemed as if light were breaking so swiftly in upon her soul that the glare dazzled her. She was helpless—almost frightened. Osmond saw that he must be careful not to startle or vex her. With a great effort he curbed his own excitement, and took a lighter tone.

"Think what a benefactor in disguise my unknown assailant has been!" he cried brightly. "What have I lost? Nothing—absolutely nothing but a pudding-basin; what have I gained?" He made an eloquent sweep of the hand. "Everything! In fact, I can hardly realise at present what my gain is. To be ill—to be tenderly nursed—to have enquiries made all day by kind friends—to have my name in all the local papers—to be interviewed at least once a day by gentlemen of the press. I assure you that I never before was the centre of attraction; I hope it will last. That day's sketching in the lane may turn out to be the best stroke of business I ever did."

"But," cried Elsa, remonstrating, "you don't count all the pain you had to bear?"

"Pain!" he said, almost incoherently. "Did I? Have I borne pain? Oh, it counts for nothing, for I have forgotten all about it."

"Really and truly? Have you forgotten it?"

"Really and truly, just now. I may remember it presently, when I am crawling upstairs to bed to-night, with my arm round Joe Battishill's neck; but just now it is clean gone, and every day I shall grow stronger, you know."

She did not answer. She saw fate, in the shape of Jane Gollop, bearing down upon her from the open farm-house door.

"Miss Elaine, my dear, you wasn't to stay but a very little while to-day; and, if we don't start back, you won't be in time to go to the station with your Aunt Charlotte to meet your brother, you know."

"To meet your brother!" echoed Osmond.

"Yes." She turned to him. "He is my step-brother; I have never seen him since he was a baby."

"Really? That sounds odd; but you are orphans; I suppose he is being brought up by other relations. I think it was cruel to separate you. How old is he?"

"Just fourteen. I am glad he is coming at last."

"I suppose so; and you will be so happy together that you will forget to come up to Poole and see the poor sick man?"

"You *know* I shall not. I shall bring Godfrey."

"Yes, do. Please come soon. But I ought not to be so grasping, and I have never thanked you properly for coming to-day. What an unmannerly brute I am. Please forgive me! Don't punish me by staying away, will you?"

She drew near, and spoke low, that Jane might not hear.

"I shall come whenever they let me," she said, with vehemence; "whenever I don't come, you will know it is because I was forbidden. If they would allow it, I'd come *every single day.*"

CHAPTER XIX

I find you passing gentle.
'Twas told me you were rough, and coy, and sullen,
And now I find report a very liar;
For thou art pleasant, gamesome, passing courteous,
But slow in speech, yet sweet as spring time flowers:
Thou canst not frown, thou canst not look askance,
Nor bite the lip, as angry wenches will.
Taming of the Shrew.

It was quite an unusual event for Miss Charlotte Willoughby to be standing on the platform watching the arrival of the London train. Her preparation for the expedition had been made in quite a flutter of expectation. She was resolved to do her duty thoroughly by Godfrey Brabourne, much as she had disliked his mother. She had hopes that a stay in a household of such strict propriety, where peace, order, and regularity reigned supreme, might perchance work an improvement in the boy, do something to eradicate the pernicious influence of early training, and cause him, in after life, to own with a burst of emotion that he dated the turning-point in his career from the moment when his foot first trod the threshold of Edge Willoughby. This was a consummation so devoutly to be wished, as to go far towards reconciling the good lady to the presence of a boy in the virgin seclusion of the house. Elsa, at her side, was stirred to the deepest depths of her excitable temperament, each faculty poised, each nerve a-quiver as she hung bashfully back behind her aunt.

There was a long wild howl, a dog's howl, followed by a series of sharp yelps and a sound of scuffling; a crowd collected round the dog-box. A small boy in an Eton suit dashed down the platform, parted the spectators right and left, and revealed to view the panic-stricken guard, with a bull-dog hanging to his trousers.

"Ven! Come off, you confounded brute! How dare you!" cried the little boy in shrill tones, as he seized the dog by the collar, and dragged him off. "Didn't I tell you, you idiot," he went on to the guard, "not to touch him till I came! What fools people are, always meddling with what ain't their concern. Why couldn't you let my dog alone, eh? I don't pity you, blessed if I do," concluded he in an off-hand manner, cuffing his dog heartily, and shaking him at the same time. "I'll teach you manners, you scoundrel," he said, furiously; "and now, what am I to be let in for over this job? Has he drawn blood?"

Elsa and her aunt were so absorbed, as was everyone else, in watching this episode, as to temporarily forget their errand at the station; but now the girl began to peer among the little crowd of bystanders, to see if she could spy anybody who looked like Godfrey.

"Auntie," she whispered, "hasn't Godfrey come?"

"I—am not sure."

A cold fear, a presentiment, was stealing over Miss Charlotte's mind. Something in the voice, the air, the face of the dreadful boy with the bull-dog, reminded her uncomfortably of her deceased brother-in-law, Valentine Brabourne. She wavered a little, while vehement and angry recriminations went on between him and the railway-officials, noticed with a shudder how he felt in his trousers' pockets and pulled out loose gold, and was still in a state of miserable uncertainty when he turned round, and demanded, in high, shrill tones:

"Isn't there anybody here to meet me from Edge Willoughby?"

Both aunt and niece started, and gasped. Then Miss Charlotte went bravely forward.

"Are you Godfrey Brabourne?" she asked, with shaking voice, more than half-ashamed to have to lay claim to such a boy before a little concourse of spectators who all knew her by sight. The guard lifted his cap, surprised, and half-apologetic.

"Pardon, mum," he grumbled, "but I do say as a young gentleman didn't oughter travel with that dog unmuzzled. He didn't ought to do it; for you never know where the beast'll take a fancy to bite, and a man with a family's got hydrophobia to consider."

"Hydrophobia! Hydro-fiddlestick!" cried Godfrey, making a grimace. "He ain't even broken the skin, and I've given you a couple of sovs.—a deuced lot more than those bags of yours ever cost." This speech elicited a laugh all round, and seemed to congeal Miss Charlotte's blood in her veins. "So now you just go round the corner and treat your friends. Why, if you had any sense, you wouldn't mind being bitten every day for a week at that price. How d'ye do, Miss Willoughby? My aunt Ottilie sent her kind regards, or something."

"Will you—come this way?" said Miss Charlotte, desperately, possessed only by the idea of hastening from this scene of public disgrace. "Come, my dear, come! If the guard is satisfied, let the matter rest. I am sure it is very imprudent to travel with so savage a dog unmuzzled. Dear, dear! what are you going to do with him?"

"Do with him? Nothing. He's all right; he's not mad. That ass must needs go dragging him out of the dog-box or something, that's all. He wouldn't hurt a fly."

Miss Charlotte paused in her headlong flight from the station.

"Godfrey, I regret—I deeply regret it, but I can on no account allow that beast to be taken up to the house. I cannot permit it—he will be biting everybody."

"Oh, he's all right," was the cool retort. "Chain him up in the stables, if you're funky. Leave him alone. He'll follow the trap right enough if I'm in it. Now then, where are your cattle?"

Miss Charlotte unconsciously answered this, to her, incomprehensible question by laying her lean hand, which trembled somewhat, on the handle of the roomy, well-cushioned wagonette which the ladies of Edge found quite good enough to convey them along the country lanes to shop in Philmouth, or call on a friend. The plump, lazy horse stood swishing his tail in the sunshine, and Acland, the deliberate, bandy-legged coachman, was in the act of placing a smart little portmanteau on the box.

"Now then—room for that inside—just put that portmanteau inside, will you? I'm going to drive," announced Master Godfrey; and, as he spoke, he turned suddenly, and for the first time caught sight of Elsa.

"Godfrey," said Miss Charlotte, "this is your sister Elaine."

The boy stared a moment. Elaine's face was crimson—tears stood in her eyes; her appearance was altogether as eccentric as it well could be, for she wore the Sunday dress and hat to do him honor. To him, used as he was to slim girls in tailor-made gowns, with horsy little collars and diamond pins, perfectly-arranged hair, and gloves and shoes leaving nothing to be desired, the effect was simply unutterably comic. He surveyed his half-sister from head to foot, and burst into a peal of laughter. It was all too funny. His aunt was funny, the horse and trap funnier still; but this Elaine was funniest of all.

"What a guy!" he said to himself, a sudden feeling of wrathful disgust taking the place of his mirth, as he angrily reflected that this strange object bore the name of Brabourne. Aloud he said:

"I beg your pardon for laughing, but you have got such a rum hat on; I suppose anything does for these lanes." Then before anyone could dare to remonstrate, he was up on the box with the reins in his hand. "Now then, Johnnie," said he to the outraged Acland, "up with you. I'm going to drive this thing—is it a calf or a mule? Or is it a cross between an elephant and a pig? I suppose you bring it down for the luggage. What sort of a show have you got in your stables, eh?"

To this ribald questioning, Acland, white with fury, made answer that the Misses Willoughbys had only one horse at present; at which the boy laughed loudly, and confided to him his opinion that "their friends must be an uncommon queer lot, for them to dare to show with such a turn-out."

This dust and ashes Acland had to swallow, watching meanwhile the stout horse, Taffy, goaded up the hills with a speed that threatened apoplexy, and dashing down them with a rattle which seemed to more than hint at broken springs.

And Elaine and her aunt sat inside, with Godfrey's portmanteau for company, and said never a word. Low as had been Miss Willoughby's expectations, little as she had been prepared to love the outcome of the Orton training, certainly this boy exceeded her severest thought; he out-heroded Herod.

Elsa was simply choked; she could not say one word. She scrambled out of the wagonette at the door with a face from which the eagerness of hope had gone, to be replaced by a burning, baleful rage. She was furious; her self-love had been cruelly wounded, and hers was not a nature to forget. Of course she said nothing to her aunts. They had never encouraged her to divulge her feelings to them, and she never did. She rushed away to her old nursery, to stamp and gesticulate in a wild frenzy of anger and hurt feeling.

Meanwhile Godfrey walked in, scowling. He had expected dulness, but nothing so terrible as this promised to be. Sulkily he ordered Venom, the bull-dog, to lie down in the hall, and stumbled into the drawing-room to shake hands, with ill-suppressed contempt, with all his step-aunts, who sat around in silent condemnation.

The Tree Of Knowledge A Novel | 143

Miss Ellen spoke first, thinking in her kindness to set the shy boy at ease.

"You will be glad of some tea after your long journey; you must be thirsty."

"Yes, I am thirsty; but I'm not very keen on tea, thanks. I'd sooner have a B and S, if you have such a thing; or a lemon squash."

There was a dead silence.

"Oh, don't you mind if you haven't got it," he said, easily; "a glass of beer would do."

After a moment's hesitation Miss Ellen rang the bell, and ordered "a glass of ale," and then Miss Charlotte found her voice, and told their guest to go and chain up his dog in the stable.

"Oh, all right! I'll go and cheek the old Johnnie with the stiff collar," he said; and so sauntered out, leaving the ladies gazing helplessly each at the other.

All tea-time the visitor was considerably subdued, perhaps by the close proximity and severe expression of the sisterhood; but after tea Miss Charlotte told Elsa to put on her hat and take her brother round the garden. Once out of sight, Master Godfrey's tongue was loosed.

"Whew! What a set of old cats!" he cried. "Have you had to live with them all your life? I'm sure I'm sorry for you, poor beggar."

Elsa's smouldering resentment was very near ablaze.

"What's the matter with my aunts?" she asked, defiantly.

"What's the matter with your aunts? By Jove! that's good. What's the matter with *you*, that you can't see it? Such a set of old cautions!" he burst into loud laughter. "But you've lived with them till you're almost as bad! I never saw such a figure of fun! I say, what would you take to walk down Piccadilly in that get-up? I'm hanged if I'd walk with you, though!"

"How dare you?" Elsa's cheeks and eyes flamed, she shook with passion. "How dare you speak to me like that? I hate you," she cried, "you rude, detestable child. I wish I had never seen you! Why do you come here? And I—I—I—was looking forward so to having you—I was! I was! I wish you had never been born—there!"

"If she isn't snivelling, I declare! Just because I don't admire her bed-gown! Pretty little dear, then, didn't it like to be told that it was unbecomingly dressed? There, there, it should wear its things hind-part-before, if it liked,

144 | The Tree Of Knowledge A Novel

and carry a tallow candle on the tip of its nose, or any other little fancy it may have. As to asking me why I came here," he went on, with a sudden vicious change of tone, "I can tell you I only came because I was sent, and not because I wanted to. Uncle Fred and Aunt Ottilie are off to Homburg, and want to be rid of me, so they shipped me off here; and Uncle Fred told an awful whopper, for he said it was no end of a jolly place, and I could ride and drive. Ride what? A bantam cock? Drive what? A fantail pigeon, for that's all the live stock I can see on the estate, unless you count the barrel on four legs that brought us from the station, and which the old boy calls a horse; and now where's the tennis-ground?"

"There isn't one."

"Not a tennis-ground? Well, this is pleasant, certainly. Brisk up, whiney-piney, and tell me where's the nearest place I can get any tennis."

"Now look here," said the girl, in a voice thick with emotion, "if you think you are going to speak to me like this, I can tell you you are dreadfully mistaken. How dare you!—how *dare* you say such things! But I know. It is because the aunts all speak to me as if I were four years old, and order me about. You think you can do it too. But you shan't. I am taller and older than you. I will knock you down if you tease me again—do you hear? I will knock you down, I tell you, you impudent child!"

Godfrey shut his left eye, poked his tongue out of the right-hand corner of his mouth, and leered at his sister.

"You only try, my girl," he said, "you only try, and I'll make it hot for you. You'll find out you had better be civil to me, I can tell you, or I'll make you wish you were dead; so now."

"I shall tell my aunts——!"

"All right! You play the tell-tale, and you see what you'll get. I twig what you want—someone to lick you into shape—you've never had a brother. Well, now I've come, I'm going to spend my time in making you behave yourself and look like a Christian."

She stamped her foot at him; she could hardly speak for wrath.

"Do you know how old I am?"

"No, and don't want to; I only know you're the biggest ass a man ever had for a sister, and that if I can't improve you a little, I won't let Aunt Ottilie have you up to town—for I wouldn't be seen with you; so now you know my opinion."

The Tree Of Knowledge A Novel | 145

"And you shall know mine. I think you the most cowardly, rude, detestable boy I ever met. I hate and despise you. I only hope you will be punished well one day for your cruelty to me."

"Well, you are a duffer! Crying if anyone says a word to you! I say, who's the old boy coming up the path, getting over the stile at the end of the terrace?"

The girl glanced up and recognised Mr. Fowler with a sense of passionate relief. He was the only person to whom she dared show her moods; in a moment she was sobbing in his arms.

"Why, Elsie, what's this?" asked the quiet voice, as he stroked back her tumbled hair with caressing hand. "Look up, child. Is that Godfrey yonder?"

"Oh, yes—yes—yes! And I hate him!... I ... hate him! I wish he had never come here to make me so unhappy! He is a bad boy! I wish I had never seen him!"

CHAPTER XX

Here all the summer could I stay,
For there's a Bishop's Teign
And King's Teign
And Coomb at the clear Teign's head,
Where, close by the stream,
You may have your cream,
All spread upon barley bread.
Then who would go
Into dark Soho
And chatter with dank-haired critics
When he can stay
For the new-mown hay
And startle the dappled crickets?
Keats.

A great bustle was rife in the little parlor of the "Fountain Head." A hamper was being packed, rugs strapped together, preparations in general being made. The excitement seemed to communicate itself to the village in some mysterious way; and small wonder. It was rarely that so many visitors from London haunted the Combe all at once; rarer still that so mysterious a celebrity attached to one of them; rarest of all that the Misses Willoughby should be giving a picnic-party.

Yet so it was; and the weather, which, under the iron rule of St. Swithun, had "gone to pieces," as Osmond said, for the past three weeks, had now revived anew, full of heat and beauty and sunshine.

In the doorway of the inn stood Osmond himself, and a tall, fine-looking girl with a brilliant complexion and large hazel eyes.

"What a day for a pic-nic!" she cried, jovially. "And this place—I must freely admit that Wyn, prone as she is to rhapsody, has *not* overdone it in describing the Combe. Oh, here comes Mr. Haldane, just in time. I hope you know we were on the point of starting without you," said she, with an attempt at severity, as a young man came slowly along the road leading from the village.

"I should soon have caught you up," he said peacefully, raising his hat with a smile. "How are you this morning, Mr. Allonby? Still convalescent?"

"I don't think the present participle is any longer applicable. I am convalesced—completely convalesced, and, it seems to me all the better for my accident."

"So you are not cursing me for having recommended the Combe as a hunting-ground?"

"Not in the least, I assure you."

"Did you ever hear, Mr. Haldane," cried the girl, with a burst of laughter, "that the detective tried to assign poor old Osmond's blow on the head to your machinations?"

"No! Really! You flatter me; what made him do that?" asked he, with imperturbable and smiling composure.

"He thought you had some *arrière pensée* in sending Osmond down here to paint."

"Well, so I had."

"You had?"

"Of course. I knew he'd like the place so much that he'd want to spend all the summer here; and then I thought you and your sisters would come down; and then I thought I'd come down; and I have, you see."

Jacqueline laughed merrily.

"We're going to have such a good time to-day," she cried, "and, please, listen to me. You and Wyn are *not* to talk shop. The first of you that mentions the R. A. Schools, or the gold medal pictures, or the winter exhibition, shall be sent to Coventry at once! Remember! You are under orders."

"Well, I don't think I'm likely to forget it, as long as you are here to remind me, Miss Jacqueline. By-the-by, aren't you getting bored down here? Surely the Combe falls a trifle flat after the gaieties of Cowes?"

"We are getting on pretty well so far, thank you; a school-treat the day after we arrived, an expedition to the quarries yesterday, a pic-nic to-day! I am managing to exist, but I can't think what we shall do to-morrow. The blackberries are not yet ripe, there are no ruins to explore, and not another school-feast for miles; there will be nothing for it but to go out in a boat and get drowned."

"All right; I'll come too."

"You can go out in a boat and get drowned to-day, if you like," suggested Osmond. "Boats are in the programme."

"So they are! I had forgotten. How late this Mr. Fowler is! Don't you think we had better go on, Osmond, and leave you and Wyn to follow?"

"Certainly, if you like. Who is packing?"

"*Need* you ask? Hilda, of course. She always does everything she should. Wyn! Wyn! Are you ready?"

"Coming!"

Wyn emerged from the dark entry, and shook hands with Mr. Haldane.

"I will send Hilda to you," she said, vanishing, and in a minute or two there appeared on the scene another tall girl, closely resembling Jacqueline in height and general appearance, and dressed exactly like her, down to the minutest detail. In fact the family likeness in all four Allonbys was strong, something distinctive in the curve of the chin, the setting on of the head, the steady glance of the eye, which made them all noticeable, whether handsome or not. They were, all four, people who, having once been seen, were not likely to be forgotten. Of his two younger sisters Osmond was justly proud. Their height, grace, and slenderness were striking, and the want of likeness in their dispositions completed the charm, by the rare virtue of being unexpected.

Hilda was as reserved as Jacqueline was communicative, as statuesque as she was animated, as diligent and capable as she was lavish and reckless. The difference between them was this morning, however, much less obvious than the likeness, for Hilda was full of spirits, the whole of her sweet face irradiated with pleasure.

They set off with young Haldane, chattering eagerly, the sound of their light laughter tossed behind them on the breeze as they climbed the steep grassy hillside to Edge, to join the rest of the party.

They were hardly out of sight when Mr. Fowler and his dog-cart appeared down the road, the black horse's glossy flanks and polished harness reflecting the brightness of the sun.

"Good morning," cried Osmond, blithely; "what a fresh lovely morning! We are ready and waiting for you."

"We? Then I am to have the pleasure of driving Miss Allonby! That's all right. Cranmer came down yesterday evening, looking rather jaded; he seemed very glad to get here. He has gone on foot to join the others," said Mr. Fowler, alighting and entering the dark cool passage of the inn.

"Are you there Miss Allonby?"

"Yes, here I am. Good morning, Mr. Fowler. Come and help me with this strap."

He entered, and took her hand.

"So you are all established here! What did Mrs. Battishill say to your desertion?"

"She was very unhappy, but I could not help it. She totally declined to accept a penny for rent, and I wanted to have Hilda and Jac down, so I was obliged to move. I could not quarter my entire family upon her, it was too barefaced. There, how neatly you fastened that buckle! Now everything is ready. I'll call Tom to carry the hamper to the carriage."

"You'll do no such thing; I shall take it myself. We are favored in our weather, are we not?"

"That we are. In fact, everything is favorable to-day. My mental barometer is up at 'set-fair.' I have a mind to tell you why, and receive your congratulations all to myself. I heard from Barclay's to-day that my novel is to be put into a second edition. What do you think of that?"

Mr. Fowler thought the occasion quite important enough to justify a second energetic grasping of Miss Allonby's little slim hand in his vigorous square palm; and the dialogue might have been for some time prolonged, had not Osmond cried out, from his position at the horse's head,

"Now then, you two!"

In a few minutes Wyn was enthroned beside Mr. Fowler in the high dog-cart, her brother had swung himself up behind with the hamper, and the swift Black Prince was off, delighted to be tearing along in the sunshine.

"I am going to enjoy myself to-day, and forget all vexations," said Henry Fowler, in his quiet voice.

"Vexations? Are you vexed? What is it?" asked Wyn, anxiously.

"I am—a good deal vexed—about my Elsie," he answered, with a sigh. "Poor little lass! I think she is deeply to be pitied."

"So do I," said Wyn, promptly; and Osmond cut in from behind.

"I should like to lick that cheeky little beast of a boy."

"There's the rub—you can't lick the child, he's too delicate," said Henry, with a sigh. "I took him by the shoulder and shook him the other day, and he turned as white as a sheet and almost fainted. He is a mass of nerves, and has no constitution; careful rearing might have done something for him, but he is accustomed to sit up all night, lie in bed all day, drink spirits, and smoke cigars—a poor little shrimp like that! It is a terrible trial to Elsie; one that I'm afraid she's not equal to," he concluded, slowly, his eyes rivetted on the lash of his whip, with which he was flicking the flies from Black Prince's pretty pricked-up ears.

"She ought never to be called upon to endure it—they ought to send the little imp away," said Osmond, indignantly.

"He does not show himself in his true colors before the Miss Willoughbys—this is where I can't forgive him," returned Mr. Fowler, sternly. "The child is a habitual liar—you never know for a moment whether he is telling the truth or not. His dog worried two of my sheep yesterday; the shepherd absolutely saw the brute in the field, and he—Godfrey— coolly told me that Ven had been chained in the yard all that morning. It was then," he added, with a half-smile, "that I shook him; I would have liked to lay my stick about him, but one can't touch such a little frail thing; and his language—ugh! That Elsa should ever hear such words makes one grind one's teeth. I never saw such a young child so completely vitiated."

"What a misfortune!" said Wyn.

"You are right; it is a real misfortune. I am very doubtful as to what steps I ought to take in the matter. Did you hear of his setting his bull-dog at Saul Parker, the idiot? The poor wretch had one of his fits, and his mother was up all night with him. Little cur! Cruelty and cowardice always go together: but think what his bringing up must have been."

"I wonder Mr. and Mrs. Orton are not ashamed to send him visiting; Osmond knows something of the Ortons, you know."

"Indeed!"

"Yes; they have one of the new big houses up in our part of London, and Mr. Orton is something of a connoisseur in pictures. Osmond is painting two for him now."

"Yes," said Osmond, laughing, "but now I go out armed, and escorted by a *cordon* of sisters to keep off murderers; landscape-painting has become as risky a profession as that of newspaper-reporter at the seat of war. I really think I ought to allow for personal risk in my prices, don't you, Fowler?"

A brisk "Halloo!" startled them all; and, looking eagerly forward, they became aware of a group gathered together at some distance ahead, at the point where the road ended, and gave way to a winding pathway among the chalk cliffs. Very picturesque and very happy they all looked—Wyn longed to coax them to stand still, and take out her sketch-book.

The wagonette stood a short way off, with two Miss Willoughbys, Miss Fanny and Miss Emily, seated in it. Acland was unloading the provisions and handing them to Jane. Hilda, Jacqueline, and Elsa were sitting on the grassy chalk boulders, with Mr. Haldane, Claud Cranmer, Dr. Forbes, and Godfrey as their escort.

As the party in the dog-cart drew near, Osmond's eyes sought out Elsa. She was looking charming, for the aunts had taken Wyn into confidence on the subject of their niece's costume, and her white dress and shady hat left little to be desired. She and the Allonby girls had been plucking tall spires of fox-glove to keep off the annoying flies; Mr. Cranmer was arranging a big frond of diletata round Hilda's hat for coolness; and over all the lovely scene brooded the sultry grandeur of early August, and the murmur of the sea washing lazily at the feet of the scorched red cliffs.

The spot selected for pic-nicking was a shelving bit of coast known as the Landslip. A large mass of soil had broken away in the middle of the seventeenth century, carrying cottages and cattle to headlong ruin. Now it lay peacefully settled down into the brink of the bay, the great scar from whence it had been torn all riddled with gull's nests. The chatter and laughter of the birds was incessant, and there was something almost weird to Wynifred in the strange "Ha-ha!" which echoed along the cliffs as the busy white wings wheeled in and out, flashing in the light and disappearing.

"They are teaching the young to fly," explained Mr. Fowler. "If you came along here next week, you would find all silent as the grave."

"I am glad they are not flown yet," said Wyn. "I like their laughter, there is something uncanny about it."

Mr. Cranmer was passing, laden with a basket.

"Characteristic of Miss Allonby! She likes something because it is uncanny!" he remarked. "Is there anything uncanny about *you*, Fowler, by any chance?"

"What has upset Cranmer?" asked Henry, arching his eyebrows.

"I don't know, really. Suppose you go and find out," said Wyn, laughing a little.

It was her greeting of him which had annoyed Claud; and Wyn was keen enough to gauge precisely the reason why it had annoyed him.

He had scarcely seen her since the evening when he and she had walked from the village to Poole together. A vivid remembrance of that walk remained in his mind, and he had been determined to meet her again in the most matter-of-fact way possible. He told himself that it would be ungentlemanly in the extreme to so much as hint at sentimental memories, when he was not in the least in love, and had no intention of becoming so. Accordingly his "How do you do, Miss Allonby?" had been the very essence of casual acquaintanceship. Wyn, on her side, was even more anxious than he that her momentary weakness should be treated merely as a digression. She had been very angry with herself for having been so stirred; for stirred she had been, to such an unwonted extent, that Claud had been scarcely a moment out of her thoughts for two days after. The very recollection made her angry with herself. She met him on his own ground; if his greeting was casual, hers was even more so. It was perfect indifference—not icy, not reserved, so as to hint at hidden resentment, hidden feeling of some kind, but simply the most complete lack of *empressement*; his hand and himself apparently dismissed from her mind in a moment; and this should have pleased Claud, of course,—only it did not.

He asked himself angrily what the girl was made of. His usually sweet temper was quite soured for the moment; impossible to help throwing a taunt behind him as he passed her, impossible to help being furious when he perceived that the taunt had not stung at all. He looked round for Elsa Brabourne, that he might devote himself to her; but she was entirely absorbed in the occupation of finding a sheltered place for Allonby, where he might be out of the sun.

Jacqueline and young Haldane were laying the cloth together, and doing it so badly that Hilda seized it from them and dismissed them in disgrace, proceeding to lay it herself with the assistance of old Dr. Forbes, who had fallen a hopeless victim at first sight. Jacqueline and Haldane went off, apparently quarrelling violently, down to the shore, and were presently to be seen in the act of fulfilling their threat of going out in a boat and getting drowned. Mr. Fowler shouted to them not to go far, as dinner would be ready at once, and hastened off to pilot dear little Miss Fanny safely down the rocky pathway to a seat where she might enjoy her picnic in comfort. Everyone had been relieved, though nobody had liked to say so, when Miss Charlotte announced that picnics were not in her line.

Wyn had been bitterly disappointed that it was not possible to bring Miss Ellen; but the invalid's health was growing daily feebler, and she was now quite unequal to the exertion of the shortest drive. So Miss Fanny, fortified by Miss Emily, had set out, with as much excitement and trepidation as if she had joined a band for the discovery of the north-west passage; and now, clinging to Henry Fowler's arm, was carefully conducted down the perilous steps towards the place of gathering. Wyn was left standing by herself, watching with a smile the manoeuvres of Jac and Haldane in their boat below, and Claud was left with a scowl watching Wyn.

After standing silently aloof for several minutes, he went slowly up to her.

"Your brother has made wonderful progress since I left, Miss Allonby," he remarked, stiffly.

"Yes, hasn't he?" she said, with a smile, her eyes still fixed on the boat. "Do just look at my sister; she is trying to pull, and she is only accustomed to Thames rowing; she does not know what to do without a button to her oar."

He did not look, he kept his eyes rivetted on her calm face.

"You look much better for your stay in Devonshire, too," he said, determined to make the conversation personal.

"Yes, so the girls say. I was rather over-worked when I first came down. How calm it is, isn't it? Hardly a wavelet. I think even I could go out without feeling unhappy to-day."

"May I take you presently? I am pretty well used to sea-rowing. My brother's place in Ireland is on the coast."

"Thanks, I should like to come; we will make up a party—Hilda and Mr. Fowler——"

"You are determined to give me plenty of work. I suggested pulling one person—not three. There are four boats; let them take another; but perhaps you don't care to go without Mr. Fowler."

This speech approached nearer to being rude than anything she had ever heard from the courteous Claud. It made her very angry. She lifted her eyes and allowed them to meet his calmly.

"It certainly adds greatly to my pleasure to be in Mr. Fowler's society," she said very tranquilly; "he is one of the most perfect gentlemen I ever met."

"You are right, he is," said Claud, almost penitently; and just at this juncture Godfrey tore by like a whirlwind, shouting out at the top of his voice,

"Dinner! Dinner! Dinner's ready! Look alive, everybody! Come and tackle the grub!"

CHAPTER XXI

Is she wronged? To the rescue of her honor,
My heart!
Song from "Pippa Passes."

The dinner was a most hilarious repast. It was impossible to resist the infectious good spirits of the Allonby girls, and Godfrey was duly awed and held in check by the presence of Mr. Fowler.

Elsa sat, her eyes wide open, drinking in, word by word, all this fresh thrilling life which was opening round her. Girls and their ways were becoming less and less of a mystery to her; the expression which had been so wanting was now informing all the pretty features, making her beauty a thing to be wondered at and rejoiced over by the impressionable Osmond. Dinner over, all dispersed to seek their pleasure as seemed best to them; and Mr. Fowler, who appeared to have constituted himself surety for Godfrey's good behavior, ordered the boy to come out in the same boat with him. But he was not cunning enough for the spoilt child.

"Likely," remarked Master Brabourne, "that I'm going to pass the afternoon dangling from that old joker's watch-chain. Not much; no, thank you; I'd sooner be on my own hook this journey, any way; so you may whistle for me, Mr. Fowler."

After this muttered soliloquy, he at once obliterated himself, so completely, that nobody noticed that he was missing, and Henry embarked with Hilda Allonby and Miss Emily Willoughby, and was half-way across the bay before he remembered the tiresome child's existence. Miss Fanny declined the perils of the deep, and stayed on shore; Wynifred remained with her for a few minutes, to see that she was happy and comfortable and, on turning away at last, found that there was nobody left for her to pair off with but Mr. Cranmer, who stood doggedly at a short distance, watching her.

"What shall we do?" he asked.

"I don't mind. What is everyone else doing?"

"Going out in boats. Are you anxious to be in the fashion?"

"Yes, I think so. Is there a boat left?"

"There is. Come down this way."

It rather vexed Wynifred to find herself thus appropriated. It had been her intention to steer clear of Claud, and now here he was, glued to her side for the afternoon. However, there was really no reason for disquiet; since her momentary lapse she had taken herself well in hand, and felt that she had the advantage over him by the fact of being warned.

As they slipped through the blue water, she turned her eyes to land, and there saw a sight which, for no special reason, seemed to cast a tinge of sadness over her mood. It was only Osmond and Elsa, side by side, wandering inland, slowly, and evidently in deep conversation. In a few seconds the chalk boulders would hide them from view; Wyn watched their progress wistfully, and then, suddenly withdrawing her gaze, found that of her companion fixed upon her.

"I ought to apologize for saying anything," he said, deprecatingly, "but that is a pretty obvious case, isn't it?"

"Is it?"

He suddenly aimed one of his shafts of ridicule at her.

"A novelist and so unobservant?"

"Oh, no," said Wyn, gravely, leaning forward, her chin on her hand, and still following the couple with her eyes. "I am not unobservant."

"Yet you don't see that your brother is attracted?"

"I see it quite well."

"Your tone implies dissatisfaction. Don't you like Miss Brabourne?"

"You ask home questions; I hardly feel able to answer you. I know so little of her."

He arched his eyebrows.

"Is hers such a very intricate character?"

"I don't know about intricate; perhaps not, but it is remarkably undeveloped."

"Don't you like what you have seen of her?"

Wyn hesitated.

"I think I ought not to make her the subject of discussion; it doesn't seem quite kind."

"I beg your pardon, it is my fault. I have been trying to make you talk about her, because I honestly wanted your opinion. I have studied the young lady in question a good deal; but I am one who believes that you should go to a woman to get a fair opinion of a woman."

"What!" cried Wyn, with animation. "Take care! You could not mean that, surely! It is too good to be true. Have I at last discovered a man who believes that woman can occasionally be impartial—who is not convinced that the female mind is swayed exclusively by the two passions of love and jealousy? This is really refreshing! Yes, I do believe you are right. A woman should be judged by the vote of her own sex. Of course, one particular woman's opinion of her may very likely be biassed. I don't pretend to say that women are not sometimes spiteful—I have known those who were. But to say that some fair young girl will be deliberately tabooed by all the girls she knows, simply because she happens to be attractive to gentlemen, is a fiction which is the monopoly of the male novelist. I have never known a woman really unpopular among women without very good cause for it."

"Exactly. Well, this being so, I shall attach great weight to your opinion of Miss Elsa."

"In that case, I had far better not give it; besides, I am only one woman, and the fact that my brother is evidently much attracted by the subject of our conversation is very likely to make my judgment one-sided. You know, I think nobody good enough for Osmond."

"Most natural; yet I would go bail for the candor of your judgment."

"Would you? I am not sure whether I would. I have not much to go upon," she said, musingly.

"You have allowed me to gather this much—that you are not particularly favorably impressed," he said, cunningly. "You had better give me your reasons."

She made a protesting gesture.

"It is not fair—I have said nothing," she answered. "I tell you I can form no opinion worth having. I only know two points concerning Elsa— she is very beautiful and very unsophisticated. I don't know that, in my eyes, to be unsophisticated is to be charming; I know it is so in the opinion of many. I should say that where the instincts of a nature are noble, it *is* very delightful to see those impulses allowed free and natural scope—no artificial restraint—no repression; but I think," she continued, slowly, "that some natures are better for training—some impulses decidedly improved by being controlled."

"I should think Miss Brabourne had been controlled enough, in all conscience."

"No," said Wyn, "she has only not been allowed to develop. The Misses Willoughby have never taught her to restrain one single impulse, because they have failed to recognise the fact that she has impulses to restrain. They do not know her any better than I do—perhaps not so well."

"Very likely," said Claud; "I see what you mean. You think it would be unjust to her to pronounce on a character which has had, as yet, no chance of self-discipline?"

"Exactly," agreed Wyn, with a sigh of relief at having partly evaded this narrow questioning. She did not like to say to him what had struck her several times in her intercourse with Elsa, namely, that there was a certain want in the girl's nature—a something lacking—an absence of traits which in a disposition originally fine would have been pretty sure to show themselves.

Wynifred was anxious for Osmond. She had never seen him seriously attracted before. Claud did not know, as she did, how significant a fact was his present exclusive devotion, and was naturally not aware of the consistency with which the young artist had always held himself aloof from the aimless flirtations which are so much the fashion of the day.

In the present state of society it needs a clever man to steer clear of the charge of flirting, but Osmond Allonby had done it, whilst eminently sociable, and avowedly fond of women's society, he had managed that his name should never be coupled on the tongues of the thoughtless with that of any girl he knew.

But now— —! Every rule and regulation which had hitherto governed his life seemed swept away. Old limits, old boundaries were no more. The power of marshalling his emotions and finding them ready to obey when he cried "Halt!"—a power he possessed in common with his sister Wynifred—was a thing of the past. Even Wyn's loving eyes, following him so sympathetically, could not guess the completeness of his surrender. All the deep, carefully-guarded treasure of his love was ready to be poured out at the feet of the golden-haired, white-robed Elsa at his side. He would not own to himself that his attachment was likely to prove a hopeless one. With the swiftness of youth in love, his thoughts had ranged over the future. He was making a career—Wyn was following his example, in her own line. Jacqueline and Hilda were too pretty to remain long unmarried.

Concerning Elsa's heiress-ship he was not half so well-informed as Claud Cranmer. But indeed the question of ways and means only floated lightly on the top of the deep waves of feeling that filled his soul. His Elaine seemed to him a creature from another sphere—isolated, innocent, and wilful as the Maid of Astolat herself. Probably few young men in the modern Babylon could have brought her such an unspent, single-hearted, ideal devotion; his love was hardly that of the nineteenth century.

The only difficulty he experienced, in walking at her side, was to check himself, to so curb his passion as to be able to talk lightly to her; and, even through his most ordinary remarks, there ran a vibration, a thrill of feeling, "the echo in him broke upon the words that he was speaking," and perhaps communicated itself to the mood of the uncomprehending girl.

"Now," he said, as after several minutes' silence they seated themselves at last, sheltered from sun and breeze, under the shadow of a chalk cliff. "Now at last I claim your promise."

"My promise?"

"Yes, you know what I asked you when we met to-day. You were looking like Huldy in the American poem,

'All kind o' smily round the lips,
An' teary round the lashes.'

You said that when we were alone you'd tell me why. What was it?"

A flash of sudden, angry resentment crossed the girl's fair face, and tears again welled up to the edges of her limpid eyes. Osmond thought he had never seen anything so lovely as her expression and attitude. If one could but paint the quick, panting heave of a white throat, the quiver of a sad, impetuous mouth.

"You can guess—it was the usual thing—Godfrey," she said, struggling to command her voice, but in vain. She could say no more, but turned her face away from him, swallowing tears.

Osmond felt a sudden movement of helpless indignation, which almost carried him away. He mentally applied the brake before he could answer rationally.

"It is abominable—unheard of!" was the calmest expression he could think of. "Something must be done—quickly too! I should like to wring the insolent little beggar's neck for him! What did he do, to-day?"

For answer she pushed up her sleeve, showing him two livid bruises on a dazzlingly white arm—an arm with a dimpled round elbow.

"I caught him smoking in the stable, which is forbidden because of setting fire to the straw," she faltered, "and I told him he ought not to do it, so he did what he calls the 'screw.' You don't know how it hurts!"

The Tree Of Knowledge A Novel | 159

Osmond's wrath surmounted even his love.

"But why don't you box his ears—why don't you give him a lesson—cowardly little beggar!" he cried. "You are bigger than he, Miss Brabourne, you ought to be more than a match for him!"

A burst of tears came.

"I don't even know how to hit," she sobbed, childishly. "I don't know anything that other people know; and, if I tell of him, he pays me out so dreadfully! He puts frogs in my bed, and takes away my candle, and the other night he dressed up in a sheet, and made phosphorous eyes, and nearly frightened me out of my senses, and I don't dare tell because—because he would do something even worse if I did! Oh, you don't know what he is. He catches birds and mice, and cuts them up alive—he says he is going to be a doctor, and he is practising vivisection; and he makes me look while he is doing it—if I don't he has ways of punishing me. He made me smoke a cigar, and I was so terribly sick, and he made me steal the sideboard keys, and get whiskey for him, and said if I did not he would tell aunts something that would make them forbid me to come to the picnic. He was tipsy last night," she shuddered, "really tipsy. He made me help him up to his room, and tell aunts he was not well, and could not come down to supper. Oh!" she burst out, "you don't know what my life is! He makes me miserable! I hate him! But I daren't tell, you don't know what he would do if I told!" Her face crimsoned with remembrance of insult. "I *can't* tell you the worst things, I can't!" she cried, "but he is dreadful. Every little thing I say or do, he remembers, and seems to see how he can make me suffer for it. I have no peace, day or night; and he is so good when aunts are there. They don't know how wicked he is."

"But surely," urged Osmond, gently, "if you were to tell the Misses Willoughby, they would send him home, and then you would be free from him?"

She dashed away the tears from her eyes, and shook her head with a smile full of bitterness.

"They wouldn't believe me," she said, "they never have believed me; that is, Aunt Charlotte wouldn't, and she is the one who rules. They would call Godfrey and ask if it was true, and he—he thinks nothing of telling a lie. Oh! he is a sneak and a coward! If you knew how he has curried favor since he has been here! Aunt Charlotte likes him—she will give him things she would never give me! She would never believe my word against his."

"Miss Brabourne—Elsa," faltered the young man tenderly, "Don't sob so—you break my heart—you—you make me—forget myself!"

He leaped to his feet. Poor fellow, his self-command was rapidly failing. It had needed but this, the sight of helpless distress in his ladylove, to finish his subjugation. He was raging with love, and a burning impotent desire to thrash Master Godfrey Brabourne within an inch of his life. Yet, as Henry Fowler had said, how could one touch such a scrap of a child, such a delicate, puny boy?

He knew well enough the power such a young scoundrel would have to render miserable the life of a timid girl, unused to brothers. Elsa had never learned to hold her own, never learned to be handy or helpful. She was most probably what boys call a muff, a fit butt for the coarse ridicule and coarser bullying of the ill-brought-up Godfrey. That helplessness which in the eyes of her lover was her culminating charm was exactly what to the boy was an irresistible incentive to cruelty.

Osmond turned his eyes on the drooping figure of the girl. She was leaning forward, her elbow on her knee. Her hollowed hand made a niche for her chin to rest in, and her profile was turned towards him as she gazed sadly seawards. On her cheek lay one big tear, and the long, thick lashes were wet.

He came again to her side, and knelt there. Flushing at his own boldness, he took her hand. It trembled in his own, but lay passive.

"Elsa," he said, tenderly, soothingly, "it will not be for long, you must not let this wretched child's mischief prey upon you so. I know how badly you feel it, but consider—he will be gone in a few days."

"Oh, no, no, that is just what is so hateful! He will be here for weeks! Mr. Orton has been taken ill at Homburg, and aunts have promised to keep him till they come back. Oh,"—she snatched away her hand and clasped it with the other, as if hardly conscious of what she did,—"oh, I can bear it now, when you are all here; but next week—next week—when there will be no Wynifred, no Hilda, no Jacqueline ... no you!... what shall I do then?"

"Elaine!"

"When I think of it, I could kill him!" cried the girl, her face reddening with the remembrance of insults which she could not repeat to Osmond. "You don't know what a wicked mind he has—he is like an evil spirit, sent to lure me on to do something dreadful! When he speaks so to me, I feel as if I must silence him—as if I could strike him with all my force. Suppose—suppose one day I could not restrain myself...."

She was as white as a sheet, as she suddenly paused.

"What was that noise?" she panted.

The Tree Of Knowledge A Novel | 161

"What noise?" he asked.

"I thought I heard Godfrey's whistle—there is a noise he makes sometimes".... Her face seemed paralysed with fear and dislike—involuntarily, she drew nearer to Osmond. "If he should have heard me!" she breathed, with her mouth close to his ear.

"How could he hurt you when I am with you?" cried he, passionately. "My darling, my own, you are quite safe with me!"

His arms were round her before he had realised what he was doing. It seemed his divine right to shield her—his vocation, his purpose in life to come between her and any danger, real or fancied.

A yell, quite unlike anything human—a rush of loose pebbles and white dust, a crash on the path close to the unwary couple, and a long discordant peal of laughter.

"Cotched 'em! Cotched 'em! Cotched 'em by all that's lovely! Done 'em brown, bowled 'em out clean! Oh, my dears, if you only did know what jolly asses you both look, spooning away there like one o'clock! I'm hanged if I ever saw anything like it. I wouldn't have missed it—no, not for—come, I say, let go of a feller, Mr. Allonby. Lovers are fair game, don't yer know!"

If ever any man felt enraged it was Osmond at that moment; the more, because he saw how undignified it was to be in a rage at all. Revulsion of feeling is always unpleasant, and nothing could be more complete than the revulsion from the purest of sentiment to the most contemptible of practical jokes.

Elsa cried out in a mingled anger and terror—the ludicrous side of a situation never struck her by any chance. Osmond, as he sprang up and collared the impudent young miscreant, was divided between a desire to storm and a desire to roar with laughter. The former gained the ascendency as he looked back at Elsa's white face.

"You impertinent young scamp," he said, between his teeth, "I've a great mind to give you such a punishment as you never had in your life, to make you remember this day!"

"You daren't," said Godfrey, coolly, "you daren't flog me, I'm delicate. You'll have to settle accounts with my uncle if you bring on the bleeding from my lungs. My tutor ain't allowed to touch me."

"You sickening little coward—you sneak," said Osmond, with scathing contempt. "A spy—that's what you are. I hope you are proud of yourself. Look how you have startled your sister."

"Pretty little dear—a great lump, twice my size," sneered Godfrey, grinning. "Look at her, blubbing again! She does nothing but blub. Stop that, Elaine, will you?"

"All right, young man," said Osmond, "I can't flog you, but I think I can take it out of you another way just as well. Don't flatter yourself you are going to get off so easily. I'll teach you a lesson of manners, and I'll make it my business that the Miss Willoughbys and Mr. Fowler know how you have behaved—not to-day only. You little cur, how dare you?"

"Who's old Fowler? He can't touch me. Keep your hair on. What are you going to do with me?"

"I'm going to keep you out of mischief for a bit," said Osmond, as he skilfully laid the boy down on the grass with one dexterous motion of his foot, and, producing two thick straps from his pocket, he proceeded to strap first his feet and then his hands together.

"Pooh! What do I care? I've had my fun, and I'm ready to pay for it. Oh, my stars, wasn't it rich to hear Elsa coming the injured innocent and laying it on thick for her beloved's benefit? I heard every word you both said!" cried Godfrey, convulsed with laughter.

"If you say another word, I'll gag you."

"Gag away! I've heard all I want to, and said all I want to, too. Good old Allonby, so you believe all the humbug she's been telling you? You old silly, don't you know girls always say that sort of thing to draw the men on? I told her she ought to bring you to the point to-day.... I say ... I can't breathe!"

He was skilfully and rapidly gagged by Osmond, who afterwards picked up his prisoner and carried him to a high steep shelf of rock, where he laid him down.

"You can cool your heels up there till I come and take you down," he said between his teeth. "If you roll over, you'll roll down, and most likely break your spine, so I advise you to be quiet, and think of your sins."

CHAPTER XXII

We walked beside the sea
After a day which perished, silently,
Of its own glory.
Nor moon nor stars were out:
They did not dare to tread so soon about,
Though trembling in the footsteps of the sun;
The light was neither night's nor day's, but one
Which, lifelike, had a beauty in its doubt.
E. B. Browning.

On turning his flushed and excited face again towards the seat where he had left Elsa, he found that she was gone. It did not surprise him, but made him resolve instantly to follow and console her. He wandered about for some time amongst the sunny windings of the cliffs before he found the object of his search.

She was crouched down on the grass, her face hidden, her whole frame shaken with sobs. It brought the tears to his own eyes to witness such distress, yet his feeling towards Godfrey was not all anathema. Only exceptional circumstances could have enabled him to assume the post of comforter, and those circumstances had been brought about by the impudent boy.

"Miss Brabourne," he said, gently, looking down at her.

She started, and checked her grief.

"Forgive my intruding," he went on, seating himself on a ledge of cliff just above her, "but I have said too much already not to say more. You must feel with me, our interview can't be broken off at this point; you must hear me out now, and, if I have shattered all my hopes by my reckless haste, why, I shall only have myself to thank for it."

She but half heard, and hardly understood him; her whole mind was at work on one point.

"What must you think of me?" she cried. "Did you believe it?—what he said of me?"

"Believe it! Believe what?" cried Osmond. "Don't allude to it, please, please don't. It makes me lose my temper and feel inclined to rave. I heard little that was said; what I did hear could inspire me only with one sensation—anger at his impudence, sympathy for you."

"Then you don't—believe—you don't think that I was—trying to make you flirt with me?"

It was out at last, and, having managed to pronounce the words, she buried her face in her hands.

"Oh, Elsa!" was all that her lover could say; but the tone of it made her lift her humbled head and seek his eyes. Whatever his look, she could not meet it; her own sank again, she blushed pitifully, quivered, hesitated, finally let him take her hand.

Consciousness was fully awake now. The girl, whose fingers thrilled in his own, was a different being from the Elaine who had watched him sketching in the lane. She knew that she was a woman, knew also that she was beloved. Years of education would never have taught her so completely as she was now taught by her lover's eyes.

He began to speak. She listened, in a trance of delight. He begged her to forgive his weakness in failing to control his feelings for her. Poor fellow, he was lowly enough to satisfy an empress. He knew that he had no right to speak of love to this girl who had seen no men, had no experience of life. He felt that he had taken an unfair advantage of her ignorance, and the thought tortured his pride. He would not ask her if she returned his love, still less demand of her any promise; he should go to Edge Willoughby that very night, he said, and apologise to her aunts for his unguarded behavior. He loved her dearly, devotedly. In a year's time he would come and tell her so again. But not yet. He was poor, and he could not brook that anyone should think he wanted a rich wife, though, as has been said, his knowledge of Elaine's prospects was by no means so minute as Claud Cranmer's. All his passion, all his regret, were faltered forth; and the result was, to his utter astonishment, a burst of indignation from his lady-love.

He did not believe her—could not trust her! Oh, she had thought that he, at least, understood her, but she was wrong, of course! He, like everyone else, thought her a foolish child, incapable of judging, or knowing her own mind.

"Do you think that I have no feeling?" she asked, pitifully. "Do you think that I can bear to have you leave me next week, and go back to London and never be able to so much as hear from you, to know what you are doing, or if you still think of me? How can you love such a creature as you think me—foolish, ignorant, inconstant——"

Could it be Elsa who spoke? Elsa, whose lovely face glowed with expression and feeling? Her development had indeed been rapid. Lost in wonder and admiration, he could not answer her, but remained mutely looking at her, till, with a little cry of angry shame, she bounded up and ran away from him.

Leaping to his feet, he followed and captured her. Hardly knowing what he did, he took her in his arms. Her lovely cheek rested against his dark blue flannel coat, she was content to have it so, for the moment she believed that she loved him.

The great red sun had rolled into the sea, when the two came up to the camping place again. Tea was half over, and they were greeted with a derisive chorus. Wyn, however, looked apprehensively at her brother's illuminated expression and gleaming eye, and Claud, noting the same danger-signals, looked at her, and their eyes met.

"Where is Godfrey?" asked Mr. Fowler.

"Jove, I forgot! I must go and fetch him," cried Osmond, laughing, as he ran off.

"Mr. Allonby put him in punishment for behaving so badly," explained Elsa, with burning blushes.

"What had he done?" asked Dr. Forbes, with interest.

"He was very rude to Mr. Allonby," she faltered.

"I'm grateful indeed to Allonby for keeping him in order," laughed her godfather.

Godfrey appeared in a very cowed state, silent and sulky. His durance had been longer and more disagreeable than he had bargained for. He was quite determined to be ill if he could, and so wreak vengeance on his gaoler; and his evil expression boded ill to poor Elsa, as he passed her with a muttered, "You only wait, my lady, that's all!"

The twilight fell so rapidly that tea was obliged to be quickly cleared away. It was not so hilarious a meal as dinner had been, for Osmond and Elsa were quite silent, and Wyn too absorbed in thinking of them to be lively.

They all went down to the shore to wash up the tea-things, and lingered there a little, watching the tender violets and crimsons of the west, and listening to the soft murmur of the lucid little wavelets which hardly broke upon the sand.

Wyn leaned her chin upon her hand—her favorite attitude—and watched. Jacqueline and young Haldane were busily washing and wiping the same plate, an arrangement which seemed to provoke much lively discussion. Claud was drying the knives and forks which Hilda handed to him. Osmond and Elsa stood apart, doing nothing but look at one another. Wyn hated herself for the choking feeling of sadness which possessed her. Osmond had been so much to her; now, how would it be? Such jealousy was miserable, contemptible, she knew; but the pain of it would not be stilled at once.

Henry Fowler appeared, took the knives and forks, and carried them off, followed by Hilda. Claud turned, and looked at Wyn.

"What a night," he said.

"Yes."

"Is that all the answer I am to expect?"

"What more can I say? Do you want me to contradict you?"

He was silent, his eyes fixed on the pure reach of sky.

"I wonder why I always feel sad just after sunset?" he remarked, after a pause.

"Do you?" said Wyn, quickly.

"Yes; do you?"

"To-night I do."

"I thought so."

"Our holidays are nearly over," said the girl, with a sigh. "I must go back to work again. I must utilize my material," she added, a little bitterly. "All the splendor of these sunsets must go into the pages of a novel, if I can reproduce it."

"It would go better into a poem," said Claud, tossing a pebble into the water.

"That is one fault I may venture to say I am without," remarked Wynifred. "I never write verses."

"I do; it amounts to a positive vice with me," returned he, coolly.

"I am sure I beg your pardon," she said, confused.

"You need not. It is only a vent. Everyone must have a vent of some sort, otherwise the contents of their mind turn sour. Yours is fiction; you don't need the puny consolation of verse, which is my only outlet."

"You are very sarcastic."

"So were you."

"If you always take your tone from me— —" she began, and stopped.

"I should have my tongue under better control, you were about to add," he suggested.

"Nothing of the sort. I forget what I meant. I am not in a mood for rational conversation this evening."

"Nor I. Let us talk nonsense."

"No, thank you. I can't do that well enough to be interesting. Go and talk to Mr. Haldane; he studies nonsense as a fine art."

"I accept my dismissal; thank you for giving it so unequivocally," he answered, huffily, and, turning on his heel, marched away, and spoke to her no more that evening.

Later, when the darkness had fallen, and the company were dispersed to their various homes, Henry Fowler, coming from the stable through the garden, was arrested by the scent of his guest's cigar, and joined him on the rustic seat under the trees.

It was a perfect summer night, moonless, but the whole purple vault of heaven powdered with stars.

The garden of Lower House was, of course, like all the land in Edge Valley, inclined at an angle of considerably more than forty-five degrees, which fact added greatly to its picturesqueness. Right through it flowed a brook which dashed over rough stones in a miniature cascade, and added its low murmuring rush to the influence of the hour.

Claud sat idly and at ease, smoking a final cigar. It was almost midnight, but on such a night it seemed impossible to go to bed.

"What are you thinking of?" asked Henry, as he sat down and struck a light.

The match flickered over the young man's moody face; such an expression was unusual with the cheerful brother of Lady Mabel. He merely shrugged his shoulders in answer to the question.

"The Miss Allonbys are certainly charming girls," said Mr. Fowler, after a pause. "The eldest, indeed, is most exceptional."

"You are right there," said Claud, suddenly, as though the remark unloosed his tongue. "I don't profess to understand such a nature, I must say."

His host looked inquiringly at him, surprised at the irritation of his tones.

"If I were a different fellow, I declare to you I'd make her fall in love with me," said the young man, vindictively, "if only for the pleasure of seeing her become human."

"And why don't you try it, being as you are?" asked Mr. Fowler, composedly, after a brief interval of astonishment. "Why this uncalled for modesty? Is it on account of your one defect, or because you have only one?"

Claud laughed, and flushed a little under cover of the friendly gloom.

"Miss Allonby is too near perfection to care for it in others," he said, with a suspicion of a sneer.

"Indeed? Do you think so? She seems full of faults to me."

His companion turned his head sharply towards him.

"Perhaps I hardly meant faults. I should say—amiable weakness. I only meant to express that to me she seems 'a being not too bright and good for human nature's daily food.' I am such a recluse, Mr. Cranmer, I must of necessity study my Wordsworth."

Claud was silent for a long time, and only the harmonious rushing of the brook broke the hush.

"Is that the idea she gives you?" he asked, at length. "Shall I tell you what I think of her? That she is incapable of passion, and so unfit for her century."

"Incapable of passion," said the elder man, slowly, "and so safe from the knowledge of infinite pain. For her sake I almost wish it were so. Have you read her books?"

"Yes."

"Don't you think the passion in them rings true?"

"True enough; she has wasted it there. There is her real world. I—we—" he corrected himself very hastily—"are only shadows."

"I think that remark of yours is truer than you know," said Mr. Fowler. "I am sure that Miss Allonby lives in a dream——"

"But you think she could be awakened?"

"If you could fuse her ideal with the real. I read a poem in the volume of Browning you lent me the other day. It told of a man who set himself to imagine the form of the woman he loved standing before him in the room. He summoned to his mind's eyes every detail of her personal appearance,— her dress, her expression,—till the power of his will brought the real woman to stand where the fancied shape had been. It is not altogether a pleasant poem, but it reminded me of her, in a way. She is standing, I conjecture, with her eyes and her heart fixed on an ideal. If a real man could take its place, he would know what the character of Wynifred Allonby really is. No other mortal ever will."

Claud smoked on for a minute or two in silence; then, taking his cigar from his mouth, he broke off the ash carefully against the sole of his boot.

"Your estimate of her is practically worthless," he remarked, "because you are supposing her to be consistent, which you know is an impossibility. No woman is consistent; if they were, not one in a hundred would ever marry at all. Who do you suppose ever married her ideal?"

"You are right, then," said his companion, thoughtfully. "The adaptability of woman is marvellous. Mercifully for us. But I have a fancy that the lady in question is an exception to most rules. One is so apt to argue from something taken for granted, and therefore most likely incorrect. We start here from the assumption that a girl's ideal is an ideal of perfection—a thing that never could be realized; and I should imagine that to be true in the majority of instances. But it's my idea that Miss Allonby has too much insight to build herself such a sand-castle. The hero of her novel is just a moderately intelligent man of the present day, with his faults fearlessly catalogued—he is no sentimental abstraction. And yet I am sure that he is not a man she has met, but a man she hopes to meet. That is to say, I am sure she had not met him when she wrote the book, but I see no reason why she should not come across him some day."

Claud made a restless movement. He tossed away the end of the cigar, threw himself back on the garden-seat, and locked his hands behind his head.

"The modern girl," he observed, "is complicated."

"Perhaps that is what makes her so interesting," said Mr. Fowler.

"Is she interesting—to you?"

"She is most interesting—to me," was the ready rejoinder.

There was no answer. In the dim starlight the elder man studied the face of the younger. He thought Claud Cranmer was better-looking than he had previously considered him. There was something sweet in the expression of his mouth, something lovable in the questioning gaze of his blue-grey eyes.

The silence was broken by the fretful barking of Spot, Claud's fox-terrier. He roused himself from his reverie.

"What's up with that little beggar now, I wonder?" he said, as he rose, half-absently, and sauntered over the bridge.

"Spot! Spot! Come here! Stop that row, can't you?"

He vanished gradually among the shadows, and Henry Fowler was left alone.

"Is he in love with her, or is he not?" he dreamily asked himself. "Talk of the complications of the modern girl—there's no getting to the bottom of the modern young man. I don't believe he knows himself."

He caught his breath with something like a sigh of regret for an irreclaimable past.

"I almost wish I were young again, with a heart and a future to lay at her feet!"

It was the nearest he had ever come to a treason against the memory of Alice Willoughby. Love in his early days had seemed such a different thing—meaning just the protecting, reverential fondness of what was in every sense strong for what was in every sense weak. Now it went so far deeper—it included so many emotions, some of them almost conflicting. Physically—in strength, size, and experience—Wynifred was his inferior. Intellectually, though she had read more books than he, he felt that they were equals. But there was a fine inner fibre—a something to which he could not give a name—an insight, a delicacy of hers which soared far above him. Something which was more than sex, which no intimacy could remove or weaken—a power of spirit, a loftiness which was new in his experience of women.

The men of his day had taken it for granted that woman, however charming, was *small*; they had smiled indulgently at pretty airs and graces, at miniature spites. They had thought it only natural that these captivating creatures should pout and fret if disappointed of a new gown, should shriek at a spider, go into hysterics if thwarted, and deny the beauty of their good-looking female friends. Such a being as this naturally called forth a different species of homage from that demanded by a Wynifred Allonby, to whom everything mean, or cramped, or trivial was as foreign as it was to Henry Fowler himself. It was not that she resisted the impulse to be small; it was not in her nature; she could no more be spiteful than a horse could scratch; she had been framed otherwise.

CHAPTER XXIII

And I said—Is this the sky, all grey and silver-suited?
And I said—Is this the sea, that lies so pale and wan?
I have dreamed, as I remember—give me time, I was
reputed
Once to have a steady courage—now, I fear, 'tis gone!
Requiescat in Pace.

Claud sat somewhat despondently at Mr. Fowler's side in the tall dog-cart as they spun along the lanes from Stanton back to Lower House. Their errand had been to convey some of the Allonbys' luggage to the station, and see the family off to London.

They were gone; and the two gentlemen who had just seen the last of them were both silent, for different reasons: Claud, because he was resenting the indifference of Wynifred's manner, and Henry, because he was secretly angry with Claud. He did not understand so much beating about the bush. Naturally Mr. Cranmer could not afford to marry an entirely portionless wife; very well, then he ought to have packed his portmanteau and taken his departure long ago, instead of following Miss Allonby hither and thither, engaging her in conversation whenever he could secure her attention, and generally behaving as though seriously attracted—risking the girl's happiness, Mr. Fowler called it. To be sure the conversations seemed usually to end in a wrangle; there was nothing tender in them. Wynifred's serenity of aspect was unruffled when Claud approached, and she never appeared to regret him when he departed in dudgeon. A secret wonder as to whether she could have refused him suggested itself, but was rejected as unlikely. Still the master of Lower House was not accustomed to see young people on such odd terms together; and it vexed him.

The last fortnight of the young artist's stay at Edge had been full of excitement; for Osmond had made full confession to the Misses Willoughby of his love and his imprudent declaration. The good ladies passed through more violent phases of feeling than had been theirs for years. Astonishment, fright, excitement, a vague triumph in the subjugation of the tall, handsome young man had struggled for the mastery in their hearts. Finally they had called in Mr. Fowler to arbitrate.

He came to the conclusion which Osmond felt certain that he would, namely: that Elsa could not yet know her own mind. She must be left for a year, at least, to gain some knowledge of society; he would not hear of her binding herself by any promise.

As to young Allonby, he had personally no objection in the world to him. He both liked and respected him, though unable to help feeling sorry that he had so prematurely disclosed his love to the girl. He would gladly see him engaged to her as soon as ever he could show that it was in his power to maintain her in the position to which she was born. But, on descending to practical details, it seemed to poor Osmond that it might be years before he could claim to be the possessor even of a clear five hundred a-year, unencumbered by sisters. Wynifred sympathized with him so deeply as to make her preoccupied during all her last days at Edge. Claud Cranmer's vagaries could not be so important as her darling brother's happiness. Though the engagement was not allowed, yet the attitude of the Misses Willoughby was anything but hostile. Osmond was a favorite with all, and Miss Ellen was privately determined that if, when Elsa was twenty-one, want of money should be the only barrier to their happiness, she should consent to the marriage, and make them a yearly allowance, with the understanding that all came to them at the death of the sisters. But first it was only just that Osmond should be for a time on probation, that they might see of what stuff he was made; and communication could be kept up by means of a correspondence between Elsa and Jacqueline, who had struck up something of a friendship, as girls will.

It was now finally settled that Elsa should go to London in November, spend a month or two with Lady Mabel, and then a short time with the Ortons. In London she would naturally meet the Allonbys, and this delightful consideration went far to dry the passionate tears she shed on the departure of her lover.

During the fortnight which had elapsed since the picnic, there had been an ominous calm on the part of Godfrey. His two or three hours' detention on the cliffs had given him a wholesome awe of Osmond, and each day afterwards he had been so meek that everyone was beginning to hope that he was not so black as he was painted.

Osmond, to show he bore no malice, had taken pains to have the boy included in all their expeditions; so that he remarked one day to Elsa:

"Allonby's not half a bad fellow, and I'm hanged if I ever lift a finger to help him to marry a wretched little sneak like you. If you'd been anything like decently behaved to me, I'd have settled some of my fortune on you, but now I'd sooner give him ten thousand down to let you alone. I should like him to know what sort you are; but the jolliest fellows are fools when they're in love."

"What money have you got that I haven't, I should like to know?" Elsa had retorted, unwisely. "I am the eldest—I ought to have the most."

"Jupiter! D'you mean to say the old girls have never told you that our papa left me all the cash? Quite the right thing, too. What's a girl to do with money? Only brings a set of crawling fortune-hunters round her. But, if you'd been anything like, I'd have settled something handsome on you when I come of age; as it is, you won't get one penny out of me."

"I don't believe a word you say!"

"All right; but you'd better be careful how you cheek me. I'm going to pay you out for all the lies you told Allonby about me. I haven't forgotten. You just keep your weather-eye open, my lady. You'll get something you won't fancy, I can tell you."

From this menace, Elsa went straight to her Aunt Ellen, to ask if it was true that all her father's fortune was left to Godfrey. In great concern at her having been told, Miss Ellen was obliged to own that it was so, though she still concealed the fact that flagrant injustice had been done, the money so bequeathed having all come to Colonel Brabourne through his first wife. This part of the story, however, was gleefully supplied by Godfrey, who had been lying in ambush outside the door to jeer at her as she came out.

"Well, ain't it true? Eh? I don't tell so many crackers as you, you see. And the joke of it is that all the money came from your mother, and now my mother's son has got it. My! weren't the old aunts in a state, too? You should hear my Uncle Fred on the subject! But if your mother was like these old cats I'm sure my papa must have been jolly glad to be quit of her!"

Elsa darted at him with a cry of rage, but he saved himself by flight. If anything had been wanting to fill the cup of her hatred to the brim, here it was. Had it not been for this child, she would have been rich—very rich. She would have been able to marry Osmond, to have a large fine house in London, to have her gowns cut like Lady Mabel's, and to possess necklaces, lace, jewels, and all things beautiful in profusion.

He had stolen her fortune, insulted her mother, humiliated herself. The violence of her wrath and rancour were beyond all limits, and she had never been taught self control. She loathed Godfrey; the very sight of him choked her; she could scarcely swallow food when he was at the table; yet she had no thought of appealing to her aunts. She had never received sympathy in all her life—why should she expect it now?

Such was the state of things at Edge Willoughby. The stagnant days of yore, when existence merely flowed quietly on from hour to hour, were no more. The spell was broken, the prince had kissed and wakened the sleeping beauty—human passion had rushed in upon the passionless calm, the tide of life from the outer world was flowing, flowing in the fresh breeze.

Partly on all these changes was Mr. Cranmer meditating as they drove back to Lower House in the dulness of an autumn afternoon.

The weather was threatening, the sea of that strange, thick, lurid tinge, which suggests a disturbance somewhere under the surface. The gulls skimmed low, with strange cries, over the sluggish heaving water. He thought of the hot bright day of the picnic, when the young gulls were not yet flown, and when their wild laughter echoed along the nest-riddled cliff walls.

A melancholy feeling was upon him, that the year was broken and gone, that there would be no more fair weather, no more violet and amber and crimson in the west.

To-morrow he was to leave the valley and go north to shoot over a friend's moor in Scotland. It was the best thing he could do, he told himself. There would be plenty of society, such different society from that he had known of late. There would be women of his set, women who spoke the social shibboleths he knew. There would be bleak moorland and dark grey rock, which would not seem so horribly at variance with cold weather as did this Valley of Avilion; for the whole party, taking their cue from Osmond, had been wont to speak of Edge always as Avilion.

At Ardnacruan he felt certain that he would regain his normal serenity, his cheerful from-day-to-day enjoyment of life; but this afternoon all influences seemed combined to make him experience that nameless feeling of misery and loss which the Germans call *katzenjammer*. The first verse of "James Lee's Wife" was saying itself over and over in his head, and he could not forget it. The mare's feet, in their even trot, kept time to it, the rolling of the wheels formed a sad, monotonous accompaniment.

> "Ah, love, but a day,
> And the world has changed!

The Tree Of Knowledge A Novel | 175

The sun's away
And the bird estranged.
The wind has dropped
And the sky's deranged,
Summer has stopped."

He wished he had had the sense to leave the place a day before instead of a day after the Allonbys. He knew that he had been due at Ardnacruan on Tuesday, and to-day was Thursday. Why on earth had he been so idiotic, so weak, so altogether contemptible?

Well, it was over now, and he meant for the future to possess his soul, untroubled by any distressing emotions; and, meanwhile, the thoughts of Wynifred, as she sat in the train, steaming towards London, were almost exactly a reproduction of his own.

Every turn of the lanes through which they drove brought back to Claud a memory of something which had taken place during the past summer. Here was a view they had admired together—here the quaint old gateway, half-way down the hill which Wynifred had sketched, the lane sloping so abruptly that the back legs of her camp-stool had to be artificially supported. In that field Hilda and Jac had laid out tea, and the whole party had enjoyed a warm discussion on the subject of family shibboleths. It began by Hilda's remarking that poor old Osmond could hardly be looked upon as a war-horse any longer; and, on being pressed to unravel this dark saying, she had explained with some confusion, that *war-horse* had been Jac's translation of *hors de combat* at a very early age, and that they had always used it since, which led on to various other specimens from nursery dictionaries, and much amusing nonsense. It was all past now.

In Claud's mind was a bitter thought which has countless times occurred to most of us, that the past is absolutely irreclaimable. We can never have our good minute again; it is gone. He knew the mood would pass, but that did not lessen the suffering while it lasted. Would he ever regret the days that were gone, with a regret that should be lifelong—was it possible that an hour might dawn in the far future when he should be prepared to give all to have that time again, that he might yield to the impulses of his heart, and speak as he felt?

"It will come, I suspect, at the end of life,
When you sit alone and review the past."

What nonsense!

As the dog-cart shot in through the gates of Lower House, he shook himself, and roused from his morbid reverie.

"How conversational we have both been!" he said, with a laugh.

"Yes," said Henry, gazing round with a sad expression in his kind eyes. "We miss those merry girls."

"They seem to enjoy life," observed Claud.

"Yes, indeed; and what makes it so fascinating is the assurance one always has of there being a solid foundation under all that fun. Many girls with twice their social advantages have not one half their fresh enjoyment."

"I believe you are right," was the answer, with a sigh which did not escape the other.

"We must not moralise," said the master of Lower House, briskly. "The day is dull, but don't let us follow its example. Would you care to walk to Edge Willoughby, take tea, and make your adieux?"

"Thanks—yes—I think I should. They have been most hospitable."

"Take a mackintosh," said Mr. Fowler, who had been surveying the threatening horizon; "we are going to have a bad night, I believe."

As he spoke, a ray of sunset light, darting through a rift in the watery sky, fell on a gleaming white sail some distance out at sea. It recalled to Claud his walk home to Poole with Wynifred.

"A yacht, a cutter," said his companion, with anxious interest. "She will never be able to make Lyme harbor to-night."

They watched the flashing thing for a minute or two in silence; then the rainy gleam faded from the sea, and the sail became again invisible.

They set off for Edge Willoughby, a short ten minutes walk.

Each now made an effort to converse, but with poor success. As they passed at the foot of a hill, crowned and flanked with arches, there was a rustling noise, and out into the path before them lightly sprang Elsa.

Claud had never seen her look more beautiful or more strange. Something in her expression arrested his eye.

Since her friendship with the Allonby girls, her whole wardrobe had become regenerated, and the beautiful proportions of her fine figure were no longer obscured by ill-fitting monstrosities. Her dress was dark blue, so was her hat, and she had knotted a soft crimson shawl over her chest. The buffetting wind had lent a magnificent glow to her skin, her eyes were shining—she had altogether an excited look, as though her feelings had been strongly worked upon.

"Why, where have you been, Elsa?" asked her godfather, as they greeted her.

"Out for a ramble," she answered, evasively.

"And what direction did your rambles take?"

"Oh, I went here and there. Are you coming to see my aunts?"

"We are; we will walk with you as far as the house. Where's Godfrey?"

She looked up at him—an odd, half defiant look.

"At home, I suppose," she said.

They had not gone far when suddenly, violently, down came the rain, and Claud hurriedly covering the girl in his mackintosh, they all took to their heels, and ran to the friendly shelter of the house.

CHAPTER XXIV

Walked up and down, and still walked up and down,
And I walked after, and one could not hear
A word the other said, for wind and sea
That raged and beat and thundered in the night.
Brothers and a Sermon.

The door was flung wide open by Jane Gollop, who had been anxiously on the alert.

"Miss Elaine! Well, to be sure! It's a good thing, that it is, as you happened to meet Mr. Fowler! Why—you ain't got wet, not hardly a drop, more you 'ave. But where's Master Godfrey?"

"I don't know," said Elsa, shortly.

"You don't know," said Jane, in accents of astonishment. "Why, where did you leave him?"

"Hasn't he come in?" asked the girl, in a hard kind of way; and, as she spoke, loosening her hat, she went to the mirror which hung against the wall of the hall, and passed her hand lightly through the soft masses of her hair, slightly dampened by the drenching shower. It was such a new trait in her—this attention to appearances—that Mr. Fowler gazed at her in sheer astonishment. Her beauty as she stood there was simply wonderful. Claud, eyeing her with all his might, was at a loss for a reason why he was not in love with her. Her style was not a common one among English girls—it was too sumptuous, too splendid. Though absolutely a blonde, the lashes which shaded her eyes were dark as night. Her complexion was a miracle of warmth and creamy fairness; and now that the final charm had come—that conscious life had permeated her being—the slowness of her movements, the comparative rarity of her speech, were charms of a most fascinating description. She was just beginning to understand what power was hers. It seemed as if the thought expressed itself in the faint smile, the regal grace with which the hand was lifted to the golden coronal of hair. She was absolutely exquisite, and yet Claud's only thought concerning her was an inward foreboding of the mischief she would work in London.

"Did you and Godfrey go out together?" asked Mr. Fowler at length.

The shadow fell over the lovely face again.

"Yes," she answered shortly.

"And where did you part company?" he went on, somewhat anxiously.

"I—I don't know, quite—I forget."

"I expect they've a bin quarrelling again, sir," observed Jane, with severity. "I do not know how it is as Miss Elaine can never get on with her brother at all. I'm sure I never see nothing to complain so about—a bit wild and rude, as most young gentlemen is, but——"

"Godfrey behaves exceedingly ill," said Mr. Fowler, shortly. "Did you have a quarrel, Elsa?"

"Yes, we did. I will never go out with him again, as long as I live," said Elsa, quietly.

"And you parted company?"

"Yes. I ran away from him. My aunts have no right to send him out with me." Her face worked, and tears sprang to her eyes. "He insults my mother," she said, with a sob.

Her god-father's brow grew darker.

"Never mind, Elsa," he said, in a voice of much feeling. "Let us hope he will grow better as he grows older; he is but a little chap."

"I wish I need never set eyes on him again, as long as I live," she said, in a low voice, audible to him alone.

"Hush, child! But now, the fact remains that the storm is awful, and that, as far as I can make out, the boy is out in it. What is to be done? Come and let us tell the aunts."

They entered the dining-room, where tea was already spread out in tempting guise. The Misses Willoughby turned to greet their guests, and Miss Charlotte in some anxiety demanded,

"Where is Godfrey?"

Her perturbation was great when the situation was explained.

"My dear Mr. Fowler! That young child—so delicate too! Out in this storm of rain! He will never find his way home, it will be dark directly! What shall I do? Penton must be sent after him. Elsa, tell me at once where you left him."

The crimson color mounted to Elsa's brow.

"I—I don't exactly remember—I wasn't taking much notice," she faltered.

"But which direction did you take? At least you can inform me of that. I am sure it is hard to believe that any girl of your age could be so foolish; speak!"

"We went along the Quarry Road," said Elsa, slowly, her eyes fixed on Claud, who stood looking at the ground.

"And where then?"

"We were going to Hooken for blackberries, but I thought it looked like rain, so I turned back."

"And Godfrey did not accompany you?"

A pause.

"No."

"He must have gone on to Brent," said Miss Charlotte, with conviction.

Brent was the tiny fishing-village which lay in a curve of the cliff between Edge Valley and Stanton.

"Does Godfrey know his way to Brent?" asked Mr. Fowler of Elsa.

"Oh, yes—he often goes there—to the 'Welcome Traveller,'" she answered.

"I think he is most probably there now," said he, turning to Miss Charlotte, "and, if so, you may be easy, they will not send him home in this tempest."

"But he is very wilful, he may insist on trying to come home, and, if so, he will be lost, he could never stand against the wind across the top of Hooken," said Miss Charlotte, full of apprehension.

Her attachment to Godfrey was a forcible illustration of the capriciousness of love. There had been every reason why she should dislike him, she had been fully prepared to do so. She had never seen one single trait in him to induce her to alter this preconceived opinion; he had openly derided her and set her authority at naught ever since their first meeting, yet she was fond of him.

Her looks testified the deepest concern. As the scream of the storm-wind dashed against the window of the warm, comfortable room, she shivered.

"Elsa," she cried, "how dared you leave that child out by himself? You are not to be trusted in the least! Where did you leave him—answer me— was it on the cliffs?"

"No!" cried Elsa, sharply, "it was not. He would not be likely to go by the cliffs, it is twice as long, you know it is. He went along the Quarry Road, I tell you. He is gone to Brent."

"Make yourself easy, Miss Charlotte," said Mr. Fowler, "he is not likely to try the cliff road home in weather like this. He will come by the quarries, if they let him come at all. How long had you parted from him when we met you, Elsa?"

"Oh, more than an hour, I should think."

"There, you see! He is as safely sheltered as we are by now!"

Miss Charlotte went restlessly to the window.

"I am anxious; he is so delicate, and so rash," she said. "I shall send Penton out along the Quarry Road."

"I will walk to Brent and back for you, Miss Willoughby," said Claud, in his quiet way.

"My dear fellow," said Henry Fowler, "you will scarcely keep your feet."

"Oh, nonsense about that. I'm all right—I have my mackintosh here. I enjoy a good sou'-wester."

"I'll come with you," said Henry at once.

Of course the ladies protested, but the gentlemen were firm; and, having first taken something to keep the cold out, they started forth into all the excitement of a furious gale on the Devonshire coast.

Once fairly out in it, Claud felt that he would not have missed it for worlds. There was such a stimulus in the seething motion of the atmosphere, such a weird fascination in the screaming of the blast and the hoarse roaring of the distant ocean.

"This is rather a wild-goose chase," yelled Henry in his companion's ear.

"Never mind; what's the odds so long as we can set their minds at rest," bawled Claud in return.

"Naught comes to no harm—the young imp is all right enough," howled Henry; and then, having strained their vocal chords to the utmost, any further attempt at conversation was given up as impossible.

They passed the narrow gorge where the mouth of the quarries lay and where the limekilns cast a weird gloom upon the night. The streaming rain hissed and fizzed as it fell upon the glowing surface, and, altogether, Claud thought, the whole scene was something like the last act of the *Walküre*—he almost felt as if he could hear the passionate shiver of Wagnerian violins in the rush of the mighty tempest.

In the low, sheltered road, they could just manage to keep their feet. Every now and then they paused, and shouted Godfrey's name at the utmost pitch of their voices; but they heard no response; and at last staggered down the little stony high street of Brent, without having met a single soul.

Usually the narrow street was musical with the murmur of the stream that flowed down its midst. To-night the storm-fiend overpowered all such gentle sounds. Claud, blindly stumbling in the dark, managed to go over his ankles in running water, but quickly regained his footing, and was right glad when the lights of the "Welcome, Traveller," streamed out upon the gloom.

They swung open the door. The bar was deserted, and Mr. Fowler's call only brought a female servant from the kitchen. Every soul in the town, she told them, was down at the quay—the word to haul up the boats had been cried through the village at dusk, and now the gale had come, and the fishing smacks had not come in.

Claud remembered how they had sat on the cliff black berrying only two days before, and watched the fishermen start, how the boats with their graceful red brown sails had danced and dipped on the sparkling blue water, alive with diamond reflections of the broad sun.

And now—the cruel, crawling foam, the black abyss of howling destruction, and the frantic wives assembled on the quay, watching "for those who will never come back to the town."

The inn servant was positive that Master Brabourne had not been in Brent that afternoon or evening, but Mr. Fowler, not quite relying on the accuracy of her statement, determined to make his way down to the shore.

The village was congested with excitement, as they approached they could dimly descry a dark crowd and tossing lanterns, and could hear the terrific thunder of the billows as they burst upon the beach. Then, suddenly, as they hurried on, up through the murky night rushed a rocket, a streak of vivid light, that struck on the heart like the cry of a human voice for help. Another—another—it was clear that some frantic feeling agitated the swaying crowd. As Claud dashed forward, he uttered a short exclamation.

"The yacht!"

"Good God, yes, it must be!" cried Henry Fowler in horror.

The Tree Of Knowledge A Novel | 183

In a moment they were down in the thick of it all, seizing the arm of one of the weatherbeaten fellows present, and asking what was amiss?

It was the yacht, as Claud had divined, and, when her exact situation had been explained to him, he felt his heart fail at the thought of her deadly peril, at the (to him) new sensation of standing within a few yards of a band of living human beings hovering over the wide spread jaws of death.

Brent lay in a break of the chalk cliffs which was more then half-a-mile in width. Through this tunnel the unbroken might of the wind rushed with terrific force, sweeping vehemently inland up the flat river-valley, and seeming to carry the whole sea in its train. The very violence of each wave, as it broke, made the bystanders stagger back a few paces; the tide was rolling in with a rapidity which seemed miraculous; already it had driven them back almost as far as the market-place, and it was not yet high water.

There was but one hope for the strange vessel. Change of tide had been known to bring change of wind; therein lay her solitary chance. If, with the ebb, the wind shifted its quarter and kept her off shore, the sea was not too heavy for her to live in; but if no change took place—if the waves continued to roll in for another hour as they were rolling now, with that screaming blast lashing them on as though the Eumenides were behind them, no change of tide could avail—no ebb could save the cutter from being driven on the sunken coast-rocks, and from being steadily beaten to pieces.

Was there a chance? Would it happen, this change of wind for which everyone was waiting in such an agony of expectation? In breathless horror the young man watched, parting, as he did so, with a few delusions he had previously cherished respecting the Devonshire climate. He had held a vague belief that storm and tempest were the portion only of "wild Tintagel on the Cornish coast," and that here, among the warm red cliffs, no roaring billows lifted their heads. He had now to hear how, once upon a time, the inhabitants of Brent built themselves a harbor and a pier, and how in one night the sea tore them up, dashed them to pieces, and bore the fragments far inland; and of how the Spanish wrecks were hurled so frequently on the coast that the fisher-folk intermarried with the refugees, which union resulted in the lovely, dark-haired, blue-eyed race whose beauty had so struck Lady Mabel Wynch-Frère.

Meanwhile, the lifeboat's crew stood with their boat all ready to launch, if they could see the smallest hope of making any way in such a sea. One old mariner watched the scarcely discernible movements of the yacht with a telescope. She was under jib and trysail only, the intention of the crew being evidently, if it were possible, to work her to windward, and so keep her off shore.

"Them aboard of her knows what to dû," said the old salt, with approbation. "They ain't going daown without showing a bit o' fight first."

"Why on earth don't they take in all their canvas?" cried the inexperienced Claud.

"If they did, they'd come straight in, stem on, and be aground in five minutes or less," was the response.

It was difficult, however, to see of what possible use any amount of knowledge of navigation could be to the fated craft. Slowly she was being borne to her doom by the remorseless gale. She pitched and rolled every moment nearer and still nearer to the coast—to the low sunken rocks which would grind her to powder, and where no lifeboat could reach her.

The women prayed aloud, with sobs and shrieks of sympathy. To Claud it was like a chapter in a novel, a scene in a play. He had never before seen real people—people in whose midst he stood—go mad with pity and terror. He had never before heard women cry out, as these did, straight to the Great Father in their need.

"Oh, Lord Christ, save 'em! Have mercy on 'em, poor souls!" screamed an old fishwife at his side, bent with age and infirmity.

It seemed as if he could hardly do better than silently echo her prayer:

"God save all poor souls lost in the dark!"

The moments of suspense lengthened. The knot of spectators held their breath. It would be high water directly, and the gale was still driving in the frantic sea, boiling and eddying. The night was cleft by the momentary gleam of another rocket sent up from the yacht. Though evidently terribly distressed, she did not seem disabled, and rose from crest to crest of the mountainous rollers with a marvellous lightness. It was easy to see that she surprised all the old salts who were watching her. As she rolled nearer, her proportions were dimly to be seen. In the gloom she seemed like a great quivering white bird, palpitating and throbbing as if alive and sentient.

"Eh, what a beauty, what a beauty! What a cruel shame if she is lost," gasped one of the men in tones of real anguish.

Then, suddenly, from further along the crowd came a shout faintly heard above the storm. Claud could not distinguish the words, but a vague sense of atmospheric change came over him. A manifest sensation ran through the assembly; and it seemed as if there were a momentary cessation of the blinding gusts of spray which had drenched him.

The Tree Of Knowledge A Novel | 185

A fresh stillness fell on the crowd, broken only by the sobbing whistling of the wind, which faltered, died down, burst forth again, and then seemed to go wailing off over the sea.

What had happened? Claud steadied his nerves and looked round bewildered. Surely that wave which broke was not so high as the last. It seemed at first as though the ocean had become a whirlpool, as though conflicting currents were sucking and eddying among the coast-rocks till the force of the tide was broken and divided. He turned to look for Henry Fowler, but could not see him. Moving further along the wet track left by one of the highest billows on the road, still clutching his cap with both hands, he found him presently superintending the lifeboat men, who were making a start at last.

There was a faint cheer as the boat was launched, and the receding wave carried her down, down, with that ghastly sucking noise which sounds as though the deep thirsted for its prey. Claud held his breath. He thought the next wave would break over her; but no! The crew bent to their oars, and up she rose, in full sight of the eager multitude, then again disappeared, only to be seen once more on the summit of a further crest. And now there was no question but that the wind was shifting. Silence fell on the watchers; silence which lasted long. Breathlessly they eyed the dim white yacht, which now did not seem to approach nearer the coast.

In the long interval, memory returned to Mr. Cranmer, memory of the purpose for which he had come there. Where was Godfrey? Nowhere to be seen. Making his way up to Mr. Fowler, he remarked:

"Don't you see anything of the boy?"

Henry gave a start of recollection, and cast his eyes vaguely over the crowd. A few minutes' search sufficed to show that Godfrey was not there. By the light of a friendly lantern he looked at his watch. It was past ten o'clock, and the thought of the anxiety at Edge Willoughby smote his conscience.

"We must leave this," he said, reluctantly, "and go back over the top of the cliff. It does not rain now, and thank God, the wind is falling."

"Will the yacht live?" asked Claud.

"Yes, please God, she'll do now," answered Henry. "But I daresay the crew will come ashore; they have all been very near death; perhaps they don't know, as well as I do, how near."

"Do you know the way over the cliff?"

"Know it? I think so. I could walk blindfold over most of the land near here," returned the other, drily.

"I do wonder what can have become of the child," said Claud, dubiously.

"Little cur!" said the ordinary gentle Henry, viciously. "I am not at all sorry if he has a fair good fright; it may read him a lesson."

Unwillingly they turned from the scene of interest, and began their scramble up the chalky slopes, rendered as slippery as ice by the heavy rains. Neither had dined that night, and both were feeling exhausted after the tension of the last few hours. They walked silently forward, each filled with vague forebodings respecting Godfrey.

The wind was still what, inland, would be called a gale, too high to make conversation possible. Overhead, rifts in the night-black clouds were beginning to appear; the waning moon must be by now above the horizon, for the jagged edges of the vapors were silver.

Claud was deeply meditating over his night's experience; it seemed years since he parted from Wynifred that afternoon. How much had happened since!

His foot struck against something as he walked. Being tired, he was walking carelessly, and, as the grass was intensely slippery, he came down on his hands and knees, making use of a forcible expression.

Thus brought into the near neighborhood of the object which caused his fall, he discovered that it was neither a stick nor a stone, but a book—a book lying out on the cliff, and reduced to a pulp by the torrents of rain which had soaked it.

"I say, Fowler, what's this?" he said eagerly, regaining his feet, the whole of the front of his person plastered with a whitish slime. "Here's a book! Does that help us—eh?"

Mr. Fowler turned quickly.

"Let me look," he said.

To look was easier than to see, by that light; but, by applying the dark lantern which, they carried, they saw it was a book they knew—a copy of the "Idylls of the King," which Osmond had given to Elsa, and which was hardly ever out of her hands.

"Strange!" ejaculated Henry, "very strange! She said they had not been on the cliffs—did she not say so, Cranmer?"

"Undoubtedly."

"She must have left it yesterday."

"We were all at Heriton Castle yesterday."

"Well—some time. Anyhow, it is her book—here is the name blotted and blurred, in the title-page. Let us search round here a little," he added, his voice betraying a sudden, nameless uneasiness.

The search was fruitless. They called till the rocks re-echoed, but in vain. Up and down they walked, in and out among the drenched brambles, slipping hither and thither in the chalky mire. At last they gave it up.

"We must go back and tell them we cannot find him," said Henry, wearily.

Standing side by side on the summit of the heights, they paused, and gazed, as if by mutual consent, seawards.

A pale silver glow came stealing as they looked across the heaving waters. The full dark clouds parted, and through the rift appeared a reach of clear dark sky. Wider and wider grew the star-powdered space, till at last the waning, misshapen-looking moon emerged, veiled only by a passing scud of vapor.

Below them the turbid billows caught the light and glittered; and, among them, riding proudly and in safety, was the beautiful yacht, like a white swan brooding over the tumultuous sea, which was still running high enough to make the noble little vessel roll and pitch considerably at her anchor.

CHAPTER XXV

I? what I answered? As I live
I never fancied such a thing
As answer possible to give!
What says the body, when they spring
Some monstrous torture engine's whole
Weight on it? No more says the soul.
Count Gismond.

In the breezy glitter of the sunshiny morning, a crowd stood on the curving beach of Edge Valley in a state of perplexity something resembling a pack of hounds at fault.

Day had dawned, full of light and motion. Billowy masses of white cumulus clouds sailed rapidly over the deep blue sky. The thick turbid sea rolled in, casting up mire and dirt from its depths. News had come to Brent that the fishing-smacks had found a refuge in Lyme harbour, and gay chatter filled the streets, as the happy wives and mothers ran to and fro, laughing as they thought on their terrors of the previous night.

Joy had come in the morning to all but the inhabitants of Edge Willoughby. Godfrey was still missing, and there was no news of him.

Mr. Fowler feared there could be but one solution of the mystery. The boy must have dared the cliff-path, and made a false step, or been swept off bodily by the gale. The sea, which had spared the yacht, most probably had drowned this heir to a great fortune.

The strangest part of the affair was the callousness shown by Elsa. It almost seemed as if she were simply relieved by the absence of her brother, and careless as to its cause. She had, however, come down to the shore with her godfather, and stood, like one half dazed, among the villagers, answering with painful hesitation the questions put to her as to where she had last seen Godfrey.

The yacht was brought up about half a mile off shore, and an examination of her by telescope had proved her to be a very smart and well-found vessel—a most perfect specimen of her kind. She was painted quite white, with a gold streak running round her, and she was flying a black distinguishing flag, upon which appeared a white swan with outspread wings, and an ensign which appeared to be foreign. The crew could be seen busy about the deck, repairing damages to paint and gear from the gale overnight. Just as Henry had dispatched two search-parties, one along the cliffs, the other along the shore, it was seen that a gig was leaving the yacht's side, and approaching with rapid strokes, pulled by two men, and a third steering. Mr. Fowler waited, knowing that most probably some injury had been sustained during the gale of the previous night, and that he might be able to make an offer of help.

As soon as the keel touched the shingle, the man in the stern-sheets stood up, and asked if there were an inn in the village. His English was fair, but his accent virulently German. Being answered in the affirmative, he next proceeded, somewhat to the astonishment of the crowd, to ask if there were a magistrate living near.

"I am a Justice of the Peace," said Mr. Fowler, amid a general sensation.

The man touched his cap. His master, Mr. Percivale, would be very glad of a few moments' conversation, if the gentleman's leisure served. He had a statement to make if the Justice could wait, he would be on shore in twenty minutes.

Henry, wondering greatly as to the statement he was to hear, inquired how much water the yacht drew, and, on being informed, explained that, if Mr. Percivale chose, he could steer her right in, within a few feet of the shore, owing to the peculiarly sudden shelve of the bay.

The man touched his cap again, and, having raised the popular feeling to fever heat by a scarcely intelligible hint that he believed there was murder in the case, pushed off, and rowed back to the yacht as fast as he had come.

The crowd on the beach had increased. Most of the villagers had seen the boat leave the yacht, and hurried down in great eagerness to know what was going forward.

Doubtful as to what course to pursue, Mr. Fowler stood irresolute in their midst, Elsa, Miss Emily Willoughby, Miss Charlotte Willoughby, and Claud Cranmer at his side.

Suddenly a sound of wheels was heard grinding sharply on the sea-road. Involuntarily all heads were turned in this new direction, and it was seen that one of the Stanton station-flies had come to a stand-still just opposite the assembled people, and that a lady and gentleman were hastily alighting.

On hearing that the name of the owner of the yacht was Percivale, Mr. Cranmer roused himself from the reverie into which he had fallen. This, then, was the Swan, the mysterious yacht of which everyone had been talking all the summer, and whose owner was so obstinately uncommunicative and unsociable. The idea of meeting the hero of the hour brought a certain excitement with it; but these thoughts were put to flight by the sudden arrival on the scene of the two new actors. In a flash he recognised Frederick Orton, whom he had occasionally seen in company with Colonel Wynch-Frère at Sandown; and this, of course, was his wife. Whence had they sprung? They were believed to be in Homburg; and Claud felt a strange sinking of the heart as he realised in what an unfortunate moment they appeared.

Ottilie sprang vehemently from the carriage, looking round her with flashing eyes. Evidently she was greatly excited. Moving hastily towards the group, she suddenly stopped short, asking, in her fine contralto voice:

"Is Miss Charlotte Willoughby here?"

With an assenting murmur, the throng divided right and left, and she moved on again, till she stood within a few inches of the lady in question. Her husband, after a word to the driver, followed her.

"Miss Willoughby, I am Mrs. Frederick Orton," she said, every word of her deep utterance distinctly audible to everyone present. "We are just arrived from the Continent, and, in consequence of complaints of unkind treatment received in letters from our nephew, we travelled straight down here. We have been up to the house, seen your eldest sister, and been by her informed that the boy is missing since yesterday. Where is he?" She raised her magnificent voice slightly, and it seemed to pierce through Henry Fowler's brain. "Where is he? What have you done with him? Bring him back to me, instantly."

Silence.

The brisk wave broke splashing and foaming along the beach. The white fleecy cloud drew off from the sun which it had momentarily obscured.

Miss Charlotte helplessly confronted her antagonist for a moment, and then burst into tears. All Edge Valley held its breath. That Miss Charlotte Willoughby could weep was a hypothesis too wild ever to have been hazarded among them.

Frederick Orton, in his faultless summer travelling attire, a look of anxiety on his weak, handsome face, stood scanning the group, bowing slightly to Claud, whom he vaguely recognised, and then letting his eye wander to Elsa.

There his gaze rivetted itself with a strange fascination. The girl was too like her father, Valentine Brabourne, for him to be ignorant of her identity; he partly hated her for it. Her beauty, too, took him utterly by surprise. He had heard that she was pretty, but for this unique and superb fairness he was quite unprepared.

His wife, after waiting a minute, or two repeated her question.

"What have you done with Godfrey?" she cried.

Mr. Fowler stepped forward, raising his hat, and meeting her scornful eye steadily.

"Who are you?" the eye seemed to demand. He answered, with his accustomed gentleness:

"My name is Fowler, madam, and I am at present engaged in the same pursuit as yourself—a search-for Godfrey. The Misses Willoughby will have told you how he and his sister went out for a walk together yesterday, and missed each other——"

She pounced upon his words.

"His sister! Yes, his sister! Where is she?"

Sweeping half round, she confronted Elsa on the instant. The two pairs of eyes met—the scorching dark ones, the radiant grey. In each pair, as it rested, on the other, was a menace. It was war to the knife between Ottilie Orton and her niece from that moment.

"So that is his sister," faltered Godfrey's aunt at length. "Do you know," cried she, suddenly finding voice again—"do you know that you are—yes, you are directly responsible for whatever may have happened to Godfrey. I know, Elaine Brabourne, more than you imagine."

A moment of horror, cold sickly horror, crept for one dark instant into Claud's brain as he saw the ashy pallor which overspread Elsa's lace. She seemed to reel where she stood.

"No," she panted, incoherently, "no, it is not true! I never did——"

Her godfather grasped her shoulder with a firm hold.

"Do not attempt to answer Mrs. Orton," he said, in a voice which sounded unlike his own. "She is over-tired—excited. Presently she will regret her words."

"Insolence!" said Ottilie, flinging a look at him. "Frederick, will you hear me spoken to like this?"

"I think it would be—a—wiser to say no more at present," returned her husband, hesitatingly. "Had we not better have a little more light thrown on the subject first?"

"More light? What more light do you want than that girl's ashy, guilty face, and the authority of this letter of Godfrey's?" she rejoined, vehemently. "Did he not say——"

"Madam, if you have any accusation to lodge, I must desire you to choose a more fitting occasion," said Mr. Fowler, peremptorily. "Here, in the presence of these people, in your present state of agitation, you are hardly able to speak dispassionately. As no one yet knows of what they are accused, your charges are, so far, fired into the air. Mr. Orton, what do you wish me to do?"

"Why, find the boy, I suppose. There'll be the devil to pay if he doesn't turn up," observed Mr. Orton; adding, as if to waive any unpleasant impression his speech might leave: "Why, Jove, there's a yacht coming right in shore. Won't she be aground?"

"Nay, she's right enough. The bay's deep enough to float one of more than her tonnage," returned Mr. Fowler; and for the moment everyone's attention was given to the movements of the *Swan*.

The sun streamed down on her dazzling white decks. Nothing more inviting, more exquisite, could be imagined. The curve of her bows was the perfection of grace; the polished brass of her binnacle and fittings gave back every beam that fell upon them.

Half reclining over the rail aft was a young man with folded arms and face intent upon the manoeuvres of his crew. His head was slightly raised, and, as the yacht luffed up gently to the breeze, his profile was turned to the gazers on shore.

It was precisely such a profile as might be one's ideal of a Sir Percivale— half Viking, half saint; not a Greek profile, for it was cut sharply inwards below the brow, the nose springing out with a slightly aquiline curve. The chin was oval, not square, as far as could be seen, but it was partially obscured by a short pointed golden moustache and beard, just inclining to red. The shape of the head, indicated strongly against the light beyond, showed both grace and power. His pose was full of ease and unconsciousness. He seemed hardly aware of the group on the beach, but kept his eyes fixed on his men, giving every now and then an order in German. At last the chain cable rattled out, and the dainty little vessel swung round, head to wind. Her owner roused himself, and stood upright, showing a stature of over six feet.

He wore a white flannel shirt and trousers, a short crimson sash being knotted round his waist. Very leisurely he put on his white peaked cap, then took a dark blue serge yachting coat and slipped his arms into it, moving slowly forward meanwhile to the gangway. A wooden contrivance, forming a kind of bridge, with a handrail, was pushed out by the crew; and one of the longshoremen pressed eagerly forward to make it firm.

Mr. Percivale stepped upon it, and walked, still with that impassive, pre-occupied air, forward towards the waiting crowd.

Now it could be seen that his eyes were bright and vivid, of the very deepest blue—that blue called the violet, which shows darkly from a distance. His hair, with a distinct shade of red in its lustre, was a mass of small soft curls, close to the head. His complexion was fair and clear, just touched with tan, but naturally pale; his features excessively finely cut.

"A man of mark, to know next time you saw," quoted Claud inwardly, as the stranger paused.

The dark blue eyes roved over the crowd but for one swift instant. Then, suddenly, they met the glance of a pair of passionate grey ones—eyes which spoke, which seemed to cry aloud for sympathy—eyes set in such a face as the owner of the *Swan* had never yet looked on. As the two glances met, they became rivetted, each on the other. There was a pause, which to Elsa seemed to last for hours, but which in reality occupied only a few seconds; then Mr. Fowler went forward and asked,

"You are the owner of the *Swan*?"

"Yes; and you, if I rightly understood Bergman, are a Justice of the Peace?"

"I am. Fowler is my name."

"I really do not know," said the stranger, his eyes again wandering towards Elsa in the background, "whether you are the proper person with whom to lodge my information, but perhaps you will kindly arrange all that for me. I merely felt that I could not leave the neighborhood without telling you what my men found this morning on the cliffs."

The silence, the breathless hush which had fallen on all present was almost horrible; the very sea, the noisy breeze seemed subdued for the moment. Mr. Fowler's face stiffened.

"We were lying midway between Brent and this place early this morning," went on the stranger who, to judge by his speech, was certainly English, "and my crew were examining the cliff with the glasses, when their attention was caught by something lying on the grass. It was a dark object, and after watching it for some time, one of the men declared that it moved. At last they asked my permission to go and examine the spot, which I willingly gave. They scaled the cliff——"

"Then what they saw was not at the *foot* of the cliff?" burst in Claud, breathlessly.

"No. It was on the summit. It was the dead body of a boy."

Elsa gave a wild cry and threw up her arms.

Mr. Fowler caught her to him, holding her golden head against his breast, stroking down her hair, murmuring to her with parched lips. Mrs. Orton never moved; she stood like a pale Nemesis, her eyes fixed on the trembling girl; and down from the breezy heights came the wind, singing and whistling, making all the poppies dance among the stubble, and the bright clouds dash over the vivid sky in racy succession.

"Go home, Elsa darling—let Mr. Cranmer take you home," whispered Henry.

"No! no! I want to hear everything!" she cried, in anguish.

The stranger's eyes dilated with a wonderful pity as he looked at her.

"I am sorry to give her such pain," he said, at length slowly, in his gentle voice.

"Go on," said Henry, hoarsely. "Go on—what did your men do?"

"They satisfied themselves that the boy was dead—that he had been dead many hours. When they were sure of this, they left the body as they found it, thinking perhaps they had better not meddle with it. The cause of death was apparently hemorrhage of the lungs, but it had been brought on, they guessed, by a violent blow on the back. The body, when they found it, was lying in what looked like an attempt by some very unskilful hands, to hollow out a hole and cover it with bramble branches, as one branch lay under the corpse. The gale had of course blown away anything which might have concealed the ghastly secret. About thirty feet from the spot was a large stain of blood, partly obliterated by rain."

"Murder will out," said Mrs. Orton, slowly, fixing her burning eyes on Elsa. Theatrical as her manner was, it scarcely seemed too emphatic at this fearful crisis. "Yes! no wonder she cowers! No wonder she is transfixed with horror! I say," she went on, raising her voice a little—only a little, yet every accent penetrated to the very outskirts of the crowd. "I say that Elaine Brabourne is her brother's murderer."

CHAPTER XXVI

Then I knew
That I was saved. I never met
His face before, but, at first view,
I felt quite sure that God had set
Himself to Satan: who would spend
A minute's mistrust on the end?
Count Gismond.

"It is an infamous falsehood!"

Every one turned in the direction of the speaker. Elsa, who had sunk on the ground, clinging to Henry Fowler's knees, made a sudden movement, and held out her hands.

It is very seldom, in our prosaic century, that a man first meets a woman in such circumstances—first sees her with all the restraints of conventionality stripped clean away—with helpless, appealing anguish written in her eyes.

To Percivale it seemed as if the whole scene dated back for about six centuries, as though he were a knight-errant, one of Arthur's knights, coming suddenly upon a distressed maiden, who claimed his help as her divine right. A long dreadful moment had elapsed between Mrs. Orton's accusation and his reply, a moment which he had expected would have been seized either by Mr. Fowler or the young man who stood by.

But no. Both were silent, for the same fatal reason. They both thought it possible, knowing what provocation had been Eisa's, that, in a moment of passion, she had struck blindly. But the sound of the stranger's frank, fearless tones seemed, for no reason at all, to make Henry feel ashamed of himself. He stooped to Elsa and lifted her to her feet.

"Take courage, my child, tell the truth," he said, tenderly.

Mrs. Orton and Mr. Percivale stood facing each other.

"May I ask by what right you are meddling in this affair, sir?" asked Ottilie, with studied insolence. "What do you know of the matter? How can you possibly presume to give an opinion? If I might venture to make a suggestion to so grand a gentleman, it would be that you return to your vessel, and continue that cruise which you so charitably interrupted to bring us this awful intelligence."

Percivale never moved his large, calm eyes from her face; but, slowly removing his cap from his bright head, made her a graceful bow.

"With all possible aversion to disobeying a lady's commands, madam, I must decline to take your thoughtful suggestion," he said, courteously. "I have just told you, in hasty words which were the result of a moment's indignation, that I believe the statement you just now made to be false. Whilst apologising for the manner in which I expressed myself, I beg to say that I meant every word I said; and you will thus see that I have rendered it impossible for me to leave this place, until it is proved that I am right and you are wrong."

She laughed insultingly, she was too excited to know exactly what she said or did.

"You will have to stay a long time," said she, with a sneer. "Why, look at Elaine Brabourne! Look at her cowering there! Doesn't her attitude speak for itself? Do you wish to be better acquainted with the situation? Will it satisfy you to be told that a fortune of eighty thousand pounds comes to this girl on her brother's death, and that it is only a week since she was made aware of the fact? And if I say further that she wants to marry a beggarly artist, and that only my little Godfrey's frail life stood between——"

"Ottilie, Ottilie, hold your tongue, my dear girl," said Frederick, nervously. "You are overwrought, you must take some rest, and leave me to search out this affair."

"Leave you!" She wrenched herself away scornfully. "Leave *you* to do it? Why, you could be made to say black was white in ten minutes by anyone who would discuss the question with you. Well"—to Percivale—"are you still mad enough to say that the matter admits of a doubt?"

The perfect quiet of his answer was a most complete contrast to her violence.

"It is unfortunate," he said, "that the consideration of the same circumstances should lead us to diametrically opposite conclusions; but so it is. You consider that the young lady's present appearance and attitude argues guilt; to me it strongly indicates innocence. This shows how necessary it is that I should have proof of the truth of my view, which proof I shall immediately take steps to find."

Henry Fowler roused himself; his face seemed to have grown ten years older during the last half-hour.

"I am grateful to you, sir," he said to Percivale, with a piteous humility. "Elsa, my darling, you must go home at once."

Raising her lovely head from his shoulder, she stood upright, for the first time since her accusation. She looked straight at the stranger, holding out her hands.

"It is false—every word they said about me," she faltered. "I could tell you——" here her voice broke.

Holding his hat in his left hand, he grasped both her small hands in his right, and, bending low, kissed them respectfully.

"I want no assurances," he said. "I do not even want you to tell me of your innocence. I know it; and all these people, who have heard you falsely accused, shall hear justice done if God grant me life and strength to do it." He smiled for the first time—a quiet, grave smile which irradiated all his face. "I do not even know your name," he said; "but I know that you are innocent."

Miss Charlotte, white and subdued, came up and took the girl's hand.

Elsa moved slightly, as if she were dreaming, and then smiled back into Percivale's eyes, a smile of perfect trust, as though an angel had appeared to champion her.

It was her only leave-taking: she never spoke; but, turning, walked through the assembled peasants with a mien as dignified, as consciously noble, as that of Marie-Antoinette at her trial.

"They can take our fly—I am going along the cliffs to find my boy," said Mrs. Orton, with a burst of tears.

Her husband and Claud followed the three ladies to the carriage. Henry Fowler was left face to face with the stranger.

"God help us," he said, brokenly. "What is to be done?"

"The first thing," said Percivale, quietly, "is to decide whether the boy found by my crew is the brother of Miss—Miss——"

"Brabourne,—true. But he is only her half-brother."

"The next thing will be to prove——"

"It is hopeless," cried Henry, helplessly, as they moved away from the crowd together. "You don't know, as I do, the weight of evidence against her. You do not—pardon me—understand the circumstances."

"No. For my enlightenment I must apply first to you. As the matter seems to be a family one, and as I am an utter stranger, I shall consider you fully justified if you decline to afford me any help at all. But I must warn you that, if I cannot get information from you, I shall apply for it elsewhere. It will take longer; but I have pledged my word."

Henry surveyed him with an interest bordering on admiration.

"I shall tell you anything you ask," he said. "Our first meeting has been too far beyond the limits of conventionalities for us to be bound by any rules. God bless you for your unhesitating defence of my poor little girl. I was too crushed—I knew too much to be able to speak promptly, as you did; and I terribly fear that when you have heard all I can tell you, though you may not waver in your belief in her, you will think the case against her looks very grave."

They paused, and turned to watch Mr. and Mrs. Orton, and Claud, who were approaching. Mr. Percivale called to one of the crew of the *Swan* to come ashore and lead the way; and after the party had been yet further augmented by the Edge Valley policeman, they set forth towards the cliffs.

Ottilie hurried on first, sweeping her husband in her train. Claud, Mr. Fowler, and Percivale walked more slowly, and as they went, the latter was put in full possession of the facts of the case, so far as they could be known.

He disagreed entirely with the inference that Elsa's odd conduct of the preceding day, and seeming uncertainty as to where she had parted from her brother, was a sign of guilt.

"We cannot," he urged, "any of us dwell for a moment on such a hypothesis as that it was a murder in cold blood. The next conclusion, then, would be, a blow struck in a fit of passion, unintentionally causing death. Now, consider probabilities for a moment. In such a case, would it not be the only impulse of any girl, terrified by the unexpected result of her anger, to rush for help? Miss Brabourne has never seen death—she would think of a swoon from loss of blood as the worst possible contingency, she would have hurried home, she would have told the first wayfarer she met, she would have been so agitated as to render concealment impossible. Besides, the poor boy's clothes were saturated with blood; how could she have lifted him—how could she have scooped any sort of hole without her clothes bearing such evident traces of it?"

"The front of her dress was very dirty," said Claud, reluctantly. "You know I always notice that sort of thing. No rain had fallen then, so it was not mud; but it was chalk, I am certain."

"You have not watched Elsa, Mr. Percivale, as I have done," said Henry, sadly. "You are ignorant of her character, and her bringing-up. She has never known what sympathy meant. Every trivial offence has been treated as a crime. Her childhood was one long atmosphere of punishment. The Misses Willoughby are good women, but they have not understood how to bring her up—repression, authority, decorum, those are their ideas. If ever Elsa laughed, she laughed alone; if she suffered, it was in secret. She is reserved by nature, and this training has made her far more so. Were she to fall into any grievous trouble, such as this, for instance," pausing a moment, he then added firmly, "I must confess that I think her first, second, and third impulse would be to conceal it."

Percivale made no reply.

"Her temper, too—she has never been taught to govern it," went on Henry, sadly; "and it is very violent. Add to this the provocation she has had——"

"Have you," asked Claud, suddenly, "have you mentioned to anyone the book we found on the cliff last night?"

Henry made a gesture of despair.

"I had forgotten that," he said, miserably. "But it is another strong piece of evidence."

Claud explained to Percivale.

"Miss Brabourne told us that she had not been on the cliffs yesterday. As we walked home, we found a favorite book of hers lying out in the rain—a book which only some very unforeseen agitation would induce her to part with."

"Of course we could suppress that evidence at the inquest," was the immoral suggestion of the Justice of the Peace.

"It will not be necessary," tranquilly replied their companion. "I shall know the truth by then."

They were out on the cliffs by this time, and presently became aware, by the halting of the sailors in front, that the fatal spot was reached. They saw Mrs. Orton cast herself on the ground in the theatrical way which seemed habitual to her, and saw her husband's face turn greenish white as he averted it from the little corpse over which she bent so vehemently. Walking forward, they too stood beside the dead boy.

Every feeling of animosity, of dislike, which Henry Fowler might have cherished, melted before the pitiful sight. It was through a mist of tears, which came near to falling, that he gazed down on the child's white face.

It was quite composed and the eyes half shut. A certain drawn look about the mouth, and the added placidity and beauty of death gave to it a likeness to Elsa which had not seemed to exist in life. It was somewhat horrible to contemplate. In her moments of dumb obstinacy Henry had seen her look so.

He turned away his face for a moment, looking out over the busy, tossing, sunlit sea, where the shadows of the clouds chased each other in soft blurs of shadow, with green and russet shoals between.

The fresh quick air swept over the chalk, laden with brine. A warm odor of thyme was in its breath, and there lay Godfrey, with stiff limbs and still heart, in a silence only broken by his aunt's sobs, and the whistling of the wind among the rocks.

"How do you know that death was caused by a blow?" asked Mr. Percivale of the sailors, at length.

Bergman explained, in his German accents, that they had made an examination of the body to see if it could be identified.

"It is not lying now as we found it, sir. It was bent together—we straightened the limbs. In pulling down the shirt to see if there was a name marked on it, we discovered a livid bruise."

Mr. Percivale knelt down by the dead boy, and, passing an arm gently beneath him, raised the lifeless head till it lay against his shoulder, and exposed the bruise in question.

Mrs. Orton, who had been silent till now, uttered an inarticulate cry of rage:

"Look there!" she gasped.

"Is anyone here ignorant enough to assert that this scar is the result of the blow of a girl's fist?" demanded Percivale, raising his head. "It has been done with a stick—a heavy stick. See, it has grazed the skin right across; you can follow the direction of it. Does Miss Brabourne carry a weapon of that description?"

"She had no stick when we met her in the lane yesterday," said Claud, eagerly.

"Idiot! As if she could not throw away a dozen on her way home from here," passionately broke in Mrs. Orton.

"Ottilie," said her husband, in a low, warning voice, "take care."

"Take care! Too late to say that now," she cried. "Why didn't I take care sooner—care of my poor little boy? Why did I ever send him to this den of assassins? But, thank Heaven, we are in England, and shall have justice—a life for a life," she concluded, wildly.

"We are willing to make all possible allowances for Mrs. Orton's feelings," said Percivale, with great gentleness. "I must agree with her that it is much to be regretted that she trusted such a delicate child, and one on whose life so much depended, out of her own personal care."

"What do you mean, sir?" cried Ottilie, suddenly.

"What do I mean? Merely what I said, madam," he answered, astonished.

"You are trying to make insinuations," she cried, too excited to think of prudence. "What depended on Godfrey's life? Do you suppose I am thinking of the paltry few hundreds a year we received for taking care of him?"

"Madam," he replied at once, "an hour since you did not scruple openly, in the presence of numbers of people, to accuse Miss Brabourne of murdering her brother to obtain his fortune; I am therefore not surprised that you imagine others may be ready to supply a base motive for your grief at his death. Believe me, however, my imagination is not so vivid as yours; what you suggest had not occurred to me until you mentioned it."

She had no answer to make; she was choking with rage; the stranger was a match for her. Her husband stood by, reflecting for the first time on the effect which Godfrey's death must have for him. The few hundreds of which his wife spoke so contemptuously had nevertheless been particularly acceptable to people who habitually lived far beyond their income, and were always in want of ready money. But beyond this—had Godfrey lived to attain his majority, the whole of his fortune would have been practically in his uncle's hands. He could have invested it, turned it over, betted with it, speculated with it; and the boy would have made a will immensely in his favor. He had never looked forward to a long life for the young heir.

Weakly, and viciously inclined, he had always imagined that four or five years of indulgence would "finish" him; but that he should live to be twenty-one was all-important. Now the whole of that untouched fortune was Elsa's, unless this murder could be proved against her. Mr. Orton began to divine the more rapid workings of his wife's mind. In the event of both children dying unmarried, the money was willed, half to Frederick, half to the Misses Willoughby.

Never had Mr. and Mrs. Orton been in more urgent, more terrible need than at this moment. The year had been a consistently unlucky one. Their Ascot losses had merely been the beginning of sorrows.

The hurried flight from Homburg had really been due, not to poor Godfrey's complaints of his dulness, but to an inability to remain longer; and they had arrived at Edge with the full intention of partaking of the Misses Willoughby's hospitality as long as they could manage to endure the slowness of existence at their expense.

And now here was this dire calamity befallen them! Frederick smarted under a righteous sense of injury. He thought Fate had a special spite against him. What was a man to do if everything would persist in being a failure? Every single road towards paying his debts seemed to be inexorably closed. This was most certainly his misfortune and not his fault; he was perfectly willing to pay, if some one would give him the money to do it with; and, as nobody would, it followed that he was most deeply to be pitied.

CHAPTER XXVII

One friend in that path shall be
To secure my step from wrong;
One to count night day for me,
Patient through the watches long,
Serving most with none to see.
A Serenade at the Villa.

Nothing could well look blacker than did the case to Henry Fowler. He could see no way out of it. Had the boy been found at the foot of the cliffs, a verdict of accidental death could so easily have been returned; but here, and with the marks of violence plainly visible on the body, the presumption seemed terribly strong.

He stood with head sunk upon his chest, feeling beaten down, degraded, stricken. Over and over in his mind did he turn the circumstances to see if there would be enough evidence to justify the coroner in committing Elaine for trial.

Absolute proof of her guilt would not, he thought, be possible; the night had been so wild, the spot so lonely. But the very fact of standing to take her trial on such a charge would be more than enough to blast the young girl's future. Supposing she had to go through life stigmatised as one acquitted of murder merely because the jury did not see enough evidence to convict? The thought was literally agony to his large, gentle heart. Was this to be the fate of Alice's daughter? He stood as one accused in his own eyes of culpable neglect; in some way such a culmination should have been avoided—he should have been able to watch over Elaine better than he had done.

Claud gently recalled him to the present by asking what was to be done with the body.

Rousing himself, he gave directions for it to be carried to Edge Willoughby; and then fell afresh into a fit of despair, realising how terribly imminent it all was.

"When will the inquest take place?" asked Mr. Percivale, approaching him.

"The day after to-morrow—I cannot delay it longer; you have forty-eight hours in which to accomplish your purpose," returned Henry, with a bitter laugh quite unlike him.

"Forty-eight hours," repeated the stranger, steadily. "One can do a great deal in that time."

He remained standing, in the perfect quietness of attitude which seemed habitual to him, his eyes fixed on the rude niche, hollowed in the ground, where the boy's corpse had lain.

"He was not robbed," he said, after a moment.

"Robbed? No! She was not clever enough for that," cut in Ottilie, with her harsh sneer. "Had she possessed wit enough to rifle his pockets and fling his watch into a thicket, she would have stood a better chance."

"Miss Brabourne is, perhaps, not so well versed in the science of these matters as you seem to be, madam," was the mild answer. "Yet, if she possessed cunning enough to conceive the plan of murdering her brother for his fortune, it would seem consistent to credit her also with cunning enough to do all in her power to avert suspicion; to me, it amounts to a moral impossibility that any young lady in her right mind should perpetrate such a deed, and then walk quietly home without so much as making up a single falsehood to shield herself."

"Murderers, especially inexperienced ones, are never consistent," returned Mrs. Orton, furiously, "as you would know, if you knew anything at all of the matter."

"Ottilie, Ottilie, come away, for goodness sake—it is snobbish to get up a row," urged her husband, in low tones; and, taking her by the arm, he led her unwillingly away from the scene of conflict.

Claud and Percivale were left confronting each other.

"The valley will have a pretty ghastly celebrity attaching to it after this," remarked the former, removing his straw hat to pass his handkerchief over his hot brow. "This is the second mysterious affair within one summer."

"The second!" echoed Percivale, keenly, turning his eyes upon him full of awakened interest.

"Yes; and with points of similarity too. Each victim had been attacked from behind, and beaten with a heavy stick; there was no robbery in either case, and Miss Elsa Brabourne in the former case, oddly enough, was the person to discover the insensible victim. Whether the incident unconsciously influenced her, whether as is the case sometimes, according to newspapers, the ease with which one crime had been committed suggested another, I cannot of course say——"

"Was the man killed?"

"No; he recovered: but had no idea as to who was his assailant. We had down a detective——"

"English detectives are no use at all, or I would telegraph for the entire force," replied Percivale. "I believe I shall get to the bottom of this matter more surely by myself. I have already formulated a theory. You say the criminal was never discovered?"

"No; never even had a clue worth calling a clue."

"Then surely the same idea at once occurs to you as to me, that both these murders are the work of one hand."

Claud was silent.

"I had not thought of it," he said at last.

"No; because your mind is full of a preconceived idea; and nothing is more fatal to the discovery of the truth. Let me show you what I mean. I suppose there is no room at all for the absurd supposition that Miss Brabourne was concerned in crime number one?"

"None whatever. She was out walking with her maid, and they found Mr. Allonby lying insensible by the roadside. He had been first stunned by a blow on the head, then so severely beaten that the bone of one arm was broken."

"And not robbed?"

"No; except for a most absurd circumstance—one which mystified us all more than anything. He had his dinner with him—he was making a sketch, I should tell you; an artist—and this dinner was packed for him by Mrs. Clapp, of the Fountain Head, in a pudding-basin, tied round with a blue and white handkerchief. After the murder the basin and handkerchief were missing, nor could they be found, though careful search was made. The detective could offer no solution of this part of the business."

"What solution did he offer of the rest of the transaction?"

"He felt certain it must be the result of some private grudge; the attack was such a vicious one—as if the one idea had been to kill—to wreak vengeance."

"What time of day was this done?" asked Percivale, who was following every word with close interest.

"As near as possible at five o'clock, one evening towards the end of June. The time can be fixed pretty conclusively, for when Miss Brabourne and her maid passed the place shortly before, he was alive, seated on a camp-stool; on their return he was lying in the grass, motionless."

"And was there any inhabitant of the village likely to bear the artist a grudge?"

"Impossible! He was an utter stranger."

"Did anyone see a stranger pass through? Let me know the circumstances more accurately. Describe the scene of the occurrence."

Claud eagerly complied, supplying Mr. Percivale with every detail, and doing it with the intelligent accuracy which was part of his nature. The other listened closely, questioning here and there, and finally gave his conclusion with calm conviction.

"Every word you utter convinces me that for a stranger of any sort to penetrate into the valley, track Mr. Allonby's whereabouts, and vanish without leaving a trace, taking with him a pudding-basin as a memento of his vengeance, amounts to a moral impossibility. It is absurd. You say, too, that Mr. Allonby has no idea himself on the subject—says he has no enemies—is as much in the dark as anyone?"

"Yes, and I believe him: he is a thoroughly simple-minded, honest fellow."

"Then it stands to reason, in my opinion, that the murderer is an inhabitant of Edge Valley."

"But then," cried Claud, "you take away any possibility of a motive!"

"Exactly; and, granting for the sake of argument that Miss Brabourne did *not* murder her brother, what motive have we here?"

Claud was silent.

"The way you argue is this," went on Percivale, "you know of a powerfully strong motive for the murder of this poor boy, and you feel bound to accept the theory because, if it be not so, you are at a loss to account for the thing on any other grounds. You say—there must be a very forcible reason to incite to murder. I answer you—here is a crime, committed in this very village, not three months back, fresh in everyone's memory, alike in many salient points, and, as far as we can learn, utterly without purpose. If one mysterious deed can be committed in this valley, why not two? Why is the homicide to stop short? If he has managed to dispose of a full-grown man on the high-road in broad daylight, he will make short work of a delicate little boy, out by himself on the cliffs in the twilight."

"But," urged Claud, "you are assuming that these outrages are committed simply for the sake of killing—with no motive but slaughter. They must then be the work of a maniac, of some one not in his right mind!"

"Exactly. That is the very same conclusion which I have arrived at. Do you know of any such in the village?"

"No, I don't. I am certain there is no such person," answered Claud, hopelessly.

"He may very likely exist without anyone's suspecting it," rejoined Percivale. "You know a man may suffer from one special form of mania and be absolutely sane on every other point. If we could leave the discovery to time, he must inevitably betray himself, sooner or later; but we have to run him to earth in eight-and-forty hours. Let us see if the spots selected give us any clue. How far from where we are now standing was Mr. Allonby attacked?"

"In quite the opposite direction—nearly four miles from here. Starting from Edge Willoughby, you would turn to your right and strike inland to get to Poole Farm; you would turn to your left and walk along the shore to get here."

"I see. That does not help us much; yet the criminal should have some hiding place within convenient distance one would think. Unless it be some one so completely beyond the pale of suspicion that his goings and comings excited no attention whatever. Is there no village idiot here? They indulge in one in most out-of-the-way spots like this?"

"Oh, yes, there is Saul Parker, an epileptic boy; but he is out of the question."

"Why out of the question?" asked Percivale, persistently.

"Why, because—because—my good sir, why are *you* out of the question, the thing is just as absurd," answered Claud, almost crossly.

"Is it? I wonder," said Percivale, thoughtfully. "We shall soon see, if you can answer a few more of my questions for me. To begin—*I* am out of the question because it can be proved that I was not in Edge Valley at the time either crime was committed. Can you say as much for this Saul Parker?"

"No, of course he was in the place at the time, but the whole idea is absurd. He is gentle, tractable, most beautiful in face, and sat to Miss Allonby as a model for a picture Mr. Fowler now has——"

"Where was he at the time Mr. Allonby was attacked?" coolly continued his interrogator.

"Where was he? I——" a sudden memory burst upon Claud of Mrs. Battishill's kitchen when he first beheld it.

"He was in the kitchen of Poole Farm," he answered, triumphantly, "for I saw him there myself. I think that proves the *alibi* all right."

"Did you see him there before or after the attempted murder?"

"After—naturally."

"Ah!... where does this Saul Parker live?"

"He lives with his mother in a cottage on the Quarry Road. She is the widow of a quarry-man."

"It was along the Quarry Road, I think, that Miss Brabourne and her brother went to the cliff yesterday? I wish you would kindly take me back to the village that way. I should like to see the idiot, foolish as you think my theory sounds. Is he very small and puny?"

"Oh, no—a great fellow, taller than I am," admitted Claud, with a vague, vague wonder growing in him as to whether, after all, the stranger had chanced upon the truth of what had baffled them all this summer.

And—the absurdity of the idea!

Even as this sentiment crossed his mind, he could not help owning that, though he could reiterate that it was absurd, he could give no substantial reasons for his opinion. Everyone would have thought it absurd—anyone in Edge Valley to whom the suggestion had been made would have passed it by with a contemptuous laugh. The idiot was probably the only person in the whole place whose goings and comings were never challenged—who wandered in and out as he listed, now in this farm kitchen, now in that, kindly tolerated for the sake of his beautiful face and his affliction. It was of little use to question him.

"Where have 'ee been, my lad? Haow's yer moother?" or any other like civility. A soft smile or a gurgling laugh would be the only response at times, or, if mischievously inclined, he might give an answer which was not the true one.

Yet, now that Claud began to think over what he knew of the boy....

His intense aversion to strangers was one point in his character which rose to immediate remembrance. He recalled Wynifred's story of how she had caught him in the act of throwing a stone at Mr. Haldane when his back was turned; and Clara Battishill's complaints of his cruelty were also fresh in his memory.

But Godfrey he knew to be the special terror of Saul's life, and the object of his untold hatred. Godfrey set his bull-dog at the idiot, laughed at him, bullied him—one blow from that heavy cudgel which Saul habitually dragged after him would be more than enough to avenge his wrongs on the frail boy. And yet—and yet——

Somehow, Elsa's guilt seemed painfully obvious. Her embarrassment, her confusion of the night before—how were they to be accounted for? Was there any other solution possible? Her untruthful equivocation as to where she had been—what else could it portend?

This idea about Saul was, after all, too wild and far-fetched. How could he have been guilty of the attack on Osmond without the Battishills being aware of the fact?

No; the theory was ingenious, but, in his opinion, it would not hold water. He said so, aloud, after a long interval of silence.

"I shall at all events see if facts fit in at all with it," said Percivale, quietly. "Drowning men catch at straws, you know." Pausing a moment he then added, almost reverently:

"If that beautiful woman is arraigned for this crime—if she has ever to stand in the dock to answer to the charge of fratricide, or even manslaughter, I shall feel all the rest of my life though as if I were stained, shamed, degraded from my rightful post of helper to the oppressed. I feel as though I could cut through armies single-handed sooner than see Frederick Orton's wife triumph over the youth and helplessness of Miss Brabourne."

He hesitated over the name, breathing it softly, as a devotee might name a patron saint.

"You know something of the Ortons?" asked Claud.

"By reputation—yes," returned Percivale, with the air of one who does not intend to say more.

Had he chosen, he could have edified his companion with an account of how, last summer, at Oban, Mrs. Orton had determined, by hook or by crook, to become acquainted with the mysterious owner of the *Swan*, of whom no one knew more than his name, his unsociable habits, and his somewhat remarkable appearance; and how she prosecuted this design with so much vigor that he was obliged to intimate to her, as unequivocally as is possible from a gentleman to a lady, that he declined the honor of her acquaintance.

He said nothing of this, however; evidently, whatever his merits or his failings, he was a very uncommunicative person.

As if by mutual consent, they moved slowly along together, their faces turned back towards Edge Valley. Suddenly it occurred to Claud that he was due at Ardnacruan in six hours' time. There was nothing for it but to drive into Stanton and telegraph; no consideration should induce him to leave the scene of action in the present unforeseen and agitated aspect of affairs. He must implore Fowler to keep him a few days longer—which request that good fellow would grant, he knew how willingly.

As these thoughts crossed his mind, Henry approached them, his kind face furrowed and drawn with pain in a manner piteous to behold. Laying a hand on Mr. Cranmer's arm, he said, brokenly,

"Claud, my lad, you're not thinking of leaving me to-day?"

A rush of sympathy filled the young man's heart. Never before had Mr. Fowler made use of his Christian name.

"No, my dear fellow, of course I shall stay," he said, at once. "If only I thought I could be of any comfort to you——"

"You can—you are. But I am selfish—your friends will be expecting you——"

"I will drive into Stanton and send a telegram, if I may have the trap. Perhaps there might be some business I could do for you?"

"One or two things, lad, if you would. I feel mazed. I can't think clearly. Let me see——"

"I'll think for you," said Claud, slipping his arm into his; "and, first, I am going to take you straight home to have a glass of wine and some food. You are positively faint from exhaustion."

"You must come too," said Mr. Fowler, to Percivale.

"Thanks."

The young man turned slowly round towards them.

During the few foregoing sentences he had been gazing out seawards, with folded arms.

"On second thoughts," he said to Claud, "I think that, before making the inquiries I speak of, I will see Miss Brabourne—if I can."

CHAPTER XXVIII

She stood on the floor,
Fair and still as the moonlight that came there before,
And a smile just beginning:
It touches her lips, but it dare not arise
To the height of the mystical sphere of her eyes,
And the large, musing eyes, neither joyous nor sorry,
Sing on like the angels in separate glory
Between clouds of amber.
Lay of the Brown Rosary.

The desolation and abandonment which had fallen upon Edge Willoughby cannot be described.

The sisters knew not what to think, or say, or do. A vague notion that all employment was incongruous when suffering under a *bereavement* led them to sit in a circle round the dining-room, gazing at each other with stiff and pale faces, wondering if this nightmare-like day would ever end, and what would follow next.

In the large drawing-room lay the motionless form of poor Godfrey, still and dead, in the gloom of closed blinds and drawn curtains. The same death-like quiet brooded over all the house. Miss Ellen lay on her couch in an agony of self-reproach, caused by the fact that it was owing to her influence entirely that the boy had come to Edge.

Oh, that he had never come—that Elsa had never been subjected to the fiery trial which had terminated so fatally.

It was all their fault, she told herself. They had grossly mismanaged the child—they had never sought her confidence, only exacted her submission. Now that Miss Ellen would have given everything she possessed for that confidence, it was, of course, obstinately withheld. No word could Elsa be made to speak, though, figuratively, they had all gone down on their knees to her.

If she would only confess the truth—whatever it was they could pardon it, had been their piteous cry. But she would not speak. The only thing they could extract was an announcement that they all, she knew, took her for a murderess, and she would therefore not attempt to justify herself; and finally, all they could do was to allow her to go away into her own room and lock herself in. The whole situation was intensely awkward: for the Ortons were quartered upon them, and it was hard to say which was the greater—their dislike to being there, or the Misses Willoughbys' dislike to having them.

On returning from the cliff, Ottilie had swept off all her belongings with a grand air, declaring that no human power should induce her to sleep under the same roof with Elsa, and had driven with her husband to the "Fountain Head," where they were met by William Clapp, who respectfully but firmly denied them admittance. "He had heard what the lady was pleased to say, aout on the beach this morning, and he warn't going tû harbor them as laid things o' that kind to the charge o' Miss Ullin as he had seen grow up, and meant to stand by to his dying day."

There was absolutely no alternative but to go back ignominiously to Edge Willoughby, and beg for an asylum there till the inquest should be over. The request was granted with freezing hauteur by the sisters, Miss Charlotte adding that she thought it would be more pleasant for all parties if Mr. and Mrs. Orton had their meals served separately.

The pair were out of doors now, wandering restlessly about, in quest of nobody quite knew what. When the bell sounded the sisters imagined that they had returned, and a tremor of excitement ran through the pallid assembly as the parlor-maid brought in a small card, on which was engraved simply:

> Mr. Percivale,
> Yacht "Swan."

The gentleman followed his card, and stood just inside the door, still in his nautical and somewhat unusual dress, cap in hand, and with his clear eyes fixed upon Miss Ellen.

"May I come in?" he asked.

"O—certainly!" fluttered Miss Ellen.

He went straight across the room to her couch and took her hand.

"I hope you will allow me to introduce myself," he said. "I am the unfortunate man who hurled such a bomb-shell into the midst of the village this morning. I am now engaged in doing my poor best to repair the mischief I have caused. Take courage, Miss Willoughby—your white dove shall not receive so much as a fleck on her gold and silver plumage."

Miss Ellen could hardly speak for tears.

"She is flecked already," she gasped. "A vile accusation has been levelled at her before a crowd of witnesses. We are disgraced."

"I think the lady who made the accusation will be the one to feel disgraced," answered Mr. Percivale, taking a seat beside her. "Keep up heart, Miss Willoughby, I feel sure this frightful accusation will be easily proved false."

She looked up with a sudden spasm of hope.

"Then you really think— —" she began, and paused.

"I think?" interrogatively.

"You sincerely believe that Elaine is quite innocent of this—that she is as ignorant of the facts of the case as we are?" There was a feverish, frantic eagerness, in her voice as she spoke.

"That is certainly my fixed belief," he said, calmly. "I fail to see how anyone could think otherwise. I know what you fear—that Miss Brabourne struck a blow in anger, and then was so horrified at its result that she dared not confess what she had done. There is a circumstance which renders this an impossible view of the case. Whoever murdered the poor boy afterwards scooped a shallow hole in the grass, partly out of sight beneath a bramble, and laid the body in it. To do this without becoming covered with blood and dirt would have been a miracle. Miss Brabourne came home last night, so Mr. Cranmer says, with the front of her dress marked with chalk; but there are plenty of witnesses, I think, to prove that she had no blood-stains, either on hands or dress, nor were her hands in the state they necessarily must have been had she dug a hole with insufficient tools."

"That is true," said Miss Ellen, eagerly. "You shall see the dress if you like—it is soiled, but not nearly to that extent! This is hope—this is life. I never thought of all this before."

"If you would allow me," went on the stranger, courteously, "I want to see more than Miss Brabourne's dress—I want an interview with her herself. Would you allow me to see her—alone?"

There was a slight pause. Then Miss Charlotte spoke.

"May I ask why you wish to see my niece in private?" she asked.

"I will tell you frankly why. I am the only person who has fearlessly asserted from the first that I believe her to be innocent. I think it likely that she will, in consequence, accord me a confidence which she would withhold from anyone else."

"He is right," said Miss Ellen, with tears. "She will not speak a word to us. We have never trusted her—we have let her see it; we have been very wrong. Take Mr. Percivale into the school-room, Emily, and see if you can induce Elsa to come down and see him."

Percivale followed his guide into the small, dull room where most of Elsa's life had been passed. There were the instruments of her daily torture, the black-board, the globes, the slates and lesson-books, the rattling, inharmonious piano. Outside was the dip of the valley, the wooded height beyond, and, nearer, the wide sunny terrace, now a blaze of dahlias and chrysanthemums. He walked to the window and stood there—very still, and gazing out with eyes that did not betray the secret of what his thoughts might be. His cap lay on the small table near; leaning against the woodwork, he folded his arms, and so, without change of attitude or expression, awaited the entrance of the accused.

Elsa came in after an interval of nearly a quarter-of-an-hour. She was white, and had evidently been weeping; but these accidents seemed scarcely to impair her beauty, while they heightened the strange interest which surrounded her, as it were, with an atmosphere of her own. Slowly closing the door behind her, she stood just within it, as still as he, and with her eyes fixed questioningly upon him, as if inquiring whether his first profession of faith in her had been shaken by what he had since heard.

The slight sound of the lock made him rouse himself, and withdraw his gaze from the horizon to fix it upon her face. Over mouth, cheeks, and brow his eyes flickered till they rested upon hers; and for several moments they remained so, seeing only one another. The girl seemed reading him as she would read a page—as a condemned criminal might devour the lines which told him that his innocence was established. Gradually on her wistful face there dawned a smile—a ray of blessed assurance. She moved two steps forward, stopped, faltered, hid her face.

He advanced quickly, stood beside her, and said,

"I thank you."

It made her look up hurriedly.

"You—thank me?"

"Yes; for your granting me this interview shows me that you are on my side—that you are going to sanction my poor efforts to help you. To what do I owe such honor? It ought to be the portion of some worthier knight than I; but, such as I am, I will fight for you if it costs me life itself."

"You are—" she began, but her voice failed her. "I cannot say it," cried she—"I cannot tell you how I think of you. You are a stranger, but you can see clearer than they can. Not one of them believes in me—not even my godfather. But you—you—" as if instinctively she held out both her hands.

Taking them, he bent over them and lightly kissed them as he had done on the beach, with a grace which was not quite English. Then, flashing a glance round the room, he selected the least aggressively uncomfortable chair, and made her sit down in it. Leaning against the piano, in such an attitude that the whole droop of her posture and the hands which lay in her lap were clearly visible as he looked down upon her, he said:

"I feel so ashamed to make you sit here and exert yourself to talk to a stranger when you are feeling so keenly. But I want you to help me by trying to remember certain incidents as clearly as you can. Will you try?"

"I will do anything you tell me."

"That is very good of you. Now forgive my hurrying you so, and plunging so abruptly into the midst of my subject, but my time is short—"

She started.

"Are you going away?"

A rush of most unwonted color mounted to Percivale's cheeks, and he hesitated a moment before his reply.

"No; not going till your innocence is established; but the inquest will be held here the day after to-morrow, and I want to be in a position to show you blameless by then."

She lifted her head and smiled up at him.

"You can do it. I believe you could do *anything*," she said, softly.

He looked at her steadily as he replied,

"It does seem at this moment as though a great deal were possible."

There was an eloquent pause, during which the hall clock struck loudly. Its sound roused Percivale, and he began his questioning.

"First of all, I want to know exactly what happened during your walk with your brother yesterday. Can you remember, and will you tell me carefully, what time you started, where you went, and how you parted? For all these things are of great importance."

"Yes; I will tell you exactly what happened. It was about half-past-two o'clock when my aunts said I was to go out with Godfrey. I did not want to go—for two reasons, both of which I will tell you. The first was that I was feeling very miserable because I had just said good-bye to my friends the Allonbys, who were gone to London— —"

"You will forgive me interrupting you one moment," he said, in a very still voice, and with a fixed expression, "but Mrs. Orton this morning said that you were going to be married. May I ask if you are engaged to Mr. Allonby, because if so I think he ought to be telegraphed for—it would not be my place—I am not privileged— —"

He broke off and waited. After a moment she said,

"I am not engaged to Mr. Allonby."

"Thank you. I hope you did not think I was unnecessarily curious?"

"No."

"And now to continue. What other reason had you for not wishing to go out with Godfrey?"

"He had been very rude a fortnight before, and Mr. Allonby punished him. I knew he would try to revenge himself on me as soon as Mr. Allonby was gone—he said so."

"Exactly; but you went?"

"Yes, I was obliged to go. So we started along the Quarry Road, and when we got some way we began to quarrel. I had a book with me that Mr. Allonby had given me, and Godfrey tried to take it away. I would not let him, and he grew very angry. I held it above my head, and he sprung up and hung on me, and managed somehow to get his foot underneath mine, so that I slipped on the road, and he got the book. I was feeling very low-spirited, and so weary of his tiresome ways that I began to cry. We were on the road leading to the cliff from the quarries, close to the cottage where Mrs. Parker lives. She has a son called Saul who is an idiot, and he hates Godfrey, because he used to set his bull-dog at him. The other day Saul threw a stone at Godfrey from behind a tree, and hit his leg, and so Godfrey was determined to pay him out. When he saw the cottage it reminded him of this, so he said he should run home to the stable-yard, and get Venom, his dog. He turned back, and ran along the road towards home, and I was too tired and too unhappy to follow him. I thought I would give him the slip, so I just went off and hid myself in the woods by Boveney Hollow. I sat in the woods and cried for a long time, and at last the wind had risen so, and the sky looked so black and threatening, that I was frightened, and I guessed that Godfrey had gone home by that time, so I came out of the woods by the shortest way, and when I reached the high-road I met Mr. Fowler and Mr. Cranmer, so I went home with them."

"And that was the last you saw of your brother?"

"Yes."

"He ran home to fetch his dog, in order to set it at Saul Parker the idiot?"

"Yes. He had done it before. He said it was to teach Saul to behave himself; for you know poor Saul doesn't know any manners, and he is always rude to strangers, he hates them so. If he so much as sees the back of a person he does not know, he begins to scream with rage."

"Is he—this idiot—considered dangerous?"

"Dangerous? Oh, no, I think he is quite gentle, unless you tease him. At least, I do remember Clara Battishill saying that he was growing cruel. He is a big boy. Mr. Fowler tried to persuade his mother to let him go to a home, where they would teach him to occupy himself; but she cried so bitterly at the idea of losing him; he is all she has to love."

Mr. Percivale was silent; his eyes perused the pattern of the worn carpet.

Furtively Elsa lifted her eyelids, and critically examined his face. A high, noble-looking head, the eyes of a dreamer, the chin of a poet, the mouth of a man both resolute and pure.

His fair moustache did not obscure the firm sweet line between the lips; something there was about him which did not belong to the nineteenth century; an atmosphere of lofty purpose and ideal simplicity. His expression was quite unlike anything one is accustomed to see. There was no cynicism, no spite, no half-amused, half-bored tolerance of a trivial world—none of that air of being exactly equipped for the circumstances in which he found himself, which belonged so completely to Claud Cranmer.

This was a nature quite apart from its surroundings—a nature which had formed an ideal, and would never mingle but with the realization of this ideal. For this man the chances of happiness were terribly few; he could never adapt himself, never consent to put up with anything lower or less than he had dreamed of. If by the mysterious workings of fate he could meet and win a woman whose soul was as pure, whose standard as lofty as his own, he would enjoy a happiness undreamed of here below by the many thousands who soar not above mediocrity; but if—if, as was so terribly probable, he should make a mistake; if, after all, he took Leah instead of Rachel, he would touch a depth of misery and despair equally unknown to the generality of mankind. For him existed no possibility of compromise; his one hope of felicity rested upon the simple accident of whom he should fall in love with. And, by a strange paradox, the very loftiness of his nature and singleness of his mind rendered him far less capable of forming a true judgment than a man like Claud, who had "dipped in life's struggle and out again," had many times

"... tried in a crucible
To what 'speeches like gold' were reducible,
And found that the bravest prove copper."

It seems a necessity, more or less, to judge human nature from one's own standpoint; and not only the bent of his mind, but the circumstances of his life, had held Percivale always aloof from the hurrying rush of modern society, from intrigue, or deceptions, or, in fact, from what is called knowledge of the world in any form.

Hence the statuesque simplicity of his expression. Meanness, passion, competition were words of which he understood the meaning but had never felt the force. His face was like Thorwaldsen's sculptures—chivalrous, calm, steadfast.

The reddish gold of his soft hair and short beard, the deep violet blue of his deep-set eyes, and the delicate character of his profile were all in harmony with this idea. He was artistic and picturesque with the unconsciousness of a by-gone age, not with the studied straining after effect which obtains to-day.

He did not feel Elsa's eyes as they studied him so intently and so ignorantly. Not one of the characteristics above indicated was visible to the girl; she only wondered how he could be so handsome and so interesting with that strange-colored hair; and how old he was; and what he thought of her; and whether he would be able to cleave through the terrible net of horror and suspicion and fear which was drawing so closely round her.

At last he raised his head, met her fixed regard, and, meeting it, smiled.

"You have told me just what I wanted—what I hoped to hear," said he. "Now I must take leave for the present. I shall come up the first thing to-morrow morning to report progress."

CHAPTER XXIX

The pride
Of the day—my Swan—that a first fleck's fall
On her wonder of white must unswan, undo!
The Worst of It.

It was evening when Percivale left Edge Willoughby, and walked slowly down the terrace, accompanied by dear little Miss Fanny, who had undertaken to show him the stile leading to the foot-path which was the nearest way to the quarries.

Jackie, the chough, was strutting along the gravel in much self-importance, his body all sideways, his bright eye fixed on the stranger, and uttering his unmusical cry of, "Jack-ee! Jack-ee!"

The young man paused, bent down, and caressed the bird, spite of the formidable-looking orange beak.

"What a queer old chap!" he said.

"Yes, he is quite a pet. Elsa is very fond of him," said Miss Fanny, seizing as eagerly as he had done on any topic of conversation which was not too heavily charged with emotion to be possible.

Of the terrible issues so near at hand neither dared to speak. As if nothing more unusual than an afternoon call had transpired, Percivale asked of Jacky's age and extraction, learned that he was a Cornishman by birth, and of eccentric disposition, and so travelled safely along the wide gravel-walk, on one side of which the garden rose abruptly up, whilst on the other it sloped as suddenly down, losing itself in a maze of chrysanthemums, gooseberry-bushes, potatoes, and scarlet-runners, till a tall thorn hedge intervened to separate the garden from the cornfield, where the "mows" lay scattered about in every direction, dispersed and driven by the tempest of last night.

So they gained the stile, and here Miss Fanny paused.

"If you go down the hill by the foot-path, you will come out on the main road," she said, pointing with her dear little fat finger.

"Thank you. Mr. Cranmer will meet me somewhere on the road—he said he would. I—I shall see you again as soon as—directly—as I said to your sister," stammered the young man, in an unfinished, fragmentary way.

He took her hand, with the graceful gravity which characterized all his greetings of women.

"Thank you," he said again, and, lifting his cap, vaulted over the stile, and walked rapidly down the foot-path.

Miss Fanny gazed after him through a mist of tears, which she presently wiped away from her fresh cheeks, and trotted back to the terrace with an expression not devoid of hope.

Her pigeons flew round her; they knew that it was past feeding-time. The gleaming wings flashed and circled in the light, and presently the gravel was covered with the pretty, strutting things, nodding their sheeny necks, and chuckling softly to each other.

"Jack-ee! Jack-ee!" screamed the chough, discordantly, rushing in among their ranks, and routing them.

"Jackie! Come here, you naughty bird!" cried Miss Fanny, interposing for the protection of her pets. "There! there! Go along, do! Go along, do!... I really don't know how it is—I do feel that I place such confidence in that young man! Quite a stranger, too! Very odd! But I feel as though a special Providence had sent that yacht our way to-day. It seems as though it had been sent purposely—it really does. Somehow, to-night, I feel as if help were near. No power can restore poor dear Godfrey, that's true; but we may save Elsa, I do hope and trust."

Claud was leaning over the low stone wall of the highroad, when a touch on the shoulder roused him, and, looking up, he met Percivale's collected gaze.

"Now, quick!" was all Percivale said; and, in a moment, both young men were hurrying along the Quarry Road as fast as their legs would carry them.

They only spoke once; and then it was Claud who broke the silence.

"Fowler thinks it hopeless—that you are altogether on a wrong track," he said.

"We shall see," was the response, in a tense voice which told of highly-strung nerves.

Claud thought of his last journey along that road, staggering blindly in darkness and rain, with the screaming wind and thundering sea in his ears. Last night! Could it be only last night? A thousand years seemed to have elapsed since then. Life, just now, seemed made up of crisis; and he railed at himself for being hatefully heartless, because he could not help a certain feeling of excitement, which was almost like pleasure, in anticipating the *dénouement* of the affair.

A growing admiration for the strange owner of the *Swan* was his dominant sensation. There was a light of purpose in Percivale's eye, an air of conviction about his whole manner, which could not fail to influence his companion.

The feelings of both young men were at a high pitch as they paused before the door of Mrs. Parker's somewhat remote cottage, and knocked. The woman opened the door and looked at her visitors in astonishment. One glance at her was enough to gauge her character in an instant. She was what country people call a "poor thing." Her expression was that of meek folly, and she wore a perpetual air of apology. Her red-rimmed, indefinite eyes suggested a perennial flow of tears, ready at the shortest notice, and her weak fingers fumbled at her untidy throat in fruitless efforts to hold together a dilapidated brown silk handkerchief which had become unfastened.

"Good evening, gentlemen," she said, "what can I do for you?"

Her air was mildly surprised.

"We called in," said Claud, who was not unknown to her, "to ask if you've heard the awful news about the discovery on the cliffs this morning?"

"Lord, no! She had heard never a word of it—nobody never took no trouble to look in and tell her any bit o' news as might be going; she might as well be dead and buried, for all the comfort she ever got out of *her* life," grumbled she, plaintively.

Even at this juncture, Claud could not refrain from a cynical reflection on womanhood, as, in the person of the widow Parker, it calmly reckoned the news of a murder among the comforts of life.

"Your son Saul—where is he? Doesn't he bring you the news?" asked he.

"Lord no! not he! he mostly forgets it all on the way home, he don't keep nothing in his head for more than three minutes at a stretch. An' he ain't been outside the place to-day, for I've had a awful night with him," whined Mrs. Parker, sitting down on a chair and lifting a coal-black pocket-handkerchief to her eyes.

"What, another fit?" asked Claud.

"He was out last night in all that gale, if you'll believe me, sir. What he was after passes me, an' I set an' set awaitin' for him, and a-putting out my bit o' fire by opening the door, when the wind come in fit to blind yer, an' at last in he come, with every thread on him drippin' wet, and what he'd been after Lord knows, for not a word would he say but to call for his supper, and afore he'd 'ardly swallowed three mouthfuls he was took——"

"Took?" put in Percivale, sharply.

The widow paused, with her last pair of tears unwiped on her cheeks, and stared at him.

"With a fit, sir—he suffers from fits, my poor boy do," she said. "*Epiplexy* the doctor do call it, and, whatever it is, it's a nasty thing to suffer with. It makes him sorft, poor lad, and the other chaps laughs at him, and it's very hard on him, for you see, now he's growin' up, he feels it. I ain't a Devonshire woman myself—I'm from London, I am, and I do say these Devonshire lads are a sight deal too rough and rude. When they was all little together, I could cuff them as hurt him, but they're too big for that now."

There was no stopping her tongue. Poor soul! she led a lonely life, for her peevishness alienated her neighbors, who did not approve of the censure their manners and customs met with at her hands. She never could talk for five minutes to anyone without insisting on her London origin; and, as a result, it was but rarely that she could get an audience at all.

The flood-gates of her eloquence were now opened, and she poured forth a lengthy string of grievances.

"It's terrible hard on a woman like me, as never was strong at the best of times, to be left a widder with a boy like that on my hands! He's a head taller than 'is mother, and strong—bless yer! He could knock either o' you gentlemen down and think nothing of it, and you may think if he's easy to manage when he's took with his fits!"

"You should send him away," said Claud, gravely. "Have you never thought that, if he is so strong, he might do somebody some harm in a fit of temper?"

The woman looked attentive.

"Well," she said, "I can't say I've ever give it much of a thought; but maybe you're right. But oh!" with a fresh access of tears, "I do call it hard to separate a poor widder from 'er only son! I do call it hard!" She set herself afresh to wipe her eyes, with shaking hands, reiterating her inconsistent complainings about the difficulties of managing Saul, and the cruelty of suggesting a separation; when suddenly, ceasing her whining and looking up, she said, "But you ain't told me the bit o' news, yet, have yer?"

"You haven't given us much chance, my good woman," said Mr. Percivale. "The news is that young Mr. Godfrey Brabourne was found dead out on the cliffs this morning."

As the words left his lips, a shuffling, thudding sound was heard, a door at the back of the little room was pushed open, and there stood Saul, leaning against the wall, attired merely in his shirt and trousers, the former open at the throat. His feet were bare, his thick yellow hair was matted, his cheeks were rosy and flushed; altogether he wore the look of having just that moment awakened from sleep.

His great eyes, of Devon blue, looked out from beneath the tangled waves of hair with a shy smile. He recognised Claud, but, when his gaze fell on Percivale, his whole face changed. A look of fear and repulsion came over him—he uttered a hoarse cry or rather bellow, and, turning away, darted down a small dark passage and was lost to view.

"There now! Did you ever!" cried his parent, indignantly. "Lord! what a fool the lad is! That's for nothing in life but because he seen you—" addressing Percivale, "and now he's gone to his hole, and nothing'll bring him out again perhaps for five or six hours, and nothing on him but his shirt and breeches! Oh, dear, dear, he'll kill me afore long, I'm blest if he won't!"

"What do you mean by his hole?" asked Percivale.

"It's a wood-shed as he's very partial to, an' hides all his treasures an' rubbish in there, out o' my reach. For it's very dark in there, and I can't get in very well, at least 'twouldn't be no use if I could, because I couldn't drive him out. I can't do nothing with him, when he's contrairy, and that's the truth, gentlemen."

"But is it impossible to get into the woodshed?" continued Percivale, holding her to her point with a patience that made Claud marvel.

"No, sir, but he's piled up the wood till you can only crawl in, and then as likely as not he'll hit you over the head," returned Mrs. Parker, encouragingly; "and it's that dark you can't see nothing when you *are* in, so it's no sense to try, as I can see."

"Why on earth don't you nail the place up when he's out, so that he *can't* get in?" cried Claud, irritated beyond measure at her stupidity.

"Well, I can't say I ever thought o' that," naively admitted the poor woman.

"You are afraid Saul will take a chill if he stays there now?" interrogated Percivale.

"I'm dead certain he will, sir!"

"Very well, I'll go and fetch him out for you."

"It ain't a bit o' use, sir," she cried, eagerly, "he'll never stir for you. He's mortal feared o' strange folks."

"Never fear, I shall manage him," was the placid reply. "Give me, a candle, will you?"

He took the light in his hand, and followed the woman through the gloomy back regions of the little cottage to the wood-shed, the doorway of which was, as she had stated, barricaded with logs, in a sort of arch, so that only the lower half of it was practicable.

"Saul! Are you in there?" cried his mother, shrilly.

An idiotic gurgle of laughter, and a slight rustling, assured them of the fact.

"If I push over this barricade, shall I hurt him?" asked Percivale.

"No, sir, no—there's plenty of space beyond."

"Here goes then," he answered; and placing his shoulder to the logs, handing the light to Claud, and getting a firm hold with his feet, he gave a vigorous heave, and the logs rolled clattering down, and about the shed.

There was a scream from Saul, so loud and piercing that both young men thought he must be hurt. Snatching the candle, Percivale hurried in, over the prostrate defences. Saul was standing back against the wall, as far as he could get away, niched into a corner, his face hidden in his arms.

"Come, Saul, my boy—come out of this dark place," said the intruder, in kindly tones. "Come—look at me—what is there to be afraid of?"

The boy removed his screening arm from before his eyes with the pretty coquetry of a shy baby. He had apparently forgotten his rage, for he laughed—a low, chuckling laugh—and fixed his look appealingly on the stranger.

"What made you run away—eh?" asked Percivale, gently.

But no answer could be extorted from Saul. He would only laugh, hide his face, and peep again, with coy looks, from under his long lashes.

Percivale flashed a look round him, and decided on making a venture to arouse some consciousness. By the light of the candle he held, every line of the lad's face was distinctly visible. Outside, Mrs. Parker was talking too volubly to Claud to hear what he might say.

"Saul," he said, "where is Master Godfrey?"

For a moment a spasm of terror crossed the beautiful face—a look which somehow suggested the dim return of intelligence once possessed; for it seemed evident that Saul had not always been absolutely idiotic, but that what brain he had had gradually been destroyed by epilepsy. His eyes dwelt with a look of speculation on those of his questioner, and his lips parted as if an answer were forced from him.

"Out there!" he whispered.

"What, out on the cliffs?"

He nodded.

"Is he dead—is Master Godfrey dead?" said Percivale, still keeping his eyes fixed on his by a strong effort of will.

Saul nodded again.

"Dead," he said, "quite dead! Naughty boy!"

CHAPTER XXX

East, west,
North, south I looked. The lie was dead
And damned, and Truth stood up instead.
Count Gismond.

Henry Fowler came out of the stables with heavy gait, and face from which the genial curves had fled. To-night you saw him in all his native plainness,—his leaden-colored eyes, unredeemed by the steady beam of cheery benevolence which usually dwelt there—his roughly-cut, ill-formed features, unsoftened by the suggestion of kindly peace which was their wonted expression.

Figuratively speaking, he was smitten to the earth—humbled, abased, as he had never dreamed he could be. No room was in his mind for doubt. He saw, as he imagined, only too plainly, the whole of the tragedy on the cliffs—saw Elsa's very attitude and expression as, goaded to fury by the impudence of the boy, she had dealt him a wild, blind blow, the outcome of weeks and weeks of pent-up rage and dislike.

Had she only told him, at once! Had she, on meeting him and Claud in the lane, only seized him, clung to him, cried for help and dragged him to the rescue, even though too late. But no! Her first impulse had been to hide what she had done. It was so fatally of a piece with his idea of her character. What to do—how to face the Misses Willoughby he could not tell.

Once before—more than twenty years ago now—his life had been laid in ruins at his feet by the news of Alice Willoughby's engagement to Colonel Brabourne. Now, by Alice's child, this second bitter blow descended on the head of him who had borne the first so well and uncomplainingly.

His one interest in life centred in Elsa Brabourne. The morning's intelligence had seemed to paralyse him. Like a man smitten suddenly in the face, he was left breathless—unable to rally or to fix on any plan of action.

He was just returned from Philmouth, where he had been to interview the coroner and to make what arrangements were necessary. But, now that it was done, he could not remember whether he had done it or not. The whole drive there and back was a confused blur in his mind—he wondered whether he had managed to conduct himself rationally, to explain himself adequately. Before his eyes, as plainly as if he saw it still, was the picture of a child's pallid face, peaked and grey with death, dashed here and there with blood, and in its expression horridly, fatally resembling Elsa.

Turn where he would, he saw it, with the lips discolored, the large eyes wide open, the little childish hands clenched in the agony of the sudden fruitless wrestle with death.

"If she saw it," he repeated to himself, "if she saw it, would it not have sent her mad? So young as she is—she has never seen death! Oh, merciful God, is it possible she could have looked at him and kept her reason?"

It was dark: the moon had not yet risen above the black hillside, and in the stables everything was very still. George the groom moved to and fro with a stable lantern in the harness-room above, and the shaft of light which gleamed down the staircase was the only light there was. George knew his master was in trouble, and longed to comfort him. Mr. Fowler was one of those who are always liked, and always well served by their inferiors. Everything about his house and estate was in excellent order. He never raised his voice, but his commands were always instantly obeyed.

Here, in the stable, everything was trim and fresh, smelling of new-mown hay. Dart, the pretty little black mare, knowing that her master was somewhere near, turned her head wistfully to seek him. But he saw and heard nothing of his surroundings. In fancy, he was standing on the cliff, in the wind and sunshine, looking down upon a child's corpse.

He felt as though he must suffocate.

Rousing himself, he groped towards the door, pushed it open, and let the night air fan him. The rush of the brook through the garden sounded in his ears. Down, away across the valley, was the dark water in the bay, the hulk of the yacht dimly discernible through the faint mist. A wild idea crossed his mind as to whether it might not be possible to take Elsa secretly on board of the *Swan*, weigh anchor in the night, and carry away the girl to some other land, where a home might be made for her. A moment's reflection served to show the absurdity of such a scheme, and he laughed bitterly to himself as he realised the impossibility of casting such a record behind in the girl's life, and starting fresh again.

Oh, to be able to go back for twenty-four hours! to be again, if but for one minute, the happy man he was when he walked at Claud's side through the storm to Brent. If the intervening minutes could be wiped out, as one wipes a child's sum from a slate, with a wet sponge!

No use, no use, to cry out against the inevitable. Somehow or another, this horror which had come upon him must be lived through. He must not only bear it, but help others to bear it too.

Slowly emerging from the stable, he shut the door behind him with a click; and, as he did so, he became aware of a sound of hurrying footsteps, of some one coming fast over the wooden bridge which spanned the brook, and making for the house with all speed.

It was Claud, and there was in his manner such unusual velocity and vehemence that Mr. Fowler started forward, and ran hastily after him.

They met in the hall. Claud had just flung the door wide, and was making the rafters ring with cries of, "Fowler! Fowler, I say!" when the owner of the name rushed in with white face and eager eyes, expecting he knew not what.

Claud was in such a state as his host had never before witnessed; his hat was off, his cheeks glowing, his collar and tie awry, his usually immaculate hair all a standing mass of fluff, blown hither and thither by the wind, and his quiet eyes like two stars in their brilliancy and excitement.

"Cranmer, my good fellow, what is it?" faltered Henry.

"What is it? Why, the best news you ever heard in all your life! That extraordinary fellow Percivale has done the whole thing! There's not a doubt of it. Saul Parker was the assailant of Allonby and the murderer of poor little Godfrey! The whole thing is as clear as daylight!" Henry put out a hand uncertainly, as if to feel for the support of the wall. Claud darted to him, took the hand, and placed it on his own shoulder instead. "Look up, old man," he said, unable to keep his lips from smiles, his eyes from dancing. "All this is true as Gospel that I'm telling you."

Henry cleared his throat once or twice. Then—

"It can't be," he said, huskily, "it can't be. It's preposterous. What proof have you?"

"The proof of Saul's coat and waistcoat soaked in blood—the proof of Godfrey's pocket-handkerchief steeped also in blood, rolled into a ball in the pocket of his jacket; and, last of all, what do you think, my friend? The proof of Mrs. Clapp's pudding-basin, tied up in the original and genuine blue handkerchief!"

The face of agitation which Mr. Fowler turned to the speaker was pitiful to see.

"You—you mean this," he said speaking thickly, like a drunken man; "you would never jest on such a subject—eh, lad?"

The Tree Of Knowledge A Novel | 229

"Jest? Is it likely? Do I look as if I were jesting? I can tell you I don't feel so. I couldn't put on that pace for a jest. My throat is as sore as if I were sickening for scarlet fever, and my heart feels as if it would burst through my ribs. I ran—all the way—from Parker's cottage—to tell you about it."

Henry was grasping him by both shoulders now, and clinging to him as if the floor were unsteady beneath his feet.

"You ran to tell me," he repeated, mechanically—"to tell me—what? Claud, if this is true, it means life to me—life to those good women yonder—it means *salvation* for her, for my poor little girl, for Elsa!"

His forehead sank on his outstretched arm, and his broad shoulders quivered.

Claud softly patted his back, his own bright face all alight with unselfish gladness.

"It's all true," he said, "true beyond your power to disbelieve. That Percivale is a wonderful fellow. Once he struck the scent, he stuck to it like a sleuth-hound. Every bit of evidence tallies exactly. The whole thing is as clear as daylight. All I marvel at now is that Saul Parker has been allowed to be at large for so long—how it was that nobody insisted on his being shut up."

"But I never knew he was really dangerous," said Henry. "Such a thing as a murderous attack, I mean—I knew that lately he had taken to throwing stones, and I told him the other day that I should flog him if I found it out again. He has sense enough to know what he is not to do—that is what makes him so difficult to deal with. But that he should attempt murder!"

"I remember him so well, in the Battishills' kitchen, the day he nearly did for poor Allonby," said Claud. "He must have hidden his pudding-basin, after eating the contents, somewhere in a hedge, and walked, calmly smiling, up to the farm, immediately after his first attempt at slaughter. Ugh! It's a grisly thought, isn't it, that we all have been walking calmly about all this summer with such a sword of Damocles over our heads. Why, those girls—the Miss Allonbys—he might have attacked them at any moment; they were all strangers."

"Yes, but they had spoken to him, and been kind to him. Poor Godfrey owes his fate to his own malignity, I am afraid," said Henry, turning away with a heavy sigh. He passed his hand over his brow as if to clear it, and then, lifting his eyes to Claud's, smiled for the first time in many hours. "I feel as if you had waked me out of a nightmare," he said—"a horror that was overwhelming—that shut out everything, even hope ... and God. Now that it is over, I wonder how I could have brought myself to believe such a thing of her." He spoke slowly, and at intervals, as each thought occurred to him. "Poor child! poor slandered child! Claud, she must know it to-night. We must save her so many hours of suffering—we must tell her now. Where is Mr. Percivale?"

"He is gone there—straight—to Edge. I parted from him at the cross-roads, and ran up here for you."

"He has every right to be first," faltered Henry. "Will anything I can do for Elsa ever atone for the wrong of my unjust suspicion? God pardon me! I was *sure* she was guilty."

"You had strong grounds."

"I never dreamed of connecting it in any way with poor Allonby's disaster. I never thought of it in connection with anything else at all. It simply seemed to flare out upon me like a conflagration, blotting out everything else in the world. It numbed my faculties."

"I know it did. Never mind, now,. It is all right, the darkness is over past, the horror is slain. Come, shall we go to Edge?"

"Yes, Claud. God bless you, my boy—you thought of me—you would not go on without me. We must be close friends after this, all our lives."

"We shall—I hope and believe."

The young man set the door wide. The lamp from the hall streamed out into the quiet night. The soft rustling of the trees mingled with the rushing of the falling brook. Walking down the grassy slope, they came upon the bridge. A silent, solitary figure stood upon it, leaning upon the parapet and gazing down upon the unseen but vocal waters as they hurried past.

"Percivale!" said Claud, with a start.

"Yes." He roused himself, and answered as tranquilly as if that day had passed in the most ordinary routine. "I thought it was unfair to steal a march upon you both, so I followed you here, and waited."

"Then you have not been to Edge?"

"Not yet."

Without another word they set off walking as fast as they could. Henry longed for words to thank and bless the young man at his side; but the tongue does not always obey the will, and he found none.

The dew was heavy on the pastures; the last remnants of wind were dropping down to sleep. Life and the world seemed now as full of repose as this morning they had been instinct with tragedy, and with rapid, terrifying motion. No glimmer in any of the cottages, no moon to light the rich purple recesses of darkness which enveloped the sea. Henry led the way among the winding foot-paths—a way which he could have trodden blindfold—the others followed in complete silence.

As they neared the house, a solitary light appeared,—it was in Miss Ellen's window.

Henry threw some pebbles up at the glass, and presently the pane was opened, and the invalid appeared. She was still quite dressed.

"Let us in, Miss Ellen," said Mr. Fowler, in subdued accents. "Let us in—we could not rest till morning. Mr. Percivale has news for you."

"One moment—I will send some one down to you."

She disappeared, and for several silent minutes they waited in the porch. A great bush of lemon-scented verbena grew there. Claud used to pull a leaf of it and crush it in his hand whenever he came in or out. Now, in the still night, the strong fragrance reeked from it, and to each of the three men waiting there, that scent always afterwards recalled that scene.

The bolts were drawn at last, and there stood Jane Gollop, in night attire of the most wondrous aspect.

"Come in, gentlemen," said she, in subdued accents and a husky voice which told of bitter weeping. "You must come upstairs into Miss Willoughby's room, if you wish to see her; as you know, she can't come down to you. Will you kindly tread very softly, please?"

"I'll wait down here for you two," whispered Claud.

"No, no, my boy. Come up with me," returned Mr. Fowler, firmly.

In single file they followed Jane up the staircase, in a silence broken only by the ticking of the great clock on the stairs.

Miss Ellen sat upright on her sofa, awaiting them. As they entered, she held up a warning finger, and said, "Hush!"

Following the direction of her eyes, they noticed that a screen had been drawn round the bed, hiding it from view. They waited, and so silent were they, that from behind this screen a low, regular breathing was audible.

Miss Willoughby looked at her visitors with a sort of defiance—a noble defiance—on her worn face. Her eyes were luminous and steadfast.

"I don't know what is your errand here to-night," she said, speaking scarcely above a whisper,—"something very important, I feel sure; but, before any of you speak one word, I have something to say, and something to show you. Henry Fowler, I believe we are wronging Elaine."

He started, and turned towards her.

"Yes; I feel sure we are wronging her—so sure, that it amounts, with me, to a moral conviction of her innocence. I want to tell you, all three, before a word has been said—before anything is proved either way—that I am confident that my niece is altogether innocent. I would say the same if a jury had condemned her to death. She had no share in this crime. I am glad you are all here—I will take your opinion. Henry, fold back the screen, as noiselessly as possible, and tell me, all of you, if that sleep is the sleep of conscious guilt."

In a dead silence Henry went forward, and moved away the screen.

Stretched on the bed lay Elsa, all her golden shower of hair loose, and streaming over the pillows. She wore a pale blue wrapper, and Miss Ellen had thrown a shawl across her feet to prevent her taking a chill. The girl's whole attitude was that of weariness, and profound, healthy, natural repose. The soft, warm rose of sleep was on each cheek, the black-fringed lids hid the large eyes, the breathing was as regular as that of an infant, and the expression exquisitely sweet.

CHAPTER XXXI

He looked,
Ocean and earth, the solid frame of earth
And ocean's liquid mass beneath him lay
In gladness and deep joy. The clouds were touched,
And in their silent faces did he read
Unutterable love....
No thanks he breathed, he proffered no request;
Rapt with still communion that transcends
The imperfect offices of prayer and praise,
His mind was a thanksgiving to the Power
That made him; it was blessedness and love!
The Excursion.

Spell-bound, the three gentlemen stood looking at the sleeping girl, till the pause was broken by Miss Ellen.

"Well?" she said, "what do you think?"

Henry Fowler opened his lips to speak, but closed them again, with a glance at Percivale.

The glance was unheeded, the young man was standing with a look on his face which, for some inexplicable reason, made Henry's heart leap in his side. So might Adam have looked on Eve when first he saw her sleeping—a look of intense admiration, mixed with a reverence that was almost worship. He seems to have forgotten everything but the fact that he stood there, by a wonderful chance, gazing at this consecrated girlish slumber.

Claud, who stood next him, at last put out his hand, and lightly touched his arm. He started.

"Will you tell Miss Willoughby?" whispered Claud.

He shook his head.

"Let Mr. Fowler tell her," he replied, gently.

"You have not answered my question—do you believe in her innocence?" said Miss Ellen, appealing to all three.

"We know she is innocent, dear Miss Ellen. Mr. Percivale has proved it."

It was too much; she uttered a cry, and, at the cry, Elsa started from sleep, and sat upright, pushing back her cloudy hair, and in speechless bewilderment at finding herself in her aunt's room, still half dressed, and in presence of three gentlemen. The lovely crimson flooded her face as she tried to collect her thoughts, and to rise.

A scene of some confusion ensued.

Miss Ellen, in her agitation, was trying to ask for an explanation, with her voice dissolved in tears. Elsa, springing from the bed, moved towards her, still half-awake, vaguely troubled—foreseeing some fresh catastrophe; and then Mr. Fowler caught her in his arms, kissing her and somewhat incoherently imploring her to forgive him, while Percivale stood at a little distance, speaking only with his eyes. And those eyes set the girl's heart throbbing and raised a wild tumult in her. So by degrees everything was explained, nobody exactly knew how; but, in the course of half-an-hour, Elsa knew that she was saved, and that she owed her salvation solely to him who stood before her, with his head lowered, and the lamplight gilding the soft, downy, curling mass of his hair. They did not stay long. It was he who hurried them away, that they might not break in too far on the girl's rest.

Miss Willoughby could hardly let him go. Something about this young man's whole appearance and manner appealed wonderfully to her sympathies. She held his hand long in hers, looking at him with eyes swimming in grateful tears.

"You know," he said, with a smile, "you will insist on so greatly exaggerating what I have done; it was quite simple and obvious; I merely set on foot an investigation."

"It may have been simple and obvious, but it never occurred to anybody but you," said Claud, bluntly.

"No; because you were all biassed. I told you so. I am very sorry for that poor mother—for Mrs. Parker. I shall go to her early next morning. It was pitiful to see her. She was so utterly without the least suspicion of what I was driving at, that I felt like a traitor, worming myself into her confidence. Good-night, Miss Brabourne. You will sleep again, I hope."

"I don't know, I don't feel the least bit sleepy," said Elsa, feverishly; "and it is nearly morning now, you know."

Henry started.

"Is it so late? I had no idea. Come, we must be off at once."

Outside, the blackness of the night was just decreasing. The clouds which had gathered in the evening were rolling away, leaving gaps full of pallid stars. A chill cold pierced the limbs, and the heavy dew of autumn bathed all the vegetation.

"You will come home with us, of course?" said Mr. Fowler to Percivale.

"No, thanks, I can't. I must go aboard my *Swan*. The men are waiting for me on the shore."

"All this time? Are you sure?"

"Quite sure. Good-night."

"Nay, nay; we'll see you down to the beach. Your crew may have grown tired of waiting, in which case you must come to Lower House."

They walked on for some time indulging in desultory conversation, when suddenly Henry remarked to Claud,

"Poor Allonby ought to know of this."

Percivale turned towards him, and looked searchingly at him. It was light enough for them to see each other's faces now.

"There is no engagement between Mr. Allonby and Miss Brabourne?" he asked.

"No, none. I see more than ever now how wise I was to refuse to allow it. He is a good fellow, but she did not really care for him—she does not know what love means—she had never met a young man till this summer. I told him he must give her time. Personally I like him. He has no money and has no prospects, but I do not think he is a fortune-hunter. Let her go through the fire of a year in London, and find out what her tastes and inclinations really are."

Percivale listened to all this with a rivetted attention, but made no reply; and now they were on the beach, their steps crunching upon the shingle.

A seaman stood, with his broad back turned to them, looking out over the smooth, leaden expanse of sea. In the boat a second man was fast asleep. Out in the bay, a lamp glimmered, showing the graceful shadowy outline of the yacht.

"Müller!" said Percivale.

The man turned at once. His master addressed him in German, in a glad voice which left little doubt as to the tidings he was relating. A broad grin gradually broke over the man's face, and he waved his cap ecstatically, shouting hurrah! Then he ran to rouse his companion, who was soon acquainted with the joyful news, and a grand shaking of hands all round took place. Then Percivale, taking leave of Henry and Claud, stepped into the boat, and the keel grated on the beach as it slipped into the chill, steely colored waters. The two on the beach stood together, watching as the oars dipped, and the waves broke softly. It was a sight worth watching, for a marvellous change was coming over the world, a change so mysterious, so exciting, so full of beauty, that they began to wonder, as all of us have wondered in our time, why they were not oftener awake to see the breaking of the day.

A scarlet flush was rimming the east, and a glow began to creep over the dull sea. Further and further it spread, while everything around took clear and definite form. The cliffs, the landslip, the coastguard station, the shore, all grew out gradually and yet rapidly from the darkness, and every moment the color waxed more bright, and the sky, which had seemed so dense, became translucent and dark blue, while one by one the pale stars went out, extinguished by the rosy-fingered Eos.

A cold fresh breeze whistled by, and Claud shivered as it passed. It reminded him of the sad sighing of old Tithonus, left helpless in the cold regions of the dark, whilst Aurora, warm and blooming, sprang up to meet the sun. Unconsciously to himself, he wished that Wynifred Allonby stood by him to watch that dawn—she would have understood. He could not talk of Tithonus to Henry Fowler. His eye roamed over

"The ever silent spaces of the East,
Far-folded mists, and gleaming halls of morn."

Ah! what was that which shivered like a silver arrow through the dull haze that brooded over the sluggish waters? The mist had become transparent, golden, luminous—such a glory as might any moment break away to disclose the New Jerusalem coming down out of the heaven of heavens.

And now the whole sea was one mass of pearly and rose and amber light, which had not as yet faded into "the light of common day." All was illusion—the infancy of day, the time of fairy-tales, like that childhood of the world when wonders happened, and "Ilion, like a mist, rose into towers."

A slight exclamation from Henry broke his musing, and made him turn his head.

The *Swan* lay motionless, her whiteness warmed and softened by the still mysterious light, till it looked almost like the plumage of the bird whose name she bore. The radiance gleamed on the motionless sails, and shimmered on the sea all round her.

Close to the prow stood Percivale. He had taken off his coat, and looked all white as he stood in the glow. Lifting his hat, he waved it to the watchers on the shore, with a gesture like that of one victorious, and, as he did so, up darted the sun with a leap above the sea, and its first ray shot straight across the sparkling water, to rest on his fair head like a benediction.

CHAPTER XXXII

But most of all would I flee from the cruel madness of love.
Maud.

There was a deep silence between Fowler and Claud as they walked homewards in that dewy autumn dawn. Every moment increased the beauty of the scene through which they walked—the little brooks which continually crossed their path rushed vehemently, swollen with the heavy rain which had fallen on the night of the storm. A balmy feeling was in the still air—a full, ripe feeling of autumn, and even now the beams of the sun were warm. It was going to be a hot day, such a day as shooters love amongst the stubble—such a day as swells the blackberry to a luscious bulk and flavor. Autumn in her warmth and beauty and her panoply of varying moods; not summer back again. She, as Claud had divined, was gone for this year, not to return again; she had died shrieking, in the storm that drove the *Swan* into Brent Bay, and the wild sou'-wester had sung her obsequies.

Is there anything more wonderful in nature than the rich moisture with which an English autumn night will deluge every spray and every leaf and every grass-blade? The pastures this morning were hoary with pearly drops, the beeches and ashes literally drenched with wet, which showered itself on the heads of the two as a light bird clung to the bough and set it swaying. Already the sun was drawing it up like steam from the contented land, making a mist which hid the windings of the valley from their view.

It pleased Claud to imagine that the old earth was at her toilette—had just emerged, dripping, from her matutinal tub. This conceit reminded him of his own tub, for which he had a strong hankering. He did not feel sleepy; a bath and a cigar were all that he desired.

What a strange night it had been!

This particular summer had brought him more new sensations, more experiences than all the rest of his life put together. He felt as if it had altered him, somehow. He was not the same person who had been stopped as he drove along the Philmouth Road by a girl with scared face and streaming hair. Circumstances over which he, apparently, had very little control had forced him to remain here in this valley, and for the space of one summer, look at life from a totally new point of view. He was wondering whether it would last. For the first time he had met men and women who, his inferiors in social standing, were yet his equals in breeding and manners—a man like Henry Fowler, probably a son of the soil, the descendant of generations of farmers, who in chivalry and in purity of mind would put many a Lord Harry of his acquaintance to shame; girls like the Allonbys, who worked for their living, yet in delicacy and refinement—ay, and looks too,—equalled all and surpassed most of the women who formed the "set" he moved in.

He had always imagined himself a leveller at heart, one who ignored social distinctions. Now he had been given opportunity to put his theories into practice; and he found, as most people do, that theory and practice are different in some mysterious way. A struggle was going on in his mind, a struggle of which he was hardly conscious, and of which, had he put it into words, he would have been heartily ashamed. The point at issue was a small one, but, like the proverbial straw, it showed which way the current flowed.

Should he, when in town, call on the Allonbys? That was the point that vexed his mind—the point that was never quite out of sight, even in all the congested excitement of the last two days. As he walked up the meadow footpath to-day, towards Lower House, it was his fixed intention to call upon them; but would that intention hold a month hence, as he strolled down Portland Place towards the parental mansion? That was the trouble. Was this fancy which possessed him now—this fancy for a life in the country, with only a small income and the society of one woman, a fancy only? Or was it something more? Would it wash? Such was the slangy but forcible way in which he expressed it. He could not be sure. His mind was so tossed and disturbed that he felt as though, either way he decided, he must infallibly regret it.

The idea of never seeing Wynifred again was anything but pleasant; the idea of having her always at his side was too vague to be wholly comforting. He believed he should like a middle course—her society when he felt inclined for it, now and then, but no binding down in the matter. And yet he felt dimly that this idea could not be worked, exactly, and this for more than one reason. First, because he felt sure that, if he ever saw her at all, his feelings with regard to her could not remain stationary. He must grow to want her either less or more. Secondly, because his notions of honor were strict, and he felt that, if he, an earl's son, sought out the Allonbys, and appeared bent on the society of Wynifred in particular, it might be unpleasant for her, if nothing came of it.

And then, suddenly, arose the reflection that all this reasoning was based on the supposition that Miss Allonby would have him if she could; a point on which, when he came to consider it, he felt by no means certain.

This was humiliating. As they came to the wicket-gate of Lower House, he finally decided *not* to call at Mansfield Road. He was not going to be made a fool of.

And, even as he made this resolution, arose the wild desire to go and narrate to Wynifred in person the tragic details of the past forty-eight hours. She would appreciate it so.... How her mind would seize on every point, how she would listen to him with that expression of eager interest which he could always awaken on any other subject but that of himself.

This brought his mind to the memory of their conversation about Elaine that afternoon in the boat. He remembered her guarded answers and the unfair way in which he had pressed her to give opinions which she had seemed sorry to have to hold.

"She was wrong about Miss Brabourne," he reflected. "We have all been wrong about her, all misjudged her—even Fowler, who ought to know her so well."

At the date of the above-mentioned conversation, his distrust of Elsa had certainly equalled if not gone beyond Wynifred's; now, the revulsion of feeling was complete.

Nothing in this world so enlists the sympathies of mankind as the victim of an unjust suspicion. Elsa had been under the shadow of the darkest of accusations. She was now declared to be innocent as the day. Claud's heart turned to her, as the heart of anyone calling himself a man must infallibly do. He felt as though his strictly neutral position had been the direst of insults—as though he wanted to kneel at her feet and kiss the hem of her garment. Percivale had not been neutral—he had seen, had known the falseness of the monstrous charge; Claud thought he would like to be in his place now just for four-and-twenty hours. He must be the hero of the moment, as Elsa was the heroine.

And what a heroine! The remembrance of the girl as she lay asleep, framed in her wealth of hair, flashed vividly upon him as they reached the hall door.

"By Jove! She is beautiful!" he said, quite unconscious that he spoke aloud.

Henry paused, with his latch-key in his hand and looked at him with an amused gleam in his eyes.

"What!" said he, "you too!"

Claud started, laughed, flushed deeply, and shook his head.

"Oh, no—not that," he said. "Not that at all. Of course I am a worshipper at the shrine of injured innocence and persecuted beauty—every knight-errant must be that, you know; but no more. I wonder why?"

"You wonder why what?"

"I wonder why I am not madly in love with Miss Brabourne. I fully intended to be, at one time. Why shouldn't I be? I don't understand it."

"I can tell you why, if you care to know," said Henry, smiling quietly to himself as he set open the door, and crossed his threshold.

"Oh, it's of no consequence; thank you," said Claud, with suspicious hurry, and reddening slightly.

"No? Well, perhaps you are wise," was the grave answer. "I find that young people mostly *are* very prudent in these days. It would be quite a relief occasionally to see a man carried away by the strength of his feelings."

Claud looked earnestly at him.

"Don't you think a man ought to have himself well in hand?" he asked.

"Oh, I suppose so; but I am not such a believer in the universality of self-discipline in the young men of the day. They don't control their desires for high play, costly cigars, horses, wine, or enjoyment generally. It is only in the matter of marriage that I have noticed this singular discretion overtakes them. Don't you think one may safely attribute it to another motive than self-control? Caution is often merely a name for selfishness."

"And you think this applies to me?" said Claud, slowly, hanging up his cap with deliberation. "I don't say you're wrong. But it's a nice point, which I should like to get settled for me—which is the least lovable course? To decline to obey the dictates of your heart from motives of prudence, or to follow the lead of your feelings, and so drag down to poverty the woman you profess to love, but in reality only desire to possess?"

"My dear fellow," said Henry, affectionately, "you are taking this too seriously. It's a question one can't well discuss in the abstract, particularly now, when you look as haggard as a ghost and are ready to drop with fatigue. Come, you must really get some rest. It is seven o'clock, I declare, and you have been on your legs for four-and-twenty hours."

Claud did certainly looked fagged now that the full light of high day fell on his pale face. He sat down on the lowest stair, yawned, stretched, and asked, sleepily,

"What time is the inquest?"

"Twelve o'clock. You go straight upstairs, I'll send you your breakfast in a quarter-of-an-hour, and then you are to lie down and get two or three hours' sleep. I'll have you called in time. Come, get up."

Claud remained immovable.

"I wonder who he is," he said at last.

"Whom?"

"Percivale. I should like to know."

"You won't find out by sitting on the staircase, my boy. Come, do go."

"All right—I'm going. Whoever he is, he's a trump, and that's something to know about a fellow."

The "trump" in question had been swimming vigorously in the glittering, lively sea for a quarter-of-an-hour. He emerged from the water invigorated and glowing, with the drops in his red-gold hair.

His crew had a hot breakfast ready for him, to which when dressed he did ample justice; and then giving orders to be waked, and for the boat to be in readiness at eleven, he stretched himself on a sofa which they had brought on deck, and prepared to sleep.

This, however, was more easily said than done. He had never felt more wide awake in his life. Stretched on his back, his arms under his head, the light motion of the blue waters lulling him gently, he lay and thought over all that had happened. The sunshine poured down upon him, and everything was very still. Now and again there was the white flash of a passing bird, shaft-like through the air; now and then a low, guttural German laugh, as his crew sat together discussing this latest adventure of their roving master.

Elaine's face was present to his fancy—so vividly that he had only to close his eyes to see every detail of it. The startled expression, the wistful gaze, the exquisite complexion, the golden shower that framed her.

The words of a favorite poetess of his seemed saying themselves over in his brain:

> "And, if any painter drew her,
> He would take her, unaware,
> With an aureole round the hair."

His heart began to beat loudly at the thought of seeing her again so soon. How beautiful she was! What would she look like if she stood there—just there on the white deck of the *Swan*, with a background of flickering sea and melting air, and a face from which horror and appeal were gone, leaving only the fair graciousness of maidenhood? The thought was delicious. Raising himself on his elbow, he looked around. How pretty his yacht was! How glad he felt that this was so. Was it good enough to bear the pressure of her little foot? Dare he invite her to come on board, even if only for a moment, that he might always hereafter feel the joy of knowing that her presence had been there?

And what when she had gone again—when the few moments were over, and she had departed, taking with her all light from the skies, and all heart from life?

He tried to fancy what his feelings might be, when again the anchor was weighed, and he should see the coast receding behind the swift *Swan*. Could he bear it? That seemed the question. Was it possible that he should bid good-bye to this valley as he had bid good-bye to so many a fair spot before?

He tossed himself impatiently over. He could not do it. No, no, and again no! Was he Vanderdecken, that he should fly from place to place and find no rest? Was this roving so very pleasant, after all?... what had been the charm of it?... And he was certainly very lonely. Doubtless it was a selfish life. He knew he had adopted it for reason good and sufficient—a reason which had not been of his own seeking. But now——

He sprang from his sofa and wandered to and fro on the deck. That restlessness was upon him which comes to all of us, when suddenly we discover that the life which we have hitherto found sufficient is henceforth impossible to us. Looking steadily into the future, facing it squarely, as his manner was, he recoiled for a moment. For he seemed to see, in a single flash, all his life culminating in one end—all the love of his heart fixed upon one object.

How much he required of her? Suppose—suppose——Oh, fate, fate, how many possibilities arose to vex his soul! Suppose she loved Allonby. Suppose she should never be able to care for him—Percivale. And then arose in his heart a mighty and determined will to carry this thing through, and make her love him. At that moment he felt a power surge within him which nothing could withstand. As he stood there on the deck, he was already a conqueror;—he had slain the monster—surely he could win the heart of the maiden, as all doughty champions were wont to do.

The mist was broken away now, and the roof of Edge Willoughby—the roof which sheltered Elsa—was visible to his eyes. He sent an unspoken blessing across the water towards it.

The restlessness began to subside.

He threw himself again on the sofa, and this time the wooing air seemed to creep into his brain and make him drowsy. His thoughts lost their continuity and became scrappy, disjointed, hazy. At last fatigue asserted its empire finally. The lids closed over the steadfast eyes; and the young champion slept, with his cheek pillowed on his arm, and his strong limbs stretched out in a delicious lassitude.

The sailors crept, one after the other, to look upon him as he slept. Old Müller, who had held him in his arms as a baby, gazed down at him with fond triumph. There was little he could not do, this young master of theirs, they proudly thought, and, as Müller noted the noble innocence of the sleeping face, it recalled to him vividly the deathbed of the young mother of eighteen, as she lay broken-hearted, sinking away out of life in far off Littsdoff, a remote village of north Germany. A tear slid down his weather-stained face, as he thought in his sentimental German way how proud that poor child would have been of her son could she have lived to know his future.

CHAPTER XXXIII

The air broke into a mist with bells,
The steeple rocked with the crowd, and cries;
Had I said "Good folks, mere noise repels,
But give me your sun from yonder skies,"
They had answered—"And afterwards what else?"
The Patriot.

The inquest was held at the school-house.

For two hours the excitement in the village had been something tremendous. A huge crowd had assembled outside the school to watch the proceedings, and had recognised the various arrivals with breathless awe. First of all Mr. and Mrs. Orton, in a hired fly from Stanton, the dark and menacing brows of the lady boding ill for all her adversaries. By special request of Mr. Fowler, who had been roused by her to the most furious pitch of which his gentle nature was capable, all tidings of Mr. Percivale's discoveries had been kept from them. They swept in, greeted by a faint hissing from the rural population, and Mrs. Orton broke afresh into loud grief at sight of the sheet which covered poor little Godfrey's body.

Next arrived the coroner, driven by Mr. Fowler in his own dog-cart, and two other official-looking personages, who walked straight in, while Mr. Fowler nodded to some of those who stood near, with a steady cheerfulness so unlike his crushed depression of yesterday that a sudden wave of indefinable hope arose in the hearts of many.

Next, followed by four members of his crew, the stranger Mr. Percivale walked quietly up the hill, and in at the wicket-gate. He was very pale and there were purple marks under his eyes telling of want of sleep; but the still confidence of his manner did not by any means quench the spark that Mr. Fowler's aspect had kindled. A faint cheer followed him as he vanished into the interior of the school-house; but in a moment he reappeared, and stood at the door gazing down the hill as if expecting some one.

And now was seen a spectacle which literally stopped the breath of the momentarily increasing crowd—a sight so unexpected, so unaccountable, that one old woman shrilly screamed out, "Lord ha' mercy on us!" and a strange thrill passed over the assembly as a cart appeared, and stopped before the entrance. In the cart was not only the Edge Valley constable, but two from the Stanton constabulary, and in their charge was the widow Parker, in hysterics, and Saul, seated with a smile on his face, and his beautiful hair just lifted by the wind.

The sensation was tremendous; and it was greatly increased when, as the sobbing, frantic widow staggered blindly up the path, Mr. Percivale was seen to touch her kindly on the arm, and to whisper a few words which had the effect of checking her loud distress and inducing her to compose herself somewhat.

But it was not for her he had waited, for still he kept his place at the door; and presently the sound of wheels was again heard, and up the hill came the Misses Willoughby's wagonette. As it approached, some of the spectators noticed that Mr. Percivale uncovered his bright hair, and so stood until the carriage stopped, when he went forward, cap in hand, to greet the ladies.

Miss Charlotte, Miss Emily, Miss Brabourne, and Mr. Cranmer were in the wagonette, and it was at once remarked, that, though sad, they did not seem to be in despair. All three ladies were in black, and the Misses Willoughby greeted Mr. Percivale with particular politeness and distinction.

As for him, he only saw "one face from out the thousands." She was there, her hands touched his, she walked beside him up the shingly path. Her eyes rested on his with trust and gratitude untold. It was enough. For the moment he felt as if he had won his guerdon. They disappeared within the school-house, and the crowd outside began loudly to speculate on the turn that things were taking. Presently up the road hurried Clapp, the landlord of the "Fountain Head," his wife on his arm, both in their Sunday best, and both in such a state of excitement as rendered them almost crazy. The neighbors gathered round to hear the startling news that Mrs. Clapp had been subpoenaed as a witness in the case, though what they had to do with it they were at a loss to know, unless it were connected with the loyal William's illegal refusal to take Mr. and Mrs. Orton in as his guests on the previous day.

"I don't care if they dû gi' me a foine," cried he, stoutly. "A can affoard to pay it, mates, a deal better 'n I can affoard to tak' vermin into ma hoose!"

A murmur of applause greeted this spirited speech, and William was plied right and left with questions. But he knew no more than they did, only, in some mysterious way, an idea gained ground amongst them that the strange owner of the white yacht had wrought a miracle, or something very like it, for the preservation of Miss Elaine.

"What shall we dû, mates, if a brings her aout safe an' saound?" cried William. "Take aout the horses and drag 'im home, say I."

"Get a couple o' hurdles an' chair 'em," suggested another eager spirit; and then the constable came to the door, and imperatively called Mr. and Mrs. Clapp; when they had vanished, the door was shut, and a breathless hush fell upon the crowd.

Oh, the sunny silence in the old house with the terrace! Oh, the slow, slow motion of the hands of the clock as they crept round. Miss Ellen's couch lay out in the sunshine, her wan hands were clasped, her eyes fixed on the white road which descended from the school-house.

The school was on the other side of the valley. The building itself was hidden by a thick clump of trees, but below, a long stretch of road was clearly visible, leading down past the lower extremity of the Edge Willoughby grounds. Here stood the smithy, and, just opposite that, the road widened out into a triangular space, used as a village lounge of an evening when the weather was fine. Every summer there was a school feast, and all the children were marched down this road on their way to Mr. Fowler's meadows where the feast was held; and it had been a custom, ever since Elaine was a little child, for the whole procession to halt when it came opposite the smithy, with waving banners and flying flags, and, facing the terrace, to sing a hymn for the edification of the pale invalid as she lay on her couch.

To-day, thoughts of Elsa's childhood came thronging to Miss Ellen's mind. She saw her once more as she used to stand in her class, in her clean white frock and blue ribbons, with her hair waving all about her.

Now, as Miss Ellen saw clearly, the past was utterly and completely the past—gone and done away with for ever. In future it would not be in any way possible to continue the life which had flowed on so evenly for nearly fifteen years. Already the sisters talked of change, of travel. Elsa must be taken away from the place where she had suffered so much. Change of scene must be resorted to; everything that could be done must be done to make her forget the horror of the last few days, and restore to her nervous system its usually placid tone.

Little Miss Fanny, who had stayed at home to keep her sister company, was trotting nervously in and out of the open door, now snipping a few withered geraniums, now mixing the chough's food, and moving the cockatoo's cage further into the shade. Jackie himself careered up and down in the sunshine like a contented sort of Mephistopheles. He had been down to the duck-pond, and chased away all the ducks, which was one cause of deep satisfaction to him; over and above which, the cockatoo was caged and he was free, so that he was able to march up and down under the very nose of the captive bird, deriding him both by word and gesture.

"My dear," said Miss Fanny, sitting down with a patient sigh, "how long it seems!"

"Long? Yes!... Oh, Fanny, if anything should have gone wrong, if any unforeseen piece of evidence— —"

"My dear," said Miss Fanny again, in a confident manner, "any unforeseen bit of evidence will be a help to our case."

"You really think so?"

"Think so? Why, the matter admits of no doubt at all. It is plain— even the poor mother can't deny it; the boy himself admits it. He told Mr. Percivale where to look for the cudgel with which the blow was struck."

"I should like to see Mrs. Orton's face. I wonder how she will take it," murmured Miss Ellen.

The clock struck.

"How late it is!" she sighed.

"Hark! What is that?" cried Miss Fanny. "What a strange sound! Don't you hear it?"

"I hear something," answered the invalid, growing white, and grasping the sides of her couch with straining fingers.

It was a hoarse deep roar, which for a moment they took to be the wind or the sea, till, as it was repeated, and again yet louder, they knew it for a sound which neither of them had ever heard before—the shouting of an excited multitude. There is perhaps nothing else in the world which so stirs the pulses, or sends the blood so wildly coursing in the veins. Neither sister spoke a word. They held their breath, strained their eyes, and waited, while the roar swept nearer, and swelled in volume, and at last resolved itself into a tremendous "Hip—hip—hip—hurrah!"

Then, on the white stretch of road down the opposite hill, appeared a flying company of boys, madly waving caps in the air. These were but the forerunners of the great concourse behind. Edge Combe, albeit so apparently small, boasted a population of a thousand souls, and quite half of them were present that morning, besides a goodly sprinkling from Brent, Philmouth, and Stanton. On they came, moving forward like a huge, irregular wave, every hat waving, every throat yelling; and then there flashed into sight a dozen or so of stout fellows, who bore on their shoulders a young man, lifted high above the heads of the throng, a young man whose head was bare, and whose conspicuously fair head caught the light of every sunbeam.

"Fanny! Fanny!" gasped Miss Ellen, in the midst of hysterical tears and laughter, "it is Mr. Percivale, they are chairing him. Who could have believed such a thing, in our quiet village! And, Fanny—see—there is the carriage—our carriage! There is Elsa—God bless the child! God bless her, poor darling!... They have taken out the horses; they are dragging them home in triumph. Look! the carriage is full of flowers; the women and girls are throwing them—they all know what she has suffered, they all sympathise, they all rejoice with us ... and that wonderful young man has done it all. How shall we ever repay him?"

And now the crowd had come to the space opposite the smithy, and here their leader, none other than the redoubtable William Clapp, waved his arms frantically for a halt. The masses of hurrying people behind stopped suddenly; there was an expectant murmur, a pause of wonder as to what was now to happen. The whole thing was intensely dramatic; the slope of the steep hillside lined with eager faces, the carriage in the midst smothered in flowers, and in the foreground the figure of Percivale, held up in the arms of the village enthusiasts against a background of deep blue sky.

"Three cheers for Miss Willoughby!" yelled William, so loudly that his voice carried back to the hindmost limits of the throng, and up to where Miss Willoughby was seated. The cheer that arose in answer was deafening, and Miss Ellen was so overcome that it was with difficulty she could respond by waving her handkerchief.

Scarcely had the sounds died away, when out burst the bells in the church tower, the ringers having raced off to set them going as soon as ever the result was known. As if with one voice the crowd broke forth into "See the conquering hero comes;" and so, with stamping feet and shouting lungs, they wound their way up the hill in the sunshine towards the drive gates of Edge Willoughby.

CHAPTER XXXIV

Where people wish to attract, they should always be
ignorant ... a woman, especially, if she have the misfortune
of knowing anything, should conceal it as well as she can.
Northanger Abbey.

It was snowing—or rather, sleeting, in the half-hearted, fitful way to which Londoners are accustomed. Out of doors, the lamps flared on wet glistening pavements, with here and there a mass of rapidly thawing, congealed ice, which made walking unpleasant. It was pitch-dark, though not yet five o'clock, and the atmosphere was full of a raw cold, more penetrating than frost.

In the suburb of Woodstead, the streets were swimming in slush, through which rolled the omnibuses, packed full inside, and thatched with soaking umbrellas under which cowered unlucky passengers who felt that they were taking cold every moment. Crowsley Road, the main thoroughfare, contained fine, solid houses, standing well back from the street—detached, for the most part, and having their own gardens. Mansfield Road was a turning out of Crowsley Road, and here the houses were small, semidetached, and unpretentious, though these, too, as is the fashion in Woodstead, had a strip of garden in front.

In number seven, the blinds had not been drawn, nor the lamps lit, though it was so dark, and the outside prospect so uninviting. The fire was the only light in the little dining-room, and on the hearth-rug before it sat a girl, her arms round her knees, her eyes fixed on the glowing coals.

The uncertain light of the flickering flames showed that the little room was furnished with several bits of handsome old oak, with a goodly supply of books, and with several oil-paintings, the quality of which could hardly be judged in the dark.

On the floor by the fire lay a number of loose sheets of manuscript, a pen, and inkstand, so arranged that anyone suddenly entering the room must of necessity knock them down. Wynifred Allonby, however—for she it was who sat alone—took no heed of her surroundings. She was miles away, in a dream-world of her own.

The expression of her face had changed since last summer. The independent, courageous, free look was gone. In its stead was a wistfulness, a certain restlessness, which, though it saddened, yet certainly infused a fresh interest. Apparently a struggle was going on in her mind, for her brows were drawn together, and at last, as she stared into the embers, she broke into a little laugh and spoke aloud.

"My dear girl, if I could only persuade you what an idiot you are," said she. "Will nothing—absolutely nothing make you ashamed of yourself? Faugh! I am sick of you—you that were always so high and mighty, you that hated and abhorred love-sick maidens, nicely you are, served out, now ... a man that chance just flung into your society for a few weeks, a man above you in social standing—whose family would think it as great a comedown for him to marry you, as you would think it to marry the butcher!... I have no patience with you, really. Haven't you read your Clough? Don't you remember the *Amours de Voyage*? Yes, that was a Claud, too; and I think he must have been something like mine—like this one, I mean. 'Juxtaposition,' my good young woman, 'is much.' And what was it but juxtaposition? Oh, didn't I know it all the time—know that it couldn't last, that he was just masquerading for the time in a country romance, that he must needs go back to his world of Piccadilly and peeresses.... And yet, I had not the sense to——Oh, it is so hard, so very hard! That I should want him so, and have to confess it to myself, the hateful truth that I do want him and can't forget—while he has no need of me at all!..."

Her face, no longer pale for the moment, dropped upon her hands, and she gave a little sound, between a laugh and a sob.

"It is so many weeks ago, now—years, it seems. I thought I should have been quite cured by the time winter set in. What in the world drew me so to that one man, when I never felt so much as a passing fancy for other people—for poor Mr. Merritt, for instance. Why couldn't I marry him? He was rich, and I liked him too; so did Osmond and the girls; but somehow it wouldn't do. And yet, now.... I can bear it, mostly, only sometimes, in blindman's holiday, it comes over me. It is galling, it is frightfully humiliating. It ought to make me arise and thrash myself for being so unwomanly. I know for a fact that he doesn't want to see me in the least; for, if he had, he would have come ... and yet—yet—if he were to open that door, and stand there this moment, I should be, for the time, absolutely and entirely happy. Oh, what a fall, what a fall for me. I was so certain and so safe. And now, is this pain to go on always? Am I never to be able to fling my heart into my books as I used? Oh, surely, if I am firm enough, I *must* be able to stop it. I will! I am determined I will!"

A footfall, running up the front door steps, made her pause, and foolishly hold her breath; then she laughed contemptuously as a latch-key was thrust into the lock. There was a stamping and rubbing of boots on the mat in the hall, sounds of a mackintosh being removed, an umbrella thrust into the stand, and then Jacqueline walked in, her eyes like stars, her cheeks glowing with the stinging cold outside.

"Are you there, Wyn?" she asked, peering into the twilight.

"Yes. Mind the ink," said the authoress, heaving a sigh.

"Why in the world don't you draw the curtains and light the lamp?" asked Jacqueline, coming forward, and unfastening the dark fur round her throat. "Why is there no tea ready? Where's Osmond? Isn't Hilda in yet? What have you been about, eh?"

"Oh, I don't know," said Wyn, stretching, and picking herself and her writing materials up from the floor. "I was writing hard all the morning, and this afternoon was so horrid, I thought I wouldn't go out; so I have been moping rather. Osmond's out. Hilda won't be in for half-an-hour—it's not five yet."

As she spoke, she drew the curtains, lit the lamp, and rang the bell for tea; then, drawing a low chair to the fire, sat down and looked at Jacqueline.

That young lady had removed her out-door apparel, and was kneeling on the hearthrug, holding her hands to the blaze. The severe weather had brought a magnificent glow to her face, and she looked excessively pretty and elegant. Wyn watched her with elder-sisterly pride. There was something evidently well-bred about Jac; something in the brilliant eyes, the tempting smile, the tall slender figure which gave her a style of her own. It was not exactly dashing, but it was something peculiar to herself, which made her noticed wherever she went, the undeniable beauty of the academy schools, and the pride of her devoted family.

Something had pleased her to-day. Wyn easily divined this, from the gleam in the big, laughing, hazel eyes, and the pleasant curves of the pretty mouth. But the eldest sister was too diplomatic to ask any questions. She knew that, when the slim hands were warmed, confidence would begin to flow, so she only sat still, and remarked casually.

"Bad light down at the schools to-day, I should think."

"Awful," was the candid reply. "I expect I shall have to paint out everything I have put in—such a pity! It looked most weird and Rembrandtesque in the rich pea-soupy atmosphere, but alas! to-morrow will reveal it in its true colors, dirty and opaque. Here comes tea. How nice! Bring it here, Sally, there's a dear."

Sally obeyed. She was a middle-aged, kind, capable woman, who had been their nurse in old days, and their factotum ever since they were orphans.

"Miss Jac," said she, in righteous wrath, "take off them wet boots this minute, you naughty girl. Nice colds you'd all 'ave, if I wasn't to look after you. There was Mr. Osmond painting away this morning with 'is skylight wide open, and the snow falling on 'is 'ed. Wants to kill himself, I think."

"Sally," said Jac, as she sat down on the floor, and rapidly unlaced the offending boots, "I've something very particular to say. What is there for dinner? Is there anything in the house?"

"There's plenty of cold beef, and, as I know Miss 'Ilda don't fancy cold meat, I got some sausages."

"Any pudding?"

"Yes, miss."

"Sausages and mashed potatoes are perhaps vulgar, but they're very nice," said Jacqueline, meditatively. "You might make some anchovy toast, Sal—and—couldn't we have some spinach?"

"Who is coming?" asked Wyn, with interest.

"Mr. Haldane. He is coming to finish that charcoal sketch of me so I told him he had better come to dinner," replied Jac, with airy nonchalance.

"Oh, bless your 'eart, I've got plenty for 'im; he don't know what 'e's putting into his mouth most of the time," said Sally, picking up the wet boots, and retiring.

"Only I do like to have things nice when he comes, because of course he is used to having things done in the proper way," remarked Jacqueline, with a stifled sigh. She was the only one of the four who felt their poverty in this kind of way.

"I never see Mr. Haldane eat anything but chocolate," said Wyn with a laugh. "Perhaps he doesn't like our food."

"Sally is a really good cook, that's my one comfort," returned Jac. "And now I have two pieces of news for you. The first is that he, Mr. Haldane, has got the gold medal."

"No!" cried Wyn, in tremendous excitement. "You don't say so! How splendid! How we will all congratulate him! Tell me all about it—how many votes ahead was he?"

Jacqueline launched into a mass of details, most eagerly appreciated by her listener.

"How we will cheer him at the Distribution to-morrow!" she cried. "I always felt sure he would do it."

"I don't think there was ever much doubt about it," was the answer, in a voice which Jac in vain strove to render perfectly tranquil. "He is very clever, isn't he?"

"Clever and nice too," said Wynifred. "One of the very nicest men we know. And, now, what's the other piece of news?"

"Oh—only that the Ortons are back in town. As I passed Sefton Lodge in the omnibus, it was all lighted up."

"Oh—I wonder if there is any chance for poor old Osmond to get his money now?"

"Don't know, I am sure; I would try, if I were he. Did you have a letter from Mr. Fowler this morning?"

"Yes," answered Wyn, pulling it out of her pocket. "Very nice, as usual. Elsa is still abroad, with her aunts, but he is back at Lower House. It is very strange that Elsa doesn't write—I haven't heard from her for six weeks."

"It is making poor old Osmond very anxious—he looks quite haggard," said Jacqueline, resentfully. "I believe she is in love with this man the yacht belongs to."

"Oh, don't say such a thing, Jac!" cried Wyn, in a quick voice of pain, "it will simply drive Osmond out of his mind if any such thing happens. Poor boy! Just see what he has been doing—how superbly he has been painting since he had this hope, and how his things are selling! How the papers reviewed his 'Valley of Avilion' in the Institute. Why, Mr. Mills said there was scarcely a doubt of his being R.I. next year. If Elsa fails him, I don't believe he will ever paint another stroke."

Jacqueline stared at the fire.

"You see," she said, "the circumstances under which she met this man were so very romantic—so remarkably unusual. And, then, he seems to be a wealthy, dazzling sort of person—with a yacht and a German *Schloss*, and other fancy fixings of the same kind. I don't see, if you come to consider it fairly, how poor Osmond can have a chance against a man who can follow her to the world's end."

"Surely she's too young to be mercenary—girls of her age usually prefer the poor one!" cried Wyn, protestingly.

"Mercenary? Oh, it's not exactly mercenary; but she is dazzled. Here is a mysterious hero, who flashes suddenly upon her with a large staff of retainers to do his behests, and a magic yacht which glides in and out regardless of wind and tide, and a face like a Viking of the Middle Ages, if that picture of him in the *Graphic* is to be relied upon. He is a sort of Ragnar Lodbrog. If she declined his addresses, he would most probably set sail alone in his yacht, set fire to it, and be found by some Channel steamer in the act of burning himself to death, and shouting a battle-cry while the leaping flames encircled him. Now, poor Osmond can't compete with this sort of thing; he has no accessories of any kind to help him along."

"Jac, you are very ridiculous," said Wyn, unable to help laughing a little; but her laugh was not very hearty.

"We shall soon see when she comes to London," said Jacqueline, flourishing the poker.

"If she comes to see us! I don't see why she should. Lady Mabel Wynch-Frère and her brother have dropped us completely," said Wyn, with some bitterness. "The Valley of Avilion was one thing, London is another."

"I'm sure we don't want them," said Jacqueline, indifferently. "From your account, Lady Mabel was not the kind of person I should take to at all."

"She was excessively artificial, but not altogether uninteresting," observed Wyn, in her trenchant way. "They were both very kind to Osmond, but that was their humanity, you know—they would have done the same for any village yokel. Like Lady Geraldine,

'"She is too kind to be cruel, and too haughty not to
pardon,
Such a man as I—'twere something to be level to her hate!"'

Jacqueline began to laugh.

"She is like Aunt Anna," she said.

Aunt Anna was the wife of a dean, and she never dared to invite any of her London-weary nieces to stay with her, lest they should unwittingly reveal to any of her titled friends the ghastly fact that they had to work for their living. Of this secret the said nieces were perfectly aware, and derived much amusement therefrom.

"Oh, I daresay she has never thought of us from that day to this," said Wyn, carelessly. "There's Hilda knocking. Let her in."

Hilda walked in like a duchess. Nature certainly had not intended the Miss Allonbys for daily governesses, and many a time had poor Hilda been doomed to hear the condemning words, "I am afraid, Miss Allonby, you are of too striking an appearance," from some anxious mother, who felt that life would be a burden when weighted with a governess so dignified that to suggest that she should take Kitty to the dentist's, or Jack to have his boots tried on, would seem a flagrant insult.

"If they only knew how meek and mild I am really!" the poor child would remark, dolorously. "If I could but make myself three inches shorter, or pad myself out round the waist till I was no shape at all! But it would be so dreadfully hot. And I really *can't* wear unbecoming hats—something in me revolts against the idea!"

To-night she had a letter in hand, which she dropped into Wyn's lap.

"I met the postman," she said, explanatorily. "Open it, do—it feels stiff, I believe it's an invitation."

Wyn opened it, drew out a square card with gilt edges, and read.

MISS ALLONBY, MISS H. ALLONBY, MISS J. ALLONBY,
MR. ALLONBY.

Mrs. MILES AT HOME.

Tuesday, Jan. 5th.

Dancing 8.30,
R. S. V. P.

INNISFALLE, THE AVENUE.

"A ball at the Miles'! Oh, Wyn, how splendid!" cried Jacqueline in ecstasies.

"Every creature we know will be there," said Hilda.

"Oh, Hilda, how glad I am we had those dresses made," said Jacqueline, jumping up and careering round the table in the excess of her spirits.

"How nice of them to ask us all three by name," said Hilda, gloating over the card. "They know we never go out more than two at a time unless specially invited."

"It's a good long invitation," said Wyn.

"Wyn!" cried Jac, suddenly stopping before her and shaking her fist in her face, "Wynifred Allonby, what have you got to wear?"

"Nothing," said Wyn, helplessly. "I don't think I shall go—you two are the ones that do us credit. You can go in your pretty new gowns."

"I hope you understand," said Hilda, with decision, "that not one of us sets foot in that glorious studio, with a parquet floor, and most probably Willoughby's band, unless you are forthcoming *in an entirely new rig-out!* Do you hear me? If I have to drag you to Oxford Street myself, you must and shall be decent! You have disgraced your family long enough in that old black rag, or in something made of tenpenny muslin! A new dress you shall have—silk it must be—thick, good silk, thick enough to stand by itself! Now, do, there's a darling!"

"I don't think——" began Wyn.

"Oh, yes, I know what you are doing," said Hilda, calmly, "paying for the housekeeping out of your own money, so that Osmond may save up; but I am going to put a stop to that; and you have heaps of money in the savings bank. Don't be miserly, it is so hateful."

Wyn looked somewhat confused by these terrible charges.

"Well," admitted she, hesitatingly, "I don't mind telling you two, that I had a cheque this morning from Carter" (her publisher). "It was not a very big one—only the royalty on about fifty copies of 'Cicely Montfort.' But I could buy a really good gown with it. Do you think I might?"

"Might? I say you ought; it's your duty," cried Jac, vehemently. "Everyone at Innisfallen will know you—every soul knows you are an authoress. You ought to do us credit—you shall. I'll have no nonsense about it."

"I don't see why I shouldn't," burst out Wyn, suddenly. "I will be welldressed for once in my life. I will enjoy myself as much as ever I can. Girls, my mind is made up. I will have a really good gown, as good as can be got; and it shall fit me well, and the skirt shall hang properly. For this once I'll have my fling; I'll go to Innisfallen and eclipse you both."

Here Sally walked in to fetch out the tea-things, and swooped on Hilda's boots as she had done on Jacqueline's. After which, retiring to cook the sausages, she set open the door at the head of the kitchen stairs, that she might hear Osmond's latch-key, and, descending on him like the wolf on the fold, rob him of his understandings if ever he came to the shelter of his studio.

CHAPTER XXXV

Juxtaposition, in fine; and what is juxtaposition?
Look you, we travel along, in the railway-carriage or
steamer,
And *pour passer le temps*, till the tedious journey be ended,
Lay aside paper or book to talk with the girl that is next
one;
And, *pour passer le temps*, with the terminus all but in
prospect,
Talk of eternal ties and marriages made in heaven.
Amours de Voyage.

"Sally, Sally, what are you doing? For pity's sake come here and lace me! I shall never be ready. What a time you are with Wyn!"

Jacqueline, in all the daintiness of white embroidered petticoat, satin-smooth shoulders, and deftly-arranged hair with a spray of lilies of the valley somewhere among its coils, hung over the balustrade in an agony of impatience.

"Wyn, Wyn, what are you keeping Sal for? She has been twenty minutes over your bodice."

A voice of agony from below responded.

"Tag has come off my lace."

"Oh!" A pause of consternation; then, encouragingly, "try a hair-pin."

"It's all right now. I have actually found my bodkin. I shan't be five minutes."

"Five minutes! My dear child, *Osmond has actually gone for the cab!*" cried Jac, in tones tragic enough to suit the most lamentable occasion.

"Jac, come here, and don't make such a fuss," said the calm voice of Hilda, as she emerged from her room, ready down to the minutest detail, fan, gloves, and wrap over her arm.

With a scream of joy at such unlooked-for relief, Jac darted into her room again, and her slender form was soon encased by her sister's deft fingers in its neatly-fitting fresh and captivating bodice.

"What a wonder *your* tags are not both off! They generally are," was Hilda's withering comment, as she performed her task.

"Yes, it is a wonder, isn't it?" returned Jacqueline, complacently. "Oh, there you are, Sal. I'm ready now, so you can go back to your beloved Wyn."

"You can't think 'ow nice Miss Wyn looks to-night," observed Sally, as she busied herself in collecting some of the scattered articles of wearing apparel which strewed the floor of Jacqueline's small chamber.

"I am so glad. I thought that dress would become her," said Hilda, in a pleased voice. "Oh, Jac, stand still, my beloved, one moment: there is Osmond back again."

"Very good; I am ready. Sally, where are my gloves? And my bracelet, and my fan, and my small brooch, and—oh, dear! Run and tell Wyn she must lend me a lace handkerchief and some elastic for my shoes. Do hurry, Sally, please, I quite forgot the elastic. Why didn't you remind me, Hilda? Oh, did you get it for me? You darling, what a blessing you are! There have I got everything? Oh, Sally, do I look as nice as Hilda?"

"You ain't so neat," observed Sally, with grim humor; "but neither of you looks bad, though I don't want to make you conceited."

"Are you girls coming?" shouted Osmond.

"Oh, yes; wait just a second, my dear boy. *Is* my front hair right, Hilda? Yours does go so beautifully to-night. You don't look like a governess, somehow." She threw a daring, tempting glance and laugh over her shoulder at the brilliant reflection in the mirror. "I wonder if I do," she said.

At the foot of the stairs stood Wyn, in her new white silk, with a little crescent of diamonds, which had belonged to their mother, in her hair.

"My dear girls, I am at peace," she remarked, gravely. "I stand at last inside a gown which *hangs* to perfection!"

"Oh, isn't it nice?" said Jac, with a deep sigh of longing. "Really, Wyn, you do look well; you pay for dressing. Why don't you give more attention to your clothes?" "There's Osmond fidgetting downstairs, run!" cried Hilda, and the three flew off, pursued by Sally's warning cries.

"Miss Jac, Miss Jac, don't let that fresh skirt sweep the stair carpets! Miss 'Ilda, cover your 'ead over, you've got a cold, you know you 'ave! Miss Wyn, see that Mr. Osmond crosses his comforter over his chest, there's a dear!"

"Innisfallen. The Avenue," said Osmond to the cabman; and the four were really off at last.

"For how many dances are you engaged, Jac?" asked the brother, teazingly.

"Little boys," was the frigid rejoinder, "should ask no questions, and then they would hear no stories;" after which, silence reigned in the fourwheeler.

Every Londoner knows, or has heard of, the celebrated house of Mr. Miles, R.A. It is one of the show-houses of London, and views of its interior appear from time to time in the art magazines, with an accompanying article full of praise for and wonder at the wealth and taste which devised such an abode. With our nineteenth-century habit of writing biographies in the life-time of their subject, of forming societies to interpret the work of living poets, and publishing pamphlets to explain the method of living painters, why not also extol the upholstery of living academicians? It is surely more satisfactory that people should admire your taste and wonder at your income in your lifetime than after you have gone the way of all flesh. Nowadays one is nothing if not in print. What! Furnish at untold cost; have your carpets imported from the East, and your wall papers specially designed, merely that these facts should go about as a tradition, a varying statement bandied from mouth to mouth and credited at will?

The age is sceptical; it will not believe what it hears, it will not even believe documents of more than a certain age—the Gospels, for instance. But it will believe anything which it sees printed in a society journal, or a fashionable magazine. If your name be blazoned there, it is equivalent to having it graven with an iron pen, and lead in rock forever; on which account Mr. Miles did not object in the least to the appearance of delicately-executed engravings representing "Hall, and portion of staircase at Innisfallen, residence of H. Miles, Esq., R.A." "Interior of studio, looking west." "Drawing-room, and music-gallery, showing the great organ, &c., &c." He was wise in his generation, and thoroughly enjoyed the caressing and honors which accrued to him from this form of advertisement. Moreover, he was a kindly man, and much given to hospitality. Nothing pleased him better than to throw open his magnificent rooms to large assemblies of very various people on an occasion like the present.

An interesting theme for observation was presented by the extraordinary variety of toilettes worn by the guests of both sexes.

First there was the artistic section of the community, drawn from all classes of society. By an odd paradox, these were they whose costumes were the most aggressively inartistic of any. Dirt and slovenliness are neither of them picturesque, yet it would seem that this singular clique held that to cultivate both was the first duty of man. They seemed to be one and all anxious to impress upon the observer the fact that they had taken no trouble at all to prepare for this party. A few had washed their faces. None had gone to the length of arranging their hair. Another feature which all possessed in common was their inability to dance, though some of them tried. Perhaps their large boots and ill-fitting garments incapacitated them for the display of grace in motion. They leaped, shuffled and floundered, but they did not waltz. These were, of course, only the younger section. Nearly everyone of them had distinguished him or herself in their own particular line; which fact seems to argue that to give especial attention to one sort of observation is to destroy the faculty for observing anything else: a saddening theory, and one which makes one tremble for the value of Professor Huxley's judgment on all matters outside his own province. Be that as it may, the fact remains that this concourse of young people, who could all admire beauty, grace, and refinement in the canvasses of the old masters, yet were themselves so many living violations of every law of beauty, and kept their refinement strictly for internal use.

The moneyed clique was also much *en évidence*. These were blazing with diamonds as to the women, commonplace and vacant as to the men. The latter seemed, in fact, to still further illustrate the theory of the evil of giving too close an attention to one thing. They were only faintly interested in what was going forward; they had no conversation unless they met a kindred spirit, who was willing to discuss the state of affairs east of Temple Bar. Their wives were for the most part handsome, and were all over-dressed, but this extreme was not so painful as that of the artists, because these clothes were as a rule well-made and composed of beautiful materials.

Then there was a large sprinkling of professional people—barristers, journalists, critics, *savants*, lady-doctors, strong-minded females, singers, reciters, actors. Also there were the great gems of the art world: academicians, who, having made their name, had promptly turned Philistine, with their wives and families, dressed like the rest of the world, built big houses, went into society, and painted pot-boilers; and, lastly, there was a fair sprinkling of the aristocracy: well-born people, not so handsome as the millionaires' wives, but with that subtle air of breeding which diamonds cannot give. All these were simply dressed, and unobtrusive in manner; and a stranger watching the Allonbys enter the room would have fearlessly classed them with these latter.

They all four looked what the Germans call "born." A certain way of carrying their heads distinguished them, and as they followed the announcement of their names, and shook hands with their hostess, more than one eager voice assailed the young men of the house with clamors for an introduction.

Mr. and Mrs. Miles were fond of the four orphans. They had known them for years, and watched with kindly interest the development of their fortunes. Wynifred's success had made her quite a small celebrity in the neighborhood, and she owed many introductions to the benevolent zeal of the academician's plain, homely wife.

"My dear," said Mrs. Miles, in a whisper, "I don't know when I've seen you look so nice."

This was a charming beginning. It raised Wynifred's spirits, which were already high. She had come that evening determined to enjoy herself. She intended to cast every remembrance of last summer to the winds. Claud Cranmer was to be forgotten—the one weakness in her life. She would wrench back her liberty by main force, and be free once more—free as on the hot June day when she had journeyed down to Devonshire, and found the slight trim figure waiting for her on the platform.

She knew plenty of people here to-night—people who were only too ready and anxious for her notice. When Wynifred had been working at the Woodstead Art School, before her novels began to pay, it had been said of her that she might have had the whole studio at her feet had she so chosen. She was an influence—a power. She had not been two minutes in the room before her ball-programme began to fill rapidly—too rapidly. She was too experienced a dancer not to make a point of reserving several dances "for contingencies."

"Don't introduce me to anyone else—please," she said to Arthur Miles, who was standing by her, inscribing his name on her card. "I shall have too many strangers on my hands, and I get so tired of strangers."

"There's North, the dramatic author, imploring me to introduce him— he wants to dramatise 'Cicely Montfort.' How that book has taken! I hope you are reaping substantial benefits, Miss Allonby?"

"Yes, pretty well, as times go, thank you," she answered, laughing a little as she remembered that her pretty gown had been earned by the industrious and popular "Cicely."

"I don't think it's much use my talking to him," she went on. "I have as good as promised to help Mr. Hollis dramatize it for the Corinthian."

"Then you and Mr. Hollis had better make haste, or North will have the start of you. He's the fastest writer I know, and I believe he has it already arranged in a prologue and three acts."

"Yes, there must be a prologue—that is the drawback," said Wyn, slowly. "But," with a sudden bright look, "you are making me talk 'shop,' Mr. Miles!"

"Am I? Very sorry. Here comes Dick Arden to take you off. I must go and find out if the beauty is here—she is fashionably late."

"The beauty? Has Mr. Miles a new beauty on view to-night?"

"I should just think he has, and no mistake about it this time. Have you not heard about her? She is a great heiress, and all London is to go mad over her. The *pater* is doing her picture in oils for the R.A. He says she is simply the most beautiful creature he has ever seen. She is coming to-night, under the escort of Lady Somebody-or-other. Hallo! There are the Ortons!"

"Where?" Wynifred turned her head swiftly. She knew them slightly, on account of the business relations between Osmond and Frederick. She watched with some interest as her brother, who was standing near the door, shook hands and entered into conversation with them. Ottilie was looking excessively handsome, in a black velvet dress, cut very low in the bodice, a profusion of jewels decorating her neck, arms, and head. She had grown somewhat thinner in the months she had lately spent abroad, but her color was as rich and vivid as ever. Wyn saw Osmond ask her to dance, and lead her away, and then Dick Arden, the pleasant looking young artist at her elbow, broke in with,

"When your meditation is quite finished, Miss Allonby, I am longing for a turn."

With a laughing apology she laid her hand on his arm, and followed him into the dancing-room.

The drawing-room at Innisfallen adjoined the studio, separated by enormous sliding-doors, and voluminous curtains of amethyst velvet. To-night the doors were folded back, the curtains looped in masses of dusky light and shade, so that the guests standing in the drawing-room could see the couples as they circled round.

Wyn began to enjoy herself. The floor was perfect, the band, as Hilda had prophesied, Willoughby's. She liked dancing, and she liked Dick Arden. Everyone knows that Woodstead is the suburb of London most famed for its dancing and its pretty girls. In Woodstead the dismal cry of "No dancing men!" is a thing unknown. On this particular night, the dancers were drawn from hundreds of neighborhoods, so that the waltzing was not so faultless as it was wont to be at the Town Hall; but Wyn knew whom to choose and whom to avoid, and her present partner left little to be desired.

Who could be sentimentally afflicted, she cried in her heart, with a good floor, a good band, and a good partner? The vivid memory of the weeks at Edge Combe seemed paler than it had ever been before. After all, it had only been an episode, and it was in the past now. Every day it receded further back; it was dying out, fading, disappearing.

The dancers flashed past. Osmond and Ottilie Orton, tall and commanding; Jacqueline and young Haldane, both talking as fast as they could, and laughing into each other's eyes; Hilda, quiet and queenly, with an adoring partner. It seemed a bright, hopeful world, a world full of people interested in other people. Was there no one in it who had a tender thought for her—for Wynifred? She did not want admiration, or fame, or notice, or favorable criticism. She was a woman, and she wanted love.

But no! This would not do. The stream of her reflections would carry her the wrong way. Forward must she look—never back, on past weakness and shortcoming. The music ceased with a long-drawn chord of strings. The waltz was over.

Wyn and her partner were at the lower end of the vast studio. As they turned to walk up the floor towards the archway, the girl caught sight of a head—a fair head thrown into relief against the dark background of the amethyst curtain. For a moment she felt sick, faint, and cold. Then she rallied, in a little burst of inward rage. What! Upset by a chance likeness?

They moved on. A crowd of intervening people shut out that suggestive head from view. Wyn unfurled her crimson fan, and smiled at Dick Arden.

"That *was* delightful," he was saying, warmly. "Won't you give me another? Do say you will. An extra—anything—only do give me one more."

The next instant she was face to face with Claud Cranmer.

CHAPTER XXXVI

"That fawn-skin-dappled hair of hers,
And the blue eye
Dear and dewy,
And that infantine fresh air of hers."
A Pretty Woman.

It was no fancy. There he stood, trim and fresh as ever, a small bunch of Neapolitan violets in his button-hole, his hands behind him, and wearing his usual expression of alert interest in what was passing around him. He was looking remarkably well, and a good deal tanned, so that the clearness of his blue-grey eyes showed more strongly than usual. His face was turned fully towards Wynifred, but he was not looking at her, but beyond, away down the room.

That trifling fact saved her self-respect. Had his eyes been upon her, he must have seen something—some sudden flash of uncontrollable feeling, which would have told him what she would almost have died to prevent his knowing. But in the few moments given to her she was able partially to rally, to tear her eyes from his face, to turn to her partner, even to smile at what he was saying, and to make a reply which, if neither long nor brilliant, was at least not wide of the mark. Those two minutes seemed really two hours to her. First the sudden shock, then the recovery, so slow as it had seemed, the turning of her head an inch to the left, the set smile, the brief answer, and then they were in the doorway ... were, passing him by.... No human power could have made her lift her eyes to his as she passed; yet she saw him without looking—knew how close he was, felt her gown brush his foot, and heard his voice an instant later ejaculate,

"Miss Allonby!"

It had come. As she paused, turned her head, raised her gaze to his, she was more thankful than ever that she had even so brief a preparation; for the expression of Mr. Cranmer's face could not exactly be considered flattering. It was made up of several ingredients, but embarrassment was predominant. There was a slight added color in his cheeks—a hesitation in his manner. He was off guard, and could not immediately collect himself.

A secret fury of indignation at her own folly helped to make Wynifred's smile most coldly sweet. As she held out her hand she slightly arched her eyebrows as though he were the last person she had expected to meet; as indeed he had been, not three minutes ago. He greeted her with some confusion, his eyes roamed over her dress, and never in all her life had she been so devoutly thankful that she was in this respect for once past criticism.

Nothing gives a greater confidence than the consciousness of looking one's best. As the girl stood before Claud, she felt that to-night the advantage was hers. He had not thought it worth while to call in Mansfield Road; he should see that the Allonby family was by no means dependent on his chance favors.

The usual tepid and stereotyped formalities were gone through.

"How do you do, Miss Allonby? It is an unexpected pleasure to meet you here."

"Really! I think it is I who ought to be surprised. I am always at Mrs. Miles' parties, and I never met you before."

"No—it is my first visit. I hope you are all well? Is either of your sisters here?"

"Yes, both; and my brother too. Are you alone?"

"Oh, dear, no: Mab is here somewhere, and Miss Brabourne——"

Here Dick Arden became restive.

"Miss Wynifred!" he murmured, reproachfully, making an onward step.

Wyn inclined her head with another small and civil smile, and made as though she would have passed on.

"Miss Allonby—stay! Won't you give me a waltz?" cried Claud, hastily.

"I have none till quite the end of the programme, and I am afraid you will have gone home by then," replied Wyn, airily, over her shoulder.

Claud went forward, determinedly.

"If you will give me one, I will stay for it," he said, with some energy.

"Well, you shall have number nineteen; but mind you don't trouble to wait if it is not quite convenient."

"Somebody else will be only too happy to step into your shoes, if you are not forthcoming," laughed Dick Arden. "Miss Wynifred—I hope that is not my promised dance you are giving away!"

They were gone—the slim, white-robed girl and her partner had vanished among the parti-colored couples who paraded the room. Claud's' glance followed them with a fatal fascination. He saw them pass through a sidedoor into a shadowy conservatory, and then, with a start, roused himself to the consideration of what had passed. He had met Wynifred Allonby again. How very nice she looked in white. How nice she looked altogether. Was there not something different about her since the summer—an altered look in her face? Her eyes! He never noticed, at Edge Combe, what pretty eyes she had; but now— —. He moved restlessly down towards the band. Why did they not strike up? This was only number four on the programme, and he had to exist, somehow, till the bitter end. He might as well dance, it would perhaps pass the time rather more quickly.

Actuated by this idea, he started in pursuit of Elsa.

Meanwhile, scarcely had Wynifred gained the shelter of the ante-room, when she turned to her partner abruptly.

"We must hunt up Osmond before we do anything else," she cried, peremptorily. "I want to speak to him at once."

Mr. Arden knew her too well to attempt to gainsay her. They hurried through the rooms till they reached the tearoom, where Mrs. Frederick Orton was seated in state while Osmond waited upon her.

"Osmond, my dear boy," said Wyn, eagerly, going up to him, "I must just say five words to you. Come here—bend down your head—listen! Elsa Brabourne is here to-night. Yes," as he started violently, "she is, I know, for I have just seen Mr. Cranmer, and he told me. I thought I would warn you. Oh, my dear, don't be rash, I implore you! Think of her changed position, since we last saw her—think what a great heiress she is! She has the world at her feet. Don't look like that, dear, I don't want to hurt you—only to warn you. Be on your guard! Don't let her trample on you!"

"Trample on me! She! You don't know her—you could never appreciate—you always misjudged her!" said the young man, resentfully, under his breath. "A more innocent, simple-minded creature I never saw than she! They cannot have spoilt her—yet!"

He was quivering with eagerness.

"Thanks for coming to tell me," he said, hurriedly. "I will go and find her. Never fear for me. I'm not a fool."

"But, oh, my poor boy, I am not so sure of that," sighed the sister, secretly, as she left the room again with her partner.

As she passed back through the drawing-room where the hostess was receiving her guests, her attention was attracted by the figure of a girl who was standing with her back to them, talking to Arthur Miles.

Dick Arden turned suddenly to her.

"Who is that?" he asked breathlessly.

Only the back, straight and slender, was visible, its white silk bodice leaving bare a neck that would not have degraded the Venus de Medici. A small head, crowned with masses of rippled golden hair, was bent slightly to one side, showing a spray of lillies and a flash of diamonds. An enormous fan of snowy ostrich feathers formed a background to this faultless head.

Dick and Wyn were both artists. Simultaneously they moved forward, to catch a full view of the face belonging to a back which promised so rarely.

As they came towards her, the beauty turned in their direction, and a sigh of admiring wonder heaved Mr. Arden's breast as he gazed. It was Elsa.

Wyn knew her in the same instant that she recognized her astonishing beauty.

This was something far more wonderful than mere good looks. Regular features, a clear white skin, large eyes, good teeth, abundant hair—no doubt these are important factors in the structure of a woman, but Elsa possessed something far more subtle, more dangerous then any of these.

The trouble, the horror through which she had passed had left something behind—an indefinable but real influence—a dash of sadness—a shadow, a suggestiveness, which gave to mouth and eyes a pathos calculated to drive the soberest of men out of his senses. Had she been brought up like other girls, among companions of her own age—gone to juvenile parties, stayed at fashionable watering places, attended a select boarding-school, she would, of course, have grown up handsome; nature had amply provided for that, but her beauty would have been robbed of what was its chief charm. As it was, she was not only lovely, but unique; and her superb physical health added a crowning touch to her dissimilarity from the pretty, delicate, more or less jaded and over-educated London girls who surrounded her.

As her eyes met Wyn's, she started, and came forward, with that bewitching shyness which was one of her great points.

"Oh, Wyn! Lady Mabel, here is Miss Allonby!"

Lady Mabel Wynch-Frère turned quickly.

"Why—so it is! I am charmed to meet you," she cried, with much *empressement*. "Of course, if I had only thought, Woodstead is your part of the world, is it not? What a charming part it seems! This house is lovely. I am so glad we came. Mr. Miles is painting Elsa's picture, you know. I think it will be a great success. And how is your work getting on?"

"Pretty well, thank you."

"I thought it must be! I have been, like everyone else, reading 'Cicely Montfort.' Is it true that it is to be dramatised?"

"I believe so."

"How proud you must be! it is so grand to feel that one has really done some good work, and swelled the list of useful women. You must come and see us as soon as you possibly can. Elsa is making a long stay with me. She is only just come back to England, you know. She has been cruising in the Mediterranean with two of her aunts, in Mr. Percivale's yacht; and my brother has been with them for about six weeks—ever since he returned from Scotland; he is here to-night, have you seen him?"

"Yes, just to speak to. He said you and Miss Brabourne were here," returned Wyn feeling greatly mollified to hear that, by all accounts, Claud had not been in London since they parted in the summer.

"It has done the child so much good," said Lady Mabel, dropping her voice. "She is fast recovering, but she was desperately ill after—after that sad affair, you know. I daresay you wonder to see her at a ball so soon; but they dare not let her mope. The doctors said she must at all risks be kept happy and amused. The yachting was the saving of her, I do believe. It was Mr. Percivale's suggestion."

"Is he here to-night?" Wyn could not resist asking.

"Yes, somewhere. I do not see him just now, Mrs. Miles carried him off. Ah! here he comes, with that girl in the primrose gown; is it not one of your sisters?"

"Yes,—Hilda," answered Wyn, with much interest. "Is that Mr. Percivale? What a fine head!"

"Is it not?" said Lady Mabel, with enthusiasm. "You are an artist, you can appreciate it. Some people say he has red hair, and that his style is so *outré*; for my part, I do like a man who dares to be unlike other men! He has a distinct style of his own, and he knows it. He declines to clip and trim himself down to the level of everybody else! but there is nothing obtrusive about him."

This was true. As Percivale advanced, Wyn was constrained to admit that a more distinguished gentleman she had never beheld. His face fascinated her. It expressed so clearly the simple nobility of his soul. He came up to where Lady Mabel was standing, Hilda Allonby on his arm, and then a number of introductions took place.

Suddenly, with impetuous footstep, a gentleman approached the group. Elsa turned her face, and one of her slow, beautiful smiles dawned over eyes and mouth as, with perfect self-possession, she stretched out her hand in greeting.

It was Osmond; he was white as death, and so excited as to be unable to speak connectedly. He took the little white-gloved hand in his, and seemed at once to become oblivious of his surroundings. Wyn was obliged to remind him of his manners.

"Osmond, here is Lady Mabel."

Mr. Percivale, at the sound of the name, turned round suddenly, and for several seconds the two men remained looking one another in the face.

They presented the somewhat unusual spectacle of a pair of rivals, both of whom were quite determined to fight fair. But Percivale's tranquillity was in strong contrast to Osmond's flushed and manifest disorder. To Wyn there was something cruel about it—the rich yacht-owner, the poor, struggling artist. It could never be an even contest.

"We ought to be acquainted, Mr. Allonby," said Percivale, after a moment.

"Indeed? I have not the honor— —" began Osmond, struggling for an indifferent manner.

"My name is Percivale," said the owner of the *Swan*. "Perhaps you may have heard it."

Osmond bowed. In the presence of Elsa, it was not possible to allude to the events which had brought the yacht to Edge Combe.

"I am glad to meet you, Mr. Percivale," he managed to say, with some stiffness. "Miss Brabourne, may I hope for the honor of a dance?"

Again the girl smiled at him, accompanying the smile with a look half mischievous, half pleading, and wholly inviting, as if deprecating the formality of his address.

"Yes, of course you may," she said, shyly. "Will you have this one?"

"Will I! May I?"

The rapturous monosyllables were all that he could command. Next instant he felt the light touch of that white glove on his coat-sleeve—he was walking away with her, out of reach of all observing eyes; he was floating in a Paradise of sudden, wild happiness. Of what was to come he recked nothing. The present was enough for him.

"Elsa!" he gasped, as soon as he could speak, "I thought you had forgotten me!"

"But I have not, you see."

"But you have not! I might have known it. Where shall we go—what shall we do? Do not let us dance, let us sit down somewhere; I have a thousand things that I must say."

But this suggestion was most displeasing to Miss Brabourne.

"Oh, but, please, you must dance," said she, in disappointed tones. "I want to practise, as I shall have to dance so much, and it is such a good opportunity for you to teach me!"

"To teach you! I expect I shall be the learner," cried Osmond; but in this he was mistaken.

His divinity could not waltz at all. He instructed her for some time, a conviction darkly growing in his mind that she never would be able to master this subtle art. But what of that? Could he regret it, when she calmly said,

"I should like to dance with you a great many times, please, if you don't mind. I feel as if I needed a great deal of teaching."

CHAPTER XXXVII

"Oh, sir, she smiled, no doubt,
Whene'er I passed her; but who passed without
Much the same smile?"
My Last Duchess.

"Our dance, I believe. Miss Allonby."

Wynifred, quietly seated by her partner, raised her eyes deliberately.

"You, Mr. Cranmer? I thought you had gone some time ago."

"Indeed? Am I in the habit of breaking my word?" asked Claud, stiffly.

"Oh," said the girl, as she rose and took his arm, "to cut a dance is not considered breaking one's word in *le monde où l'on s'ennuie*, especially when to keep it would be to make the horses stand in the cold!"

"The horses are not standing now, so be easy on that score. I have not carried my heroism to that extent. Now, what made you say you thought I had gone?"

"Lady Mabel has been gone some time."

"Does that entail my going too? Had she not a gentleman in attendance? Are there no hansom cabs in London? Do you think I am tied to Mab's apron-strings?"

"I have usually met you together."

Claud made no answer. He was slightly piqued.

How could he know that for these few minutes the girl on his arm had hungered and longed all the evening, that all other interests had seemed to be merged in the one question—Would he stay, or would he not? How could he know that for the moment she was tasting a happiness as brief and delusive, though more controlled, than poor Osmond's?

Like most men, he only saw what she chose to show him—a disengaged manner, a sharp tongue, and her customary indifference.

It exasperated him. What! When the sight of her had moved him so unusually, was she to treat him as any one of the crowd! What a fool he was, to waste a thought upon her! He was in a frame of mind approaching the vindictive. He would have liked to make her suffer; as she, poor child, was feeling every moment as if the strain were becoming too severe—as though her store of self-command were ebbing, and she must betray herself.

They began to dance.

It has been truly said that our very waltzes are melancholy, now-a-days. This was a conspicuously sad one. It seemed to steal into Wynifred's very soul. It was as though the burden of useless longing must weigh down her light feet and clog her easy motion. She could not speak, and for some minutes they waltzed in silence. At last—

"I have not forgiven you for thinking I should fail to keep my appointment," said he.

"You seem very much exercised on the subject," she laughed back. "I am sorry it entailed so much effort and self-denial."

"You wilfully misinterpret, as Darcy said to Elizabeth Bennett."

"You are not much like Darcy."

"Now why?" said Claud, nettled for some unaccountable reason, "why am I not like Darcy? Your reasons, if you please."

"Don't ask me to make personal remarks."

"I insist upon it! I will not have my character darkly aspersed."

"Well, you have brought it upon yourself. The difference is that, whereas Mr. Darcy seemed excessively haughty and unapproachable on first acquaintance, yet was, in his real self, most humble, unassuming, and ready to acknowledge himself in error; Mr. Cranmer, on the contrary, seems easy, debonair, and ready to fraternise with everyone; but on closer knowledge he is found to be exceedingly proud, exclusive, and—and—all that a peer's son should be. There! what do you not owe me for that delicate piece of flattery?"

"What do I owe you? A deep and dire revenge, which I will take forthwith by drawing, not a contrast, but a likeness between you and Elizabeth Bennett. She was deeply attracted by the shallow, insincere, and fraudulent Wickham. She began by grossly underrating poor Darcy, and imputing to him the vilest of motives; she ended by overrating him as unjustly. In other words, her estimate of character was invariably incorrect. In this respect there is a striking resemblance between you."

"I can almost forgive you your unexampled rudeness, on account of your knowing your 'Pride and Prejudice' so well," cried Wyn, in delight.

"But, alas! what is a poor novelist to say in answer to such a crushing charge! I must retire from business at once, if I am no judge of character."

"Oh, you are young, there is hope for you yet if you will but take advice."

"Willingly! But it must be from one competent to advise!"

"And who is to settle that?"

"I, myself, of course!"

"You have great confidence," said Claud, "in that judgment which, as I have just told you, is incurably faulty."

"Pause a moment! One step further, and we shall have rushed headlong into a discussion on the right of private judgment, and, once begun, who knows where it would end?"

"We have a way of trending on problematical subjects, have we not?" said Claud, with a gay laugh.

He wondered at himself—his good humor was quite restored. Just a few minutes' unimportant chat with Wynifred, and he was charmed into his very best mood. She annoyed and fascinated at the same moment, she acted like a tonic, always stimulating, never cloying. What she might say next was never certain, and the uncertainty kept him always on the *qui vive*. He could imagine no pleasure more subtle.

He began to understand his danger more completely than heretofore. To-night he realised that a continued acquaintance with Miss Allonby could have but one end. Was there yet time to save himself? Would he do so if he could?

The glamor which her presence shed over his spirit showed itself by outward and visible signs, in the genial light of the grey eyes, the smiling curve of the mouth, in the whole expression of the pleasant face. In her society he was at his best, and he felt it. Everything was more enjoyable, life more vivid when she was there, she was the mental stimulus he needed.

Yielding to this happy mood, which each shared alike, they sank into seats when the music ceased, scarcely noting that the dance was over. Suddenly, in the midst of his light talk, Claud broke off short, ejaculating in surprise,

"By George, there's the tragedy queen!"

Wyn, looking up, saw Mrs. Orton in the centre of the polished floor, gracefully bidding "good night" to her hostess.

"I wonder—oh, I *wonder* if she came across Percivale," said Claud, eyeing her intently. "I would give my best hat to see them meet! How she does hate him! I never saw a woman in a rage in my life really, until I saw Mrs. Frederick Orton at the inquest."

"Ah, you were there! I wish," said Wyn, "that you would tell me all about it. I have heard so few details. All that I have heard was from Mr. Fowler. He is very kind, but not a clever writer of letters. I think he is unaccustomed to it."

"Very probably. So he writes to you! I think," he looked keenly at her, "I never saw a more thoroughly first-rate fellow."

"I go every length with you, as Jac would say. He is good. I think I rejoiced over Elsa's innocence as much for his sake as for anything."

"Yes. He was splendid at the inquest. He and Percivale are a pair for never losing their tempers under any provocation. That woman contradicted him, insulted him, abused him, but he never let her get the better of him for a moment. What a curious thing human nature is! She had so nursed some sort of grudge against Miss Brabourne that it has grown into a blazing hatred, which is the ruling passion of her life. I honestly believe that to have proved the girl guilty of murder would have afforded her the keenest satisfaction. She was furious at being baulked of her revenge."

"Oh! Such a thing is inhuman—incredible! If I put such a character into one of my books, people would call it unpardonably overdrawn," said Wyn, in horror.

"I daresay; but it is true. Remember she was in a desperate frame of mind altogether. They were literally without money, and they came down there to find that the boy, from whom came their sole chance of funds, was dead. It seemed only fair that somebody should be made to suffer for Mrs. Orton's exceeding discomfort. That was all. But I believe she would do Percivale a bad turn, if she could."

"Who *is* Mr. Percivale?" asked Wyn.

"That's just what nobody quite knows," said Claud, with a puzzled laugh. "All I know about him is that he is a gentleman in the word's truest sense. He is very reserved; never speaks of himself, and one can't exactly ask a man straight out who his father was. He is a good deal talked about in society, as you may guess, and the society journals manufacture a fresh lie about him, on an average, once a month. He evidently dislikes publicity, for he never races that beautiful yacht of his, or gives large donations to public institutions, or opens bazaars, or lays foundation-stones, or in any other way attracts attention to himself. That made it all the more generous of him to espouse Miss Brabourne's cause so frankly. He knew what it would bring upon him. You can't think how much he had to suffer from the idiots sent down to interview him, the letters imploring him for his photograph, the journalists trying to bribe his crew to tell what their captain withheld. He could not prevent surreptitious newspaper artists from making sketches of the *Swan* as she lay at anchor; but his full anger blazed up when the *Pen and Pencil* produced a page of heads—you saw it, of course—including portraits of him, Fowler, myself, the idiot Saul, poor Godfrey, and Miss Brabourne. Where they got them from is to this day a mystery. We suppose most of them must have been done at the inquest. Ah! that was an exciting day. I can feel the enthusiasm of it now. It was splendid to see that fine fellow held up in the arms of the fisher-lads, with the sunshine blazing on him, and the bells clashing out from the tower!—the sort of thing one sees only once in a lifetime. It sounded like a bit of an old romance. I often tell Percivale he is an anachronism."

"He has a wonderful face; but it does strike one as strange that he should be so mysterious," said Wynifred. "Has he no family—no relations—no home?"

"He has no near relations living—he told me that himself," answered Claud. "He also told me that his mother died when he was born, and his father two months before. He was brought up in a castle in Bavaria by an English clergyman who had known his parents. This man was a recluse, and a great scholar. He died some years ago. Percivale has had as little of ladies' society as if he had been a monk. Now you know exactly as much as I do of his antecedents, Miss Allonby."

"I am afraid I seem very inquisitive; but to a writer of fiction there is a certain attraction about such an unusual history."

"And such an unusual personality. He is unlike anyone else I ever knew. I wonder," said Claud, feeling in his pockets, "if I have a note from him that I could show you. Yes. Here, read that. It is not like most people's notes."

Wynifred unfolded the stiff sheet of paper, and read. The hand was rather small and very peculiar. It seemed as though the writer were accustomed to write Greek. It was particularly clear.

"Dear Cranmer,
"Please help me. The German Opera Company is in
London, and Miss Brabourne has often expressed a wish
to hear some Wagner. If I take a box, could you bring your
sister, Lady Mabel Wynch-Frère, and Miss Brabourne to fill
it? If you think they would care to come, let me know what
night they are free. It is the "Meistersinger" on Tuesday,

and "Lohengrin" on Thursday. I wish you would answer this personally, rather than in writing. Dinner this evening at 7.30, if you care for the theatre afterwards. It is a week since we met.

"Affectionately yours,
"Leon Percivale.

"7, St James' Place, Thursday."

"Is there not something unique about that?" asked Claud, as she gave it back. "He always signs himself mine affectionately, in the most natural way possible. I am glad of it; I have a very sincere affection for him."

"I like his note very much," said Wyn, with a smile. "Thank you for letting me see it. You and he are great friends."

"I was with him seven or eight weeks on the *Swan*. He insisted on leaving England the moment he found that he had become a public character."

"Is he English? His note reads like it."

"I believe his father was English and his mother German; so I presume it was through her that he inherited his beautiful *Schloss*."

"Have you seen it?"

"Yes, I spent a week there. It is among the most northern spurs of the Tyrolese Alps. When there, you cease to wonder that Percivale is so unlike other people. It is like going back into a past age. The peasantry are Arcadian to a degree, the spot remote beyond the imagination of English people. The nearest railway station leaves you a day's journey from Schwannberg. Do you know Defregger's Tyrolese pictures? All the people are just like that. Over the door of every room in the castle is carved the swan, which is the family crest."

"But his father was English, I think you said?"

"Why—yes—I never thought of that. The arms must belong to the other side of the family, I suppose," said Claud, thoughtfully. "That is rather odd, certainly."

He turned with a start. Osmond Allonby was standing before them.

"Wyn, I'm sorry to interrupt you but we must really be going. We are almost the last."

The girl rose at once, and held out her hand to Claud.

"Good-night, Mr. Cranmer. I wish I had time to hear more about the inquest. I had been longing for news, and it is kind of you to have told me so much."

He rose too, and took the offered hand.

"Must you go?" he said, scarcely knowing that he said it.

In another moment she had released her hand and was walking calmly away. Not a word had she said about hoping to see him again. He was conscious of an intense wish that she should not go; he was not strong enough, he found, to let her depart thus. He made a step forward.

"Miss Allonby."

She paused.

"I shall be in town for some weeks now, probably. May I come and see you at Mansfield Road?"

She turned to her brother.

"We shall be pleased to see Mr. Cranmer, if he cares to come, shall we not, Osmond?"

"Certainly," said Osmond, cordially.

"Which day is most convenient for you?"

"You will not find Osmond on Mondays or Thursdays, as he conducts a life-class at the Woodstead Art School on those days; any other day. Good-night."

She was gone. He felt half-angry that she had so easily led him on to waste time in talking of indifferent topics. Yet, had she left him to choose a subject, what would his choice have been?

CHAPTER XXXVIII

She should never have looked at me if she meant I should not
love her! There are plenty ... men, you call such, I suppose
... she may discover All her soul too, if she pleases, and yet
leave much as she found them: But I'm not so, and she knew
it when she fixed me, glancing round them.

Cristina.

A variety of reasons kept the Allonbys very silent as they drove home
that night.

When Mansfield Road was reached, they walked into the hall, still in
the same silence. Osmond dismissed the cabman, followed them in, and
made fast the bars and bolts for the night.

"Good-night, old man," said Jac, coming up for a kiss.

"Good-night, young woman," he replied, with the air of one who does
not intend to be drawn into conversation.

"Girls," said Hilda, over the stairs. "Sal has put a fire in my bed-room.
Come along."

Jac flew upstairs. Wyn lingered a moment.

"Are you coming to bed, Osmond?" she said, anxiously, as she saw him
unlock the door leading to the studio.

"I think I'll have a pipe first," he answered, in a constrained voice. "Run
to bed and don't bother."

She hesitated a moment, but, seeing that interference would be useless,
went on upstairs, and joined the *séance* round Hilda's fire.

"Well," said Hilda, with a long sigh, "it *was* a delightful dance, wasn't
it?"

"The nicest I was ever at," returned Jac, with smiles dimpling round
her mouth.

Wyn did not echo these comments. She sat down with a sigh, and pulled
off her gloves.

"How well our lilies have lasted, Hilda," said Jac, spying at her own head in the glass. "Not a bit faded, are they? Wyn, you old wretch, you did look well. How everybody praised you up. I should think your head is turned."

"Humph!" was Wyn's discontented reply.

There was a pause, during which Jac secured Hilda's programme, and stealthily examined it.

"Well!" said Wyn, suddenly. "Now you have seen Lady Mabel, what do you think of her."

"She is exactly what I expected," observed Jac, who was possessed of considerable acumen. "That impulsive, frank manner is of great service to her. Nothing escapes her notice, I can tell you! She has decided not to take us up as a family. She does not feel quite sure as to what we might do. Vaguely she feels that Hilda and I are formidable, and poor Osmond, of course, is to be steadily discouraged. She will ask you, Wyn, because you are rather a celebrity just now; but nobody else."

"Jac—I think you misjudge— —"

"All right. Wait a fortnight. If an invitation comes for Osmond, Hilda, or me, to Bruton Street, I will humbly apologise for my uncharitable judgment."

"Jac is right," said Hilda, suddenly. "I spied Lady Mabel's eye upon me when I approached with Mr. Percivale!"

"By the way, do you like Mr. Percivale?" asked Wyn.

"I should think so!" was the emphatic answer.

Wyn passed her hand wearily over her brow.

"You look very tired, dear child," said Hilda, sympathetically.

"I am worried—about Osmond," she sighed. "I would give so much if—all that—had never taken place between him and Elsa. One sees now how hopeless—how *insane* the bare idea is; but I am afraid he doesn't think so, poor fellow!"

"Lady Mabel was very off-hand with him," said Jac. "I was near when she was ready to go, and Elsa was dancing with Osmond. Do you know, she danced five times with him."

"It was too bad of her!" cried Wyn.

"If she does not mean to marry him, it certainly was," said Hilda.

"Mean to marry him! They would not let her! I am thankful at least that there was no engagement," returned Wynifred, with energy. "That would just save his dignity, poor fellow, if one could restrain him, but I know he will rush like a moth to his candle, and get a fearful snub from Lady Mabel." She covered her face with her hands. "I can think of nothing else—I can't forget it," she said. "He will never get over it. He was never in love before in all his life."

"Won't his pride help him? I would do anything—anything," said Hilda, with vehemence, "sooner than let her see I was heart-broken.... I suppose she will marry Mr. Percivale."

"Or Mr. Cranmer," suggested Jac, in an off-hand way. "That is what Lady Mabel intends, I should think."

Wynifred winced painfully. It seemed as though Osmond's case were thrust before her eyes as a warning of what she had to expect. It braced—it nerved her to the approaching struggle. She would never be sick of love; and she determined boldly to face the sleepless night which she knew awaited her—to work hard, go to parties, anything, everything which might serve as an antidote to the poison she had imbibed that fatal summer.

When at last the girls separated for the night, Osmond was still in his studio. It was not till six o'clock had struck that Wyn's wakeful ears heard his footstep on the stairs, and the latch of his bed-room door close quietly.

Jac's prophecy was fulfilled. A few days brought an invitation to Wynifred from Lady Mabel to meet a few friends at dinner in Bruton Street. No mention was made in the note of either Osmond or the girls.

"I shall not go!" cried Wyn, fiercely.

"Wyn, my dear child, listen to me," said Hilda, with authority. "You *must* go. Beggars musn't be choosers. Look here what she says—'to meet several people who may be of use to you.' Oh, my dear child, you have published one successful novel, but your fortune is not made yet, is it? Think of poor old Osmond—think how important it is that we should all do the best we can for ourselves. In my opinion you ought to go. What do you say, Jac?"

"I suppose you must; but I should like to let Lady Mabel know my opinion of her," said Jac, grudgingly.

"Be just," urged Hilda. "Lady Mabel very likely thinks that to take us out of our sphere and to plant us in hers for a few hours would be to unfit us for our work. I believe she is right. What good would it do us to sit at her table and talk to men who would only tolerate us because we were her guests? Answer me that."

Jac said nothing.

"You see I am right," went on Hilda, triumphing. "She merely thinks, as Aunt Anna does, that we had better remain in our humble station; and it would be simple cruelty of her to invite Osmond under existing circumstances. It would be tantamount to giving him encouragement, would it not?"

Osmond himself, somewhat to his sister's surprise, when he heard of the invitation, was most anxious that she should accept it. It seemed as if anything which brought the two families together, however indirectly, was pleasant to him. On the subject of himself and Elsa he, however, quite declined to talk; and this reserve of his was to Wyn a dangerous symptom. However, he was very quiet, and had not yet made the suggestion his sisters dreaded, namely, that one of them should go with him to call on Lady Mabel.

Sometimes Wyn almost hoped that he had realised the futility of his desires, since Elsa would not be twenty-one till the following Christmas, and it was madness to suppose that Mr. Percivale would not press his suit before then. Sometimes she dreaded that, as we say of children, he was quiet because he was in mischief—in other words, that he was corresponding with Elsa, or otherwise intriguing; though this was not like Osmond.

With surmises she was forced to rest content, however. The invitation to dinner was accepted, and then came wretched days of hesitation and cowardice—days when she endured continual fluctuations of feeling, at one moment feeling as though all her future hung on that dinner-party, at another that nothing should induce her to go when the time came.

She had not, however, very much leisure for reflection just at this period. One of the monthly magazines wrote to ask a serial story from her on very short notice, and she was obliged to devote her attention to the expansion and completion of an unfinished fragment for which, before the appearance of "Cicely Montfort," she had tried to find a publisher in vain. On the third day after the Miles' ball, as she returned from a walk, she found Claud's card in the hall. After the first moment of keen disappointment, she was glad that she had not seen him.

What use to feed a flame she was bent on smothering?

She learned from Sal that the visitor had been into the studio and seen Mr. Osmond, and to the studio she accordingly bent her steps. Osmond was not working. He was seated on the edge of the "throne," his palette and brushes idle beside him, his face hidden in his hands. At the sound of the opening door, he leaped to his feet, and faced his sister half angrily.

"You startled me," said he.

"I am sorry. I hear you had a visitor to-day, so I came to know what he said."

"Oh, yes—Cranmer. He didn't say very much. Asked after you all; said he hoped you were not very tired after the dance; said he was looking forward to seeing you at his sister's. Not much besides. He seems very thick with this Mr. Percivale."

Turning aside, he aimlessly took up a dry brush and drew it across a finished canvas in slow sweeps.

"Wyn," he asked, "who *is* this Mr. Percivale?"

Wyn made a gesture of ignorance with her hands.

"I don't know," she said. "Nobody knows much about him. Mr. Cranmer told me all he knows the other evening." She related the meagre facts which Claud had given her. "But everyone seems agreed that he is very much all that can be wished," said she. "What made you ask me, dear?"

"I have been talking to Ottilie Orton," he said; and paused.

"To Mrs. Orton! And what had she to say, if one may ask?"

"You appear," observed Osmond, "to have taken a dislike to the lady in question."

"Well, I cannot say she fascinates me. She is so big and bold, and she looks artificial. She reminds me of that dreadful middle-aged Miss Walters who married the small, shy young curate of St. Mary's."

"She is a very handsome woman," said Osmond obstinately.

"Well, never mind her looks. What has she been saying to you?"

"Oh, she merely remarked," was the reply, as Osmond picked up his palette and charged a clean brush with color. "She merely made a remark about this Mr. Percivale whom everyone is so ready to take for granted."

"What was the remark?"

"She said there were several ugly stories afloat about him, and that—" he paused to put a deliberate touch upon his almost completely finished picture—"that his antecedents were most questionable."

CHAPTER XXXIX

Love is a virtue for heroes—as white as the snow on high
hills,
And immortal, as every great soul is, that straggles,
endures, and fulfils.
Lord Walter's Wife.

A long, dark, panelled room, with a low flat ceiling carved with coats-of-arms and traversed with fantastic ribs. A room so large and long that a small party could only inhabit one end of it. Its age was demonstrated by the massive stone mullions of the small windows ranged along the wall on one side. There were four of these windows, each of them with three lights. Beneath each group of three was a deep, cushioned recess.

Opposite the windows were two fireplaces, the elaborately-carved black oak mantels reaching to the ceiling. In the further of these a great fire burned red and glowing, flinging out weird, suggestive half lights into the dim recesses of the chamber, and flecking with sudden gleams the multitude of curious things with which every corner was stored.

The room was very still, the air heavy with the scent of flowers; the early January darkness had fallen over the great city, but something very unlike London was in the warm, fragrant silence of this place. One of the diamond-paned casements was open, but through it came no hoarse rumble of cart or waggon. An utter peace enfolded everything. Presently the door at the near and most densely dark end of the room opened and closed softly. From behind the great embossed screen which was folded round the entrance a flash of vivid light gleamed. A man-servant emerged, carrying a large silver lamp. He traversed the whole length of the room, and set down the lamp on a black oak table with heavy claw-feet.

The circle of radiance illuminated the scene, rendering visible the mellow oil-paintings on the panelled walls, the rich Oriental rugs which covered the floor of inlaid wood, and the treasures from all parts of the globe, which were ranged in cabinets or on shelves, or lay about on brackets and tables. A grand piano stood open not far from the fire, and beyond the groups of windows, in the corner, a curtain looped back over a small arched entrance looked darkly mysterious, till the servant carried in two small lamps and set them down, revealing a fine conservatory, and accounting for the garden-like fragrance of the place.

Silently the man moved to and fro arranging various lights, daintily shaded according to the present fashion; then, stepping to the windows, he closed them, and noiselessly let fall wide curtains of Titian-like brocades shot with golden threads.

This accomplished, the general aspect of the lighted end of the room was that of sumptuous elegance, warmth, and comfort; while the shadows slowly deepening, as you gazed down towards the door, left the dark limits indefinite, and conveyed an idea of mysterious distance and gloom.

Just as the servant's arrangements were completed, a bell sounded, and he hastily left the room as he had entered it, leaving once more silence behind him. So still was it that, when the shrill notes of the dainty sunflower clock on the Louis Quatorze escritoire rang out the hour in musical chimes, it seemed to startle the Dying Gladiator as his white marble limbs drooped in the rosy radiance of the big standard lamp.

Again that door opened, away there among the shadows; and slowly up the room, in evening dress, with his crush hat, and his inevitable Neapolitan violets, came Claud Cranmer, looking about him, as if he expected to see the master of this romance-like domain. Percivale was not there, however; so, with a sigh of pleasure, Claud sank down in one of the chairs set invitingly near the wide hearth, and leaned back contentedly.

Apparently, however, solitude and firelight suggested serious thoughts, for gradually a far-off look came into the young man's eyes—a tender light which seemed to show that the object of his meditations was some person or thing lying very near his heart. Presently he leaned forward, joining his hands and resting his chin upon them; and was so completely absorbed that he did not hear Percivale, who, advancing through the conservatory, paused on the threshold, gazing at his visitor with a smile.

Reaching out for a spike of geranium bloom, he threw it with such exact aim that it struck Claud on the face, startling him so that he sprang instantly to his feet, and, facing about, caught sight of the laughing face of his assailant.

"Good shot," said Percivale, coming in. "Sorry to keep you waiting, old man."

His hands were full of lilies of the valley, which he laid down on a small table, and then saluted his guest.

"You told me to come early," said Claud.

"Yes," was the answer. "I wanted to have a talk with you before the ladies arrived."

"Delighted. What do you want to talk about?" asked Mr. Cranmer, as the two young men settled themselves in comfort.

"It is a subject I have never touched upon before," said Percivale, hesitatingly. "Not to you or any man. I hardly know why I should expect that you should listen. I have no claim on your attention. I want to talk about—myself."

"Yourself?" Claud set up with keenly awakened interest.

"Myself. It is not an interesting topic...."

Breaking off, he leaned forward, supporting his chin on his left hand as he stared at the fire. Little flames sprang up from the red mass, cast flickering lights on his serious face, and glowed in his dark blue eyes. Claud thought he had never seen so interesting a man in his life. Whether on board the *Swan*, in his white shirt and crimson sash, or here in these quaint London rooms of his, in modern Philistine dress-clothes, he seemed equally at home, yet equally distinguished.

Mr. Cranmer waited for what he would say—he would not break in upon his meditations.

"Have you ever," slowly he spoke at last, "have you ever given your really serious attention to the subject of marriage? I mean, in the abstract?"

Claud started, tossed his head combatively, while an eager light broke over his face.

"Yes, I have," he replied, quickly. "I have considered very few things in my life, but this I have seriously thought over."

"I am glad," said Percivale, simply. "I want to know how you regard it. What place ought marriage to take in a man's life? Is it an episode? Ought it to be left to chance? Or is it a thing to be deliberately striven and planned for as the completion of one's existence? Is happiness possible for an unmarried man?—I mean, of course, happiness in its deepest and fullest sense? Can a man whose experience of life is partial and imperfect, as a single man's must be—can he be said to be a judge at all, not having tried it in its most important aspect? What do you think?"

"I do wish," said Claud, in an irritable voice, "that you would not put your question in that way. I wish you would not follow the example of people who talk of marriage in such an absurdly generic way, as if it were a fixed state, a thing in which the symptoms must be the same in every case, like measles or scarlet fever. I have always thought the subject of marriage left remarkably little room for generalising. One marriage is no more like another than one man is like another. The Jones marriage differs essentially from the Smith, because they are the Jones, and the Smiths are the Smiths. Yet people will be absurd enough to argue that because Jones is unhappy Smith had better not try matrimony. If he were going to marry the same woman there might be a show of reason in such an argument; but even then it wouldn't follow, because he is not the same man."

Percivale's eyes were fixed on the speaker.

"I see," he said, reflectively. "Your view is that the individual side of our nature is the side which determines the success or failure of marriage."

"Certainly—especially in this age of detail. In the Middle Ages, when life was shorter, people took broader views; and, besides, they had no nerves. Any woman who was young and anything short of repulsive as to her appearance would suit your feudal baron, who would perhaps only enjoy her society for a few weeks in the intervals of following the duke to the wars, or despoiling his neighbor's frontier. When they did meet, it was among a host of servants, men-at-arms, poor relations, minstrels and retainers; they had no scope for boring each other. A man's value was enhanced in his wife's eyes when it was always an open question, as she bade him adieu, whether they ever met again in this world. Moreover, in those days the protection of a husband was absolutely necessary to a woman. Left a widow, she became, if poor, a prey for the vicious—if rich, for the designing. Eccentricities of temper must have been kept wonderfully in the background, when issues like these were almost always at stake; the broad sympathies of humanity are, generally speaking, the same. Any woman and man will be in unison on a question of life or death; but now-a-days how different! Maid, wife, or widow can inhabit a flat in South Kensington without any need of a male protector to "act the husband's coat and hat set up to drive the world-crows off from pecking in her garden"—which Romney Leigh conceived to be one, though the lowest, of a husband's duties. And your choice of a woman becomes narrowed when one cannot live in London, another will not emigrate, a third differs from you in politics, a fourth disdains all social duties, a fifth can only sit under a particular preacher, and yet another dare not be out of reach of her family doctor. Times are changed, sir. Marriage to-day depends on the individual."

"Of course it must, to a large extent; and, to meet the requirements of the age, women are now allowed to marry where they fancy, and not where they are commanded. Yet, as one looks around at the marriages one knows," continued Percivale, "there is a sameness about matrimony."

"Just so," broke in Claud, eagerly. "Because, as we look round, we see only the outside life. There is a sameness about the houses in London streets; but strip away the wall, and what a difference you will find in each! I will find you points of likeness between Rome and Manchester. Both are cities, both have houses, streets, shops, churches, passers-by, palaces, hovels. So with Jones and Smith. Both are married, both have servants, children, houses, bills, all the usual attributes of marriage. Yet you might bet with certainty that the general atmosphere of Jones' life is no more like Smith's than the air of Rome resembles the air of Manchester. It makes me quite angry," went on the young man, with heat, "to hear fools say with a smile of some young bridegroom, 'He thinks his marriage is going to turn out a different affair from anyone else's.' If he does think so, he is perfectly right. It *will* be different. He will have an experience all his own; but it will give him no right at all to generalize afterwards on the advantages or disadvantages of marriage in the abstract—there is no such thing as marriage in the abstract!"

"You take it to heart," said Percivale, smiling at his earnestness.

"I do. Such balderdash is talked now-a-days about it. As if you could make a code of regulations to suit everyone—the infinitely varying temperaments of nineteenth-century English people!"

"Yet we find one code of laws, broadly speaking, enough to govern all these infinite varieties."

"Precisely! Their outer lives. But happiness in marriage does seem to me to be such a purely esoteric thing. 'It's folly,' says some one, 'to marry on a small income.' I hold that no one has the least right to lay down any such thing as a general proposition. It may be the height of folly—it may be the most sensible thing in the world. Nobody can pronounce, unless they know both the parties who contemplate the step. It seems to me that, granted only the right man and woman come together, the spring of happiness is from within. I can believe in an ideal marriage—I can fancy starvation with one woman preferable to a stalled ox with any other; but it must be one woman"—again that most unwonted softness in his eyes—"a woman who shall never disappoint me, though she might sometimes vex me; who shall be as faulty as she pleases, but never base; and then—then—'I'll give up my heart to my lady's keeping,' indeed, and the stars shall fall and the angels be weeping ere I cease to love her:—a woman, mind you, an imperfect, one-sided, human thing like myself!—no abstraction, but just what I wanted to complete me—the rest of me, as it were, placed by God in the world, for me to seek out and find."

There was a complete silence in the room after this outburst. Claud, half-ashamed of his spontaneous Irish burst of sentiment, stared into the fire assiduously. Percivale's hand was over his eyes. At last he said,

"You and I think much alike; and yet— —"

"Yet?"

"You want to bring your love out into the broad daylight of common life; you want to yoke her with yourself, to bear half the burden. For me, I think I would place mine above—I would stand always between her and the daily fret—she should be to me what Beatrice was to Dante: the vision of all perfection."

"You must not marry her, then," said Claud, bluntly.

"Not marry her?"

"No woman living would stand such a test. Think what marriage means! Daily life together. Your Beatrice would be obliged to come down from her pedestal. Not even your wealth could shield her from some thorns and briars; and then, when you found a mere woman with a little temper of her own instead of a goddess, you would be disillusioned."

After another pause—

"I don't agree with you," said Percivale. "I would make life such a paradise for the woman I loved that she should lead an ideal life—my experience will be, as you say, solitary. Perhaps other men's marriages will never be as mine shall. I speak with confidence, you see; because"—he rose, and stood against the mantel-piece, his head resting on his hand—"because I have seen the realization of my fancy. It is a real woman I worship, and no dream."

Claud raised his eyes, earnestly regarding the fine, enthusiastic face.

"The lady in question is greatly to be envied on most grounds," he said. "I only trust she will be able to act up to the standard of your requirements."

"My requirements? What do I require of her? Only her love! She shall have no trials, no vexations, no more loneliness, no more neglect—if only she will let me, I will make her happy!——"

"In point of fact," said Claud very seriously, "you ask of her just what God asks of men—an undivided allegiance, a perfect faith in the wisdom of your motives, and a resignation of herself into your hands. You ask no positive virtues in her—only that she shall love you fervently; in return for which you promise her a ceaseless, tender care, and boundless happiness. It does not sound difficult; yet human beings seem to find it amazingly so; and your beloved is unfortunately human. You see one does not realize at first what love implies. No love is perfect without self-denial——"

"I require no self denial," cried Percivale.

"I tell you no two people can live together without it."

"I am going to try, nevertheless. When I have been married a year and a day, you shall own that I have illustrated your theory, and had an experience all my own!"

"Agreed," was the answer, as the honest gray eyes dwelt on the dark-blue ones with an affection which seemed tinged with a faint regret. "But will you bear to confess failure if—if by chance failure it should be?"

"There is no question of failure," was the serenely confident answer, "always provided I attain the desire of my soul. But we have strayed wide of the mark in this interesting discussion. What I really wanted to consult you about was—was the difficulty of mine." He lapsed into thought for some minutes, and seemed to be nerving himself to speak.

"I wonder," he said at last, "if it really is a difficulty, or whether I have been making mountains out of mole-hills. Or, perhaps, on the other hand, I have not considered it enough, and it may form a serious obstacle...."

Claud's attention was now thoroughly aroused.

"It is—it is—" went on Percivale faltering, "it is a family secret—of course I need not ask you to consider this conversation as strictly private?"

"Of course—of course," said Claud, hastily.

"Well—it is a secret—a secret connected with my—father." It seemed a great effort for him even to say this much. "I never opened my lips on this subject to any human being before;" he spoke nervously.

"Don't say any more, if you had rather not," urged Claud, gently.

"I want to tell you, and I may as well do it quickly. Percivale was my father's christian, not his sur-name. The sur-name was one which you would know well enough were I to mention it—it was notorious through most parts of Europe. That name was coupled with undeserved disgrace;" he paused a moment, to strengthen his voice, then resumed:

"I entreat you to believe that the disgrace was utterly undeserved. It broke his heart. He went abroad with my poor young mother; they buried themselves in a small, remote German village. There he died; and she followed him when I was born. It was believed that he committed suicide: that was also untrue; he was murdered, lest the truth should come to light. I heard all this from Dr. Wells, a clergyman who had been my father's tutor.

He was a real friend—the only man to whom my father appealed in his trouble. At my birth, he took me to Schwannberg, the Castle of which my mother was heiress. She was an orphan when my father married her—twenty years younger than himself. Dr. Wells alone knew all the exact details of the whole affair. He made a statement in writing, which is in my possession, setting forth his knowledge of my father's blameless conduct and the manner of his death. I could not show you this paper without your knowing my father's name—and that, I hope, is not at present necessary. Now, to come to the point. I have always used the name of Percivale, because it was my mother's most earnest entreaty on her deathbed, that, if I lived to grow up, I should do so. I have not a relation living, so far as I know. Do you think that I should be justified in marrying without mentioning what I have told you? Should I do anyone any wrong by leaving the story untold? You will see that to half-tell it, as I have just done, would be impossible. I should have to mention names; and—and——" he dropped into a chair, covering his face with his hands.

"Dr. Wells was father and mother both to me," he said. "When his health failed, I had the *Swan* built that his life might be prolonged. He liked to roam from place to place in the strong sea-air. I think it did serve to keep him with me for some time. When I lost him there was no one.... He made me promise him to respect my mother's wish, and keep the name by which my father had been known a profound secret. The reasons for this are partly political. I think he was right, but I find that, from having lived so little in the world, I do not always think as others do; so I determined to consult you. Do you see any reason to drag this Cerberus to the light of day? or should you let it alone?"

Claud sat plunged in thought.

"There is no possibility of its ever getting about unless you mention it?" said he at last.

"None, so far as I can see. Even old Müller, on my yacht, who was a servant in the house when my mother died, does not know of my father's changed name nor false accusation. No one in England of those who knew him under his own name knew of his marriage, still less that he had left a son. I have exercised the minds of all London for the past seven years, but nobody has ever guessed at anything dimly resembling the truth. Were I to proclaim aloud in society that I was the son of such a one, nobody would believe me. The secret is not a shameful one. Were I the son of a criminal, I would ask the hand of no woman without telling her friends of my case; but my father was a gentleman of high birth and stainless honor. May I not respect the silence he wished observed as to his name?"

"I think so," said Claud, with decision. "I should not even hint at there being a mystery surrounding your parentage."

"Naturally not. I must tell all or nothing."

"Then I should tell nothing. I see no reason why you should. Your father's secret is your own; I would not blazon it to the world."

"That is your deliberate opinion?"

"Certainly—my deliberate opinion. I am honored, Percivale, that you have trusted me so generously."

"I knew you were to be trusted," said Percivale, simply; then, turning his face fully towards him with a fine smile, he added—"I shall, of course, tell my wife the whole story when we are married."

"What, names and all?" said Claud anxiously.

"Names and all. I will marry no woman unless I feel that I can safely lay my life and honor in her hands."

Claud had no reply to make; in the silence which followed, the door at the obscure end of the room opened, and the servant, advancing to the borders of the lamplight, announced,

"Lady Mabel Wynch-Frère and Miss Brabourne."

CHAPTER XL

Beat, happy stars, timing with things below,
Beat with my heart, more blest than heart can tell,
Blest, but for some dark undercurrent woe
That seems to draw—but it shall not be so:
Let all be well, be well.
Maud.

"Dinner at once, Fritz," said Percivale to his servant, as he advanced to meet his guests.

"Are we late?" cried Lady Mabel, as she swept her silken skirts up the long room, and greeted her host with extended hand. "It must be Elsa's fault, then—she was so long dressing."

"Oh, Lady Mabel!" cried Elsa, in lovely confusion, as she came forward in her turn.

She was in black to-night—some delicate, clinging, semi-transparent material, arranged in wonderful folds, with gleams of brightness here and there. It caused her neck and arms to seem a miracle of fairness; the arrangement of her golden hair was perfect, a diamond arrow being stuck through its masses.

To the chivalrous poetic mind of her lover, she was a dream of beauty—a thing hardly mortal—so transfused with soul and spirit, that no thought of the mundane or the commonplace could intrude into his thoughts of her.

Disillusioned! Could any man ever be disillusioned who had the depths of those lake-like eyes to gaze into?

She gave him her little hand—*bien gantée*—and lifted those eyes to his. Lady Mabel had passed on to speak to her brother.

"I have no flowers," said Elsa, softly "you told me not to wear any."

"I wished you to wear mine, will you?" said Percivale.

Her eyelids fell before his eager glance: but she made a little movement of assent.

He turned to the table, and taking up the fragrant bouquet of lillies, placed it in her hands; then lifting another of mixed flowers, which lay beside it, he offered it to Lady Mabel, with an entreaty that she would honor him by carrying it that night.

As he spoke, a pair of dark curtains, which hung at the upper end of the room, were drawn back by two men in livery; and Fritz, appearing in the aperture, solemnly announced,

"Dinner is served."

Percivale offered Lady Mabel his arm, and led her through the archway, followed by Claud and Elsa.

"Claud, will you take the foot of the table for me?" said he.

"Which do you call the foot?" laughed Claud, as he sat down opposite his host at the daintily appointed round table.

The room was very much smaller than that they had quitted, but was quite a study in its way. Vanbrugh had designed the ceiling and carvings, and a fine selection of paintings adorned the walls. A beautiful Procaccini was let into the wall above the mantelpiece; a Sasso Ferrato was opposite. Two Ruysdaels lent the glamor of their deep gloomy wood and sky, and the foam of their magic waterfalls. The whole room was lit with wax candles, and fragrant with the violets which composed the table decorations.

"I am so sorry to seem to hurry you," said Percivale, apologetically; "but I want Miss Brabourne to hear the overture; one ought not to miss the overture to 'Lohengrin,' though I find it is the fashion in England to saunter in in the middle of the first act."

"Oh, dear, yes; but we don't go to the opera to hear music in England," laughed Lady Mabel. "It is to see the new *prima donna*, or study the costumes of the ladies in the stalls."

"I should have no objection, if these laudable objects could be attained without spoiling the pleasure of those who are sufficiently out of date to wish to listen to the performance," replied Percivale. "It is the one thing in England which I cannot bear with temper! It would not be allowed in Germany."

"Germany is the land of the leal for those that love music."

"Yes, indeed; there one can let oneself go, in utter enjoyment, knowing that there can be no onslaught of large and massive Philistine, sweeping her ample wraps, kicking your toes, struggling across your knees, banging down the seat of her stall with a report that eclipses and blots out a dozen delicate chords. No loudly whispered comments, no breathless pantings are audible, no wrestling with contumacious hooks and clasps sets your teeth on edge. For the unmusical and vociferous British female, if she have arrived late, will be forcibly detained at the door till the first act is over, and even then will enter despoiled of most of her weapons for creating a disturbance, having been forced to leave her superfluous clothing in the *garde-robe*."

They had never seen Percivale so gay, nor so full of talk. He chatted on about one subject and another, addressing himself mostly to Lady Mabel, whilst Claud was constrained to listen, since Elsa was even more silent than her wont.

The dinner was excellently cooked and served.

"You are a perfect Count of Monte Cristo, Percivale," laughed Claud. "I feel myself waiting for the crowning point of the entertainment. Will not your slaves presently bring in a living fish, brought from Russia in salt water to die on the table? Shall we each find a Koh-i-noor diamond in our finger-bowl as a slight mark of your esteem? Or, at a given signal, shall we be buried in a shower of rose-leaves like the guests of Heliogabalus!"

Percivale laughed, and reddened.

"Sorry to disappoint you, but I have prepared no conjuring tricks to-night," he said. "Another time, perhaps, when we have more leisure. Lady Mabel, you must not judge of the entertainment I like to offer my guests from this hurried little meal; you will do me the honor to return here after the opera, and have some supper? I am afraid we have no time to lose now."

"Mabel neither eats anything herself nor thinks that other people ought to," complained Claud. "I suffer a daily martyrdom in her house, and I am sure I begin to perceive signs of inanition in Miss Brabourne. You see, it demoralises the cook. She thinks that to live on air is the peculiarity of the upper ten, and wants me to dine on a cutlet the size of half-a-crown with a tomato on the top, followed by the leg of a quail."

"How can you, sir?" cried Lady Mabel, in mock indignation, shaking her fist at her brother.

"I tell you it's the literal truth; that is the real reason why poor Edward is wintering abroad. He cannot reduce his appetite to the required pitch of elegance."

"If elegance consists in eating nothing, Mr. Percivale may take the prize to-night," observed Lady Mabel, significantly, as she and Elsa rose from table.

"I—have not much appetite to-night," stammered the young man, in some confusion, as he started up and held the curtain for the ladies to pass through.

He remained standing, so, with uplifted arm, for several seconds after the sweep of Elsa's black skirts had died away into silence; then, letting the curtain drop suddenly into place, turned back and tossed his crushed serviette upon the table. She had been there—in these lonely rooms, which year by year he had heaped with treasures for the ideal bride who was to come. Now the fancy had taken shape—the vision was realised; the beautiful woman of his dreams stood before him in bodily form. Would she take all this treasured, stored-up love and longing which he was aching to cast at her feet?

Claud broke in upon his reverie.

"I wish you luck, Leon," said he, coming up and grasping his hand.

His friend turned round with a brilliant smile.

"That is a capital omen," he said, "that you should call me by my name. Nobody has called me by my name—for five years. Thank you, Claud."

He returned the pressure of the hand with fervor; then, starting, said:

"Come, get your coat, we shall be late," and hurried through the archway, followed by Mr. Cranmer.

The opera-house was crowded that night. There were the German enthusiasts occupying all the cheap places, their scores under their arms, their faces beaming with anticipation; there was the fashionable English crowd in the most costly places, there because they supposed they ought to say they had heard "Lohengrin," but consoling themselves with the thought that they could leave if they were very much bored, and mildly astonished at the eccentricity of those who could persuade themselves that they really liked Wagner. And lastly, there were the excessively cultured English clique, the apostles of the music of the future, looking with gentle tolerance on the youthful crudities of "Lohengrin," and sitting through it only because they could not have "Siegfried" or the "Götterdämmerung."

A very languid clapping greeted the conductor of the orchestra as he took his seat. Percivale, watching Elsa, saw her eyes dilated, her whole being poised in anticipation of the first note, as the *bâton* was slowly raised. There was a soft shudder of violins—a delicate agony of sound vibrated along the nerves. Can any operatic writer ever hope to surpass that first slow sweep of suggestive harmony? From the moment when the overture began, Percivale's beloved sat rapt.

The curtain rose on the barbaric crowd—the dramatic action of the opera began. At the appearance of her namesake, the falsely accused Elsa of Brabant, a storm of feeling agitated the modern Elsa as she gazed.

At last she could keep silence no longer. Turning up her face to Percivale's, who sat next her:

"Oh," she whispered, "it is like me—and you came, like Lohengrin, to save me."

He smiled into her eyes.

"Nay," he said, "I am no immortal or miraculous champion; you will not induce me to depart as easily as he did. Besides, I do not think he was right—he demanded too much of his Elsa—more than any woman was capable of. You will see what I mean, when the next act begins."

To these two, as they sat together—so near—almost hand-in-hand, the music was fraught with an exquisite depth of meaning which it could not bear to other ears.

As the notes of the distant organ broke through the orchestra, and rolled sonorous from the cathedral doors, it was like a foreshadowing to Percivale of his own future happiness.

And when, in the twilight of their chamber, Lohengrin and Elsa were left alone, and the mysterious thrilling melody of the wonderful love-duet was flooding the air, unconsciously the hand of the listening girl fell into that of her lover, and so they sat, recking nothing of the significance of the action, until the curtain fell.

"Now you will see," spoke Percivale, softly, "that Lohengrin did what I could not do; he left his—Elsa."

She did not answer; she could not. Ashamed of her late action, and with a tumult of strange new feelings stirring in her heart, she turned her head away from him, and would not speak again until the end of the opera.

"I want to offer an apology," said Percivale to Lady Mabel, as he arranged her cloak. "Will you condescend to drive back in a hansom? My coachman has rheumatism, and I told him he was not to come for us."

"Certainly. I have a great partiality for hansoms," answered Lady Mabel, readily; she was rather disconcerted, however, a moment later, to find that it was her brother who was at her elbow.

"Where is Elsa? Claud, you should have taken her," she said, rather irritably.

"I? Thanks, no. I don't care to force my company on a young lady who would rather be with the other fellow. No hurry, Mab. I want to light a cigar."

"Nonsense, Claud. Get me a cab at once. Am I to wait in this draughty place?"

"You must, unless you are prepared to walk in those shoes as far as the end of the street."

"But where are the other two? Are they behind?"

"No; got the start of us, I fancy," said Claud, with exasperating calmness. "Wait a moment. I will go out and catch a cab if you will stay here."

He vanished accordingly and his sister was constrained to wait for him. When at last he returned, she was almost the only lady still waiting.

"You have no idea," said Claud, apologetically, "of the stupendous difficulty of finding a cab. They all say they are engaged. I feel quite out of the fashion, Mab; I think I ought to be engaged."

"I'm not in a mood for nonsense, sir. I am vexed with you, and with Mr. Percivale, too. He could not have meant to treat me like this—he had no right to make off in that manner and leave me in the lurch."

"To be left in the lurch *is* sometimes the fate of chaperones," observed her brother, pensively, as he piloted her out of the theatre. "I am afraid you hardly counted the cost, Mab, when you offered to chaperone a beauty. It is hardly your *rôle*, old lady."

This was too true to be pleasant. Lady Mabel was so accustomed to male admiration that she usually took it for granted that she was the attraction. The great influx of young men which inundated Bruton Street had caused her, only a few days back, to congratulate herself that her charms were still potent. Percivale's good looks, riches, and generally unusual *entourage* had led her to imagine that a platonic friendship with him would enliven the winter. The idea suggested by her brother's words was like a douche of cold water. If he were such an idiot as to be in love with the pretty face of the foolish Elsa—well! But he was so fascinating that one could not help regretting it! He was raised all of a sudden to a much higher value than the crowd of adorers who in general formed her ladyship's court. Surely he could not intend to go and tie himself down at his age! The thought greatly disturbed her.

"Claud, you must throw away that cigar, and tell him to let down the glass—I am frozen."

Claud complied.

"He's going in a very queer direction," observed he, presently. "Hallo, friend, this is not the way to St. James's Place."

"Thought you said St. James' Square, sir."

"Well, I didn't; it's exactly the opposite direction, down by the river——"

"Right, sir. I know it."

"I suppose you will get there some time to-morrow morning," observed his sister, icily.

"I am tearing my lungs to pieces in my efforts to do so," was the polite response.

Percivale and Elsa stood together in the lamplight.

Thanks to Claud's kindly manoeuvres, a precious half-hour had been theirs. The young man's arms were round the slim form of his beloved and there was a look in his eyes as though, to him, life had indeed become the "perfumed altar-flame" to which Maud's lover likened his.

A deep hush was over the whole place, and over his noble soul as he held his treasure tenderly to him.

Presently, breaking through his rapturous dream, he led her to the window, and, pushing it open, they gazed down on the wide dark waters of the Thames, lighted by a million lamps.

"We stand together as did Lohengrin and his Elsa," he murmured. "Oh, love, love, love, if I could tell you how I love you!"

"It is sweet to be loved," said the girl. "I have never had much love, all my life. When first I went abroad, and began to read novels, I used to wonder if any such thing would ever happen to me."

"But—but," faltered Percivale, a sudden jealous pang darting through his consciousness, "did not some one speak to you of love before—before I ever saw you, sweet?"

"Oh, Osmond Allonby. Poor Osmond!" Leaning back against his arm she turned her beautiful face to his. "I did not know what love meant, then," she said.

He bent his mouth to hers.

"You know now, Elsa?"

Even as he kissed her, a sudden unbidden memory of Claud's warning words rushed in and seemed just to dash the bliss of that caress.

"You ask more than any woman can give?" No, he fiercely told himself, he asked of her nothing but to be just what she was. Was it her fault that Osmond could not look on her without loving? Most certainly not.

Love and happiness, the two things from which this rich young man had been debarred, seemed all his own at last.

Farewell to lonely cruising and aimless travels. His heart's core, his life's aim was found; the birthday of his life had come.

CHAPTER XLI

Well, you may, you must, set down to me
Love that was life, life that was love;
A tenure of breath at your lips' decree,
A passion to stand as your thoughts approve,
A rapture to fall where your foot might be.
James Lee's Wife.

"Come in," was the languid reply, as Lady Mabel knocked briskly at her young guest's bed-room door.

Lady Mabel had been up for hours. If there was one thing upon which she prided herself, it was on being an exemplary mother. She had breakfasted with her little girls and their governess at eight, had seen her housekeeper, made arrangements for her dinner-party that night, send Claud out shopping for her with a lengthy list of commissions, written several notes, and now, trim, freshly dressed, and energetic, presented herself at Elsa's door to know how she felt after the fatigues of her first opera.

Elsa was just out of her bed. She was lolling in a deep luxurious arm-chair, with all her golden hair streaming about her. Her room was in a state of the utmost disorder, and her French maid stood behind her with an expression of deep and embittered sulkiness.

"My good child, what is the meaning of all this mess?" cried Lady Mabel, somewhat aghast. Miss Brabourne's habits daily set all her teeth on edge; though her shortcomings were probably only the natural rebound after the state of repression and confinement in which she had been brought up.

At Edge Combe there had been no shops, and she had been allowed no pocket-money; consequently she now never went out for a walk without lavishly purchasing a hundred useless and costly trifles with which she strewed her room. Under the regime of the Misses Willoughby no untidiness had been permitted; Miss Brabourne had darned her own stockings and repaired her own gloves. Now she let the natural bent of her untidy disposition have full play, flung her things about in all directions, and never touched a needle. In her childhood she had been obliged to rise at seven, and practise calisthenics for an hour before breakfast. Now that this restraint was removed, she never rose to breakfast at all, but usually spent the entire morning dawdling about in her bed-room in a loose wrapper, and with her hair hanging over her shoulders.

Like Lady Teazle, she was more self-indulgent, and gave far more trouble to her maid, than if she had been reared in habits of the greatest luxury. All her tastes were expensive and elegant. Dress was almost a mania with her, and no sooner had she been allowed to plan her own than she manifested a wonderfully correct taste. The rustic nymph, on whom Percivale's eyes had first fallen when he landed on Edge Beach, had entirely disappeared in the Miss Brabourne who lived only for fashion, admiration, and amusement.

She knew exactly what suited her—how daring her perfect complexion and fine shape permitted her to be in her choice of color and style—how the greatest severity only showed up and enhanced her beauty the more. Her whole time was devoted to the planning of new toilettes; her lengthiest visits were to her dressmaker.

Henry Fowler had not thought it prudent to make an exceedingly large allowance to a girl who had never had money to spend before; but this in no way circumscribed Elsa's movements, since before she had been a week in London she found out that unlimited credit could be hers.

The account-books carefully prepared by Aunt Charlotte before taking leave of her young niece lay at the bottom of her trunk, the virgin whiteness of their pages unmarked by a single entry. She had come to London to enjoy herself, and she meant to do so. Her visit could not last more than a few weeks, and then she would have to go back to Edge.

This thought was horror and misery unutterable. She loathed the place. Every association was hateful to her. She never wished to behold it again. As each day brought her nearer to the hideous prospect, her spirit shrank from it more and more. There was no other house in London where she could become a visitor, as the break with the Ortons was of course complete and final. And there was no hope at all of the aunts bringing her to town. The agitations of the past summer had greatly aggravated Miss Helen's weakness, and Miss Charlotte and Miss Emily had declared, on returning from their four months abroad, that they should not dare leave Fanny again in sole charge.

The thought of living the spring and summer through mewed up in lonely captivity at Edge, after the intoxicating taste of life and pleasure which she had had, was too terrible to be borne with gratitude.

Elsa could see no way out of the dilemma but to be married.

But Osmond Allonby could not help her here. He could not afford to marry yet; and to be married at once was her aim. And now, suddenly, unexpectedly, dazzlingly, here was Mr. Percivale, the wonderful owner of the yacht, the stately gentleman, the rich, mysterious stranger, offering her his heart as humbly as if she had been an empress.

The girl felt her triumph in every fibre of her nature. It had not occurred to her to think of Percivale as her lover.

His stately courtesy and distant reverence had seemed to her like pride. He had never been openly her slave, as was Osmond, whose infatuation had been patent from the first moment of meeting. Her admiration for the hero had been always mixed with a certain fear and great shyness.

She had heard him discussed wherever they went—here in London as well as all along the Mediterranean—when, wherever the yacht put in, it had been the cause of boundless excitement and interest, heightened to fever-heat when it was discovered that the solitary and mysterious owner had friends on board.

She knew that he was considered one of the "catches" of society—that to be on intimate terms with him was the aim of some of the leaders of the world of fashion. Town gossip never tired of his name, and whatever it had to say of him had been listened to with eager ears by Elsa.

Gossip and scandal had never been heard at Edge Willoughby; they had all the charm of novelty to the uninitiated girl, who absorbed the contents of every society journal she could get, and was far better versed in the latest morganatic marriage or the Court sensation than was Lady Mabel, who, being genuinely a woman of intelligence, usually let such trash alone.

Thus were filled the blank spaces which Elsa's training had left in her mind. Wynifred's dictum had been perfectly accurate. Not knowing their niece's proclivities in the least, the Misses Willoughby had not known what to guard against in her education. They had regarded her as so much raw material, to be converted into what fabric they pleased; now, her natural impulses began to show themselves with untutored freedom.

She was acutely alive to the importance of her conquest, but she was, let it be granted her, perfectly honest, as far as she knew, in telling Percivale that she loved him. She liked him very much; she admired his personal appearance exceedingly; she was beyond measure flattered at his preference; she preferred him, on every ground, to either Osmond Allonby, or any other man she had ever seen.

Of what love, in its highest and deepest sense, meant—such love as Percivale offered her—she was intensely ignorant; but few men will quarrel with incomprehension, if only it be beautiful; and how beautiful she was! Even Lady Mabel confessed it, much as the girl irritated her, as she sat supine before her in the easy-chair, lightly holding a hand-mirror.

"My dear Elsa, are you aware that Mr. Miles will be here in half-an-hour for a sitting?"

"I know," said Elsa, in her laconic way; adding, as if by an after-thought. "It isn't my fault; Mathilde is so stupid this morning. I must have my hair properly done when Mr. Miles comes, and I have had to make her pull it all down twice."

"There is no satisfying mademoiselle," muttered Mathilde.

"Mathilde, don't be rude," said Elsa, calmly.

Poor Mathilde! To her were doled out, day after day, all the countless small grudges owed to Jane Gollop by her young mistress. Like all oppressed humanity, when once the oppression was removed, Elsa tyrannised. The maid proceeded to lift the luminous flexible masses of threaded gold, and to pack them afresh over the top of the small head in artistic loops, the girl keenly watching every movement in the mirror.

"Don't wait, please, Lady Mabel," said she, abstractedly, arranging the soft short locks on her brow. "I shall be down in ten minutes; I want to say something to you particularly."

Lady Mabel, after a significant glance round the room, shrugged her shoulders, and went out.

"Her husband need be rich," she soliloquised as she descended the stairs.

Claud was seated in her morning-room, his youngest niece upon his knee. This fascinating person, whose age was three, was confiding to her uncle the somewhat unlooked-for fact that she was a policeman, and intended to take him that moment to prison. If he resisted, instant death must be his portion. Two plump white fists were clenched in his faultless shirt-collar, and he hailed his sister's entrance with a whoop of relief.

"Just in time, Mab! My last hour had come," he cried, as he relegated the zealous arm of the law to the hearth-rug, stood up, and shook himself. "Why do children invariably select the tragedy and not the comedy of life for their games? I should think, Mab, for once that you and I assisted at a wedding we took part in a hundred executions—ay, leading parts, too; the bitterness of death ought to be past for us two."

"Have you been taking care of this monkey?" said Mab, rubbing her face lovingly against his arm. "What a comfort you are to have in the house, dear boy; far more useful than my visitor upstairs, for instance. She is not handy with children, to say the least of it."

"She has not had my long apprenticeship," returned Claud, good-humoredly. "Hallo, Kathleen mavourneen, I draw the line at the poker, young lady."

"Baby, be good," said baby's mother, as her daughter was reluctantly induced to part with her weapon. "You make excuses for Elsa, Claud; why don't you admit that you are as much disappointed in her as I am?"

"Because I am not at all disappointed in her. You know, after the first few days, she never attracted me in the least."

"I know. I used to wonder why. Now I give you credit for much discrimination. She will never make a good wife."

"I say, that is going too far, Mab. She may develop—I hope—" he paused, and his voice took an inflection of deep feeling—"I devoutly hope she may."

"Why?"

"Because the happiness of the best man I know is absolutely dependent on her."

"Claud! He told you?"

"Yes."

The young man leaned his arm on the mantelpiece, fixing a meditative eye on his niece as she crawled up his leg.

"Did you—did you not—dissuade him in any way?"

"No," was the slow reply.

"I think, Claud, if he asked for your opinion—"

"Well, he didn't—that is, not on the lady. He did not even mention her name. I told him that, broadly speaking, I thought everything depended on compatibility of disposition; but what on earth is the use, Mab, of cautioning a man who is head over ears in love, as he is? You might as well try to stop Niagara; he is beyond the reasoning stage. Besides, what could I urge? That I believed the lady of his choice to be selfish, vain, and not too sweet-tempered? I couldn't say that, you know; and of course he thinks he is likely to know about as much of her as I do; he has been with her, on and off, ever since the autumn."

"Oh, you men, you men!" cried Mab. "Caught by a pretty face, even the best and noblest of you!"

"Not I," interrupted Claud, shortly. "No! That beautiful girl upstairs doesn't know what it means to love as I would have my wife love me. She has no passion in her! And she does not know the value of love! She does not know that it is the one, only central force of life—the thing without which any lot is hard—with which any hardship is merely a trifle not worth noticing. How should she know the power of it, that flame which, once lit, burns slowly at first,—cold, perhaps, and faintly—for the loves that flare up at once are straw fires, they burn out. This that I mean grows slowly, steadily, till all the heart is one glowing, throbbing mass, flinging steadfast heat and radiance around. This is love."

Lady Mabel's susceptible Irish eyes were wet. She had missed her life's aim, not through her own fault: which fact perhaps helped to make her brother so tender to her failings, so anxious for her happiness.

"You speak feelingly, Claud," she said.

"Do I?" said the young man. He lowered his eyes to the carpet, and blushed, smiling a little.

"Claud!" vehemently cried his sister, "you are in love!"

"If I am, it is with my eyes open. I am not a boy, Mab."

"No, indeed; but who can she be. Won't you tell me, dear?"

"I can't tell you, because I'm afraid I am in the ignoble case of loving without return. You see," he faltered, "there is nothing very heroic about me—nothing that I ever said or did, as far as I know, would entitle me to the slightest respect from any woman with a high standard. Look at my life. What have I done with it? Just nothing. Why, Kathleen mavourneen," cried he, diving down to the rug, and catching the warm white child in his arms, "the most onerous of my duties has been to carry you up to bed on my shoulder, hasn't it?"

"Claud, my dear old man, you mustn't! Why, what an untold comfort you have been to me when Edwar—when I could not have lived but for you!" cried Mab, the tears splashing on her cheeks. "I envy your wife! She will have the most constant, loving care of any woman under heaven—you will be an ideal husband—the longer she is married the better she will learn to appreciate you!"

"I never shall have a wife at all, Mab, if I cannot get this one," said Claud, with a ring of determination in his voice which was quite new.

Lady Mabel contemplated him for a moment.

"Is she rich, Claud?"

"No," said he, laughing a little.

"So I expected. Trust you never to love a rich woman. You would sit down and analyse your feelings till you became perfectly certain that some greed of gain mingled with your affection. But, my dear boy, forgive the pathos of the inquiry, but how should you propose to set up housekeeping?"

"I should take a post—cut the Bar and take a post."

"Charming, but who will offer the post?"

"A friend of mine," was the mysterious reply.

"Percivale, of course. Well, I suppose he has influence. Poor fellow! I could wish him to have a happier future than seems to me to lie before him."

"Tell you, Mab, you take too serious a view. I will sketch his married career for you. The first six weeks will be bliss unutterable, because he will himself turn on his own rose-colored light upon everything and everybody, and his bride will be beautiful, amiable, and passive. Then will come a disillusioning, sharp and bitter. He will be most fearfully upset for a time, there will be a period of blank horror, of astonishment, of incredulity, almost of despair. Then will dawn the period when the bridegroom will discover that his wife is neither the angel he first took her for, nor the fiend she afterwards seemed, but a very middling, earthly young person, with youth and beauty in her favor. Once wide awake from the dream that was to have lasted for ever, he will pull himself together, and find life first tolerable, then pleasant; but for the remainder of his days he will never be in love with his wife again, even for a moment. Now in my case——"

He had never mentioned his love before to anyone; in fact, until last night's talk with Percivale he had scarcely been sure of it himself. To use his own metaphor, his friend had stirred the smouldering hot coals, and they had burst into blaze at last. The earth and air were full of Wynifred. The end of life seemed at present to consist in the fact that she was coming to dine that night.

His sister's thoughts still ran on Percivale.

"Claud," she said, "do you really think it will be as bad as that?"

"More or less, I am afraid so. He is a man with such a very high ideal— with a rectitude of purpose, a purity of motive which do not belong to our century. Miss Brabourne *must* disappoint him. But she is very young, and one can never prophesy exactly ... marriage sometimes alters a girl completely, and his nature is such a strong one, it must influence hers. I think she is a little in awe of him, which is an excellent thing; though how long such awe will last when she discovers that his marital attitude is sheer prostration before her, I cannot tell. Besides, he does not really require that she shall love him, only that she shall permit him to love her as much as he will; at present, at least, such an arrangement will just suit her."

As he spoke the words, the door opened to admit Elsa herself.

She entered, looking such a picture of girlish grace and sweetness as more than accounted for Percivale's subjugation. She wore the semi-classic robe of white and gold, in which Mr. Miles had chosen to paint her; and, as it was an evening dress, she had covered her shoulders with a long white cloak, lined with palest green silk.

"Oh!" she stopped short, laughing. "Good-morning, Mr. Cranmer! I did not know you were here. I feel so crazy, dressed up like this in broad daylight. I wonder if I might be rude enough to ask you to turn out for a few minutes? I want to speak to Lady Mabel."

CHAPTER XLII

He either fears his fate too much,
Or his deserts are small,
That fears to put it to the touch
To win or lose it all!
Marquess of Montrose.

Lady Mabel's dinner-party was a very cultured but also a somewhat unconventional one. Twelve was the number of guests, and all of them were young, lively, and either literary, scientific, artistic, or otherwise professional.

Wynifred had been invited, as Jacqueline's penetration had divined, solely on the score of "Cicely Montfort's" success.

If there was one thing that Lady Mabel loved, it was a gathering of this sort: where everything imaginable was discussed, from anthropomorphism to the growing of tobacco in England—from Egyptian hieroglyphics to the latest *opera bouffe*. The relations of her ladyship's husband would have had a fit could they have peeped from the heights of their English starch and propriety at the *mixed* company in Bruton Street. But, not greatly to his wife's regret, Colonel Wynch-Frère's health had entailed a sojourn in Egypt for the winter, and his relations were conspicuous by their absence. Claud, her unconventional, happy-go-lucky brother, made all the host she required. However little he might care for the young actors and journalists who adored his sister, he was always genially ready to shake hands and profess himself glad to see them; and when his eldest brother, the earl, complained to him of Mabel's vagaries, he would merely placidly reply that he did not see why the poor girl should not have some pleasure in her life— let her take it how she pleased.

Her ladyship was, of course, a holder of that unwritten axiom which governs modern culture, *Intelligence implies infidelity.*

If she met anyone who had read, or thought, on any subject whatever, she took it for granted that they had decided that the gospels were spurious, and St. Paul, as Festus discovered, beside himself. Of course she, in common with everyone else equally enlightened, kindly conceded the extreme beauty of the gospel narrative and the great force of St. Paul's reasoning on false premises—as furnishing a kind of excuse to those people who had ignorantly accepted them as a Divine message for so long.

The great charm of holding these opinions was that she found so many to sympathise with her, and she had invited a selection of these to dinner that night, sure that the conversation would be most interesting and instructive. Concerning Wynifred's views on this point she had no definite knowledge. "Cicely Montfort" spoke of Christianity as still a vital force, and of the Church Catholic as bearing a Divine charter to the end of time; but, of course, Christianity is a very artistic theme, with highly dramatic possibilities, and the most utter unbeliever may use it effectively to suit the purposes of fiction. Anyway, Lady Mabel's breadth of view constrained her to hope the best—to expect enlightenment until ignorance and superstition had been openly avowed; so she invited Miss Allonby to dinner.

Her pretty drawing-room was as complete as taste could make it; she herself was a study, as she stood on the fur hearth-rug, receiving her friends, with all her Irish grace of manner.

Wynifred was in anything but high spirits when she arrived. To begin with, she was overworked. In her anxiety to render Osmond independent, she had been taxing her strength to its utmost limits all the winter through. In the next place, she was angry with herself for having accepted the invitation; she thought that it showed a want of proper pride on her part. Finally she was very unhappy over herself, on account of her utter failure to drive the thought of Claud Cranmer from her heart. Her self-control seemed gone. She had exacted too much from the light heart of girlhood—had employed her powers of concentration too unsparingly. Now the mainspring had suddenly failed; she felt weak and frightened.

What was to be done if her hold over herself should give way altogether? A nervous dread was upon her. If her old power over her feelings was gone, on what could she depend? All the way to Bruton Street she was calling up her pride, her maidenliness, everything she could think of to sustain her; yet all the time with a secret consciousness that it was like applying the spur to a jaded horse—sooner or later she must stumble, and fall exhausted.

She looked worn and pale as she entered the room. Claud took note of it. Had he been on the brink of falling in love, it might have checked him; but, as he was already hopelessly in that condition, it merely inspired him with tenderness unutterable. It no longer mattered to him whether she were plain or pretty, youthful or worn; whatever she was, he loved her.

It so happened that she was obliged, after just greeting him, to take a seat at the further side of the room, and politeness forced him to continue the discussion on Swinburne into which he had been drawn by the last new poetess, a pretty little woman with soft eyes and a hard mouth, who was living separated from her husband, but most touchingly devoted to her two children. She was a spiritualist, and had written a book to prove that Shakespeare was of the same following, so that her conversation was, as will be divined, deeply interesting.

Wyn, for a few minutes, sat without speaking to anybody, taking in her surroundings gradually. It seemed as if things were on a different footing—as if all were changed since the old days at Edge. Claud, in his simple faultless evening attire, with his smooth fair head under the light of a yellow silk lamp-shade, and the last new book balanced carelessly between his fingers as he leaned forward in his low chair, was in some indefinable way a different Claud from him who had stood with her in the garden of Poole Farm in the glowing twilight of the early summer night, which had brought back life to Osmond.

The room was a mass of little luxuries—trifles too light and various to be describable, all the nameless elegáncies of modern life, with its superfluities, its pretence of intellect, its discriminating taste. It was not exactly the impression of great wealth which was conveyed—that, as a rule, is self-assertive. Here the arrangement was absolutely unconscious; there was no display, it was rather a total ignorance of the value of money—the result of a condition of life where poverty in detail was unknown. Lady Mabel had often experienced the want of money, but that meant money in large quantities; she had been called upon to forego a London season; she had never felt it necessary to deny herself a guinea's-worth of hot-house flowers.

Wynifred sat in the circle of delicate light, feeling in every fibre of her nature the rest and delight of her surroundings. The craving for beautiful things, for ease and luxury, always so carefully smothered, was wide awake to-night. Lady Mabel seemed environed in an atmosphere of her own. The short skirts and thick boots which she had used in Devonshire were things of the past. Her thick white silk gown swept the rug at her feet, her emeralds flashed, her clumps of violets made the air sweet all round her. It was something alien from the seamy side of life which the girl knew so well. That very day she had travelled along Holborn, in an omnibus, weary but hopeful, from an interview with her publisher. Now the idea of that dingy omnibus, of the yellow fog, muddy streets, dirty boots, and tired limbs;—of the lonely, ungirlish battling for independence, sent through her a weak movement of false shame. It was repented of as soon as felt; but the sting remained. It was not wise of her to visit in Bruton Street. What had she in common with Lady Mabel, or—Lady Mabel's brother? Her unpretentious black evening dress, though it fitted well, and showed up the delicate skin which was one of her definite attractions, seemed to belong to a lower order of things than the mist of lace, silk, sparkles, and faint perfume which clad her hostess.

No, she was not wise, she told herself, in the perturbation of her spirits. What besides discontent could she achieve here?

This unhappy frame of mind lasted about a quarter-of-an-hour. Then she began to call herself to order. Lady Mabel's attention was diverted by a young man who was yearning to rave with her over the priceless depths of truth revealed in the latest infidel romance, and the fearless manner in which the devoted author had stripped Christianity of its superstitions, to give it to the world in all its uninspired simplicity. Like the authoress of the book in question, Lady Mabel had imbibed her Strauss and her Hegel somewhat late in life, as well as a good deal late in her century. Doctrines burst upon her with all the force of novelty which, in the year 1858, a champion of Christianity had been able calmly to describe as "a class of objections which were very popular a few years ago, and are not yet entirely extinguished."

The calm disapproval with which Miss Allonby found that it was natural to listen to the two speakers restored to her a little of her waning self-respect. A wave of peace crept into her soul. Social distinctions seemed very small when coupled with the thought of that divinity so lightly discussed and rejected in this pretty drawing-room. A movement at her side interrupted her thoughts. Claud had moved to the seat next her.

"I wonder how you like Belfont in 'The Taming of the Shrew?'" he said, as though purposely to turn her attention from what she could not avoid hearing.

It was done, as she had learnt that all his graceful little acts were done, with a complete show of unconsciousness; but her gratitude made her answering look radiant with the vivid expression which was to him so irresistible.

Yet, even as she met his kind eyes, she experienced a pang. Why was this man placed out of her reach—this one man whose sympathies were so wonderfully akin to her own? He could interpret her very thoughts; the least thing that jarred upon her seemed to distress him also.

"You were out, when I called," said he, after a few minutes.

She could find nothing more striking in reply than a bare "Yes."

"I saw your brother," he went on, diffidently. "Did he mention our conversation to you?"

"No; that is, nothing particular."

"Ah! I was afraid I had put my foot into it," said Claud, taking up the black lace fan from her knee and playing with it.

"What did you say?" asked the girl, with eager anxiety.

"It was a thankless task—one usually burns one's own fingers by trying to meddle with other people's affairs; but I thought," said the young man, "as I had seen a good deal of Allonby last summer, that I would be doing him a good turn if I let him know the state of affairs?"

"The state of affairs?"

"Yes: with regard to my friend Percivale and Miss Brabourne. You see, she knew nothing and nobody when your brother spoke to her last summer. It was unfortunate ... but it could not be helped ... the long and short of it is, however, that I am afraid she has changed her mind."

Wynifred controlled herself; after all, it was only a definite statement of what she had known must be the case.

"You—told Osmond this?" she faltered.

"I tried to; I daresay I bungled; anyhow he took it in very bad part. Said it was a pity for outsiders to meddle in these things, especially when they were so imperfectly informed."

"Oh!"

"I daresay it was entirely my fault; but I thought, in case he had been abusing me, that I must justify myself with you.... I mean, I want you to believe that my motive was kind."

"I do believe it."

How thankful she felt that the room was full of people! Had they been alone she must have broken down. As it was, he must see that her eyes were full of tears; and, had her life depended upon it, she could not have helped answering his tender gaze of sympathy with such a look as she had never given him before. It was a look of utter, defenceless weakness—a look of girlish helplessness—it sent his heart knocking wildly against his side. He drew his breath in sharply, through his set teeth. Had there been no audience he would have tried his fate there and then.

Surely it was the subdued woman's heart that appealed to him from those pathetic eyes. Ah, would she only overlook his inadequacy, his short-comings, and let him be to her what an inner consciousness told him that he alone could! He sat gazing at her, oblivious for the moment of his surroundings; she scattered his dream by a hurried question—the eloquent silence was more than she could bear.

"Forgive my asking,—but—is anything decided yet?"

"I think you have every right to know as much as I do of the matter. Percivale proposed to her last night, and was accepted. Of course, nothing can be announced until the Misses Willoughby sanction the engagement. He has written this afternoon; but I cannot imagine that any difficulty will be made on their part; he is so altogether unexceptionable."

As he spoke, a door opposite them opened, and Elsa appeared in the doorway. She was smiling—her soft dreamy smile—and her hands were full of flowers. Her lover was just behind her, his face aglow with happiness and satisfaction. They came in together; a sudden shade dropped over Elsa's face as her eyes met those of Wynifred. A slight color rose to her cheeks, and she hesitated.

Wynifred rose, went forward, shook hands, and inquired after the Misses Willoughby in a perfectly natural manner; but she failed to reassure the girl, who answered hurriedly, with a look of guilty consciousness, and escaped as soon as she possibly could to the other side of the room.

"It is very natural," said Wyn, with a sad little smile to Claud, "that she should be shy of me; but she need not. I do not blame her in the least; if anyone is to blame in the matter it is poor Osmond. I fancy he is likely to suffer pretty severely for his imprudence."

"Miss Allonby," said Lady Mabel, approaching with the young man she had been talking to, "I want to introduce you to a most interesting person to take you down to dinner. He is an esoteric Buddhist—so earnest and devoted, as well as intensely enlightened. Mr. Kleber—Miss Allonby."

CHAPTER XLIII

No man ever lived and loved, that longed not,
Once, and only once, and for one only,—
Ah, the prize!—to give his love a language.
One Word More.

At an earlier period in her career, the esoteric Buddhist would have amused Wynifred beyond measure. She would have regarded him as material for a sketch of character, and drawn him out with such intent; but she was past this, to-night.

She had burst all barriers—all care for her professional career was gone; she recked nothing of whether she ever again wrote a line, or not; everything which made up the sum of her daily existence was forgotten, or if remembered seemed poor, trivial, unimportant, beside the present fact of Claud sitting at the foot of the table, with the spiritualist poetess on his right and a lady politician on his left, each talking across him without intermission, as it seemed, and sometimes evidently amusing him, for he smiled a pre-occupied smile from time to time. But ever his eyelids were lifted to where sat the pale girl in black separated from him as far as circumstances permitted, eclipsed and blotted out by the vivid color of the young actress who sat near her, and by the regal beauty of Elsa opposite.

Usually, Wynifred easily held her own among women with twice her charms, by the spell of her conversation; but to-night she was silent—abstracted—trying to give her best attention to her neighbor, but with ears stretched to catch the accents of the low, hearty Irish voice at the end of the table. Lady Mabel, who had heard something of the girl's brilliancy, was quite cast down. Wyn absolutely declined the *rôle* of Authoress to-night, and was almost stupid in some of her answers, avowing that she did not believe in the astral fluid, and getting hopelessly wrecked on the subject of Avatars, which dimly recalled to her mind Browning's poem, "What's become of Waring?"

When the move was made, and the ladies rose from table, it was almost with a pang that she left the room in which Claud remained. She dared not lift her eyes to his, as he stood holding back the door for them to file out, yet the bent, shy head inspired in him a hope unfelt before. Was consciousness awake at last;—that consciousness which for his own amusement he had tried to stir at Edge, and which had annoyed him so greatly by falling to sleep again and declining to be roused? A dream of utter personal happiness enfolded him, and made him a more negligent host than was his wont; and, as Percivale too was aching to be in the drawing-room, the male contingent soon made their appearance, to the delight of the ladies and the chagrin of the professional gentlemen, who most of them found a good deal of wine necessary to support their enormous and continuous brain-efforts.

But no further word with Miss Allonby was possible for Claud.

A sudden suspicion had flashed across the mind of Lady Mabel—dismissed as unlikely, but still leaving just enough weight to make her determine that no unnecessary words should pass between them. She did not like Wynifred, and she had never imagined for a moment that her brother did, until to-night. Even now she was by no means sure of it; only Claud seemed abstracted and unlike himself. She dexterously kept him employed with first one person, then another, using the same tactics with the girl, until the cruelly short evening was past, and Wynifred had to rise and make her adieux, feeling something as if she had been through a surgical operation—that it was over—and that she was living still.

Never would she visit that house again, she truly vowed, as she dragged her tired limbs upstairs. This was the limit of her endurance. Not any motive, whether of self-interest, or of foolish, worse than foolish infatuation, should drag her there. As she came down Claud stood in the hall at the foot of the staircase, waiting.

"Are you driving home alone, Miss Allonby?"

"Yes; I could not ask Osmond to fetch me from this house, could I? But I am not nervous, thank you."

"But I am, for you. Will you not allow me to come with you?"

Now, if ever, must be the moment of strength—now one last effort of self-command. Let the heart which is bleeding to cry, "Come!" be silenced—let maidenly pride step in. What! allow Claud Cranmer to drive home with you when you are in this mood—when one kind word would draw the weak tears in floods—oh, never, never, never!

"Come with me, Mr. Cranmer? On no account, thank you,"—a chilly manner, a spice of surprise at the offer. "It will break up your sister's party. Good-night."

At the same moment the drawing-room door above opened quickly, and Lady Mabel's voice was heard.

"Henry! is Mr. Cranmer there? I want him."

"You see," said Wynifred, with a little smile. "Good-night again."

She was gone.

A moment later, and the tears had come—had gushed freely as the rain. Alone in the London cab, the girl bowed herself together in the extremity of her pain. It was no use to argue or ask herself why; only she felt as if all were over. Had she done right? Was it indeed wise to be so proud? Was it possible that really, after all, he loved her as she loved him? If so, how she must have hurt him by her cold refusal! And yet—yet—the sons of earls do not marry girls in Wynifred's position. Better a broken heart than humiliation, she cried bitterly. Did not the warning of poor Osmond's hideous delusion loom up darkly before her?

Yet where was the comfort of right-doing? Nowhere. If this were right, she had rather a thousand times that she had done wrong. Oh, to have him there beside her, on any terms—recklessly to enjoy the delight of his presence, caring not what came after. So low does love degrade? she questioned.

After a few minutes, her wildness was a little calmed. An appeal had gone up to the God Who, in Lady Mabel's creed, was powerless to save, yet the thought of Whom seemed the only remedy for this misery; she felt anew that she was in reality neither reckless nor degraded, only worn out, mind and body.

The cause of her wild longing for Claud was as much the feminine desire to rest on the strength of a masculine nature as the weaker yearning to be loved. With Osmond she had been always the supporter, never the supported; to the girls she had been forced to stand in the light of father and mother, as well as sister; and it had come to be a family tradition that Wyn was indifferent to anything in the shape of a love-affair—impervious as far as she herself was concerned, though sympathetic enough in the vicissitudes of others.

It seemed, indeed, a hard dispensation both for brother and sister that, when at last their jealously-guarded and seldom-spent store of sentiment found an object, it should be in each case an object out of reach.

It seemed to Wynifred as if to-night a climax was reached. The point had come when she could bear no more; she could do nothing but sit and suffer, with a keenness of which a year ago she had not deemed herself capable.

Mansfield Road was reached at last.

Somewhat to her surprise, lights were in the dining-room window, and, as the wheels of her vehicle stopped, a hand drew aside the blind, and, some one looked eagerly out. Almost at once the hall door was flung open, and Wynifred painfully conscious of red and swollen eyelids, walked slowly in.

Osmond was holding back the door with such a pleasant, happy smile, as drove a fresh knife into her heart. Was she to be the messenger to dash his cup of joy from his lips, and tell him that his hopes lay in ruins all around him? She felt that it was impossible—at least, yet; and, before she had time to think more, Hilda's voice broke in from the dining-room:

"Is that you, Wyn? Do come in—there's some news—guess what has happened! Osmond and I waited up to tell you."

She walked in, feeling stiff, mazed, and as though the familiar room was strange to her. Sally, who was also standing by, participating in the general excitement, burst out—

"Bless me, Miss Wyn, whatever is the matter? You look like a ghost!"

"I am tired, Sally—dead beat—that is the only expression that conveys my meaning. I told you I was done up before I started, did I not?... I shall be—well again to-morrow. What is the news?"

Hilda's eyes were soft and almost tearful.

"Can't you guess?" she said.

Wyn flashed a look round, noting Jac's absence.

"Jac!" she said, involuntarily.

"She would not stay up to tell you herself," smiled Hilda.

"Not—oh, Hilda, not—Mr. Haldane?"

"Yes; they are engaged," said Osmond, brightly. "It will be a wrench, at first, to lose Jacqueline out of the house; but think what a match it will be for her! Such a delightful fellow! Ah, Wyn, I am not too selfish to be able to rejoice in their happiness. They have nothing to wait for! He can well afford to be married to-morrow, if it please him. She is a fortunate girl!"

"She deserves it!" cried Hilda, loyally. "Oh, Wyn, they are so deliciously in love with one another!"

In the midst of this family sensation, Wyn could not bear to launch her thunderbolt. To destroy, at a word, all Osmond's peace was more than she felt herself equal to. The little drop of balm seemed to blunt for a few minutes the keen edge of her own pain.

In Jac's little room, with her arms about the pliant young form, and the blooming head hidden in her neck, she could feel for the time almost happy in the hushed intensity of the girl's love.

It was what the others had longed for, but scarcely dared to hope. In fact, much as she liked young Haldane, Wynifred had never encouraged his visits much, for fear of breaking Jacqueline's heart. But now all was right. The young man had chosen for love, and not for gain. Jacqueline would be a member of one of the oldest county families in England. No wonder that the engagement shed a treacherous beam of unfounded hope over Osmond's path. If Ted Haldane could marry for love, other people equally exalted might do the same.

For a few hours he must go on in his fool's Paradise. Wynifred *could not* speak the words which should wake him from his dream.

All night long she lay with eyes wide open to the winter moonlight, watching the pale stars hang motionless in the dark soft sky, bright things which every eye may gaze upon, but no man may approach. Their measureless distance weighed upon her as if to crush her. A leaden clamp seemed bound round her aching temples. To live was to suffer, yet the relief of sleep was unattainable. Faster and faster the thoughts whirled through her tortured brain. There was no power to stop them. Over and over again she lived through the events of last evening; over and over again she heard each word that Claud had uttered; again she saw the open doorway, the regal girl with her flowers, her lips curved with laughter, her lover attendant at her side. One after the other the pictures chased each other through her mind, in never-ending succession, till it seemed as if she must go mad. There was no respite, no moment of blissful unconsciousness till the laggard January dawn had come, and Sally was filling her bath with the customary morning splash.

It seemed a bitter irony. Was this morning, then, like any other morning, that the habits and customs of the house were to go on as usual?

"Am I to get up?" asked she, in a dazed way. "Why yes, of course. I must get up, I suppose."

"Ain't you well, Miss Wyn?" queried Sally, in a doubtful voice.

"Not quite, Sal. I have been working too hard, I think. But now I remember, I must get up, for my proofs are not corrected. When they are finished, I think—I think that I must take a little rest."

CHAPTER XLIV

Unwise
I loved and was lowly, loved and aspired,
Loved, grieving or glad, till I made you mad,
And you meant to have hated and despised,
Whereas you deceived me, nor inquired.
The Worst of It.

It was the second morning after Lady Mabel's dinner-party. Claud and his niece sat together in the morning-room, discussing the affairs of the nation. A large picture-book was spread out across the young lady's knees, and her most serious attention was being bestowed on a picture of Joseph in the pit, which subject her uncle elucidated by a commentary not exactly remarkable for Scriptural accuracy.

He was preoccupied and bothered, and did not find the child's chatter so engrossing as usual, for he had many things on his mind.

There came an imperative knocking at the street door. He heard it, but without any particular anxiety. No visitor would penetrate into Mab's sanctum. It was not until the steps of the butler sounded along the tiled passage outside that he leaped to his feet with Kathleen in his arms, acutely conscious of the shabbiness of his brown velvet morning-coat.

There was a sharp rap on the door, then it was thrown broadly open, and in the aperture appeared the sturdy square figure, sun-browned face, and grizzled hair of Henry Fowler.

"Any admittance?" said his kind voice, cheerily. "I wouldn't let the good gentleman outside announce me. I think he took me for a country farmer, come to pay his respects—and he might have made a worse guess. How are you, my lad, how are you?"

Claud had swooped upon him, dragged him in, shut the door, and now stood shaking the two firm hands in their tawny doe-skin gloves as though he would shake them off.

"If anything in the world could make me feel good-tempered at this moment, it's the sight of you!" he cried, joyously. "Where did you spring from? What brought you up? How long can you stay? Tell me everything. This is a surprise of the right sort, and no mistake!"

"Not so very surprising, is it?" asked Henry, as he drew a letter in Percivale's unmistakable hand from his breast-pocket. "I thought I must come and settle this in person. I am the Misses Willoughby's delegate."

"Capital! Don't care what brings you. I only know how glad I am to see you."

"Not more so than I to see you, my lad. You don't look as well, though, as you did when you left Lower House. You must come down again as soon as ever you can get free of dissipations. Your chair still looks vacant at table, and your horse is eating his head off in the stable. George took him for a gallop the other day, and managed to lame him slightly. 'Eh,' says he, 'there'll be the devil to pay when Mr. Cranmer comes down!' So you see you're expected any time."

"How good that sounds!" cried Claud, sitting on the table and swinging his legs boyishly. "Ah, I would like to be there at this minute! You have had some fine seas rolling up in Brent Bay, I'll go bail! I fancy I can still feel the salt sting of that sou'-wester we faced together. And the excitement in which the *Swan* made her *début*!"

"Ay! That storm had consequences we little recked of," said Henry, thoughtfully fingering the letter in his hand. "To think of little Elsa! Well! Miss Ellen always said so. She was right, as usual. She is a woman of talent, is Miss Ellen, as well as being a saint on earth. But now, Claud, tell me, how have matters been arranged? I am an old stager, you see, and doubtless I don't march with the times; but this seems to me to be a very rapid business! 'Off with the old love and on with the new!' What has become of young Allonby? Has he quitted the lists, or how has he been disposed of?"

Claud put his hands over his ears with a gesture of despair.

"You may as well not waste your breath," he cried, in mock anger, "for not one word shall you get out of me on the subject of Miss Brabourne's love-affairs! I am sick of it! From morn till dewy eve do I hear of nothing else! It is my sister's one topic of conversation, and Percivale talks of it unceasingly! He has been here already once this morning pestering me to go with him to get her a necklace, or a plaything, or something! I'm hanged if I do! I have nothing to do with the matter—what's more, it doesn't interest me much! And now you come, on the top of everyone else, and gravely ask my opinion, or advice, or anything you please. Seriously, Fowler, you must excuse me; I will have nothing to say in the young lady's affairs, either to meddle or make. It is no business of mine whether she marries you, or the prime minister, or a crossing-sweeper, or anyone she chooses. I have worries enough of my own without puzzling over her the whole day long!"

"Poor fellow! Are you worried?" asked Henry, kindly, looking doubtfully at him. "You should come and live with me—I am sure the life would suit you. I have just lost my overseer—Preston—you remember him! His work would do admirably for you, young man—much better than lounging about up here in London in hot rooms, doing nothing."

"Doing nothing? I am minding the baby," said Claud, lightly, but the color flew to his fair face and he looked confused. "It is no good trying to reform me," he said, after a moment, his hot cheek against Kathleen's floss-silk curls; "I am an incorrigible idler."

"I never knew a man less idle by disposition than you are," was the answer, as Henry regarded him with a look at once wistful and disapproving.

"You're not thinking of getting married, then?" he asked, after an interval.

"Married—I? No," stammered Claud, incoherently, as he rose, set the child on the rug, and walked to the window.

There was a short, uncomfortable silence. Henry's puzzled gaze still followed the young man. At last, as if resigning the subject in hand as hopeless, he asked, abruptly:

"Where's Elsa?"

"Miss Brabourne? Oh, in bed."

"In bed? Is she ill? You should have told me."

"Oh, dear no, she is not ill. These are merely fashionable habits. Percivale thought, like you, that she must be ill; I had great difficulty in restraining him from rushing up to obtain the latest bulletin."

"But—your sister—the butler said she was out!"

"Oh, my sister is an early riser. She always breakfasts at eight."

"So used Elsa—she was the soul of punctuality."

"A compulsory punctuality, perhaps?"

"Well—I suppose so; but why—what on earth can induce her to stay in bed till this hour?"

"I am sure I don't know. Perhaps it is to take care of her complexion."

"Take care of her complexion!... The child must have altered strangely— —"

"No; I don't think she has altered much; she has merely developed."

As he spoke, the door was flung open, and Miss Brabourne, in her riding-habit, entered.

"Lady Mabel, my horse is late again— —" the frown died away from the pretty forehead, the great blue eyes grew wide with surprise.

"God-father!"

"Well, god-daughter! Are you surprised? Not more than I am. My little girl is a woman of fashion now!"

"Oh, how can you? Poor little me," said the girl, with an affected little laugh which jarred upon his nerves. "I am so pleased to see you! Are you come to stay here?"

"Of course," put in Claud, hurriedly.

"Thanks, Elsie, I shall perhaps be in town for a few days, but I prefer my own old room at the Langham."

"My sister won't hear of such a thing," urged Claud.

"Lady Mabel is more than kind, but I am an old bachelor, and I like my liberty. And so, Elsie, you are very well and blooming?"

"Oh, very, very! I am enjoying myself so much here!"

"I have a great deal to say to you, but you are going out now, I see?"

"Yes," she said, composedly, "I am going out now, but of course you will stay to lunch, and I shall see you afterwards. Mr. Cranmer, did you see Mr. Percivale?"

"Yes; he was very disappointed not to see you."

"He should not come before lunch. I must tell him so; he might know I should not be visible," said Percivale's betrothed, coolly.

The butler appeared.

"Captain and Miss St. Quentin are at the door, and your horse is round, miss."

"At last!" She caught up her gold-tipped riding-whip with her gauntleted hand, and waved it merrily at her god father. "I am going for a gallop round the Park with the St. Quentins, and then I shall see you again," she cried. "Mr. Cranmer, come and mount me, please, the groom is so awkward." She paused a moment at the door. "I have a great deal to tell you," said she, nodding, "so mind you are here on my return! I must not keep my friends waiting."

She was gone.

Mechanically Mr. Fowler went out into the hall and looked. Through the open door the gay winter sunshine shone on the glossy horses and the young, well-dressed riders. Claud helped the heiress to her saddle, gathered up the reins, gave them into her hands, bowed, patted the mare's glossy neck, and the party started away.

"She never asked after her aunts," Mr. Fowler was reflecting. "Not one word. And they brought her up."

Claud hardly liked to meet his eye as he returned slowly up the hall. His sympathy for the elder man was at that moment deep and intense. Henry had never been blind to Elsa's failings, but had always ascribed them to her bringing-up, and believed that, in a more genial atmosphere, they would vanish; that, when treated with love, the girl would grow loving. She had always in old days been so fond of him, clung to him, cried at his departure. He forgot that at that time his was the only notice she ever received, whereas now she had more notice from everyone than she knew what to do with. Collecting himself with an effort, he turned to Claud.

"I have some business I must see after just now," he said. "Am I likely to find Lady Mabel if I come about five?"

Claud thought it was kinder to let him go for the present. He had forgotten with what suddenness the change in the girl would come upon one who had not seen her for some months.

Henry left the house in a reverie so deep that he walked on, hardly knowing where. He was mystified, staggered, what the French call *bouleversé*. If a girl could so develop in a few months, what would she be in another year? Was it safe to let anyone marry such an extraordinary uncertainty? The problem was no nearer to being solved when he discovered that it was past two o'clock. Sensible of the pangs of a country appetite, he went to a restaurant, lunched leisurely, and then decided that it was not too early to present himself at Mansfield Road for a morning call.

It was strange how his spirits rose and his thoughts grew more agreeable as he walked briskly on. It was so pleasant to think that he was going to see Wynifred. Of course she might, and very probably would, be out; but he should not be discouraged. He meant to see her; if not to-day, then to-morrow; and he was a person who resolved seldom and firmly.

The aspect of the little house pleased him. The small garden strip was black and bare with winter, but indoors through the window could be seen a row of hyacinths in bloom, and a warm curtain of dull red serge was drawn across the hall, visible through the glass lights of the front door.

With a glow of pleasurable anticipation, he applied his hand to the knocker. Before he had time to breathe, the red curtain was torn aside, a girl had darted forward, seized the handle, and ejaculating, "Well?" in a tone as if her very life depended on the answer, fell back in confused recognition and apology.

It was Wynifred—but what a Wynifred! She looked all eyes. Her face was sheet-white, her hair thrust back in disorder from her forehead; her expression conveyed the idea of such suffering that her visitor's very heart was riven.

"Mr.—Fowler," she said, faintly. "Oh, I beg your pardon. Come in. We are in—trouble."

He closed the door, tossed his stick into a corner, and, taking both the girl's hands, drew her into the little dining-room.

"Miss Allonby," he said, in tones whose affectionate warmth was in itself a comfort—"Miss Allonby, if you are in trouble, I must help you. I have come at the right moment. Now, what is it? Do you feel able to tell me?"

She sank upon a chair, turning her quivering face away out of his sight.

"Oh!" she said, "how can I tell you? How can I? It is all so miserable, so.... What a way to receive you!... You must have thought me mad."

"I thought nothing of the kind. I could see that you were utterly over-wrought. For pity's sake, don't make apologies—don't treat me as if I were a stranger. Tell me what the trouble is."

She lifted her eyes, the lashes drowned in tears that could not fall.

"I will show you, I think," said she. "Come."

Rising, she hastily went out, he following, expecting he knew not what. She led him into the studio.

It was a fair-sized room, built out behind the small house. Usually it was a charming place. Girlish fingers had arranged quaint pottery and artistic draperies—placing lamps in dark corners, flowers in vases, and tinting the shabby furniture with color. The piano stood there, and near the fire a well-worn sofa, and two or three capacious wicker chairs.

To-day a nameless desolation overspread the very air. Mr. Fowler entered, and looked straight before him. An enormous canvas was mounted on a screw easel in the best light the room afforded. The landscape had been put in with masterly freedom, and was almost finished. But a hole a foot square gaped in the centre of the picture, and the canvas was hacked and torn away in strips, some lying on the floor beneath. Near this ruin was a gilt frame, the portrait from which had been slit clean out, torn across and across, and left in fragments. So all round the room. Picture after picture had been torn from the wall, and dashed to the ground as if by a frenzied hand. A pile of delicate water-color studies on paper lay in the grate half charred, wholly destroyed. The whole scene was one of utter and hopeless wreckage. The mischief was irremediable.

The visitor uttered an exclamation of consternation. "What does it mean?" he asked.

"I don't think I ought to tell you," said the girl, who was standing against the wall as if for support, her head thrown back, her eyes raised as if to avoid seeing the desolation which surrounded her.

"Nonsense. You *must* tell me," said Henry, bluntly.

Slowly she took a letter from her pocket, went forward, and laid it on a table which stood near the centre of the room. The table was heaped with a confusion of brushes, tubes of color, palette knives, varnish bottles, and mugs of turpentine, all of which had been pushed hastily together, that the letter might occupy a prominent position by itself.

"When I went to call my brother this morning," said Wyn, obeying his mandate as if she could not help herself, "I could not make him hear. At last I went in. He was not in his room; he had not been to bed at all. It seemed to give me a terrible shock: I—I—partly guessed ... I knew I ought to have told him; but I...."

"Don't reproach yourself—go straight on," said Henry, anxiously.

"I rushed down here: for he has done such a thing as sit up all night. He was gone; the room was as you see it. That letter was on the table."

He possessed himself of the envelope. It was hastily scrawled on the outside in pencil, "For Wynifred." In a tremor of apprehension, he drew out the enclosure. It was in Elsa's hand-writing.

"Dear Mr. Allonby,

"I am afraid this letter will make you very angry, and this makes me sorry to write, as I have always liked you so much, ever since I knew you. But I think I ought to let you know that I have found out that I do not love you well enough to marry you some day, as you hoped. I am engaged to be married to Mr. Percivale, who was so kind and good when everyone else thought that I had killed my brother. I hope this will not disappoint you too much, and that we shall always be friends. I send my love to your sisters, and remain,

"Yours sincerely,
"Elaine Bradbourne.

"P.S.—You see I had not seen Mr. Percivale when I said I would marry you."

CHAPTER XLV

Now I may speak; you fool, for all
Your lore! WHO made things plain in vain?
What was the sea for? What the grey
Sad church, that solitary day,
Crosses and graves, and swallows call?
Was there nought better them to enjoy,
No feat which, done, would make time break
And let us pent-up creatures through
Into eternity, our due?
Dis aliter visum.

At this letter Mr. Fowler stared, as though some magnetic power rivetted his eyes to the sheet.

At last he slowly lifted his gaze, to fix it on Wyn.

"Is this the only intimation—the only explanation she has given him?"

The girl assented.

"It is my fault," she said, huskily. "I knew it two days ago, Mr. Cranmer told me, but I had not the heart nor the strength to tell Osmond; I could not!"

"It is monstrous, heartless. I cannot understand it," he said, in a harassed voice. "Something should be done—she should be made to feel—I think Percivale should see this letter!"

"Oh, no! No! You must not think of such a thing!" Leaping up, the girl caught the letter from his hand. "It is not her fault—not her fault—it was poor Osmond's!... What she says is true. She had seen no one when he spoke to her. She did not understand what it meant! Her mind was like a child's—unformed. She could not have remained as she was then. It is natural, it is what I felt would come."

"But this unnatural, insolent brevity!" cried Henry, indignantly. "See here: 'To be married, as *you* hoped.' 'I hope *you* will not be disappointed.' Nothing of what it costs her to write and own her change of feeling. I call it intolerable."

"Oh, it is better so! Better any brevity, however crude, than hollow professions, or—or useless regret. You must not blame her, please, Mr. Fowler. It will be all right soon, as soon as I hear that he is safe," panted poor Wyn, biting her pale lips.

"How can you take her part, here in the ruin she has caused?" demanded Henry, fiercely.

"She did not cause it. I will be just," said Wyn, faintly but firmly. "Osmond has deluded himself. She never loved him—he should have known it. She had forgotten him in a month. She never came here, never wrote to us, never took any steps to renew the intimacy, yet he would go on, hugging his folly, though I told him what it would be."

Even in his agitation he had time for a passing feeling of fervent admiration for the woman who could be just at such a crisis.

"I will spend no more time in lamenting over spilt milk," he said, "but see if I cannot help you, Miss Wynifred. I suppose your brother's absence is the chief trouble?"

She answered by a movement of the head.

"What steps have you taken?"

"Mr. Haldane, who is engaged to Jacqueline, has gone to Scotland Yard. I thought it was his knock when you came—that was why I went to the door. The girls are gone together to telegraph to a friend of his who lives in a little remote village; he sometimes goes there, we thought it was possible he might have done so to-day."

"Just so; then you have no idea of where he went, or what he meant to do?"

"None at all. Oh," she began to shiver nervously, "you do not think he has—do you? People do such fearful things sometimes ... and he is one of those gentle, passive men, with a terrible temper when once he is roused; you can tell, by this room, what a state of mind he was in. I knew it would be so! I said, if she failed him, he would never do a stroke of work again. Oh, if that were really to be true!"

She gave a cry of helpless pain.

"Say you don't think he has done it!" she gasped.

"I am sure he has not. He is a brave man and a Christian. No man who had your love left to him would take his own life," cried Henry, incoherently. "Keep up your courage, Miss Wyn, you have so much nerve."

"Not now—not now. It has gone. Come away, come out of this room, I cannot bear it, it stifles me."

She moved uncertainly towards the door, almost as if she were groping.

"My head aches till I can scarcely see," faltered she, apologetically.

His eyes were fixed apprehensively on the slight figure which moved before him. Just as she reached the dining-room door, she swayed helplessly. It was well that the sturdy Henry, with his iron muscles, was behind her. He took her in his arms as if she had been a little baby, laid her on the sofa, and fetched the water from the sideboard. Her faint was deeper, however, than he had anticipated, and, after ten minutes of absolute unconsciousness, he was constrained to go to the top of the kitchen stairs and call Sally.

"Fainted again, has she?" said the good woman, grimly. "I knew she would. She's overdone, is Miss Wyn, and this here nonsense of Master Osmond's has been the finishing touch. Don't talk to me! He's no right to go off like that, nor to carry on like a madman because he's disappointed. But men are poor things, and he don't know nor care what he makes his sisters suffer. Here I comes down this morning to see Miss Wyn fainted dead off in the middle of all that rummage on the studio floor; and I can tell you, sir, it give me a turn, for I thought, from the state of the room, as somebody had been a-murdering of her. Dear, dear, she is dead off. I suppose you couldn't carry her upstairs, sir, could you?"

"Half-a-dozen of her weight," said Henry, laconically.

"My pretty dear, my lamb," said Sal, pushing up the heavy hair. "She do look ill, don't she, sir?"

"Very," said Henry, speaking as well as he could for the lump in his throat. "I am horrified at her. Let me take her upstairs. You had better put her straight to bed."

He lifted the unconscious girl in his strong, tender arms, and carried her up, directed by Sally, into the little room which was her own. Reluctantly he laid her down on the bed, looking with pitiful love upon the whiteness of the thin sweet face. How much would he have given to kiss the pure line of the pathetic mouth! How far away out of his reach she seemed, this pale, hard-working girl whom other men passed unnoticed by. One cold hand he lifted to his lips, and held it there lingeringly a moment.

"Now," said he to Sally, "I will go and fetch the doctor, if you will direct me. She must have every care, and at once."

From leaving a message with the doctor, he went straight to his hotel.

The sudden rush of events had somewhat confused him, and he could not tell what was best to be done. It seemed no use to go hunting for Osmond, when his sisters did not possess the slightest clue to his whereabouts. Yet he had an uneasy conviction that it might go badly with Wynifred if it could not be proved that her brother was alive and safe, and he would cut off his right hand to serve her.

Oh reaching his sitting-room, the fragrance of a cigar assailed his senses, and, not much to his surprise, he discovered Claud, ensconced in a deep arm-chair near the fire.

"Just thinking of going to the police-station after you," said the young gentleman, composedly. "Thought you were lost in London."

Henry did not answer. Approaching the fire, he slowly divested himself of his heavy overcoat and gloves. Claud, flashing a look at him, caught the expression of his face.

"You take it too seriously, Fowler," said he.

"Oh, I take it too seriously, do I? You know all about it, of course. After the intimacy which existed between you and Miss Allonby in the summer— after the exceptional circumstances which brought you together, you would naturally take a great interest in her, and go to see her frequently; but I hardly think you would be likely to say I took matters too seriously."

"Fowler! Miss Allonby!"

The young man sat forward, thoroughly startled, his cigar expiring unheeded between his fingers.

"What do you mean?" he asked, breathlessly.

"Mean? That I am disappointed in you, Cranmer. Yes, disappointed. I don't care in the least if I offend you, sir—I have passed beyond conventionalities. You have missed what should have been your goal— missed it by aimless trifling, by this accursed modern habit of introspection, of tearing a passion to tatters, of holding off and counting the cost of what you want to do, till the moment to do it has gone by. Sir, there comes an instant to every man in his life, when the only clean and honorable course is to go straight forward, even if that be to incur responsibility—why, in Heaven's name, tell me, are we not born to be responsible? Isn't that the pride of our manhood? Do you call yourself a man, living as you live now, without aim, without cares, getting through your life anyhow? It is the life of a cur, I tell you—ignoble, unmanly, base."

"I am prepared to stand a good deal from you, Fowler," said Claud, very white, "but I will ask you kindly to explain yourself more fully."

"You understand me well enough, lad," said the elder man, with a stern straight glance which somehow sent a consciousness of shortcoming into his victim's mind; "but, as I have taken upon myself to open this subject, I'll say out frankly all that's in my mind. Do you suppose blind chance took you to Edge Combe this summer? Do you suppose a mere accident placed near you such a woman as—I speak her name with all reverence—Wynifred Allonby? Now listen to me. She was no pretty, shallow girl, to catch the eye of any idle young fellow. Hers was a charm that only a few could feel; and, Claud, *you felt it.* Don't deny it, sir. You knew what she was; you could appreciate to its utmost the beauty of her mind, and the strange charm of her personality. Do you suppose it is for nothing that God Almighty gives such sympathy as that? Now hear me further. She needed you, she was lonely, she was poor. She wanted a man to stand between her and the world, to afford her opportunity to unfold the hidden tenderness that was in her, and give her a chance to be the gentle loving woman God meant her for. Was not your mission plain? Yet you would not read it—and why? For reasons which were one and all contemptible. I say downright contemptible. She was not rich, she was not precisely in your rank of society. Your self-indulgent selfishness winced at the prospect of a life of work for her sake. So you put aside the chance of an undreamed-of happiness which lay there clear before your eyes. And I say you should be made to feel it. Strip off all your self-delusions, all your sophistry, and tell me what you think of yourself, Claud Cranmer. Are you proud of your insight? Do you congratulate yourself upon your prudence? Faith, it's a marvel to me how few men read the purpose of their being aright. Why do you suppose women were made weak, but for us to be their strength? What calls out the very highest points in a man's nature but a woman's need of him? I say there was not one grace of Wynifred's that escaped you, not a word she uttered that had not power to influence you; yet you deliberately resisted that influence and strove to forget those graces. You are despicable in my eyes."

The room rang with his low, tense tones. Flinging himself into a chair, he shaded his eyes with his powerful, work-hardened hand, and a long silence reigned.

Claud did not move. His face looked stony as he stared into the fire. In the main, every word that Fowler uttered had been true; for, though in the last few days the young man's love had taken definite shape, yet the old habits of ease and carelessness had still held him back. The sudden rush of rugged eloquence had been like a flash of lightning, shivering delusions to fragments, and laying bare before him the manner in which he had dallied with the high possibilities offered him.

The moments ticked on, and still he sat, not uttering a word. The other did not move from his position. Nothing moved in the room but the even pendulum of the clock. At last Claud nerved himself to speak.

"Is Miss Allonby in trouble?" he said, in a constrained way, stooping as if to recover his cigar, but in reality to conceal the flush which accompanied his words.

"She is ill. I found her alone, in bitter grief. Her brother has disappeared—they do not know where he has gone. It is in consequence of Elsa's engagement. She—Miss Allonby, is utterly over-strained. She fainted whilst I was there, and I went to call the doctor. You have heard my denunciation. Now hear my determination. I am going to try for the treasure you have tossed on one side."

Claud started violently, and raised his eyes to those of his companion in astonishment.

"Yes, you may well be astonished. I know I have not a chance, but what difference does that make? I know that, but for one thing, it would be intolerable presumption in me to dream of it; but hear me. She is lonely and unprotected—yet, she has a brother, I know, but see—the brother has ends of his own, he is an anxiety, not a helper. She has need of some one to stand between her and the bitter necessities of life. The long struggle is wearing out her youth. If I could take her"—the voice vibrated with intense feeling—"and put her down in my Devonshire valley, with sunshine and sweet air, and every care that love could devise, what a heaven it would be to see the color come in her white cheeks, and the natural bent of girlhood return with the removal of unnatural responsibility." He made an expressive gesture with his hand. "Look at my niece, Elsa! She has more money than she can spend, she has beauty of the sort all men rave over, all her life she will have dozens of adorers, she will never be in want of loyal slaves to obey her lightest behests. And yet, with all her beauty and money, she is not worth the little finger of one of those three Allonby girls. As for Wynifred" ... he paused for a moment, and cleared his throat, "she will not have me," he said. "She is too absolutely conscientious to marry where she does not love; yet I hope it may comfort her—a little—to know that one man would—not metaphorically but literally—die for her, that to one man her womanhood is a nobility no title could give, and her happiness the most fervent desire of his heart."

He ceased abruptly. The feelings of his large heart were too deep for utterance. Another eloquent silence succeeded. Claud's face was hidden in both his hands. When he raised it, it was white and fixed.

"Fowler," he said, "I can't stand this."

He sprang to his feet spasmodically, pushed his hand up through his hair, then, thrusting both hands deep into his pockets, walked quickly across the room and back.

"I suppose you don't expect me to stand on one side and let you take my chance?" he asked, between his teeth.

Henry rose too, and faced him.

"I don't know," said he, speaking with slow scorn, "why I should have told you my intention, except for the purpose of showing you how another man could prize what you hold so lightly. I have no fear of wounding you; a love which can shilly-shally as you have done is not worth the having—is not capable of being hurt. Perhaps my reproaches have galvanized it into a sort of life; but it will die again when the friction ceases."

"You are unjust to me now," said Claud, sharply. "What you said at first was mainly true. I did not at once realize how deep it had gone, and, when I did, I tried to stop it—to turn my thoughts. But all that is past—was past before you spoke. My deliberate intention is, and has been for a month past, to tell Miss Allonby what I feel for her."

"Then why have you not carried out your intention?"

The young man was silent for a moment; at last:

"Love makes a man modest," he said. "I was not sure she would have me."

"And pray what does that matter? Are you prepared to risk nothing to obtain her? Lad, you don't know what love is or you would lay yourself at your lady's feet and feel yourself the better man for doing it, even though she sent you empty away. With such a woman as Wynifred, you know full well you need fear the taking of no undue advantage. In my eyes you are without excuse."

"At all events, I am not too far sunk not to resent your language," retorted Claud, angrily. "Are you going to offer yourself to Miss Allonby in the midst of her domestic trouble?"

"Yes, certainly. I am no fancy lover to sing madrigals in my lady's bower. If I have any merit in her eyes, it shall be as one ready to help her in her hour of need. I can at least say to her, 'Here am I, my house, my lands, my money, all to be spent in your service; use them all, for they are freely yours.'"

"And I," faltered Claud, in an undertone, "can only say, 'I have no house, no lands, no money; all I can offer is myself, and that I withheld as long as I could.' I congratulate you, Fowler. You ought to win in a canter."

Henry laughed somewhat bitterly.

"Ought I? Perhaps, if Miss Allonby were likely to be swayed by such considerations. But she will marry for love, and only for love. Claud, what makes me rail against you so is that I believe she loves you. You don't deserve it, but I am afraid she does. And you—if you do not value it as you should——" he paused, for there was a knock at the door. "Come in," he said, irritably.

A waiter brought in a telegram for Claud. Hastily scanning it the young man turned to his rival.

"I am to bring you to dinner in Bruton Street," he said, after a pause. "I am afraid you must come. Percivale is to be there."

"I will be ready in fifteen minutes," answered Henry; and he disappeared into the inner room.

Claud stood gazing into the red embers in the grate with an awful sinking of the heart—a horrible depression he had never felt before. Now that he felt the possibility of losing Wynifred, he knew at last what his love was worth—knew that she was his life's one possibility of completion. Yet he had deserved to lose her.

Resting his arms on the mantel-piece, he let his fair head fall disconsolately upon them.

"My love, my dear," he whispered, "he is more worthy of you than I; and yet I believe that you belong to me—that I, with all my faults, could make you happier than he could. Choose me, Wynifred—my beloved, choose me!"

CHAPTER XLVI

To have her lion roll in a silken net,
And fawn at a victor's feet.
Maud.

The news from Mansfield Road next morning defeated for a time the designs of both the aspirants after Wynifred Allonby's hand.

Ted Haldane had been able to bring a certain amount of comfort to Hilda and Jacqueline. He had been to Osmond's bankers, and found that the young man had that morning drawn out a considerable sum. This certainly seemed to negative any idea of suicidal intentions. But no further clue was forthcoming. The porter believed that Mr. Allonby, on leaving the bank, hailed a hansom and drove off; but even on this head he was by no means sure.

It was the opinion, however, both of Henry Fowler and Mr. Haldane that Osmond would himself send news of his present whereabouts in a few days' time, when he had cooled down somewhat. But Wynifred was unable to derive comfort from the news, such as it was, for when she recovered from her long fainting-fit she was quite delirious. For the next few days the two poor girls had a time of terrible anxiety. The third morning brought a brief, reckless note from Osmond in Paris. It was merely to let them know that he was alive. He could not say when he was likely to return, or what he should do. He gave no address.

No words could express the comfort which Mr. Fowler was able to afford the desolate girls. He saw that Wynifred had the best advice in London, and everything that money could procure; and when, in a week's time, the doctors were able to declare with confidence that the dreaded brain-fever had been averted, it was hard to tell who most rejoiced in the fact.

Meantime, the engagement of Elsa to Mr. Percivale was publicly announced. The marriage was to take place immediately after Easter, and, as the young lady totally declined to be married in Devonshire, two of the Misses Willoughby were coming to town almost immediately to take a furnished house for a couple of months. After all, it was but natural that the girl should shrink from a place which had such terrible associations for her.

Percivale sympathised entirely with her in this matter, as in everything. It was extraordinary for outsiders to watch the utter subjugation of his strong nature by the power of his love. Only one thing did certainly trouble him. His betrothed could not bear the quaint old dark house overlooking the river. It was exactly suited to the disposition of the young man who, as Claud said, always seemed to be trying to escape from his own century, somehow. He had improved the house, spent large sums of money upon it, and it was, indeed, the one spot in the modern roar of London wherein he felt entirely at home. His life of seclusion had, of course, rendered him shy. Going much into society was a trouble to him. But who wanted to find Elsa must needs go into society to seek her, and he thought she more than repaid the effort. Of course, if she found the house dull, it must be sold; but he had persuaded her graciously to consent to live in it for a few months first, just to try. Immediately on their marriage, he was going to take her to Schwannberg, that she might see the bursting of the glorious South German spring; but here again occurred a slight difference between them. He would have liked to linger, but this did not suit his bride. It would be dreadful, she urged, to waste these precious months cooped up in such a remote corner of the world. She must be in town by the middle of May, to have her first taste of a London season.

This was a definite trial to Leon; but all his tastes were gradually undergoing such a complete revolution that he was willing on all occasions to think himself in the wrong. When first Elsa had fixedly declared that a month was the longest honeymoon she would suffer, the idea had greatly ruffled him. They had parted in much offence on the lady's part, and some unhappiness on the gentleman's.

Next day he presented himself with a mixture of feelings at Burton Street. Fate was propitious. Lady Mabel was out at a calisthenic class with her children and the governess. Elsa was alone in the boudoir, attired in a tea-gown of delicate silk, and seated near the fire with a little sick terrier of his which she had undertaken to doctor. At her lover's entrance she half looked up, then turned slowly away and devoted her attention to the dog. Percivale stood in the doorway, his hand on the lock, his fine head thrown back.

"May I come in?" he asked.

"Pray do," said a small and frigid voice.

He closed the door and came forward, his daily offering of flowers in his hand. Pausing before her—

"Are you angry with me, Elsa?" he asked, miserably.

"I thought *you* were angry with *me*," she said, in low and injured tones.

"My darling, no." He knelt down beside her. "Only I was a little disappointed to think—to think that you would not be happy alone with me——"

She shot a shy glance at him from beneath her heavy lashes.

"I do not know you very well yet," said she softly.

"Are you afraid of me, Elsa?"

A suggestive pause, during which he hung breathless on every change which swept over the lovely face.

"I do not quite understand you," faltered she at last.

"I only plead to be allowed to explain myself," he murmured. "What is it, love? I am so unused to women, you must be good to me, and help me, and forgive me if I am not gentle enough. What is it you do not understand?"

"Is our honeymoon only to last as long as our wedding journey?" slowly asked the girl. "Will you not love me as well in London as in Tyrol? Will you change when that little month is over? For me, I shall love you as dearly, wherever we are."

"My beloved!" he flung his arm about her in a rapture; for Miss Brabourne, as a rule, was very wisely sparing of her professions of attachment. "You are right—I was wrong. Our honeymoon will last for ever—what matters where we spend it?"

"That was what I thought—no, Leon, you must not kiss me again—once is quite enough. Be good and listen to me while I talk to you a little."

She passed her arm round his neck as he knelt, and, with her other hand, pushed up the soft curling rings of his bright hair. He closed his eyes with rapture as he felt the touch.

"You say," said Elsa, stroking softly, "that you do not care for society, that you dislike London in the season."

"And that is true, my own——"

"Now, how do you know? Have you tried society?"

"No, never. I have always avoided it!"

"And how many seasons have you been through?"

"Not one."

"There, you see! Now, Leon, look at me!" Daintily placing a finger beneath his chin, she turned his face up to hers. "Is it fair to say you dislike a thing you have never tried? How can you tell beforehand? Is it not, perhaps, a little wee bit selfish of you?"

"Yes, it is," promptly replied he. "I am a brute, my darling."

"No, but you had not thought. I think, perhaps, if I—if I had a wife; and if I were foolish enough to be very proud of her, as you are of poor little me, that I should be pleased for people to see her, and to see how happy I made her—and to let all the world know that I loved her so—and—and—oh, Leon, you are laughing at me," and, with a burst of childish merriment, she hid her face in his neck.

"Elsa," cried her lover, as soon as he could speak coherently, "my life, do as you like, go where you will—if you please yourself you please me! I live to make your happiness, mind that!"

This was merely a specimen of the way in which Elsa carried her points. Percivale was a mere child in her hands; she had a knack of making others feel themselves in the wrong, which was little short of genius.

Her presentation was a triumph. London was unanimous in pronouncing her undeniably the beauty of the year; and her engagement to the mysterious Percivale, as well as the romantic story of their first meeting, surrounded them both with a perfect blaze of interest. Nothing else was talked of. The marriage would be the event of the season. The world was more than ever anxious to know more of the owner of the *Swan*.

"Miss Brabourne has never asked you anything about your belongings, has she?" asked Claud one day of Percivale.

"Never. She has not alluded to the subject."

"Take my advice," said Claud, "and don't volunteer that information which you mentioned to me."

"Oh, I must. I shall tell her everything when we are married. I have all along determined on that."

"People are so busy with your name, that it occurs to me that you are saddling a young girl with a great responsibility in giving her such a secret to keep."

Percivale smiled.

"Cranmer, are you in love?" he asked.

"Yes, I am. Why?" said Claud, bluntly.

The other looked surprised.

"Well," he said, "you have not honored me with your confidence; and it is quite new to me to hear that you are; but to the point. Would you not trust the woman of your choice with any secret?"

Claud hesitated a moment.

"Well, to be honest," said he at last, "yes. I certainly should."

"Should you not think it an insult to her to hold her debarred from the innermost recesses of your mind?"

"Undoubtedly I should."

"Well! Do you expect me to feel differently?"

Claud had no more to say. His own state of mind in these days was one of deep depression.

Henry Fowler had been obliged to leave town directly. Wynifred was announced to be convalescent; and, two days after his departure, Miss Ellen Willoughby had written to ask Hilda to bring her sister down to Edge Willoughby as soon as ever she was strong enough to travel, there to remain as long as she pleased, and grow strong in the soft sea air.

Claud's only comfort was in calling every day at Mansfield Road for news, and now and then leaving a basket of grapes or some flowers from his sister; but he could never gain admittance to see Wynifred, though his face, as he once or twice made a faltering petition, went to Hilda's heart. His suspense was costing him a great deal, as was manifest from his countenance of settled gloom, his pale face, and the purple marks under his eyes.

Lady Mabel received a shock one day.

"Claud," said she, "I have been most astonished. Lady Alice Alison has been calling, and she tells me that the youngest Miss Allonby is going to marry one of the Haldanes of Eldersmain. I suppose I shall have to call; and she tells me also that their father was a colonel, and a nephew of Lord Dovedale. It is rather annoying; we ought to have known that before."

"Why?" asked Claud, aggressively.

"Why? Because I ought to have been told—I should have shown them more civility."

"Why, what do you know of the Dovedales?"

"Nothing, personally; but they are in society."

"Well? Are not the Allonbys in society?"

"Claud, how idiotic you can be when you like."

"It is a matter of necessity, not choice, my sister. My brain never did work as fast as yours. But the speed of yours is abnormal. However, I should not lay myself open to a snub by calling in Mansfield Road now."

"Why?"

"Because, if they have any pride, and I fancy they have a good deal, they will not return your call."

"Claud! Not return my call?"

"I think not. They are very stiff with me."

"That is just because I have not called."

"And now you are ready to do so on the strength of their great-uncle having been in 'Debrett,' Mab. I thought you were beyond that sort of thing."

"If it is being in love that makes you so unpleasant, my good boy, I do hope you will soon get over it."

"Get over it. You talk as if it was measles. Does one get over these things? But, if you find my company irksome, I can go to Portland Place, you know."

"Don't be offended; only you have been so terribly in the dumps lately. Why don't you propose, and have done with it?"

"I am waiting for leave," said Claud, with a laugh which ended in a sigh, as he hurriedly left the room.

CHAPTER XLVII

A man may love a woman perfectly,
And yet by no means ignorantly maintain
A thousand women have not larger eyes;
Enough that she alone has looked at him
With eyes that, large or small, have won his soul.
Aurora Leigh.

Elsa Brabourne had been transformed into Elsa Percivale with the assistance of two bishops and a dean. Drawings of her *trousseau* and of her bridesmaids' dresses had appeared in the ladies' newspapers. Her aunts had given a reception to about a hundred people of whom they had never heard before, and who, in return, had presented the bride with much costly rubbish which she did not want; and at last Leon had carried off his wife, in an ultra-fashionable tailor-made travelling dress, to Folkestone *en route* for the Continent and Schwannberg.

Claud Cranmer had officiated, somewhat gloomily as best man at this wedding, the courtship of which had been so romantic, the realization so entirely Philistine.

All the technicality and elaboration of this modern London ceremony had been most trying to Percivale, who, as has been said, hated coming before the public as a central figure; and, at this particular marriage, the mysterious bridegroom had, contrary to custom, attracted quite as much notice as the lovely bride.

The young man was beginning dimly to realize that Claud had spoken truly when he said that life now-a-days could be neither a dream nor an ideal. There seemed so much that was commonplace and technical to take the bloom off his romance. He literally panted for his Bavarian home—for foaming river, wide lake, rugged steep, glittering horizon of snow-peaked Alps in which to realize the happiness that he so fervently anticipated. As to Elsa's mental state on her wedding-day, it must be owned that, when the excitement was over—when the admiring crowds were left behind, and she found herself alone with her husband, she was a good deal frightened. She did not understand him in the least. Her nature was so utterly devoid of the least spark of romance or sentiment that she could not interpret his thoughts or his desires. There was a still firmness about him which awed her. Docile as he was, subjugated as he was, there yet had been times during their short engagement when she experienced great uneasiness. Chief of these was the evening when he heard of Osmond Allonby's disappearance. There had been something then in the low, repressed intensity of his manner which had made her quail.

True, she had been able to change his mood in a moment. A couple of her easily-shed tears, lying on her eye-lashes, had brought him to his knees in an agony of repentance. But still there remained always in her mind a kind of rankling conviction that her lover expected of her something which she could not give, because she did not know what it was. When Percivale gave rein to the poetic side of his nature, and talked of sympathies, of high aims, of beauty in one's daily life, he spoke to deaf ears. Vaguely she comforted herself with the reflection that this would last only for a little while. Men had a way of talking like that when they were in love; but, while it lasted, it give her a feeling of discomfort. She could never be at her ease whilst she was in a state of such uncertainty; for uncertainty begets fear.

Her depression was increased by the serious words which her godfather had spoken to her on her wedding-morning. She hated to be spoken to seriously. It was like being scolded—it carried her back to the unloved memories of her dull childhood. Why could he not have given her her gold necklace with a gay declaration that most jewels adorned a white neck, but that in her case the neck would adorn the jewel—or some other such speech—the kind to which her ears were now daily accustomed.

Why did he think it necessary to entreat her never to allow her husband to be disappointed in her? Was it likely that any man could ever be disappointed in her? It seemed more probable that she might one day come to feel bored by him, handsome and eligible though he was.

Somehow, being engaged to him had not quite fulfilled her expectations. More than once she had felt—not exactly consciously, but none the less really—that she was more in touch with Captain St. Quentin, or others of the well-born ordinary young men of the day who formed her set, than with the idealist Leon. He was a creature from another sphere, his thoughts and aims were different, she knew; and, as her own inclinations became daily more clearly defined, she could not help feeling that they grew daily more unlike his.

"But she is so young, he will be able to mould her," said Claud, hopefully to himself. He guessed, more clearly than any one else, that Percivale was mismated; and foresaw with a dim foreboding that a bad time was in store for him when he should discover the fact; but, on his friend's wedding-day, he would not be a skeleton at the feast. He was willing to hope for the best.

Slowly he turned from the shoe-flinging and rice-scattering which formed the tag-end of the wedding. Leon's face haunted him. The expression of it, as he spoke the oath which bound him to Elaine, had been so intense, so holy in the purity of its chivalrous devotion, that it had awed and impressed even the crowd of frivolous triflers who lounged and chatted in the church, whispering scandal, and criticizing each other's appearance as others like them did at Romney Leigh's wedding. There was in fact something about this day which recalled the poem forcibly to Claud's mind: not, of course, the ghastly *dénouement*, but the character of the man, the same loftiness of aim, the same terrible earnestness in its view of life.

Something, too, about his friend's farewell had struck him with a sadness for which he could scarcely account.

A little, trifling slip of Percivale's tongue, dwelt in his memory in a manner altogether disproportionate. In the hurry and bustle of the departure, as he grasped Claud's hand, instead of saying, "Good-bye," as he meant to, Leon had said, "Good-night."

He was unconscious of it himself, and in an absent way he had repeated it, in that still voice which always seemed to convey so much meaning.

"Good-night, Claud, good-night."

Now that he was gone, the words rang in Cranmer's ears, as Romney's words lingered in Aurora's. As he turned back into the house and slowly went upstairs, he was repeating softly to himself the line,

"And all night long I thought *Good-night*," said he.

Walking into the drawing-room with its showy display of wedding-gifts, its fading flowers and vacant, desolate aspect, he was confronted by Henry Fowler.

They had hardly spoken before, as Henry had only arrived in town late the preceding night. Now they stood face to face, and the elder man was painfully struck by the haggard aspect of the younger.

Wynifred Allonby had now been for some weeks at Edge Willoughby, and his only way of hearing of her was from the two Misses Willoughby who were in town, for the little house in Mansfield Road was shut up. Hilda was with her sister in Devonshire, Jacqueline staying with her future relations, Osmond still in Paris, his address unknown, his letters few and unsatisfactory.

"Well?" said Mr. Fowler, interrogatively.

"Well," said Claud, defiantly, "I am glad to have the chance of speaking to you, Fowler. I will begin with putting a straight question. Are you engaged to—to Miss Allonby?"

"No, lad; that question is soon answered. She will not see me."

"Well, then, I give you fair warning, I am coming down to the Combe. I can bear this suspense no longer."

"Come as soon as you will, and stay as long as you can; but she will not see you. She will see nobody. She seems well, they say; her strength is coming back, she can walk, and eats pretty well; but she is sadly changed, her pretty sister tells me. She does not seem to care to talk. She will sit silent for hours, and they are afraid she does not sleep. She will go nowhere and speak to no one. If you call upon her, she will decline to see you."

"I shall not give her the chance to decline or to consent. I shall insist upon seeing her," said Claud, calmly. "Fowler, some words you said to me that night at the Langham have been with me ever since: 'There comes a time to every man when the only clean and honorable course is to go straight forward.' I have passed beyond that. For me now, the only *possible* course is to go straight forward. I *will* see and speak to her, if only to ask a forgiveness from her. I have piled on the sack-cloth and ashes this Lent, Fowler. I have found out at last what I really am; and for a time the knowledge simply crushed me. But now I am beginning to struggle up. I have grown to believe in the truth of the saying that men may rise on stepping-stones of their dead selves to higher things. If—if I could have *her* for my own, I honestly think I might yet be a useful man. Now you know my intentions, sir, as well as I know them myself. You can't be mad enough to ask such a declared rival down to stay with you."

"Mad or sane, I must have you to stay with me. Can you start to-morrow?"

"With the best heart in the world; but, Fowler, I don't understand you."

"See here, lad. I trust Miss Allonby entirely. She will not have you if she does not love you; and if she does love you, I am willing she should have you, for my life's aim is her happiness, whether she find it in me or in another man. Ah! you are young; no wonder you think me mad. Time was when I should have felt, as you do now, that the thing was a blind necessity, that either she and I must come together, or the world must end for me. In those days there was a woman,"—he halted a moment, then went on serenely, "there was a woman made for me. I was the only man to make her happy; but she chose another. It was then I knew what desolation meant. Now I can feel tenderness but not passion. I can wish for Wynifred's happiness more fervently than I desire my own; I do not feel, as you feel, that her happiness and mine are one and the self-same thing. Yours is the love that should overcome, I am sure of that, now. It is the love that will tear down barriers and uproot obstructions; the only love a man should dare to lay at the feet of a woman like Wynifred Allonby."

CHAPTER XLVIII

Write woman's verses, and dream woman's dreams:
But let me feel your perfume in my home,
To make my sabbath after working-days.
Bloom out your youth beside me,—be my wife.
Aurora Leigh.

Wynifred stood idly at the window.

It was a lovely day—one of those real spring days which we in England so rarely enjoy—perhaps one, perhaps half-a-dozen in the whole year. A brief interlude in the east wind's unfailing rigor; a breathing time when the black shadows leave the land and color begins to dawn over copse and meadow. The sea-ward slopes of the valley were beginning to grow green. The borders of the garden were purple and gold with crocuses, and sweet with violets.

Hilda had yesterday brought in a sumptuous handful of Lent lilies from the woods, lighting up the room like a flash of condensed sunlight. There were countless ripples on the sea, a breath of life and spring in the warm air. The birds were twittering and building, and the long hazel-blooms fell in pale gold and crimson tassels on the pathway. Miss Ellen lay on her sofa, anxiously watching the silent pale girl at the window.

They were alone. Hilda was out riding with Henry Fowler.

Miss Ellen had been watching the clock, wondering how long Wynifred would remain speechless and in the same position if left to herself. When the silence had lasted more than fifty minutes, she felt it unbearable.

"Wynifred, my dear, a penny for your thoughts," said she.

Wyn started violently, and faced slowly round. Her eyes wore a dull look, as if she was not quite fully awake.

"I don't think I was thinking of anything in particular," said she, sitting down listlessly and taking up her work, which lay on a table near. Miss Ellen watched her keenly, as she turned the embroidery this way and that, smoothed it with her hand, threaded a needle with silk as if she felt that some pretence of employment was necessary, but, after five minutes' spasmodic working, let it drop idly in her lap, leaned back in her chair, and again became apathetic.

It was disheartening indeed to watch her.

Miss Ellen recalled the energetic, slender Wynifred of last summer, with her eager, vivid interest in everything, her ready tongue, her gay laugh, her quick fingers.

How could the girl tell at what precise amount of work she would have to stop short? How should she recognise the signs of overfatigue? To spur herself on had been her only care,—to check her cravings for rest and leisure, as something to be crushed down and despised.

Now she was like a clock with damaged works. If you shook her, she would go fitfully for a few minutes, and then relapse into her former lethargy.

Of course, the completeness of her breakdown had been greatly aggravated by her own private unhappiness, and by the terrible trouble of her brother's total inability to stand up against his reverse of fortune. It seemed as if the consciousness of Osmond's utter weakness had sapped all her strength, had struck away her last prop. From such a depth of sickness and depression, she would, naturally take some time to re-ascend. Miss Ellen comforted herself with the thought that her cure must be gradual, but she could not feel that it had yet so much as begun.

Wynifred could not be made to talk on any subject except the sun, the flowers, the chough, the villagers, or some such indifferent theme. To talk about books made her head ache, she said, and she never put pen to paper. Hilda had now and then tried her, by casually leaving writing materials about in the room where she sat; but, alone or in company, she never touched them.

She spoke of no one and asked after no one but Osmond, and of him she would now and then speak, though never mentioning Elsa, or anyone else connected with the episodes preceding her illness.

Miss Ellen watched her daily with a tenderness and penetration which were touching to behold. The whole of her gentle heart went out to the girl, the deepest depth of whose malady she hardly guessed. She had an idea that what was wanted was the sight of some thing or person vividly recalling the trouble, whatever it was, which had made such an impression. She believed that a moment of excitement, even if painful, would break up the dull crust of indifference, and bring relief, even if it should flow in tears. But she had not clue enough to go upon in order to bring such a thing about; and Hilda was profoundly ignorant of her sister's secretly-cherished love-affair.

"Wynifred," said Miss Ellen.

The girl looked up quickly.

"It is such a lovely day, dear; why don't you go for a walk?"

"I did not like to leave you, Miss Willoughby; not that I am very enlivening company."

"You will be much more enlivening if you can bring me news of the primroses beginning to bloom in the woods. Get your hat and be off, bring back a pair of pink cheeks and an appetite, or you won't be admitted."

Wynifred rose slowly and folded her work. Painfully Miss Ellen recalled words that Henry Fowler had spoken last year as he watched the blithe young company out at tea on the terrace:—Elsa, the Allonbys, young Haldane, and Claud Cranmer.

"How those Allonby girls do enjoy themselves!" he had said.

Their enjoyment was infectious, it was so spontaneous, so fresh. The change was acute.

"What is to be done with her?" pondered Miss Willoughby, as the girl went out, apathetically closing the door behind her.

Hardly knowing why, Wynifred chose the road that led inland, along the further side of the valley, to Poole Farm.

Had Miss Ellen only known how inwardly active was the mind that outwardly seemed almost dormant! All yesterday the bells had been clashing from the little church in honor of Elsa's wedding. In fancy the girl had gone through the whole ceremony—had seen Claud attending his friend Percivale to church, in his capacity of best man. To-day it seemed as if the bells were still ringing, ringing on in her head until she felt dizzy and unnerved.

Why could she not expel unwelcome thoughts and order herself back to work, as heretofore? No use. She had taxed her self-control once too often, and stretched it too far. It had snapped. There was no power in her.

"There was a time," she thought, "when I could have saved myself. At the Miles' ball I was comparatively free—I could take an intelligent interest in other things. Why—oh, *why* was he sent there to force me to begin all over again?"

Lost in reverie, she wandered on until she found herself opposite the spot where Saul Parker had attacked Osmond.

There was a fallen tree lying on the grass at the other side of the lane, and, overcome with many memories, she sat down upon it. Here it was that she and Claud had exchanged their first flash of sympathy, when strolling back to Poole together in the summer twilight. Closing her eyes, she rested her brow on her two hands, as she lived again through the experiences of those days.

What was this strange weight which seemed to make her unable to rise, or to think, or to cast off her abiding depression? Had there really been a time when she, Wynifred, had possessed a mind stored with graceful fancies, and a pen to give them to the world?

That was over for ever now. Her literary career was stopped, she told herself in her despair; and when her money came to an end she must starve, for her capacity for work was gone. Yet all around her was the subtle air of spring, instinct with that vague, indescribable hope and desire which sometimes shakes our very being for five minutes or so, suddenly, on an April day, however prosaic and middle-aged we may be. She did not weep, her trouble was too dull, too chronic for tears.

She sat on, idly gazing at the farm-house windows and at the flight of the building rooks about the tall elms, till a footstep close beside her made her turn her head; and Claud Cranmer stood in the lane, not ten paces from her, his hat in his hand, his eyes fixed on her face.

For a moment his figure and the landscape surrounding it swam before her eyes, and then, in a flash, the woman's dignity and pride sprang up anew in her heart and she was ready to meet him. All the feeling, the force of being which, since her illness, had been in abeyance, started up full-grown in a moment at sight of him. She knew she was alive, for she knew that she suffered—as poignantly, as really as ever; and for the moment she almost hailed the pain with rapture, because it was a sign of life.

She must take his outstretched hand, she must control her voice to speak to him. She was childishly pleased to find that her strength rose with her need—that she could do both quite rationally. She did not rise from her log. As soon as Claud saw that she was conscious of his presence, he came up to her with hand extended, and, in another moment, hers was resting in his hungry clasp.

He was more unnerved than she. His heart seemed beating in his throat, his love and tenderness and shame were all struggling together, so that for a few minutes, he was dumb; the sight of her had been so overpowering.

They had told him not to be shocked—to expect to find her greatly altered; but they had not calculated on the instantaneous effect of his appearance on her. Thin indeed she was—almost wasted—her eyes unnaturally large and hollow. But the expression was as vivid, as fascinating as ever, the color burnt in her cheeks—it was merely an ethereal version of his own Wynifred, inspiring him with an idea of fragility which made him wild with pity.

She spoke first—her own voice, so unlike that of any other woman he had ever known.

"I did not expect to see you," she said. "Are you staying with Mr. Fowler?"

"No. I came down yesterday."

Her hand, which seemed so small—like nothing, as it lay in his own—was gently withdrawn.

"You have brought spring weather with you," said she, quietly.

"It is beautiful to-day," he answered, neither knowing nor caring what he said. "May I sit down and talk a—a little? It is—it is—a long time since I saw you last."

He seated himself beside her on the log, hoping that the beating of his heart was not loud enough for her to overhear. He could hardly realize that he had accomplished so much—that they were seated, at last, together, "With never a third, but each by each as each knew well,"—and with a future made up of a few moments—a present so intensified that it blotted out all past experience; a kind of foretaste of the "everlasting minute" of immortality, such as is now and then granted to the time-encumbered soul.

Whether the pause, the hush which was the prelude to the drama, lasted one moment or ten he could not say. He was conscious, presently, of an uneasy stirring of the girl at his side.

"I think I ought to be walking home," said she.

"Not yet; I have not half enjoyed the view," said he, decidedly.

"Oh, please do not disturb yourself," she faltered, breathlessly, as she made a movement to rise, "I can go home alone—I would rather——"

"So you told me the last time we parted, and, like a fool and a coward, I let you go. I am wiser now. You must stay."

She had lifted up her gloves to put them on. Taking her hands in his, he gently pulled away the gloves, and obliged her to resume her seat. She began to tremble.

"Mr. Cranmer—you must let me go. I—am not strong yet—I cannot bear it. Oh, please go and leave me. I cannot talk to you."

The words were wrung from her. Feebly she strove to draw her hands out of his warm clasp, but he held them firmly.

"The reason I followed you here was because they told me you would refuse to see me if you could," he said calmly. He had regained his composure now, and his quiet manner soothed her. "I was quite determined to see you. I came down to Edge for that reason alone. It is merely a question of time. If you will not listen to me to-day, you must to-morrow. I have something which I *will* say to you. Choose when you will hear it."

"Is it—is it about Osmond?" she said, feverishly.

"About Osmond? No, it has nothing to do with him," said Claud, rather resentfully. "It is only about me."

She was silent for a long moment, gazing straight before her with a strange, wild excitement growing in her heart. At last, with one final effort at self-mastery, she deliberately lifted her eyes to his. "About you?" she said faintly.

"About you and me," he answered.

She made an ineffectual struggle, half-rose, looked this way and that, as if for flight, then sank back again into her place, in absolute surrender.

"Say it," she whispered, almost inaudibly.

"Wynifred," he said, his voice taking from his emotion a thrill which she felt in the innermost recesses of her heart. "I have a confession to make to you—a confession of fraud. Pity me. Perhaps the confession will deprive me of your friendship for ever; but I must speak. There is something in my possession which belongs to you—it has been yours for nearly a year. You ought to have had it long ago. I have kept it back from you all these months. Do you think you can forgive me?"

She gazed at him uncomprehending.

"Something of mine? A letter?" said she.

"No, not a letter." It was exquisite, this interview; he could have prayed to prolong it for weeks. He held her attention now, as well as her hands; he felt inclined to be deliberate. "It is worth nothing, or very little, this thing in question," he went on. "You may not care for it—you may utterly decline to have it—you may tell me that it is worthless in your eyes, and throw it back to me in scorn. But, since it is yours, I feel that I must just lay it before you, to take or leave. It has been yours for so long, that I think that very fact has made it rather less good-for-nothing, and, Wynifred, it has in it the capacity for growth. If you would take it and keep it, there is no telling what you might make of it."

"I do not understand," cried Wynifred.

The Tree Of Knowledge A Novel | 351

"You do not understand why your own was not given to you before?" he asked, softly. "That is the shameful part of the story. I kept it back only for mean and contemptible reasons; because I was afraid to give it absolutely into your keeping, not knowing certainly whether you would care to have it. But I have been shown that this was not honest. Whether you will have it or not, my dearest, I must show my heart to you, I must implore you to take it, to forgive its imperfections, to count as its one merit that it is all your own. It is myself, my beloved, who am at your feet. My life, my hopes, my love, are all yours, and have been for so long.... Can you forget that I withheld them when they were not mine to keep? Can you forgive that they are so poor, so imperfect, so unworthy?"

She had given a little cry when first the meaning of his riddle became apparent to her, and, snatching away one hand, had covered her face with it.

All the Irish fervor and poetry of Claud's nature was kindled. He was no backward lover,—the words rushed to his lips, he knew not how.

Determinedly he put his arm round his love as she sat, speaking with his lips close to her ear.

"Wyn," he said, with that sweetness of voice and manner which had first won her heart. "Wyn, I'll give you no option. You are mine; you know it. I deserve punishment; but don't punish me, dear, for I tell you you can't be happy without me, any more than I without you. Is that presumption? I think not,—I believe it's insight. There are times, you know, when one seems to push away all the manners and customs of the day, and my heart just cries out to yours that we are made for one another. My own, just look at me a minute, and tell me if that isn't so."

Drawing her closer to him, he gently pulled away her hand from her eyes and made her look at him.

"Is it true? Dare you contradict me, sweetheart?" he said, tenderly. "Don't you belong to me?"

The authoress could find no eloquent reply. No words would obey the bidding of her feelings. With her head at rest at last on her lover's heart, like the veriest bread-and-butter miss, she could only murmur a bald, bare, "Yes,—I—I think so."

"You think so, do you, my love?" he said, ecstatically. "Tell me what makes you think so, then, sweet?"

She closed her eyes, and, lifting her arm, she laid it round his neck with a sigh of bliss.

"I—can't," said she, weakly.

It sounds very inadequate, but the fact remains that this entire want of vocabulary in the usually self-possessed and ready Wynifred was the highest possible charm in the eyes of her lover. To his unutterable delight, he found that his very loftiest dream was realised. He himself was the great want of the girl's life. He comforted her. She was able at once to let go the burden of care and sorrow she had borne so long, and to rest herself utterly in his love. The expression on her white face was that of perfect rest. Her soul had found its true goal. Claud and she were in the centre of the labyrinth at last. Above them on the hillside stood the grey farm, still and lonely in the sunlight as it had stood for more than three centuries. Never had it looked on purer happiness than that of these two obscure and poorly-endowed mortals who yet felt themselves rich indeed in the consciousness of mutual sympathy.

The air was musical with streams, the stir of spring mixed subtly with their joy. This betrothal needed no pomp of circumstance to enhance its perfection. To Claud and Wynifred to be together was to be blessed.

CHAPTER XLIX

To marriage all the stories flow
And finish there.
The Letter L.

It was sunset when at last they rose from the fallen log. To Wynifred it was as though every cloud of trouble had melted away out of her sky. Grief was grief no longer when shared with Claud. His sympathy was so perfect and so tender. It seemed to both of them as if their betrothal were no new thing, as if, in some prior state of being, they had been, as he expressed it, *made to fit each other.*

"Vaguely, I believe I always felt it," he said. "I was always at ease with you. You suited me. I felt you understood me; at times it almost seemed as if you must be thinking with my brain, so wonderfully similar were the workings of our minds. Wyn, we can never be unhappy, you and I, whatever our lot. We are independent of fate so long as we have each other. I wonder how many engaged couples arrive deliberately at that conclusion?"

"I did not think you would ever arrive at it," said Wyn, smiling. "I thought you were a Sybarite, Claud."

"You thought right—I was. But by habit, not by nature. It was Henry Fowler who awoke me to a sense of my own contemptibility. God bless him."

"God bless him," echoed the girl, softly.

"Look!" cried Claud, "how the sun catches the windows of the farm-house, and makes them flame. So they looked the first evening I ever saw them—before I knew you, my darling. Shall we go and tell Mrs. Battishill that we mean to get married? She will be so pleased."

"Ah, yes, do. I had no heart to go and see her, the place was so full of memories of you. But now!"

It was quite dark when Henry, who had been smoking at the open door of Lower House, heard Claud's quick footfall cross the bridge.

"Well, lad," said he, as the young man came buoyantly towards him, "I'm to congratulate you, I know. There's triumph in your very step."

"I'm about as happy as it's possible for a man to be," said Claud simply, as he gave him his hand. "I believe I should be too happy if it were not for the thought of you."

"Don't you fret for me," was the steady answer.

The moon was up, and threw a clear light on Claud's features as he stood bareheaded, just against the porch. Moved by a sudden impulse of affection, Henry laid his hand on the fair hair, and drew it closer, till it rested against his sturdy shoulder.

"Claud," he said, "I believe I care more for you two than for any other living creatures. I know you will find your best happiness together, so I'll just not intrude my feelings on you any more. My head's full of plans for you, lad. Do you care to hear them?"

"I should rather think so. Fowler, what a brick you are!"

"Glad you think so. Now, listen. You'll accept that post of overseer I offered you?"

"I should like it of all things."

"Very well, then. I'll build you a house for my wedding gift. She can choose her own site, for most of the land round here is mine, as you know; and she can choose her own plans. I'll have them carried out, whatever they are. All I have will be hers when I'm gone; for Elsa will not want it. She has a large fortune of her own, and her husband's is larger. If my life is spared it will be my happiness to plan for your children, Claud. Do you think you can be happy leading such a retired life—eh?"

"My happiness will be with Wynifred, wherever she is," was the tranquil answer. "I am not a boy, Fowler, and, as you know, my love has not been a fancy of an hour. She has told me that she is delighted at the idea of living here in the Combe; and, as for me—you know how I can enjoy myself in the country."

"I foresee a long useful life for you both," said Henry, as they slowly went indoors in response to the supper-bell and reluctantly shut out the spring moonlight. "I wish I could feel as sure about Elsa."

"Oh, that will be all right," said Claud, encouragingly. "What makes you despond about her?"

"I feel so uncertain of her. What Miss Ellen always said about her is so true. She has a most pronounced character of her own, but nobody as yet knows what it is. I am afraid her husband expects too much of her."

"Everyone who expects perfection in a woman must needs be disappointed," returned Claud. "He will get over it, and find out how to manage her. He is a dreamer, you know—an idealist, any bride must needs fall short of his requirements. He is in love with an abstraction, and there is something particularly concrete about Mrs. Percivale."

"There are some natures, I have heard of, that never trust again where their faith has been once shaken," said Henry, in a low voice. "I—I cannot consider Elsa reliable. She was not to be trusted as a child. I have a horrible suspicion that her husband would feel it terribly hard to forgive deceit."

"She will have no occasion to deceive him," said Claud soothingly. "He will allow her to do whatever she pleases."

"Well, I daresay I am wrong, I wish devoutly that I may be. But I have all along thought the marriage unsuitable. Of course, I foresaw it—from the moment when he saw her lying asleep in her aunt's room, the night we brought the news of her innocence. The circumstances were such as could not fail to attract such a romantic mind as his. And yet, Claud—yet—I wish things had fallen otherwise. She would have suited Allonby better."

Claud was thankful that Henry was ignorant of the fact which, even now, was causing him the gravest anxiety. If he, Fowler, the gentlest of men, could sorrowfully admit that Elsa was not to be trusted, it was somewhat agitating to reflect that she was probably even now in possession of a secret which the entire London public was burning with curiosity to know. Henry did not believe in the existence of a secret at all. He thought that it was merely gossip, the natural result of Percivale's odd habits and secluded life.

But suppose the entire facts were blazoned abroad—suppose the tale was in everybody's mouth!—Claud shrugged his shoulders. He had warned his friend, he could do no more. The sequel lay between the dainty hands of Percivale's wife. What would she do with it?

CHAPTER L

"Eyes," he said, "now throbbing thro' me are ye eyes which
did undo me?
Shining eyes, like antique jewels set in Parian marble stone?
Underneath that calm white forehead, are ye ever burning
torrid.
O'er the desolate sand desert of my heart, and life alone?"
Lady Geraldine's Courtship.

It was a beautiful May evening. The air seemed full of incense, the
trees which clothe the heights of Heidelberg were just one sheet of snowy
blossom. The dull red castle was gilded by the slanting rays of the sun, and
for a few moments stood out more decidedly that it is wont to do from
the background of hills which surround it. The Neckar lay broad and calm
under the light, at one end of the view lost in a narrowing gorge, at the other
emerging wide into a seemingly limitless plain.

Down the stream a boat was slowly floating. The current was taking her
down quite fast enough to please her inmates. The young man's sculls lay
idly skimming the surface of the shining water, and his eyes were turned
up towards the bowery heights and the romantic ruin which lay to his right.

The lady in the stern lay back with one hand and wrist clasped lightly
on the rudder-lines; but there was little need for very accurate steering, as
the season was too early and the stream too strong to tempt many boats out
on the water.

"By Jove, how lovely everything looks this evening! like a city in a
dream," said Osmond Allonby, for it was he, turning up a face of artistic
enjoyment to the lovely scene, with its quaint old roofs clustering down to
the river, and its faint blue haze enveloping city and pinewoods alike in the
mystery and stillness of evening.

"Charming," said his companion, Mrs. Frederick Orton, as she roused
herself, and let her eye follow the direction of his. "Let us land, and stroll up
to the *Schloss*. It will be fine to see the sun set from that height."

"Ah! you are improving, I see. Learning, under my tuition, to appreciate the beauties of nature," said Osmond, in a tone which seemed to imply considerable intimacy.

He was a good deal changed for the worse in the few short months which had elapsed since the shattering of his hopes. It seemed as though his entire will had concentrated itself towards one aim, which, when removed, left his whole moral nature in fragments. His mouth looked hard and mocking, his eyes like those of one who sat up late, his whole manner had degenerated and taken a different tone.

His falling in with the Ortons in Paris had been about the worst thing which could possibly have befallen him. Ottilie's bitter hatred of Percivale and Elsa made her a dangerously sympathetic confidante. With one of those impulses of kind-heartedness which she was not wholly without, she had commissioned the forlorn young man to paint her portrait. This was at the time when his utter solitude and misery were so great, that his better nature was on the point of reasserting itself and sending him back to his forsaken home. But the daily sittings in Mrs. Orton's luxurious boudoir supplied his craving better than a return to duty would have done. She made a *protégé* of him. He was good-looking and had plenty to say for himself, his present sardonic and bitter frame of mind was amusing. He fell into the habit of escorting her about when, as frequently happened, her husband was too indolent to accompany her. When they moved from Paris, he went with them. She declared she should be dull without him. For several reasons it suited them better to remain abroad, and Osmond had grown to believe that he could not set foot in England till after Elsa's marriage. The notice of that event in the newspapers did not, however, seem to quicken his desire to go back and take up the broken threads of his life. He was content to dawdle on at Ottilie's side, railing at fate, sneering at the world, and growing every day less able to retrieve himself, and face disappointment like a man.

Ottilie laughed at his remark, as she laughed at all his sneers, whether directed against herself or others.

"Oh, you'll do wonders with me, if you keep on the course of training long enough," she said. "Now pull a few strokes on the bow side. I want to go in."

"This is a sweet place.... I should like to make some stay in it," said Osmond, musingly.

"Like most Edens, you would find there was a snake in it," said she, laughing.

"Might I ask whether you mean anything particular by that remark?"

"What makes you ask?"

"I fancied there was a hidden meaning in it, somehow."

"My dear boy, your penetration is fast becoming a thing to dread. Yes, if you will have it, there *was* a special meaning. I looked at the visitors' list this morning, and saw, among the arrivals——"

She paused. They were just in shore. The young man shipped his sculls, leaned his arms on his knees, and faced her steadily.

"Well—who were among the arrivals?"

"Mr. and Mrs. Percivale," she answered, rising. He sprang up to help her to land.

"What a mercy all that folly is over and done with," he said; and laughed, the harsh and dreary laugh proving the falsity of his words as he uttered them.

Turning to the boat he collected her wraps, paid the boatman, and then turned absently towards the town.

"We were going to the castle, I think?"

They set off walking in silence. At last Osmond abruptly broke out:

"They are returning from their honeymoon, I suppose."

"Doubtless. They are soon tired of seclusion; but Mrs. Percivale is no lover of seclusion; she had too much of that in her youth. What she wants now is to have her fling; and that is the very thing which does not by any means meet her husband's wishes."

"Why not? Is he jealous of her?" asked Osmond, in dry, hard tones.

"Jealous? He may be. I daresay she will give him cause; but that is not his reason for not wishing to appear very conspicuously before the public."

"Do you know the real reason?" asked Osmond, after a pause, staring at the ground.

"Broadly speaking, yes, I do. But not the details; they are too carefully concealed. Osmond, my young friend, if you want to be revenged on your successful rival, as is the fashion in the story-books, I could surely show you the easiest way in the world to do it."

"You could?" he said, with a momentary flash of unmistakable interest.

"I could indeed. I mean it."

"Rubbish," he said, in the unceremonious way of addressing her which he had rapidly acquired.

The Tree Of Knowledge A Novel | 359

"Oh, very well, if you contradict me flatly—"

"I didn't contradict. I only thought it was another flight of that brilliant fancy of yours."

"It is no fancy, but a solid fact," said she, vehemently, "that nobody knows who Percivale's father was. There! You have it in black and white."

Osmond gave a long whistle, and mused a few minutes in silence. At last—

"Won't do, my friend," said he. "She would never have been allowed to marry a man who could give no account of his antecedents."

"Oh—you think so! You are as clever as all the rest of them! I tell you the man is an adventurer—a mere adventurer! He had no difficulty in bamboozling that old idiot Henry Fowler, who was taken in by him from the first moment he saw him. As for the women, they could none of them see beyond his red beard and his red sash. It is as clever a case of fraud as I ever saw."

Osmond laughed bitterly.

"If it were fraud how can you prove it?" he said. "It is of no use to set indefinite reports afloat. There are hundreds of them already, but nobody believes them. And how can you get at facts?"

"Let me have Mrs. Elsa alone for half-an-hour, and I will engage to know as much as she does by the end of that time."

"And how much does she know?"

"Everything there is to tell."

"How in the world do you know that?"

"Because, my friend, I am, unlike you, a student of character. Percivale is besottedly in love, and, with his idiotic, romantic notions, would be sure to think he must tell his precious Elsa everything."

"Your inconsistency pains me, Mrs. O. Does this tally with the character of the deliberate adventurer? Surely he would have more prudence."

"Well," said she, after a pause, "if she does not know it now, she could certainly make him tell her, if it were put into her head to ask."

"You would be a bad ambassadress. If there is one person on the face of this earth whom she hates, I imagine it to be yourself."

"Oh! Pooh! Let me have her for an hour, I would be her warmest friend."

He smiled.

"You are sanguine," he answered.

"Osmond, you think I am talking nonsense," she said, impetuously. "I tell you I am not. Will you bet on it? Will you bet me that I don't get an interview with Elsa Percivale, win her over, and extract her husband's secret?"

"Yes, I will. Twelve pairs of gloves—anything you choose. You won't do it. To begin with, is it likely her husband will ever leave her alone? Besides, I think you are all wrong. I don't believe in any mystery except what is the invention of gossip."

"Very good. We shall see," was the lady's oracular answer. "Remember, it's a bet."

"Certainly. What am I to have if you fail?"

"A couple of boxes of the very best cigars."

"Done."

No more was said, for they were in the very steepest part of the ascent, and even Osmond's breath began to fail.

At last they were at the summit, repaid by a view which more than atoned for past struggle. As they leaned over the terrace, and gazed down, there was nothing beneath their eye but a foaming sheet of white, spray-like blossom and tender green foliage. The whole air was heavy with its fragrance. It was like a fairy sea, and inspired a longing to plunge one's weary limbs into its flowery midst and be at rest. As Osmond gazed around him, a sadness, born of the evening consecration, stole meltingly over his passion-twisted heart. The monotonous iterance of a little vesper bell somewhere in the valley, hidden by the orchard bowers, added the finishing touch. Leaning over the parapet, he felt unmanly tears welling up from his heart. All around spoke of peace, and it seemed as though the force of an invisible yet all pervading love flung around him.

"A slow arm of sweet compression felt with beatings at the breast."

Not for long had nature had the power so to move him; not since the fair June day when, in the Devonshire Combe, had first shone on him the eyes of the girl who was to prove his undoing. Remorseful memories swept over him all in a moment. A wholesome sense of failure, not in his worldly career, but morally, weighed down his spirit.

Ottilie, seated on the parapet, with her jewellery and her gorgeous parasol, looked out of place. At the moment it seemed as if he loathed her company, and must leave her.

A great yearning to be at peace, and forgive, flooded his heart. All the springs of sentiment were touched. Perhaps if any spot could lift up the degraded soul, and speak to it intensely of its own high possibilities, that spot is Heidelberg at the blossoming of spring.

A bough of lilac swayed close to his lips. Its surpassing freshness drifted past him on the breeze. The wallflower in the cleft of the red sandstone wall gave out with odorous sighs the store of warm sunlight which it had imbibed all day. He covered his face with his hands. Had he been alone, he would have fallen on his knees. There, on the bounteous hill-side, was the ruin of a palace—one of those "little systems of this world, which have their day, and cease to be." The kings who had erected it and lived in it, the men who had, may be, broken their hearts there, as he, Osmond, had lately done, were all past and gone, like a dream. But all around the woods were yet green, the fruit-trees blossomed still; and, encircling the decaying works of man, the works of God took on the semblance of the endless youth of immortality.

No such thought as this took definite shape in Osmond's mind; but the influence spoke all around him in the eloquent silence, teaching him, as God is apt to teach, without words, by the stress of the unseen upon his soul, felt without being comprehended. He had wandered away from Mrs. Orton's incongruous presence, and was alone in the most lonely part of the terrace.

Steps on the gravel roused him—low voices. Then the light ripple of a girl's laugh, like a splash of musical water, made him almost leap from his attitude of musing, every fibre of him alive and quivering with a rush of memory.

She stood before him—Elsa Percivale. Inwardly he said over the strange name that was now hers. One hand was in her husband's arm, the other was full of lilac and cherry-blossom. Her shining eyes beamed from beneath the most alluring of large hats. They looked, at that moment, an ideal bride and bridegroom.

Osmond whitened to the very lips as he faced the pair. He had no moment of preparation. Though he had just heard that they were in Heidelberg, the idea of meeting them face to face had not occurred to him very forcibly.

But, after the first moment of confusion, he felt that he could perhaps more easily have achieved such a meeting in this particular spot, than anywhere else in the world. His mood was that of being lifted above disappointment. He raised his hat with a hand that hardly trembled, and then stepped forward with a low word of greeting.

As for Elsa, when she saw who confronted her, the color flew to her face, and she glanced up at Leon's face with a guilty start. He scarcely looked surprised, but advanced with frank courtesy, saying.

"How do you do? What a lovely spot in which to meet."

"It is indeed," said Osmond, wondering at the calm with which he was able to proceed to offer the customary hopes as to the bride's health, and inquire what sort of weather they had had for their honeymoon.

Elsa was in radiant spirits this evening. She was on her way to London — that London which she loved so well. She was travelling, too, from place to place. Almost every night they stopped at a different hotel, and she sunned herself in the admiring glances of fresh *tables-d'hôte*. Whatever she expressed a wish for was immediately hers. Marriage, so far, suited her exactly. Certainly it was rather dull at Schwannberg and Leon had been rather tiresome sometimes, talking in a manner she could not understand. But that was over now; and honeymoons are not, as a rule, of frequent occurrence in one's career.

Whether Percivale was equally satisfied was a problem not yet to be answered. His thoughts were always hard to guess. Osmond could only note afresh every grace of his person and bearing with a bitterness which not even his late musings could take away.

"Are you here alone?" asked Elsa of Osmond, after her first panic; she was so relieved to find that he shook hands like any other mortal, and attempted no denunciations, that she felt quite at ease.

"No," he said, "I am with the Ortons."

"The Ortons!" cried she, with a gesture of dislike, and then she turned her head, and saw Ottilie Orton just behind her.

"I don't wonder at that involuntary expression of opinion, Mrs. Percivale," said Ottilie, in the soft low tones she could employ when she chose. "I am afraid you will never be able to forgive me for the wrong I did — for the greater wrong I intended to do you."

Ottilie dearly loved a little melodrama, anything approaching a "scene" was quite in her line. After the above speech she looked imploringly at Elsa, not holding out her hand, yet seeming by her whole attitude and expression, to denote that from one so good and beautiful she dared to hope much.

Elsa looked at her husband, and her husband hesitated. His distrust of the lady was profound, yet he did not wish to be rude.

"You cannot know, how can anyone tell," pleaded she, "what little Godfrey was to me? Ah, you saw only the bad side of his nature, you never knew what he could be to those he loved. I—never," here the rich, expressive voice broke, "I never had a child of my own—he was all I had to love. Cannot you imagine the burning sense of wrong—the feeling that my darling was dead, that some one must and should pay for his death? I was blind—mad! I lost all sense of right. I never thought of you, I only wanted vengeance for my boy."

It was beautifully done. The fervent tones took fresh meaning from the picturesque ruin and the lovely surroundings. Two of her auditors listened eagerly, the third, Osmond, turned away sick with disgust. He knew Mrs. Frederick pretty well by now. He had heard her conversation as they climbed the hill together, he knew that, if she possessed one sensation more prominently than another, it was hatred of the two standing before her. Yet she could speak thus to compass her own ends.

Almost before he knew what had happened, both the husband and wife had shaken hands with her, and she had seated herself on the parapet, holding Elsa's hand in hers. He stood apart, hearing as in a dream the conversation which Ottilie knew so well how to sustain—hearing her faltering statements of contrition, and her pitiful complaint of sleepless nights, spent in the wonder as to whether chance would ever give her the opportunity to crave that forgiveness which she so sorely needed.

What the influence of the calm, spring sunset had begun, the violent revulsion of feeling completed in Osmond. A stinging contempt for himself, in that he had worse than idled away three months in this woman's society, overcame him. The thought that, in his cowardly desire of revenge, he had well nigh plotted with her the destruction of this young Elsa's golden dream of happiness seemed to strike him like a lash.

No more—no more! A little fount of longing for his despised and deserted home broke over his barren heart. Home, straight home, now. To sever instantly all connection with the Ortons was his one fixed intention.

"The Castle Hotel!" Ottilie was saying, "why, that is ours. We shall meet at the *table-d'hôte* to-night."

CHAPTER LI

A lady! In the narrow space
Between the husband and the wife!
... She showed a face
With dangers rife.
A subtle smile, that dimpling fled
As night-black lashes rose and fell.
The Letter L.

"You are an excessively foolish boy," said Ottilie, angrily. "It is idiotic of you, Osmond. Leave the place by express train because of the Percivales! Why, they will probably leave themselves the day after to-morrow, at further. They are making no stay."

"It is of no use to argue," said Osmond, turning his haggard face away from the window, where the twilight was growing obscure. "I am off, Mrs. Orton. I seem an ungrateful brute, I know, but I can't help it. It's my lot, I think, to disappoint everybody who expects anything of me. I have, the feeling upon me that I must go; but, before I go, I want to say one thing."

He stopped short. From the depths of an easy chair, Ottilie made an impatient exclamation.

"Well, then, say it, do," said she, "if it's worth hearing."

"I want to say that the bet's off, as far as I am concerned."

She laughed loudly.

"O ho, that is it, is it? No, no, my friend, you don't get off in that way. When you betted so valiantly, you thought you were putting your money on a certainty; but, since the specimen of my ability I gave you up on the terrace, you begin to tremble. You find that I am not such a fool as you took me for! Excellent! But you shan't beat such a cowardly retreat as that."

"You mistake, partly," said the young man, hurriedly. "I admit that, when I dared you to try a reconciliation, I thought the whole thing was out of the question; and now I see I was mistaken. But don't think I withdraw for fear of loss. You shall have your gloves without the trouble of winning them; sooner than that— —"

"Dear me! Then what is all the fuss about?" she asked, sneeringly.

He came up to her chair, laying a clenched hand on the back of it.

"Don't try to do harm—to make mischief," he said, in a low voice. "It's devil's work."

"O—oh! Are we there? It is a sudden attack of virtue you are laboring under, is it? My good friend, don't attempt the part. It doesn't suit you nearly as well as the one you have lately appeared in."

"And what is the part I have lately appeared in?"

"Well, something very nice and fascinating, and easy to get on with. If you are going to be all over prickles, and object to everything on high moral grounds, you will make yourself an emphatic nuisance, as Artemus Ward observed."

"Much better that I should take my departure, then. We shall never agree. But, Mrs. Orton, you have been very kind to me——"

"Oh! don't allude to your gratitude. It is so patent."

"You are bitter. I am glad, perhaps, to think that you will regret me a little bit. But won't you promise me this one thing—the only favor I ever asked you, I believe. Let Percivale's wife alone."

"Osmond, you are a poor, chicken-hearted coward. I am ashamed of you. Why your reasons for hating those two ought to be even stronger than mine. Here lies revenge ready to your hand. Yet you drop it and sneak away. You are worse than Macbeth."

"And you," he rejoined, excitedly, "are worse than Lady Macbeth—a woman who hounded a man on to crime. Thank God I am not so completely under your influence as that, Mrs. Orton."

"You are too complimentary, Mr. Allonby. One would think that I was anxious to murder the Percivales in their beds."

"You are anxious to do them all the harm you can."

"Now listen to me, if your generous rage will allow you to be impartial for a moment. What is all this rhodomontade about? If Percivale is an adventurer, he deserves to be exposed—it is a kindness to his wife to accomplish it. If he is not, my shaft will recoil harmless. I shall do no injury in either case."

"Pardon me. She is his wife. If he is unworthy, for Heaven's sake spare her the pain of knowing it. If he is not, you will most probably achieve the wreck of his married happiness by making her suspect him. Either way you cannot fail to do infinite harm."

"Dear me! You ought to have been a lawyer, not an artist. You have such a logical mind. One would think you cherished no grudge against that empty little jilt for her treatment of you."

"You would think right. I love Elsa. I always shall. Mine is the kind of love that is immortal; I wish it could die. But it cannot. Like Prometheus, it must live for ever, though a vulture gnaw at its very heart. Her treatment of me makes no difference at all. I would die to save her from pain."

"You are a contemptible fool, then!"

"Possibly. My folly may make me happier than your revenge will make you." He walked once or twice through the room, then stopped again at her side. "Won't you give me a promise?" he said, wistfully. "I am going away, and you won't see me again for some time. Won't you promise?"

"I decline to speak to you at all. I am disgusted with you; sorry I ever troubled myself to be kind to such a poor-spirited — —"

She rose with passion, flung past him, and left the room. Osmond put his hand over his brow and stood silent for several minutes. Ought he to warn Percivale that Mrs. Orton's pretence of friendship was only specious? Perhaps he ought. And yet——He could not control his jealous dislike so far as that. No, it was impossible. If he washed his own hands of the whole affair, surely that was enough. It was the husband's duty to protect his wife; it was certainly not Osmond's place to interfere. Percivale had obtained possession of the treasure. Let him keep it. So said he vindictively to his own heart.

The sound of the opening door made him start. It was so dark that he could hardly see Frederick Orton as he walked in.

"Is Ottilie here?" he asked, lazily.

"She has just gone out," returned Osmond. "I'll wish you good-bye, Orton; my train goes in half-an-hour."

"Your train? Where the deuce are you off to?"

"England. I have played long enough. I am going back to work."

Frederick stuck his hands in his pockets and whistled.

"Oho! I see daylight. Mr. and Mrs. Percivale are in the hotel," he drawled. "Pooh! what does that matter? Stay and cut him out. Easily done. He's too virtuous to keep any woman's affection for long."

Osmond laughed bitterly.

"Which means that I am not?"

Orton laughed too.

"Look at Ottilie, she is hand and glove with them; sharp girl!" he said. "Thinks they are rich enough to be useful acquaintances, I suppose. Bury the hatchet, old man, and get the happy bridegroom to give you a commission."

"Might manage it seven years hence, but it's no good to try yet," said Osmond, with an effort to copy his tone. "I am afraid Mrs. Orton doesn't like my defection, but she will soon get over it. Remember me to her. I must not wait now, or I shall miss my train."

After all, he had to wait for the next train. Firm in his purpose, however, he declined to go in to the *table-d'hôte*, but walked out into the gardens of the hotel, and sat down in the spring starlight, meditating. He recalled the gush of feeling with which the castle had inspired him, and the meeting, so laden with emotion of the most poignant kind.

Meanwhile, Elsa had asked in surprise what had become of Mr. Allonby. She was excessively disappointed not to see him again. She had decked herself in one of her most radiant *trousseau* gowns, in order to inspire him with fresh despair at sight of what he had lost. In point of fact, she had never regretted her treatment of him until that day. He was greatly altered, and, in her opinion, much for the better. His world-worn air and cold cynicism were just the very things to attract her. How much more interesting he would have been if he had always had that air! He was her timid slave no longer. A desire to subjugate him afresh fired her bosom. He was far better worth thinking about than she had previously imagined. And now, just when she wanted him, he had disappeared.

He was not far off, had she known it. He slowly paced the walk under the trees in the shadow until the dinner was over, and the ladies came out on the balcony. He saw Elsa, in the shimmer of her pale dress, with the moon on her golden hair. She leaned over the balcony and laughed at Ottilie, who was down in the fragrant garden below. Osmond heard Mrs. Orton ask her to come down—it was so cool and fresh among the flowers; and, after a few minutes' hesitation, the girl disappeared within doors, fetched a wrap, and came gliding like a silver moonbeam down the staircase to the lawn.

The young man held his breath as he saw the two walk away together into the gloom of the garden. He was tempted for a moment to emerge from his concealment, join them, and defy Ottilie.

At the moment a clock struck. He started. He must not lose his sole chance of escaping from Heidelberg that night.

Slowly he turned and moved away, his eyes still on the two ladies, the dark and the fair, as they strolled in the picturesque setting of the purple night together; and the sound of Elsa's joyous laugh was the last memory he took with him from the enchanted spot.

It was in this wise that Osmond returned to his duty and his senses.

Hilda and Wynifred had just left Edge Combe, and returned to Mansfield Road in preparation for the wedding-day of the latter, which was to be on the first of June, when, to their delighted astonishment, arrived a letter from Cologne, from Osmond, warm, loving, and penitent, announcing that he was travelling back to them as fast as train would carry him. It is needless to describe the joy with which the sisters and Sally prepared the little house for the wanderer's reception, carefully hiding away out of the studio any picture or study which might bring unpleasant memories in its train.

When he experienced the delight of their welcome, and the sweet surrounding atmosphere of home, he was more ready than ever to marvel at the folly which had led him, in his dark hour, to fly from such a prodigal wealth of sympathy. It seemed, after all, as if trouble had strengthened him. His total failure to bear up like a man against disappointment had taught him a lesson. The ease with which he had lapsed into a "lower range of feeling" was also serviceable in showing him his inherent weakness. Only for the next few months his heart was overshadowed by a deep misgiving. He could not banish from his conscience the idea that he ought to have warned Percivale against Mrs. Orton. His quitting the field, as he had done, washing his hands, like Pilate, free from the guilt of destroying a just man, seemed a despicable piece of pusillanimity. Every day he feared to hear ill tidings of some sort—to learn from the Wynch-Frères, or Henry Fowler, that some unpleasantness had arisen between Elsa and her husband.

But time went on. Wynifred's wedding-day came and went, the Percivales were in town, Elsa's name figured at all the best receptions. She and her husband were seen everywhere together, and though, certainly, there were those who said that he looked very ill, still, the world is always prone to calumny. They were leaving the old house by the river, and moving into an enormous mansion in one of the fashionable squares. The decorating and furnishing of this abode was the delight of the bride's life. Society said that she grew every day more gay and entrancing, her husband more pale and silent. He was not used to the confined life of London—to being up all night in heated rooms, in noise, glare, and crowd. Physically, it told upon him. Lady Mabel Wynch-Frère saw it, and told Elsa, she must take her husband away as soon as possible,

"Yes, poor fellow, it is unfortunate we cannot manage to get away yet, is it not?" said Elsa, brightly. "But you know what upholsterers and decorators are unless one is personally there to superintend them? It is impossible to leave town until things are rather more finished. It is that hateful house in St. James' Place that makes Leon ill, I am sure of it. He will be a different creature when we move."

Certainly no results had as yet followed from Mrs. Orton's enmity. Osmond grew at last to believe that all her talk had been at random, that no mystery existed, that she had done nothing, and that he was a fool to have distressed himself over an angry woman's idle threats.

Yet there were moments,—times of deep thought and solitude, when, on pondering over what he knew of Ottilie's character, this explanation hardly satisfied him. There was a power for evil about this woman which was undeniable—a keenness, a mental activity which were at times formidable. Was it possible that she had obtained the knowledge she sought for, and as yet held it in her bosom like a concealed weapon, waiting a favorable opportunity to strike?

CHAPTER LII

Duchess.	*What have they said?*
Bertuccio.	*Ask never that of man.*
Duchess.	*What have they said of me?*
Bertuccio.	*I cannot say.*
Duchess.	*Thou wilt not, being my enemy. Why, for shame,*
	You should not, sir, keep silence.
Bertuccio.	*Yet I will.*
Duchess.	*I never dreamt so dark a dream as this,*
Bertuccio.	*God send it no worse waking!*

Marino Faliero.

A pleasant autumn afternoon shed its mellow light over Edge Combe. The fields were golden with harvest, and the air was warm with sunshine. In the porch at Lower House, Wynifred Cranmer stood leaning against the arched doorway, her needle-work in her hands. Near her, in a capacious wicker chair, her husband was enjoying his afternoon "weed."

Very contented and serene did Claud look, in his countrified suit of rough cloth, his leggings and thick boots. The costume suited him admirably, and the healthy out-of-door life had already given a glow of red-brown to his fair complexion. His gun lay near at hand, ready for him to clean, when so disposed; but at present life seemed to offer no more perfect enjoyment than to sit still, smoke, and look at his wife's delicate head in a setting of sunny sky and purple clematis blossom.

"Penny for your thoughts, Wyn," he remarked, after a more lengthy pause than usual; for they were, on the whole, rather a talkative pair.

"I was thinking about saucepans," said Wyn, peacefully, as she drew her needleful of silk out of the cloth and stuck in her needle with a click of her thimble.

"Saucepans, my dear girl?"

"Yes, saucepans. Where is my penny?"

"Do you think pots and pans are worth such a sum?"

"I wish they were not. It would be pleasant if we could stock our house with them at the price. No; it was Miss Willoughby's lovely preserving-pan that filled my thoughts. We must drive into Philmouth and get one to-morrow. You are so terribly addicted to jam that I expect I shall pass my whole career in boiling and skimming fruit!"

"Yes, let us have plenty of jam," returned Claud, with interest. "Dear me, how entertaining all the little details of life are, to be sure. I don't know when I have been more excited than when I had successfully contrived those bookshelves; and the sinking of the well in our garden kept me awake two whole nights."

"You silly boy! New brooms sweep clean," said his wife, laughing. "You will get tired of it all one day. No! I don't believe you will! We shall always be planning some improvement, we two. Housekeeping is a great pleasure."

"To think we shall be under our own roof in a month's time, my child," cried Claud, gleefully. "It sounds ungrateful to dear old Fowler, who is such a first-rate fellow; but it will be nice to be all to ourselves, won't it?"

"Won't it!" said Wyn, rapturously, letting fall her work, while she gazed at her husband with devotion.

"Mrs. Cranmer, come here and sit on my knee. I want to say something."

"Can't you say it as we are?"

"It's private and confidential."

"You must put down your pipe then. I can't talk to you if you puff smoke in my face."

He obediently laid aside the pipe and held out his arms invitingly.

Wyn decorously took a seat, still armed with her work.

"A gardener is sure to come by in a moment," she remarked, primly.

"The entire staff of domestics may march past in procession, for aught I care. Don't be silly," said her husband, pinching her ear.

"Well, now, what did you want to say?" asked she.

"Why, that something has upset dear old Henry. I expect it is to do with Elsa. I know he is very anxious about her. I was down at the quarries this morning, and he rode up to give me the message I gave you—that he would not be in to dinner. I thought he seemed not quite himself, and I asked him what it was. He said he would tell me later. He looked most horribly put out."

"Oh, it can't be Elsa. Why, they are coming here in the yacht to-morrow, to spend a week at Edge Willoughby. Something connected with business, it must be."

"I don't think so, from his manner; but we shall see. Imagine those other two honey-moonists turning up to-morrow. I wonder if they enjoyed themselves as much as you and I did?"

"They couldn't!" cried Wyn, letting her work slip from her knee, while she took her husband's face between her hands and caressed it. "No wedding-journey was ever like ours, or ever will be, will it?"

"I don't quite see how it *could*," he returned, with an air of candid reflection. "Ours was jolly. We'll have another next year, and go further afield, if we can save up enough out of our income."

"My dear silly, we shall save *heaps*! We are *rich*, I keep on telling you, but you won't believe it. Do you remember my last month's accounts?"

"They were absurd; but we have not tried housekeeping yet."

"And, as we are going to keep such a great deal of dinner company, our expenses will be heavy indeed."

"My dear girl, reflect! Think of the cost of your preserving-pan!"

"As to you, you have just bought that expensive fowling-piece. Whenever my weekly balance is low, I shall send you out shooting. No more butcher's meat till things come right again."

"Ah! Henry Fowler speaks the truth. I am indeed a hen-pecked husband."

"Claud! How dare you? I am sure Mr. Fowler never said such a thing."

"I never said he did."

"You are quite too foolish; and now you must let me go, for here comes George, and he is bringing the tea-tray out here."

"Well done, George," said Mr. Cranmer. "Just what I feel to want. And there comes the postman over the bridge. Run like a good little girl and bring me my letters."

"None for you," said Wyn, returning. "Only one for the Honorable Mrs. C. Cranmer, from Lady Mabel."

As she stood by the rustic tea-table, opening and reading her letter, her husband, for the hundredth time, thought how pretty she looked. Fresh and dainty as to her gown, her face just tinged with color, no longer unnaturally thin, but alive and sparkling with animation. Her soft hair waved about her in the pleasant air, her sole ornaments were the two wide gold rings on the third finger of her left hand. Henry Fowler had witnessed the change he had so longed to effect in her—the combined result of happiness and the Combe air.

From her serene brow to her neatly-shod feet, this doting Claud had not a fault to find with her. She was his own, the darling of his heart, the fulfilment of every need of his soul.

But, even as he gazed, Wyn's happy face clouded; a furrow came in the smooth forehead.

"Oh, Claud!" she said, hurriedly, "here is something very disagreeable. I wonder if Mr. Fowler can have heard this; it would be enough to make him feel very disturbed, at least. Mabel is at Moynart, and Edward joined her yesterday, and he says there is a hateful story about Mr. Percivale going the round of the clubs."

"My child, there usually is a hateful story about him going the round of the clubs— —"

"Yes, but Colonel Wynch-Frère seems to think there is something in this one. The names and dates are so accurate. I—it was before my time. Did you ever hear of R— —?"

She named a notorious political offender, who, nearly thirty years before, fled to Germany, and there committed suicide on the eve of his arrest.

"Yes," said Claud, thoughtfully, "I remember hearing of it. I was in the nursery at the time. I think Mabel and I acted the whole scene together. We liked a violent death of any sort. But what about him?"

"They say Leon Percivale is his son."

Claud raised his eyes to the scene before him. There lay the bay, there was the spot where the white *Swan* had anchored. There in the dawn, a twelvemonth ago, he had seen the sun rise over Percivale the victor— Percivale, who had saved Elsa Brabourne from a stigma worse than death.

Now the blow had fallen. The girl whom he had rescued had betrayed him, as Claud had feared she would. The blood rushed to his face, a storm of angry sorrow to his heart. Why, why had such a man wasted his heart on so slight a thing as Elsa?

Wynifred's eyes rested keenly on her husband. She saw his silence, his consternation.

"Oh, Claud, it is not true, is it?"

"No, darling, I know that it is not true; and yet—yet—I fear there is some truth in it."

She came close to him, laying her hands on his shoulders.

"Who can have spoken of such a thing?" she said, earnestly.

"There was only one human being who knew the facts," was the answer. "That was—his wife."

"Claud, no!" Her vehemence startled him. "You should say such a thing of no wife!" she cried. "It is impossible—unnatural! She never could have betrayed such a secret!"

He rose, and slipped an arm round her neck.

"You judge all women by your own standard, dear."

"I don't! I don't do anything of the kind! I do not think highly of Elsa—you know I never did! But that would be too horrible. It has come out some other way. No wife could be such a traitor."

As she spoke the words, Henry Fowler came over the bridge; and instinctively they held their breath. His face looked calmer and he was smiling.

"Well, young people," he said, brightly, "my eyes are getting old, you know, but I don't fancy I'm wrong. Claud, look out to sea. Isn't there a sail out there towards Lyme? Isn't it the cutter?"

Claud turned his eyes in the direction indicated.

"Right enough," he said. "If this breeze holds, she'll be here in no time. She has made her journey a day faster than was expected."

"Ay lad! It's a year to-day since she came sailing into the bay! Yesterday was the night of the great storm."

He turned to Wyn. "I got a bit upset to-day by some foolish talk that I heard in Stanton about Leon. But I've decided to think no more of it. As soon as I see him I know I should feel ashamed of myself to have thought ill of the lad—God bless him! Now, Mrs. Cranmer, a cup of tea, if you please, for I must be off down to the shore."

Wyn slipped her letter into her pocket, and betook herself to the tea-pot. Her husband hastily got up, leaving his own tea almost untasted, and disappeared into the house to collect himself a little; for he felt as though his meeting with Percivale might be agitating.

The Tree Of Knowledge A Novel | 375

CHAPTER LIII

A lie which is half the truth is even the blackest of lies.
For a lie which is all a lie may be met with and fought
outright,
But a lie which is half a truth is a harder matter to fight.
The Grandmother.

An excited crowd had quickly collected on the beach when the news spread like wild-fire through the village that the *Swan* was sailing into the bay.

The premature arrival of the yacht was almost a disappointment to William Clapp, Joe Battishill and others, who were rigging up a triumphal arch in preparation for the morrow.

Elaine's London wedding had been a great downfall to the hopes of the natives of the Combe; and now they desired to make up for it by welcoming her in a manner suitable to the triumphs she had achieved.

Leon, leaning against the rail aft, as he had done a year ago, saw the assemblage of excited people, and a crowd of memories arose within him. So they had stood, a dark, eager group, on the breezy morning when first the Valley of Avilion had broken upon his gaze. How calm had been his mood, then! How serene his horizon! A tranquil peace was his habit of mind, no storm of passion had come to lash that deep heart of his into swelling waves.

Since that day all had changed. His whole being had suffered revolution. How many sensations had successively dominated his soul! Emotion, excitement, longing, passion, triumph, and reaction.

Yes. It had come. He had realized fully now that the glittering Eden of his dreams was a *mirage* on desert sand. It was, he judged, his own fault from beginning to end. He had started on a wrong tack. He had begun life all theories and no experience, and one by one his sweet delusions had suffered shipwreck.

He had married with no practical knowledge of women, their wants and their ways; for of course he imagined that all women were like Elsa. He found her unreasonable, exacting, pettish if thwarted, absolutely unsympathetic, and with a mind incapable of comprehending his. All these failings he unhesitatingly ascribed to her sex. He believed that he ought to have been prepared to find her thus merely because she was a woman.

He was passing through the bitter stage of disillusioning which Claud had prophesied for him.

This afternoon he was feeling specially unhappy, for Elsa so disliked the idea of coming to Edge at all that she had been sulky ever since they embarked. He had been impressed with the conviction that it was imperative that she should pay a short visit there, as Miss Ellen, who was failing rapidly, was longing to see her. Accordingly, he had exerted his naturally strong will and carried her off, and she had been making him feel it ever since. To add to her vexation, her maid was always ill on the water; so that Leon was devoutly thankful that the wind had enabled him to make his cruise shorter than he had anticipated.

As the smiling shores of the lovely bay became distinct, he rose and went below to the dainty and exquisite little saloon, where his wife was reclining with a novel.

"Elsa, we are nearly there," he said, "and there is quite a mob collected to watch our arrival."

"No! really! is there?" she said, sitting up with some appearance of interest. "I never thought they would think of giving us a reception. What a pity I did not change my gown! Is it too late?"

"You look perfectly well as you are," he answered, with a sorrowfully tender gaze at the graceful form in its natty blue serge and coquettish sailor-hat.

"Oh, that is like you—you never care what I wear! I really think I'll change. What a bother Mathilde is to be sick like this! But you can hook my skirt, can't you, Leon?"

"My dear little woman, we shall be on shore in five minutes. You must come on deck directly. Be quick—I want to see who is there to greet us."

"How tiresome! Why didn't you remind me that the people would turn out to look at us?" she complained. "I do hate to feel shabby."

"Elsa! you look perfectly charming! Do you suppose the villagers can distinguish between the prices of your gowns?" He coaxingly put his arm round her. "I want to feel proud of my wife," he said. "Put on your best smile for the people, darling."

In this wise he managed to persuade her into showing herself on deck just in time. As the *Swan* drew on gracefully close in shore, a hearty cheer greeted the young couple as they stood side by side.

"There are Cranmer and his wife, besides dear old Fowler!" cried Leon, gladly, as he waved his cap. "How pleasant to have Claud here—it seems so long since I saw him—not since our wedding-day!"

"Humph! You are a civil bridegroom! I am sorry that time has passed so tediously," said Elsa, in some real and some pretended annoyance. "But is that really Wynifred Allonby—Cranmer, I mean? How she has improved in looks! I suppose it is because she is better dressed. Mr. Cranmer looks well, too."

In a few minutes they were all on shore together, in the midst of greetings.

As Claud and Percivale joined hands, their eyes met in a long, searching, mutual inquiry. One moment showed Claud that his friend had not found perfect happiness. He was changed; he looked older, and the expression of his eyes and mouth seemed to tell of mental suffering.

Claud's own obvious, radiant content was in sharp contrast.

"Well, Claud, my dear friend, I was astonished, I confess," faltered Leon. "But I must congratulate you. You look very happy."

"Happy! I should think so. I have my heart's desire," smiled Claud. "The only times that anything has power to vex me are the moments when she is out of sight; and I believe they will always be few and far between."

Leon looked earnestly at him.

"That *is* happiness," he said.

Mr. Fowler and the Cranmers dined at Edge Willoughby.

It was a hot night—so sultry as to suggest the proverbial thunderstorm, though the sky was clear and starry.

All dinner-time Percivale's sad eyes haunted Wynifred uncomfortably. He seemed to be studying her own and her husband's entire sympathy with a wistful appeal, as if wondering how it was that he and Elsa had come so terribly short of it.

Mrs. Leon Percivale was in her most gracious mood. The public reception had gratified her, and to trail her new gowns up and down the familiar corridors of Edge Willoughby, to the awe of Jane Gollop and the rest of the staff of elderly retainers, was not without its charm. She wore a dazzling evening toilette, and looked like a beautiful apparition as she sat between her godfather and Claud in smiling quiescence, talking, as was her wont, very little.

The company separated early, as was their country fashion,—Wynifred to walk peacefully home to Lower House with her husband and Mr. Fowler, through the meadow foot paths.

They went in silence for some distance. Percivale had strolled as far as the end of the terrace with them, and bidden them good night at the stile. His tone appeared to have cast a gloom over all three; something there was in his whole manner which was inexpressibly sad. They felt it without knowing why. Henry spoke at last.

"Percivale does not look well," he said.

"No; Mabel has several times said so in writing," replied Claud. "She thinks London life does not suit him. I daresay a cruise will set him up. That is why she made this suggestion of his fetching her from Clovelly. I think he seems to like the idea."

"Yes; but Elsa does not care to be left here alone while he goes; so I am afraid he will have to give it up," returned Mr. Fowler, with a sigh.

Lady Mabel had taken a farm house at Edge for her children and their governess, and had written to say that, if the *Swan* was really there, it would be very delightful to be fetched, and enjoy a cruise round the Cornish coast. The suggestion had brought a ray of brightness to Leon's face. To be at sea again, in his beloved *Swan*, was what he relished. He would like to go; but Elsa did not approve. She declined to accompany him, and declined to let him go without her.

"I will not go cruising with a sick maid," she said, simply, "and I will not go cruising without a maid; and I will not be left in this dull place by myself. So you can't go, Leon."

"I am glad, on the whole, that my wife does not require a maid," said Claud, with Wyn's hand held closely against his side.

"You make such a charming lady's-maid that I require no other," she laughed. "Imagine, Mr. Fowler! He can do my hair beautifully. What it is to have a husband who can turn his hand to anything!"

CHAPTER LIV

There is nothing to remember in me,
Nothing I ever said with a grace,
Nothing I did that you care to see,
Nothing I was that deserves a place
In your mind, now I leave you, set you free.
How strange it were, if you had all me
As I have all you in my heart and brain,
You, whose least word brought gloom or glee,
Who never yet lifted the hand in vain
Will hold mine yet, from over the sea!
James Lee's Wife.

Percivale strolled back alone up the garden path. The night was motionless and heavy. A lethargy seemed to lie on his soul like a weight. To-night he had realized a new thing. He had seen that the wedded bliss he had figured to himself was no dream, but a human possibility, which some attained, but which he had missed. How had he missed it?

Was it possible that he had married the wrong woman?

"Oh, Love, Love, no!" he cried, in his remorse. The fault was his, in some way, of that he was very sure. Had that unknown mother of his lived, she would have been his counsellor, and have shown him where he failed. His deep eyes filled with tears as the thought of that mother beyond the stars came vividly upon his soul. He felt a longing to be comforted—to have his unbroken loneliness scattered and dissipated by tender hands which should draw his weary head down lovingly to rest on a sympathetic breast, and, while telling him what had been his error, whisper consolation.

If there was one thing more than another for which he could not possibly look to his wife, it was for this. Elsa expected him to have his attention always fixed on her and her requirements. The idea that he could ever ail in mind or body never occurred to her.

He stood in the porch of Edge Willoughby, the suffocating sweetness of the verbena-bush, which grew beside the door, suffusing the air all round him. He remembered the night when he stood there with Fowler and Claud, just a year ago, bearing the news of Elsa's innocence.

If he could but charm away this bitter sense of failure!

A sudden determination to make one desperate appeal to his wife dawned in his heart. When first they were married he told himself she was in awe of him, she had not understood him. Now that she knew him better, was there not a chance that she might comprehend the fierce hunger which was in his heart? Surely yes.

Meditatively he walked down the hall.

As he passed along, his eye was attracted by a newspaper lying on the ground, folded tightly together as if it had fallen from some one's coat pocket.

Stooping absently he picked it up, with intent to lay it on the hall-table near. As he did so, his eye fell on a paragraph scored at the side with a pencil-mark. One word in that paragraph struck him like a blow. He started, stared, half laughed like one whom a chance coincidence has disturbed; then, his eyes travelling on, he slowly whitened and stiffened where he stood, his attitude that of a man thunder-struck.

For a couple of minutes or more he remained motionless, then put up an uncertain hand to his eyes as if to clear away a mist.

After another pause, he laid his left hand firmly against the hall-table near which he stood, and, so fortified, read the passage through.

The word which had first caught his eye was Littsdorf, the name of the obscure village of North Germany where his father and his mother lay buried. Glancing higher on the page he saw his father's name printed in full, and his own relationship to him openly proclaimed. So far, true; but the account then became inaccurate, repeating the old story of corruption and suicide which had so long passed current.

As it stood it was not the truth as he had told it to his wife, yet there were certain things in it which surely no one could have known except from his wife's lips.

Violently he repelled the thought, as if to think it were a sin. She! What, she! To whom he had trusted his honor—in whose hands he had laid his life and love—at whose feet he had heaped up the incense of a devotion which was all hers, and had never for a moment leaned towards any other woman!

And yet—yet—*Littsdorf*!

The writer of the paragraph must evidently have visited the place, to collect the names, dates, and inscriptions on the lonely grave of his mother in the little *Friedhof*. Chance might have taken him there; but could chance connect the name of R—— with the name of Percivale?

In comparison with the horror of this thought, the publication of this strange hash of truth and falsehood troubled him but little. Too many false reports of him had been circulated for the public to pay much extra heed to this last. If Henry Fowler questioned him, he could easily tell him the truth; but this thought—this ghastly chill which crept over him—this horrible suspicion that his wife had discussed the innermost core of her husband's heart with some casual acquaintance!

It was not true. It could not be. It must not be, or there seemed an end to all possibility of living on in the shattered temple of his broken idol. No! It must be some other way; some strange, marvellous coincidence must be at the root of it.

He would go to his darling and look her in the face—feel the pressure of her little hand, and curse himself for the unworthiness of his thought.

With a strenuous effort, he steadied himself mentally and struggled for his habitual calm. He determined not to go to his wife in the present excited condition of his nerves, lest he might say something which he should regret. He had not yet fully considered the bearings of the subject. Perhaps after all his fear was groundless. Was not some other solution possible?

Again he went out into the night, and for half-an-hour his restless feet trod the terrace, up and down, up and down, while he tried to banish suspicion.

What a coward and traitor was the man who could doubt his own wife without proof! Anything else might happen—a miracle might have revealed the closely hidden secret; anything but *that*.

The big hall clock striking midnight made him start. He must go indoors or he would waken Elsa, and nothing so put her out of temper as to be waked from her first sleep.

He went indoors, shutting out the hot and heavy darkness of the night with a sigh almost of relief, drew the bolts into their places, extinguished the hall lamp, and quietly went upstairs through the silent house.

He expected to find his room in darkness, but, rather to his surprise, lights were burning, and Elsa sat in an armchair, reading a novel. She glanced up, and yawned as he entered.

The room was transformed since the arrival of Mrs. Percivale's trunks and Mrs. Percivale's maid. A mass of various articles of apparel strewed the chairs and sofa, the dressing table groaned under its load of silver-topped essence-bottles, ivory brushes, hair-curling apparatus, and so forth. The mantel-piece was adorned with knick-knack frames containing photographs of a certain tenor who sang in the opera in Paris, and for whom Elsa had conceived a violent admiration.

The young lady herself was in *déshabillé*; she never looked more beautiful than when half-dressed. She wore a white embroidered petticoat and low bodice, much trimmed with lace. Her golden hair streamed all over her creamy neck and arms.

Tossing away her book, she yawned and laughed, lifting said arms and folding them behind her head.

"Oh, is it you? Just fancy! How late it is. I was so tired of trying to undress myself, for Mathilde went to bed the minute she arrived, and I won't let old Jane touch me. So I felt so hot, and I sat down to rest; and this book was so fascinating that" (yawn) "I've been reading ever since." The last five words were almost lost in a large yawn. "Isn't it hot, Leon?"

"Very," he said, as he closed the door, and, drawing up a chair, took a seat at her side. "I am glad you are up still, though. I was afraid I should wake you."

"No; I am not very sleepy. I feel inclined to sit up and finish my book."

"Sit up and talk to me instead," he said, taking one of her hands in his, and looking down lovingly at its slender grace. "The coming back to this place has put me in mind of so many things, my darling, I have been remembering the night—just such a night as this—when I saw you lying asleep on Miss Ellen's bed, dressed in blue— —"

"Oh, yes!" her laugh broke in. "That fearful old dressing-gown of Aunt Ellen's! What a fright I felt! I was so ashamed for you to see me. It had shrunk in the wash. Did you notice?"

"My own, I thought you were the most perfect creature I had ever looked upon—as I think still."

"It is rather disappointing, Leon, to find that you don't like me a bit better, now that I really do dress properly, than when I was such a frump. Look at that now," indicating, with a white satin-shod foot, the wondrous toilette she had worn that evening, which lay across a chair near. "That really *is* pretty, if you like; but it is nonsense to tell me that I looked well in that old blue dressing-gown."

"I tell you that you looked lovely—lovely! There you lay, calmly sleeping, with your life shadowed over by a false accusation!" Falling on his knees beside her chair, he caught her in his arms in an irresistible access of love. Could he suspect her—he, the champion of her innocence when everyone else forsook her?

His head, with its soft curls, lay against her neck. In a passing impulse of affection, begotten of the novel she had been reading, she bent down, kissed him, and stroked his hair.

"Be a good boy, and don't suffocate me quite," said she. "It is very hot to-night."

He did not lift his head, but still clasped her close.

"Elsa, my sweet," he said, "I am ashamed to look in your face. I feel a traitor; I have been thinking evil of you, my heart! I want to confess—to tell you of it. May I?"

"I"—yawn—"suppose so. Yes. But don't be long. I think I'll go to bed now."

"To think that I was mean enough, poor-spirited enough, in face of a few suspicious circumstances, to dream that my wife would break her word to me, would shatter my trust in her, by talking of my private affairs, of the secret which I gave her to guard——"

He felt the girl start in his arms, and a corresponding thrill, a sudden sense of horror, went through him. Letting her go out of his clasp, and lifting his eyes to her face, he saw her crimson from brow to chin.

"What made you say that, Leon?" she asked sharply.

"This," he said, as, scarcely knowing what he did, he laid the paper on her knee.

She took it up and read it quickly through, the color ebbing and coming as she sat.

His heart was beating so fast he could hardly breathe, his whole soul sick with an awful fear. The paper fell on her lap, and she remained still, as if not knowing what to say.

"Elsa," he cried, "how could those words have been written unless the writer of them knew—what you know?"

The girl tossed the paper from her, flinging herself back in her chair defiantly.

"That mean, hateful woman," she cried, with passion. "She deserves—what does she not deserve?—when she solemnly vowed to me not to tell a soul——"

She stopped short, the words died away. The blaze in Percivale's eyes seemed to wither and strike her dumb.

"Elsa!" Rising, he stood before her, laying his hands on her shoulders. "Do you mean to tell me that you have been speaking of what should be sacred in your eyes—no, no! Consider what you are saying."

"Nonsense, Leon!" Angry tears sprang to her eyes. "Let go of me—you hurt! You speak as if I were a criminal."

His face, as his hold relaxed and stepped back, was pitiful to behold.

"To a woman," he said. "To what woman?"

"To that odious Mrs. Orton."

"Elsa, you are mad! *Mrs. Orton?*"

"Leon, you don't know what hateful things she said of you. She said she knew them for facts. I was obliged to tell her the real truth, I could not stand to have her pitying me, and telling me she knew better than I did. And she declared she would not tell. I made her promise."

He laughed harshly.

"So, though you could betray your husband's confidence, you did not think that she could betray yours! Oh, Elsa! Elsa!... God help me!"

"Leon, it is very inconsiderate and unkind of you to frighten me so! I—I—shall faint or something. What harm so very great have I done? They often put stories about you in the papers. Nobody will know that this is true."

"The world may know, for aught I care. What is the world to me? Less than nothing. All my life I have never valued public opinion. I could bear with perfect fortitude to be an outlaw—tabooed by society, if—if I knew there lived on earth one woman I could trust."

He went to the window. The purple darkness outside seemed in sympathy with him. The verbena scent welled up in waves of perfume. Elsa began to cry bitterly, and then to let fall a torrent of excuses.

She had done it for him, because she hated to hear a spiteful woman speak ill of him. It was because she loved him so that she had been tempted; and there was no great harm done, and now he spoke to her as if she were a dog. He was unkind, he terrified her. She would not bear to be so scolded, she was not a child any more, etc.

Through it all Percivale stood immovable by the window, wondering what could possibly happen next. He felt rather like a man who, having received his death-blow, awaits with a dumb patience the moment when death itself shall follow. Was this woman really the Elsa of his adoration? Had he indeed to this slight, trifling, deceitful nature surrendered himself body and soul as a slave? How could he live on, a long life through, with a wife whom he despised?

Despised? His feeling came nearer to loathing than to contempt as he looked at her. Her very beauty sickened him—the outer covering which had won his fancy. He hated himself for ever having loved her.

She could not see that it was the act itself, not the consequences of it, which he so condemned. So small was her nature that she was unable even to comprehend her transgression. He could not make her understand the horror with which he must regard such a breach of trust.

"There was no great harm done?" was her cry.

"Harm!" he said, brokenly. "There is murder done. You have killed my faith, Elsa, for ever more."

"It is very rude and unkind to say that you will never tell me anything again, just because I let out this one thing. And I only told one person. I never so much as mentioned it to anyone else. I might have published it all over London, to hear you talk!"

It was impossible to answer a speech like this. She had *only* betrayed him to one person! She had *not so much as mentioned it* to anyone else! And this was his wife, his ideal!

Claud Cranmer had said,

"If you wish to preserve your ideal, you must not marry her."

He sank into a chair, covered his face, and groaned.

"Come, Leon, don't behave like that—you are the most unreasonable person I ever met!" cried Elsa. "Go away, please, to your dressing-room, and leave me alone. I want to go to bed. You have made me cry so that my eyes are scarlet, and my head feels like lead. I think you are extremely unkind; when I have told you I am very sorry, and begged you pardon. I don't see what more I can do."

"No, Elsa," he said, rising, "you can do nothing more. You cannot make yourself a different woman; and nothing short of that would avail to help us much."

He passed her without looking at her, and shut himself into his dressing-room.

His wife crossed the room, and stared at herself in the glass.

"I know my eye-lids will be all swelled to-morrow," she thought, with a keen sense of injury. "I never saw Leon in such a rage. I hope he will soon get over it. I don't think he is a very good-tempered man; I call him rather sulky. Osmond was much greater fun."

A few minutes after she was in bed, the door opened and Percivale came in. He had changed his dress clothes for his yachting suit, and his cap was in his hand.

"Leon! Are you mad?" cried Elsa.

"I think not," he said, gravely, as he came to her bedside, "but—but—Elsa, forgive me, I cannot stay here and go on as if nothing had happened. You have given me too severe a shock for me to recover from all at once."

"Leon, what nonsense! You talk in such a strange way sometimes I think you cannot be quite right in your head. I do not understand you."

"No," he said, his voice almost a cry, "that is the trouble, Elsa. You do not understood me. I have not understood you either. I have been mistaken. I was ignorant of life. I did not know you, and now that, suddenly, I have seen you *as you are*, and not as I fancied you, I must have time to grow used to the idea. Poor child, poor child! You could not help it. It is I who am to blame, far more than you. Forgive me that I expected too much."

"What are you going to do? Go away and leave me alone here with the aunts for a punishment?"

"I am going to take the yacht round to Clovelly for Lady Mabel, as was suggested. It will not be very long, and by the time I come back I shall be calmer. I shall be able to face this new aspect of things better. Elsa, Elsa, have you no word for me—nothing to heal the wound you have made? Do you not see, my child, what you have done? Can't you realize how despicable a part you have played! Elsa, face this conduct of yours—what should you say of another man's wife who had betrayed her husband's confidence to his enemy—abused the trust confided to her? Can you not even see the nature of your fault as it is?"

"I have said I am sorry, and I will say it again if it will please you. I know it was stupid to tell her. I thought so several times afterwards. I did not like to tell you; but I do think you make too much fuss, Leon. A thing is out before you know it, but I can't see that it is such a sin as you want to make out."

He tried no more. He bowed his head to utter failure.

Stooping, he gently put his lips to his wife's pure brow, shaded with its innocent-looking curls of gold.

"Poor child," he said, tenderly, "poor, beautiful child. Sleep, Elsa, I must not keep you awake, or make you grieve. It would spoil your beauty; and it is your mission to be beautiful. Good-night!—good-night! I am not angry with you."

"Then why do you go rushing off in the middle of the night instead of coming to bed like a Christian?" she cried, pitifully. "Leon, Leon, why are you so strange—so unaccountable! You make me so unhappy—without my knowing why! You—you are—so very *very* hard on me!" Suddenly she burst into a passion of tears. Lifting herself from her pillows, she cast both arms round him, clinging to him. "I—I do love you," she gasped, "don't be so cruel to me, don't!" The tears welled up in the young man's beautiful eyes in sympathetic response.

He drew the lovely head down upon his breast, and soothed her with infinite compassion. Like Arthur, the stainless gentleman whose wife had failed him in another—a worse way—"his vast pity almost made him die," as he held her closely, caressing her like a child until her sobs had ceased.

"You are not angry any more?" she asked at last, lifting her wet eyelashes with a wistful, appealing glance.

"No, Elsa, no. I am not angry. I am penitent. There is no need to make yourself unhappy. Go to sleep."

"I am very sleepy," she sighed, "but you will wake me if you move me."

"I will sit here until you sleep."

"Thank you. You are a good, dear boy. Good-night, Leon."

"Good-night, Elsa."

There was stillness in the room—utter stillness as at last Percivale laid his sleeping wife down, and, bending over her, bestowed a parting kiss.

He felt somewhat as a man who gazes upon the dead form of one beloved.

His dream-Elsa was a thing of the past—vanished, dead.

What would the fresh life be like which he must begin with her? A life of strain—of the heavy knowledge that never while he lived could he hope for sympathy, could he satisfy the mighty craving of his soul for a wife who should be to him what Claud Cranmer's wife was to her husband.

Everything was changed.

Never, in all his solitary youth, in all the remote wanderings of the *Swan*, not even when he laid to rest his tutor, the one friend of his childhood, had he felt the terror of loneliness as he felt it now. It was grey dawn when he came down to the beach. Müller, who was on the look-out, saw the misty figure of his master standing upon the shore, and at once launched the gig and took him on board.

With the gradual dawn, a faint breeze sprang up and lifted the mist that hung over the sea.

It filled the *Swan's* white wings as it rose and freshened, and just as the sun rose, she sailed out of the bay, her master, silent and pallid, standing on the deck, watching the dim roof which covered his perished hopes.

There lay the Lower House, snug in the valley. He sent an unspoken farewell to the good Henry, and to the happy husband and wife who were probably just awaking to a fresh day of love and hope and mutual help.

The warm sun-rays gilded Percivale's bright head, and glorified the still features as he stood. Old Müller looked anxiously at him. Something was wrong, he guessed, and yet—oh, the joy to be putting to sea again as in old days, free and untrammelled by the fashionable wife or the sick maid!

The old man's spirit leaped up with the red sun. His blood rose, his eye kindled.

The bonnie yacht bounded over the freshening waves, the day laughed broadly over the sea, and the crew, animated by Müller's delight, sang their *Volkslieder* as they went about their work.

That night, the last sultry heat of autumn burst in a storm more violent than Edge Combe had known for half a century. The first of the equinoctial gales raged from the south west, thundering against the battlemented crags of Cornwall, shrieking up the Devonshire valleys.

More than one large ship went to pieces on the wild coast; and fragments of wrecks were washed ashore at Brent and in Edge Bay.

But no trace of the *Swan* or of any of those on board of her was ever carried by the relentless ocean within reach of the hearts that ached and longed for tidings of her fate. She had vanished as she had first appeared, mysteriously, in a tempest.

To the fisher-folk there seemed to be something supernatural alike in her arrival and her disappearance.

For months they cherished among themselves the belief that she would return one day—that somewhere, in some distant port, or in far sunny seas she was gliding like a big white bird along her mysterious course.

They argued that some trace of her must have come ashore somewhere—she was cruising so near the coast, some fragment of her must have been washed up at some point—some dead sailor have been floated in on the tide wearing the white *Swan* worked on his jersey, to be a silent witness of the destruction of the yacht.

But no! No news, no sign, no trace of her end was ever forthcoming. She seemed to have melted away like a mythical ship into the regions of legend.

And it has now become a tradition in the Combe that if ever the day should come when some wrong done there shall cry aloud for justice, and there is none to help, that, on that day, will be seen the white *Swan* sailing into the bay in the sunshine, and her owner standing on her deck like a hero of ancient story, as he stood when first he approached the Valley of Avilion ready to champion the Truth.